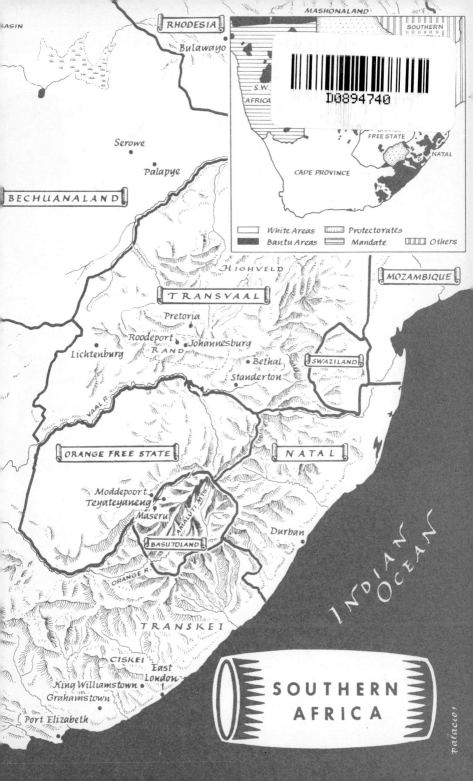

BASIN

RHODESIA

Bulawayo

MASHONALAND

SOUTHERN

S.W.
AFRICA

FREE STATE

NATAL

CAPE PROVINCE

White Areas | Protectorates
Bantu Areas | Mandate | Others

Serowe

Palapye

BECHUANALAND

HIGHVELD

MOZAMBIQUE

TRANSVAAL

Pretoria

Roodeport

Johannesburg

Lichtenburg

RAND

Bethal

SWAZILAND

Standerton

VAAL R.

ORANGE FREE STATE

NATAL

Moddepoort

Teyateyaneng

Maseru

Durban

BASUTOLAND

ORANGE R.

INDIAN OCEAN

TRANSKEI

CISKEI

East London

King Williamstown

Grahamstown

Port Elizabeth

SOUTHERN AFRICA

Patacior

Charles M. Good
March, 1961

American Committee on Africa
Carnegie Institute
New York City

A TIME TO SPEAK

A TIME TO SPEAK

1958   *Doubleday & Company, Inc., Garden City, New York*

MICHAEL SCOTT

Library of Congress Catalog Card Number 58–11325
Copyright © 1958 by Guthrie Michael Scott
All Rights Reserved. Printed in the United States of America
Designed by Patricia Walsh
First Edition

To every thing there is a season, and a time to every purpose under the
    heaven:

A time to be born, and a time to die; a time to plant, and a time to pluck
    up that which is planted;

A time to kill, and a time to heal; a time to break down, and a time to
    build up;

A time to weep, and a time to laugh; a time to mourn, and a time to dance;

A time to cast away stones, and a time to gather stones together; a time
    to embrace, and a time to refrain from embracing;

A time to get, and a time to lose; a time to keep, and a time to cast away;

A time to rend, and a time to sew; a time to keep silence, and a time to
    speak;

A time to love, and a time to hate; a time of war, and a time of peace.

What profit hath he that worketh in that wherein he laboureth?

I have seen the travail, which God hath given to the sons of men to be
    exercised in it.

He hath made every thing beautiful in his time: also he hath set the world
    in their heart, so that no man can find out the work that God maketh
    from the beginning to the end.

ECCLESIASTES iii, 1–11

Southward, shining and snakelike, the mighty Ganges River sweeps swiftly through the pass of Heridwar—the gateway of God—and out into the plains where it is lost in the mists of distance.

To the north are range upon range of the Himalayas—for them no word is mighty enough. And there, scarcely discernible from the clouds, are the snows that never melt but are blown from the peaks like still white plumes by winds which no man alone can withstand.

Since this story has no beginning and no ending, I may as well begin it somewhere midway. It is 1950.

We had come here to India in search of peace. We had come from the ends of the earth—I from the United Nations where I had gone to make a petition for some South West African tribes. Others from America, from Japan, Germany, England, Canada, France, China, Pakistan, India, New Zealand, West Africa, Burma, Australia, the Philippines, Denmark, Norway, Holland, Egypt, Israel.

There had been an exacting Quaker conference on peace, and the methods and tasks of peace, and now here we were, some of us, after a day's climb, relaxing on the top of Mani Kot.

The spurs of the hills were terraced in a marvel of contour cultivation. Below us an eagle was wheeling and banking, alert for a sign of his prey. Faintly, to the ears straining for a sound, came the faraway crowing of a cock, the barking of a dog. Voices of children calling to one another were swallowed up with their distant echoes in the silence—a scene as ageless as perhaps anything human can be.

As the story unfolds it will, perhaps, more clearly be seen to be not only a story of Africans, or of a particular African tribe, much less of an individual in search of justice and peace, but a story of the crisis of our time and age—a story of how people, not great people, but ordinary people in the humdrum occupations of our utilitarian civilization, can rise out of their little ruts to propel and to be themselves propelled by a cause greater than themselves. Their individual acts of choice may have seemed trivial, may have been instinctive gestures with no thought of their deeper or more long-term implications, yet they were more far-reaching than each could measure.

By such acts, insignificant in time, are mountains moved, the rocks worn smooth, and the steep slopes terraced. The whole is formed into a landscape touched by the hand of man, as a sudden trifling sound of a cock crowing down in the valley can give life to a scene and charge the whole with meaning.

It was only a little while ago that the harsh metallic clatter of our civilization in New York had formed the background of an historic debate at the United Nations—a debate between East and West, as the controversy between capitalism and communism has come to be known.

The flight to India had been swift, and there they were again, the sights that had sent me across the world from South Africa to the United Nations. The millions of landless and homeless, the dispossessed of the earth living in tents and shanties made of sackcloth and cardboard, fleeing from the wrath of some ignorant bigotry, some half-understood truth disseminated by ambitious prelates or politicians in the minds of the masses, driving them to insensate acts of cruelty and depredation. On the pavements in Karachi the refugees had set up their little shacks and stalls in front of the regular shops. In Calcutta the population had increased from two to four million, and refugees from Pakistan were still pouring in. A million were sleeping in the streets, wrapped in thin cotton blankets, silent spokesmen of our disorder and the ineptitude of our statesmanship.

It was for the dispossessed that a band of unlikely helpers strewn along the path from the edge of the Kalahari to the shores of Lake Success had joined in an effort to enable the voices of an obscure African tribe to be heard by the United Nations.

Mostly they were white people drawn from small scattered groups of volunteers and amateurs separated by thousands of miles in a country where the whole white population, Dutch and British, does not amount to more than the population of a large town in Europe or America (three million). There the political life is mainly influenced by the powerful monopoly groups, the mining industry, the farmers, and the white trade unions. And there are few white people who do not find themselves attached by some economic or social tie to one or another of these groups which are all concerned to maintain the colour bar and cheap migrant labour.

My very grateful thanks are due to Mary Benson, Mrs. Gibson, and Mrs. Cruickshank for all the hard work they have devoted to this manuscript, pruning and piecing it together, typing and retyping it in order to make it a more connected and readable story than it could otherwise have been. This encouragement has repeatedly stimulated my flagging efforts to complete this book while trying to do many other things at the same time.

Contents

A TIME TO SPEAK

1　First Impressions

As a boy I used to worry much about the "question." In fact I cannot remember any time in my life when it was very far from my thoughts. Not that it was a question which I ever really formulated; it was more a feeling of doubt which was always interfering, sometimes with my pleasures, sometimes with my beliefs. I would sense it as a rock beneath the surface of my sea where all else was plain sailing. Sometimes when, for no particular reason, I could feel an inner joy welling up inside me, it would wag an admonitory finger or clutch me by the coat tails. Sometimes it would impishly mock at the things I believed in and would poke out an impudent tongue at the person I thought of as me.

Most of my childhood that I can remember was spent in my father's parish on the banks of the river Itchen, where the people lived who worked in the shipbuilding yards, on the Southampton docks, or as the crews of trans-Atlantic liners and other passenger ships to India, South Africa, and the Far East. It was said at that time to be the second worst slum in England. That was during the First World War. There were living there, in a place called Northam, ten thousand people in an area of half a square mile.

My father was an Anglican clergyman, the son of an Anglican clergyman who was the son of a naval captain during Nelson's time. Our pride in this rugged old sailor, whose red-faced portrait and sash always hung in the hall, was dimmed a little, however, by the fact that he had been disowned by his father for reasons which were rather obscure.

This was my father's first living. He had come from a more prosperous parish near Southampton, and before that was curate at a place called Lowfield Heath on the borders of Sussex and Surrey, where my two elder brothers and I were born.

I understood my father and loved him very much, which I had to admit was more than I could honestly say about God, hard as ever I tried. My father was more of an athlete than a scholar. In fact he was a better than average all-round sportsman. He had played cricket for Scotland and always regretted a frost that had spoilt a chance he had been given in a Scottish rugby trial. In England he had played "soccer" as an amateur for Charlton and Sheffield United. All this stood him in good stead in that poor parish. He was a devoted "High Churchman" at a time when this was by no means popular amongst the episcopate. He was not a theologian or a sociologist in the tradition of Scott Holland, but had caught some of the fire of his convictions from Bishop King of Ely. He was never tempted to try any other path to the Kingdom of God, whether in Heaven or on Earth, than "the Faith." The Gospel story was to him a vital reality. The Incarnation, Cross, and Redemption were a living drama without which life was meaningless; and without the Sacraments it was unbearable. His faith and infectious enthusiasm carried him on, and others with him, in face of all the impossible tasks that were then expected of him and my mother in their lonely fight against the most degrading poverty and ignorance, at a time when human suffering and need were not dealt with at the political level or by National Health schemes and when there was little voluntary effort in the provincial slum areas.

My mother was not of the "managing" or condescending type which is often "attracted to social reform." She was then, and always remained, shy and diffident and nervous both of physical dangers and of other personalities more vigorous than her own. She came from a prim and sheltered home that belonged to a seemingly different world. Her forbears also belonged to the traditions of the Church and the navy. "I was the youngest of a family of ten," she wrote. "My mother was the daughter of a country clergyman brought up in the strictest early Victorian manner. She was a lovely girl and my father when paying a visit to the squire had fallen in love with her. After a very short courtship he took her out to Singapore where he had an appointment as Marine Magistrate, and there all her children were born and six of them died. When I was six months old my father was killed in a carriage accident and my mother brought me to England, where we lived in a large house with my grandfather and grandmother, a great uncle, a great aunt and a brother and sister of my mother and my own three sisters—truly a patriarchal household.

"We children had our day nursery or 'school room' as it was called and a large 'play room' and a 'night nursery' where we all slept with one of our nurses. We had all our meals in our school room with our nurses, except our dinner which we had with the grown-ups—a rather trying experience for we were not allowed to speak unless we were spoken to. On Sundays we were taken to Church. Everyone went, my grandparents, uncle and aunt, and we children, my mother and the nurses. But it was not considered 'the thing' for us to sit with our nurses in the pew at the front which was rented. They were relegated to the back of the Church."

If it had not been for my mother's sense of humour and her strong evangelical faith, I dread to think what the effect on her would have been of her arrival with us in that slum and the eleven years we were to spend there.

"I must confess," she wrote, "that when I first saw the place that was to be our home my heart sank within me. The house was large and damp and dirty, and the poor bit of grass (the only grass in the parish) which was the garden looked unkempt and untidy. The Church, though a good building, was dark and not very clean. One of the workmen who was doing work in the house said to me, 'That Church of yours, Mem, is that dark and dreary it fair gives me the pip.' When I told my husband that he said 'We won't rest until that is altered.' And it soon was and became a beautiful place and real home to many dear people.

"Of course it was all very difficult at first and I made all sorts of stupid mistakes. But my husband was splendid always, all the time, he never lost heart or courage, and the people, some out of that ten thousand, loved him. Of course we had no leisured people to help in the work of the Church and so we had to teach people to teach others. All the Sunday-school teachers were drawn from the elder girls and boys and we had a Sunday-school of about seven hundred.

"One of the things that worried me most was having to bring up my three boys in such a place. They went to school, first in the nearby town, and then to King's College, Taunton. But of course all their holidays were spent at home, and I used to wonder how it would affect their after life to see such a great deal of poverty and suffering and the work of the Church at its very hardest. But I was very wrong and faithless and, with a father like theirs as an example they were safe."

My brother Nigel's phrase in later life when he was campaigning for slum clearance in London with Father Jellicoe was "symphony of suffering," and it seemed to describe all that was life in that place as we grew up to understand it.

For my own part I wanted to believe all that my father and mother believed. It was really impossible to think of not believing it. Often I had a joyous overflowing feeling that it was all true. Too good to be true. "Too good to be true," my little imp would echo. If it is true, "Your heavenly Father knoweth that ye have need of all these things." Then why did it have to be like this? In any case if everybody believed what they said they believed—all the other people in the town and in England —why did they do nothing about it? Why was it left to my father and mother? For them to be possibly wrong was a thought too hideous, too cruel, too evil to be contemplated.

I could not and would not contemplate it, I had a horrible feeling that it must come from something evil and horrible in me. And always I came back to that half a square mile with its ten thousand people, and their houses built back to back in their long, narrow streets, all leading down to the river from which it had all been reclaimed. Periodically, the river overflowed in winter time and came within a few yards of our gate, flooding the cellar. Most of the houses in the parish would be flooded, and the people, already overcrowded, would have to exist as best they could in the upper rooms, often ten people of different ages and sexes in a single room. When the river receded the streets and lower floors of the houses were covered with a thick carpet of evil-smelling slime.

When these half-expressed doubts cast their shadow over my mind everything seemed bleak and dreary. The rain on a vast sea of slate roofs against a grey sky and a chill mist from the river shrouded the life of the people and stifled my thoughts and feelings.

My mother used to love reading more than any other form of recreation. She used to read both to old and young women some of her own favourites, especially Jane Austen, Dickens, *Pilgrim's Progress,* and even Shakespeare. Many used to come, some because they enjoyed hearing what she read to them, others perhaps to get away from the squalor, noise, and overcrowding of their own homes. The impossibility of being quiet by oneself is surely one of the most soul-destroying deprivations of slum life. My mother told me of one old lady who always carried about with her in a string bag her few precious possessions. She had only one leg and lived in a back room in a filthy house. She told my mother how much she enjoyed coming to her readings. "You see, my dear," she said, "when you are reading to us I can have a nice sleep. Of course I can't sleep of nights because of those others and the nasty bugs, and besides my landlady would try and pinch my bits of sugar and tea."

My mother was not very good at speaking to people about their shortcomings, and when they ridiculed her or were rude she became acutely embarrassed.

"One evening," she wrote, "I was coming home from a meeting in the little tram that came down from the town to our part of the world. One of the ladies of the parish was also coming home rather hilariously intoxicated. She did not see me at first as the tram was full. But presently she did see me and stopped short in her rather exuberant behaviour, threw her eyes to the roof, clasped her hands together and said 'Let us pray.' Of course everyone laughed and so I am afraid did I."

The possibility of evoking amongst the young people any appreciation of what she read, or enthusiasm for the things she believed in, strong enough to counterbalance all the pressures that were exerted on them in other directions, must have seemed to her very slight. Yet she was never tempted to apply the test of "results" to what she was trying to do.

Nor was it possible for me to fit in the harsh realities of Northam with other experiences I had of the world, with what I always thought of as "treats" such as outings to the New Forest and occasional plays, concerts, or pantomimes in the town.

Inside the church that had been so dark and grim when we first went there my father had worked wonders. It was brightly lit, and there were gaily coloured hangings and banners and brocade curtains and carpets with intricate designs which I could follow with my eye if the service got dull. My father put in a carved oak screen with a cross and Calvary group on top, and at Christmas we would erect a crib underneath. Every year there was a pageant in which we all took part, my brothers and I dressing up perhaps with a sword and a shield cut out of cardboard and silver paper to signify Faith or an Anchor for Hope or a Heart for Charity.

My mother took the part of Mother Church which to her was a great nervous strain, though no one would have known it. She did it with such simplicity and sincerity that it all seemed perfectly and wonderfully true though we knew it was make-believe. She was very much hindered by her shyness and diffidence from helping people who needed her help and whom she loved.

"My time," she wrote, "was largely taken up with my three children and with cooking. I was entirely ignorant of both jobs so had rather a hectic time. I remember being dreadfully agitated by being asked to see and speak seriously to a girl who, as her mother told me, had 'got into trouble.' The poor dear did come to see me and as far as I can remember we talked about everything else except her 'trouble.' But I loved to think that my husband was always 'Father' to all these dear people, and their Church was their home and they loved it. It was our refuge and strength and stay and our little Lady Chapel was a source of sure hope and confidence. We had the Blessed Sacrament reserved there; it made a tremendous difference to us all. I remember one day I was kneeling there when a woman came in and touched me. I looked up and she whispered 'My child'—it was her only one—'is dying: pray for us.' That was one who hardly ever came to Church and was too shy to come to a Mothers' Meeting. The child did die but the woman and her husband found God and were very faithful and loving worshippers in the Church and out of it. We had a guild of girls. All of them working girls busy the whole week. But the Church was their joy and pride. After we had left the parish one of the girls got T.B. When she was dying she asked for my husband and me to be sent for. We went to her and I could see something was troubling her. When I asked what it was she said 'I am only afraid I love you and Father more than Jesus.' I told her perhaps He had given us our love for each other to help us to understand His Love for us and she was quite happy."

The vicarage which was our home seemed to be the focus of so much of the misery and unhappiness of the place. Everyone who was in trouble or needed something seemed to come to the vicarage. As a small boy I would hear "grown-ups" crying in my father's study. Then after a time he would go out and dig furiously in the garden without saying a word for hours, till at last we would persuade him into a game of cricket. He would correct our style and show us the importance of a "straight bat" and how, though it was more difficult than taking a cross swing, it increased the chances of really hitting the ball.

The problem of keeping a straight bat was of course a technical one, but also a very personal problem of how to keep one's head in face of a fast-moving ball directed towards head, hands, or feet—how to keep one's control in face of surroundings which constantly evoked feelings of fear and dread, resentment, pity, or hostility.

When I went away to school it seemed as if I were going into another world. But always when I came back to Northam, dark, unformed doubts clouded over my mind, so that despite whatever I was taught and whatever I wanted to believe, it seemed as though the real world was a world of cruelty, of men and women swearing at one another, at their children, at other people's children, and at the Church too.

I remember there was an old cobbler to whom we used to take our shoes to be mended. He used to talk about the "rich and the poor." I was very lucky to have boots. Most of the children in the place at that time used to run about the streets even in the ice and snow of winter without any shoes or stockings on. A lot that the old cobbler used to say seemed true, and I liked to take my shoes and wait for him to patch them because he told me stories, stories he said they would never teach me at the Church or in school, about rebel leaders and peasant risings and the persecution of the despised non-conformists. "Why won't they tell me?" "Because," he would say, "you was born with a silver spoon in your mouth." That sounded absurd—like many of the things he said I should have to wait and see before I should understand. He said he had never been to school to learn how to read and write. Perhaps the history books I read were all written by people who could read and write, but a lot of history was written by people who couldn't read or write. One day perhaps I should learn about that too.

Then there were other things to worry about. My red school cap always seemed to be attracting a lot of attention. The other children used to think I was trying to put on airs. I looked like a red-top match, they said. And gangs would waylay me and want to fight. If I got the better of one boy, another would take his place, until I was so exhausted and battered I had to give in. The garden was "our" garden, and other children could not be allowed in without permission. This of course was the cause of a lot of jealousy. But if they were allowed in they would swarm all over it and trample flowers and cut down sticks from the shrubs, and would even use it as a lavatory. So they were forbidden to come in and sometimes when they did the police would be called in.

At times, though, I would slip out with some tin soldiers in my pocket to play with those children in an alleyway. I was proud of my little possessions and perhaps I wanted to show them off. I did not see any reason why I should not play with the others. They spoke a little differently perhaps, and some were a little dirtier, but there was not any real difference that I noticed. However, once I was seen playing with them in the street and it was reported to my mother, who sent for me in a great state of mind. I was to be punished for "playing in the gutter." When I said I didn't know there was anything wrong, my mother looked as though she did not believe me at first; but then, after a long searching look, she went away and came back with her eyes all red and said I would not be punished and could stay up to supper and afterwards get on with my homework. Then I had a feeling that I must have cheated and got myself out of a punishment by saying I could not see it was wrong when it was wrong and I ought to have known it as otherwise my mother would not have been so upset about it. But there was homework to do, and my mind could not cope with so many difficulties at once.

At school I had a very strict form-mistress. For our homework she would insist on our getting sixty marks out of a possible hundred or it would mean a spanking. When others were looking on, awaiting their turn, there was of course the double indignity of being put across someone's knee with one's trousers down, as well as the physical pain inflicted. However the victim might try his best to "take it like a man," it was always continued until his spirit of resistance was broken. Then afterwards, for the rest of the day, there was the ridicule to be faced from enemies and friends alike.

Looking back, it seems that such an excessive use of corporal punishment as a corrective was harmful for all concerned, inducing a semi-permanent state of fear, as well as an abhorrence for those studies which we found most dull or difficult and which the teachers seemed unable to bring to life.

When it came to correcting our homework, with all its fateful implications, the teacher would read out the correct answers and we then had to mark our own exercise books. Then there was the breathless business of adding up the marks at the end. All too often there was the even more breathless moment of saying I had sixty marks when I had only fifty or fifty-five. If I were caught it would mean a double dose for lying as well as laziness. If not, I would be free from fear for a whole day until tomorrow, unless I was unskilful enough to be caught out over something else. Before and after the punishment was inflicted there was always a good deal of talk about how they really loved me and hated this being necessary. As a rule there was also a prayer in school chapel afterwards about the need of forgiveness for our wrongdoings and asking for help to make us more obedient or truthful in the future so that I felt very confused both about love and truth.

Of my mother's and father's love I had no doubt. My father certainly believed all that he taught, and sent me to schools where I should be taught the same faith. The headmaster believed it too. We would often hear him saying his prayers in the chapel and singing hymns all by himself to his own accompaniment on the harmonium. He used to bring the boarders at the school to my father's church, walking them in "crocodile" more than two miles in time for the Sung Eucharist on Saints' days at 6.30 in the morning.

Yet my father seldom used to speak in terms of duty and obedience. He made religion so real, and the things he believed in so much alive, that religion corresponded to my own little inner joy. My father was a good man and a very good sportsman too. He was a better man than any other man I knew, and if he could believe it all, that should be good enough for me too.

Life was not always sombre though. There was a great deal of good humour and excitement and a great deal of pleasure to be had, especially when we went on "excursions" to the New Forest for the day. One source of great pleasure and excitement was a small sailing boat someone had given my father. It was a 22-foot ship's gig off the King's yacht *Alexandra,* which came to one of the yards to be scrapped. We used to keep her down at one of the shipyards and would go off sailing for the day with an old "salt" acting as skipper. She was fitted with a lug sail and jib and a false keel and two pairs of oars. We would go right down past the shipyards—Day and Summer's and Camper Nicholson's—on the banks of the Itchen, past the docks and the big ships coming up Southampton Water, and out into the Solent. Old Skipper Garnett would tell us of all sorts of adventures on ships he had sailed in, of waves as tall as poplar trees, and queer fish and creatures which looked like little red men swimming under water. We used to pass astern of some of the big trans-Atlantic liners and would turn to head up into their wake after they had towered above us and glided majestically by.

For one glorious summer month in the year we would go away to the sea for a holiday or to the New Forest, where with long poles we went jumping over marshes on the heath. We jumped from one mound to another and when we landed on a tuft of grass the turf all around us would sway and heave. Showing above the surface were the horns of cattle which had sunk and been swallowed up by the bog, which made it seem very dangerous.

These pleasures all helped me to put off thinking about the "question." But my mother would get very worried sometimes by my raising "problems" and would tell me not to "sit staring like that" or to "stop frowning," which would irritate me, as I was not aware that I was frowning. Momentarily I would rather resent not being allowed to follow my own thoughts through but would often, since they did not seem to lead anywhere, find some comfort in self-pity and be secretly glad of the diversion from trying to think things out.

Once I remember finding a small book amongst some things that had been sent to the house for a jumble sale. I glanced at it and slipped it into my pocket. I remember it was entitled *Vive la Commune,* though written in English, and it was all about Paris after the French Revolution. One evening, when I thought everyone else was out at a rehearsal and I was left to finish my homework, one of the young women whose guild was organizing the jumble sale asked me what I was reading. Was it one of my school books and was it part of my homework? Guiltily I said yes, it was a history book, but when she tried to take it to look at I tried to hold on to it, and she asked me what it was all about. I said sulkily it was about Paris. And she asked suspiciously that I let her see it and twisted my wrist till I was forced to let it go. Then she accused me of stealing the book from the room where things were being sorted for the jumble sale, since she had seen it there. She said it was a very serious matter as it was not a book that was meant for me and I had no business to be reading it. She thought she would have to report me to my school-teacher for neglecting my homework in the first place and for stealing this book and then lying to her about it. She asked me if I would prefer to take my punishment from her or whether I would prefer to have it reported at the school. I was horrified, for as I told her tearfully I had already been punished at school that day for not doing my homework and that was why I had not gone to the rehearsal with the others.

She said in that case she would not report me, but would think over herself what she was going to do to cure me of stealing and telling her lies. She was going to take the book with her with a page of some of my writing in it as evidence. She went away with the book, leaving me pale and frightened to go on with my homework, but unable to apply my mind to it for wondering what would happen. I felt very guilty, partly from a knowledge of having stolen the book, but also for stealing thoughts from the book on matters which were for some reason not meant for me. She kept the book and used it afterwards to keep me in suspense and make me do things for her, threatening that one day she would have to teach me my lesson.

All the doubts and fears that I had about these and many other matters seemed to loom larger and larger in the back of my mind without ever being formulated or expressed in any particular way. Somehow I knew that one day they would catch up with me. Even at that time I used to have terrifying dreams that I was being pursued by something. I could never discover what it was, but my legs could not carry me at more than a snail's pace. I often have this dream even to this day, but with the additional variant that I manage to reach a car or vehicle of some kind, only to find then that I am being carried away by something which I can no longer control.

Though at this time I had not really formulated any of the questions which never seemed to lead to any solution, they were all, I think, part of the same question of human suffering, of hatred, cruelty, and evil in the world—not merely the conscious cruelty of deliberate acts but the often greater cruelty of indifference to suffering and the unawareness of the consequences of actions or of inaction. This, so it later seemed to me, is all part of the problem of war and peace. With the false beliefs which enable human beings to act as they do towards one another, goes their remoteness from the consequences of their acts so increasingly characteristic of modern life and modern warfare.

Perhaps there is a "lie in the soul" of each of us which forever tries to escape the real issues, to pretend that one day we will really turn and face them, and continuously postpones the day. But of course all this did not occur to me then.

The times in which we lived and events in the great outside world did of course affect us. There was the disaster of the *Titanic,* many of whose crew were drawn from my father's parish. She was thought to be unsinkable when we saw her off from the docks on her maiden voyage. Then there came the First World War with the never-ending stream of infantry and artillery en route to the docks or returning from the front. Our bright school caps were always being asked for as souvenirs as the men rode by on their mules and gun carriages. I remember the Seventh Division going through from their remount depot to the docks. All day long there was the sound of their songs mingling with the clatter of hooves and wheels on cobblestones.

They were all so gay, so lighthearted, to have been going to their deaths, as we were afterwards told so many of them had, on the battle-fields of Ypres. They seemed to have no care in the world as they rode by rising in their stirrups with a slight swinging swagger, so strong and sure in their handling of frightened mules and pack-horses.

Unlike the Second World War, the First seemed then to us children to be more of a crusade. There were no doubts about our aims or con-fusion about our allies. It was a fight for freedom, right, and justice. The marching of long columns of troops gave to the drab streets and slate roofs of Northam a new sense of significance, a sense of being caught up in a great world drama, though it was of course a significance which we could not very well understand. Gradually it all became more sombre, the march of the troops less carefree, and their songs less spontaneous. Sometimes a band or the skirl of the pipes made up for the silence of the men as they marched. Now they carried as part of their equipment ugly looking gas masks with long corrugated windpipes; and replacing the Royal Field Artillery came the more inhuman but grimly determined and efficient looking tanks, with their caterpillar wheels and the men con-cealed inside them.

All through this time of war my parents seemed to have an infinite capacity for entering into the troubles and fears of the people, sombre enough in the light of the workaday world, but overshadowed at night by the searchlights lacing and stabbing at the darkness all through the long hours. Their own faith was joyous and infectious, not an evasion or denial of the reality of suffering, but rather an entering into it and a triumphing over it.

I remember one day when it seemed to me as if the "question" was about to catch up with me. We were all in the garden with a lot of other children. I was having a swing. My father was pushing a wheelbarrow-ful of small children. They were swaying about, and he was trying to keep them balanced. Then the wheelbarrow fell over sideways and the children tumbled out on the grass, delightedly squealing and wriggling.

I roared with laughter and we all thought it a great joke. Then I noticed that my father did not move or get up. He was pretending he could not. That was funnier still. The children started pulling him up, but they could not. He fell back every time. It was so funny I thought I must surely burst with so much laughter.

Some grown-up came up and stooped to help him. Then they began taking the children away, and somebody went running towards the house. Something had happened to my father. My laughter shrivelled up. I began to be afraid. Something in my mind was falling, falling. I jumped from the swing and ran towards my father, but they would not let me get to him. They were trying to carry him. I struggled and fought with some grown-ups who were holding on to me. But they were too strong for me, and I cried with frustration and fear. Then somebody said there was nothing to be frightened about. My father was just a little bit giddy and would be all right in half a jiffy. I was only making a fool of myself, they said. So I gave in.

They carried him into the house. For days and nights he hung between life and death. People spent hours praying for him. My mother was always going off into church whenever she could get a few minutes. She put a brave face on it, but what with the parish and the family her burdens and anxieties must have been almost unbearable.

It was one day when my father's curate, whom we were all rather inclined to poke fun at, was with us praying with him that my father opened his eyes and looked round the room.

What a wonderful feeling when I knew, inside myself, that he was not going to die and they were not telling lies to me any more. Slowly, day by day, he got better. And every moment that I was allowed to spend with him was precious. My whole world was secure at the feel of his hand on my head and I hugged him. I never wanted to let him go. It must always be like this. "As it was in the beginning," the curate was finishing with the words of the *Gloria Patri* . . . "As it was in the beginning, is now and ever shall be, world without end." And I said "Amen" more fervently than I had ever said it, because I believed in it now and realized I had not been praying as I ought, and it might be thought I had not been believing in it. I felt the vibration of my father's chest as he said it too; it was like an affirmation of life and it dispelled that terrifying loneliness which had come over me when I first knew something was wrong with him.

It was some time after this when I was eleven or twelve that I was prepared for Confirmation, and my first Confession and Communion. The eagerness with which I listened to the explanations of the Catechism and Creed and the meaning of Creation and Redemption, and the joy I had in a more confident faith, were overshadowed to some extent by the bewilderment I experienced when my father took my brothers and me one at a time for a walk in the churchyard, as he quite often did when he had something serious to talk about. This evening he told us about the "facts and mysteries of life." To my brothers who were older than me this explanation may have corresponded to some inner experience of sex. I felt completely bewildered. My father warned me of temptations and abuses I might be subject to either at school or at the hands of grown-ups. I was very much taken aback. I had often heard blasphemies and obscenities. They were the commonplace talk in the streets and trams and shops, but I had never associated them with sex or the origin of life. I had never thought about the origin of life before, much less the origin of my own life. The thought that my own life was the result of what my father described, with the implication that this had taken place between him and my mother, simply did not bear thinking about. And because it meant nothing to me in the realm of actual experience at that time, I put the thought of it away and refused to accept what he had told me, though I could not doubt that he had meant what he said and that he meant me to believe it as much as any other serious thing that he told me.

When I came to make my first Confession to the curate I was puzzled by his questions and the rather suspicious but understanding way in which he persisted in asking them. He warned me that boys and girls had to face many difficulties, both at school and when they went out to work. Many of them had to face deliberate attempts by other boys and girls or young men and women to corrupt them. He told of initiation rites in which they might be forced to show they were growing up by having natural or unnatural experiences in front of their other workmates. The more I thought about it the more horrifying it became, so I tried not to think about it. I remained bewildered that the knowledge of it had come from my father and the curate, from whom had also come my knowledge of the most holy and beautiful things in life. It was not till some six or seven years afterwards that I remember having any strong or direct experience that I could identify as sex. Meanwhile I built up my defences and grew up to hate and fear something which I had not really as yet experienced.

I was very puzzled by what I was taught about the Crucifixion. The story itself was horrible but quite intelligible. What I could not understand was how my sins could have affected it or how Christ's death could bring about my salvation. We were always being told that by our sins we were crucifying Christ afresh. By my disobedience, my cheating or lying, I was actually nailing Christ to the Cross. If I was sorry, He would forgive me; and if I loved Him and wanted to please Him, He would give me the grace to do His will. Yet I could not help a feeling of revulsion at the idea of eating His body and drinking His blood especially if I was responsible for His death. When I went up to receive the Holy Communion I would feel very self-conscious, and when I turned round to walk back to my place I would feel strangely flat. I ought to be feeling as if I could fly, but here I was putting one foot in front of the other and feeling rather foolish. On the other hand sometimes I had a strange sense of belonging to God when I got back to my place, and I would be filled with a great sense of wonder and joy. I could not relate it to the doctrine of the Crucifixion and of salvation by the Body and Blood. That seemed revolting, but there must be something wrong with me because of the fervour with which other people sang hymns about being "washed in the blood of the lamb." If people really believed that by their sins they were actually driving nails into His hands and feet, surely they would not keep on doing it. How could they all come trooping out of church and start talking and laughing as though it made no difference, or as if it were only true when we were in church? Outside it almost seemed as though other people's sufferings did not matter so much or must just be accepted as part of their share in the sufferings of Christ.

I had a horrible feeling that it really did not all make sense, but I put away the thought; because if it failed to make sense, then nothing would make any sense. I would be alone, I would not belong to anyone. And it was terrifying to think of not belonging to anyone in an impersonal world of meaningless suffering.

Some time after my father had recovered from his illness, and after the war had ended in tumultuous victory celebrations in the streets, we went for our summer holiday to Milford on the sea. We set out in the

Alexandra from Day and Summer's yard. My mother and the skipper's wife went ahead by rail with the luggage.

It was a wonderful holiday, and in the middle of it my father heard from the squire of a small village in Suffolk. He had heard about my father's illness, and asked him if he would care to come and see him in connection with the living of Stoke by Nayland, which was under his patronage. During the last few days of our holiday my father went off to see Sir Joshua Rowley and the village of Stoke by Nayland. We secretly dreaded the return to Northam in a day or two and the long grey winter ahead, though as if by common consent we never spoke of our dread. That evening we walked down the road to meet my father, who would be returning on his bicycle from Lymington station.

He looked very depressed as he came up to us and got off his bicycle. Our hearts sank. My mother began talking very quickly about the best holiday we had ever had, and about how we would be coming back again next year if something else did not turn up before then as it quite probably would. Then my father started laughing at our long faces. Excitedly we realized he had been joking. We could hardly wait to hear as he began telling us about Stoke by Nayland—how its great thirteenth-century church stood high up on a hill and was renowned all over the county as an example of perpendicular architecture. He described the lovely old village with its timbered houses and spoke of Tendring Hall where there was a cricket pitch as good as a county ground. He said it was right in the middle of the Constable country and the church figured in some of his landscapes. Questions came tumbling one after another before he could begin to answer them. My poor father began to realize he was perhaps making a mistake. First he had cast us down, now he was lifting us up. We were already delighting in a new and unbelievably wonderful world.

He knew, and my mother knew, that there were many weighty matters to be considered. He could not let himself be rushed into taking any decision, but our own minds were already being made up as we walked along the road. Anything else was unthinkable. Excitedly we pulled him along, tugging at him to answer our questions. An impossible situation was being created for a man as devoted to his Church and his parish as he was to his family.

How weighty is a weighty matter? And how free is the conscience of a married priest with a family in such a lonely outpost of the Church's salient against evil? Without his wife and family life, the work of our parish would not have been what he had made of it. His faith expressed itself through his family life as well as his work and worship, and it was thus it revealed its meaning to many who would hardly have understood it otherwise. He himself might not have been the same person. Another priest who was a bachelor came to the parish afterwards and destroyed so much of the good work he had done by his failings under the strain. Moreover, these failings eventually resulted in his imprisonment.

In the days that followed, my mother, who had suffered more than anybody else from anxiety and the extra work and worry which had fallen on her during my father's illness, tried hard not to influence him to accept the offer of the living, which Sir Joshua, we learned, had made my father simply in order to give us a period of peace and quiet. Eventually he was prevailed upon by the doctor to leave the slums for a while at least.

He knew, and we all knew in our different ways, that we were leaving something unfinished—though I also had a feeling of escaping out of some dark and seemingly interminable tunnel.

In Suffolk we began to grow up into some of the delights of the countryside, the small unspectacular quietness of the Constable country with all its mellowing human features—a church, a mill, or a wagon merging in the smoky mist of winter or the hot haze of summer—such as appear in Constable's pictures.

There were tennis parties and cricket matches in summer and the otter-hounds and beagles for those who could not afford fox-hunting. I was ashamed of myself for being ashamed of following hounds and would never let on to my brothers that I was ashamed. I thought it was part of the "question" which was following me and which, one day, would surely catch me up.

My two elder brothers went up to Oxford. I hoped to be a doctor and to join the Universities Mission to Central Africa after all that I had heard from Bishop May, who always used to visit us at Northam whenever he came on leave from his diocese of Northern Rhodesia. I had a great admiration for him and for Bishop Weston, whose controversy over the Kikuyu (a theological controversy between Christian denominations) meant little to me at the time, though I have since wondered how far the subsequent situation in Kenya might have been altered had a different spirit prevailed amongst Christians.

I wonder, also, whether my own ambition to become a doctor was not part of my own inward controversy over the "question," part of the search for the inner secret of life?

At this time, during my last year at school, I was also a little concerned that something was not right internally which was affecting me physically. It was not part of the code at school to worry about health, however, and I put the thought aside. I had won my rugger colours during the last autumn term at school, but did very badly in athletics the following term. I attributed this partly to smoking with my friends and to being caught when I was a sub-prefect. In spite of the fact that I received eight with a cane for this from the headmaster, I was made a senior prefect, but I felt very unhappy and nervous in this role and could not bring myself to inflict corporal punishment, which at that time in the school made one appear weak and ineffectual and fair game for small boys who had a sure instinct for such weakness in a prefect.

My inner feeling grew into a very definite pain which left me sweating at nights until one night I could no longer conceal it and was hurried off to the local hospital. There I was very embarrassed by the attentions of a young nurse. I made light of the pains which by that time had grown less acute, and was allowed to leave on a negative diagnosis. When I returned to school for my last term I knew there was something wrong and told my housemaster that it was due to an internal strain during a tug-of-war. Being little use at cricket or athletics, my physical weakness was not so conspicuous during my last summer term at school as it would have been if it were a football term.

When the result of the School Certificate examinations came through after my last term I found that, though I had passed, I lacked a credit in one subject and could not be excused responsions before going up to Oxford. So in order to earn some pocket money I was to go as junior master to a prep school for a year and put in some study by correspondence course. I was extremely nervous about my new responsibilities and my lack of qualifications. I was able to interest the elder boys in such subjects as English and history, but I did not know how to cope with the very junior boys and was afraid of the elder ones in those subjects where my own lack of qualifications could hardly be concealed if I were stumped by a Latin translation or made a mistake at mathematics. I was determined to try and get back into training before going up to Oxford. So I took to smoking a pipe instead of cigarettes and went for cross-country runs. Also, every Saturday that I was not on duty I went off to play "rugger" for the Dorking R.F.C., but I lacked the zest for it that I used to have.

The question of discipline was a nightmare, both in school and when out for walks on the downs. A climax was reached one night when a woman member of the staff who was on dormitory duty surprised some of the boys at a midnight feast. She threatened them with a beating from me if she had any more nonsense and an hour later she was knocking on my door. Not wanting to appear soft, I ordered each one to bend over and applied the sole of my slipper. My prestige never recovered from that inadequacy, either amongst the staff or the boys.

Not long after this I began to experience a recurrence of my former attacks of pain, which grew in intensity until I finally had to be admitted to hospital. There the pain and fear I experienced while awaiting an operation greatly increased my dread of hospitals and their ways. Finally I was operated on for the removal of my gall bladder. In the course of the operation they discovered some T.B. mesenteric glands and I was advised to go to Dr. Rollier's sun cure clinic at Leysin in Switzerland.

My father was able to take the English chaplaincy at Leysin and he and my mother both came out with me. It was a new world to us. We had left England by the night-boat from Harwich during the General Strike of 1926. My two brothers were having the time of their lives acting as special policeman and railway porter.

We arrived in cloud and rain which lasted for ten days with hardly a glimpse of anything but pine forests on the immediate slopes. And then one day we awoke to a blue sky and the sun gleaming on the white snows of the mountains, and the Rhone valley five thousand feet beneath us. From my bed I could see right across to the peaks of the Dents du Midi and the steep slopes of the Chamoissaire with the waterfalls tumbling down its sides. The mists of the valleys were quickly drawn up into the sun, and I began to feel within myself the radiant heat, vibrant with new life and hope.

Nevertheless, I could not help recalling a remark of the famous surgeon who operated on me. When he asked me what I was going to do with my life I told him I had been thinking of becoming a doctor but might go into the Church. He waved his hand at a row of test tubes and jars containing specimens and said: "There is my God. If I had thought you were going to waste your life I might not have taken so much trouble over you."

I lay in the sun and tried to think things out. I had had no grounding in philosophy, but I felt the time would come when I should have to turn round and face the "question" before it caught me unawares. Which was I to think of as reality? The might and majesty of the mountains, dazzling white in the sun, or the grey lines of slate roofs shrouded in a mist which concealed the silent suffering in places like Northam, where people were less privileged than I was? Where was the truth to be found —in life and beauty and creation, or in the denial of life, in disease, corruption, and death? The question began to formulate itself.

I would press on in the hope or expectation shared by others that

> *Somewhere beyond the railheads*
> *Of reason, north or south,*
> *Lies a magnetic mountain*
> *Riveting sky to earth.*

My parents returned to England, and as the months went by and I lay there still in the sun, I could find no certainty in my alternating moods of exalted confidence and futility and defeat. Had my father not left Northam, had I gone on living there, Dr. Rollier said I should probably have been dead, like thousands of others there who had been dying of the same disease.

When it was time for me to return the doctors all advised me against trying to study medicine at one of the London hospitals or going up to Oxford because of the damp climate. However, one of my father's churchwardens in Suffolk, Henry Engleheart, had a brother who was an archdeacon in the Cape Province of South Africa. He was in charge of a leper settlement on Robin Island and was opening a new settlement on the mainland for those who had been partly cured and could not live with their families and for those families which still had to live in isolation. The archdeacon invited me to go out there and help him, though I had no qualifications for doing so. The doctors said I was clear of T.B. and agreed to this plan.

The family came down to see me off on the *Carnarvon Castle's* maiden voyage from Southampton docks. My father and brothers shook hands stiffly with me on the deck and then went off and waved from the dockside. We all tried to be very matter-of-fact about it and were rather contemptuous of those passengers who held streamers of coloured paper till the slow movement of the ship broke them one by one.

My father's old parish still lay huddled behind the shipyards, grey and dim in the mists of a late autumn afternoon, and the mud flats of South-ampton Water reminded me of the many times we had sailed away from it in the summer time. We had left that problem unsolved—my father and I. Then it was different when we sailed away. Now I was leaving him too for a new life in Africa and it was not without some foreboding.

When I had told my doctor in Switzerland about my future plan he had questioned me about where I had been living and what I intended to do. When I had told him about Northam and about the invitation to South Africa, he had stiffened his fingers and, with a little shrug of the shoulders, had murmured, not intending to be heard, *"Plus ça change plus c'est la même chose."*

2 South Africa, First Visit

There is something symbolic of Africa about Table Bay. The huge mass of the mountain stands up stark and clear against the sky and dwarfs civilized little Cape Town, at its foot, to the size of a few dolls' houses and toy trams and trains. So it seemed at first, at least, because I saw nothing and really wanted to see nothing of "the question." I had been greatly excited by the chance of getting away from civilization. I had looked forward for so long to the prospect of another world of beauty and adventure, a world which, however untamed and uncivilized, would at least be free in its unsophistication from the hypocrisy and inhumanity of the civilized life I had known, where my father's tireless devotion and enthusiasm had so often seemed like a private war against society.

Perhaps it was some sickness of soul and body in myself that was responsible for heightening and fostering the illusion of the great mass of Table Mountain. It symbolized the height and spaciousness I had longed for in contrast to mean city streets, the world I had read about in the life of Livingstone and heard so much about from Bishop May.

So from the deck of the *Carnarvon Castle* as she berthed I scanned the docks and streets of Cape Town and speculated on all that lay beyond the mountain.

The Cape had a beauty beyond all my expectations. The mountains seemed to come right down to the sea. The vineyards flowed like a green sea to the foot of the mountains and over their sunlit lower slopes. Range after range could be seen till mauve mists enveloped them and merged in the blue sky. Some of the upper valleys and hills are almost covered with the blossom of fruit trees, like fleecy clouds delicately tinted as a flamingo.

On the Cape Flats there is an infinite variety of succulents and heaths. The abundance of colour in the gardens of old Cape homesteads, with their flowering trees and shrubs and tumbling bougainvilleas and morning glory, overwhelmed me with a sense of such richness and variety of beauty that at first it seemed impossible to keep my eyes still. Yet unless one's eyes rested on these splendours each new impression could not be so fully and exquisitely felt.

By the time we had motored out from Cape Town to St. Raphael's Faure I felt quite exhausted with delight. It was late afternoon when we drove up to Archdeacon Engleheart's house. His house and the chapel alongside it, forming three sides of a quadrangle, and a little summerhouse which was to be my study could be seen from the drive. His little garden in the courtyard was alight with every colour, and there were most exciting flashes from big bright butterflies and hummingbirds.

This beauty seemed almost too prolific, almost wasteful, for how could it all ever be appreciated? As I watched, fascinated by a small lizard, I was startled by the sound of the chapel bell. It rang out the three threes and a nine of the Angelus. I could not move; I seemed for a moment to be transported back to Northam, and a host of half-formed memories and emotions rushed through my mind so that I could not think of the words of the Angelus and it all seemed incongruous. The bell for Compline followed, and I could hardly find my voice to sing the familiar chant:

> *Before the ending of the day*
> *Creator of the world we pray*
> *That with thy wonted favour thou*
> *Wouldst be our guard and keeper now. . . .*

Archdeacon Engleheart was a very saintly man with a very strict code of orthodoxy and convention. A conservative, and in many ways an autocrat, both in religion and politics, his somewhat irascible manner was tempered by a courtesy derived from a well-to-do Victorian upbringing and a deep human kindness and generosity, which were as much a product of his supernatural religion as were his strictness and conservatism. These latter, however, were the only things about him that seemed at all out of keeping with his environment. He was saturated with the sunshine and beauty of his garden and of the Cape Peninsular and the Hottentot Holland Mountains, which could be seen from his stoep and from the open door of my summer-house when I lay in the sun and read.

The little chapel where we sang Compline every evening, and where he celebrated Communion every morning, was of a different order of beauty, not exactly incongruous but belonging to an order of things seemingly different from the untamed beauty and the prolific life which abounded everywhere else.

My first impression of the Africans was of a rather aloof people, inclined to be suspicious of anyone whom they did not know who tried to speak to them about anything other than the practical details of the work at hand, yet not wanting to offend, a people with an unusual anxiety to please. I did not understand either of these characteristics at the time.

I lived a rather secluded life in South Africa at first. St. Raphael's was a settlement for lepers—or so it was regarded ("and non-Europeans at that, poor devils," as someone put it)—and was almost completely isolated from the surrounding countryside. But the archdeacon used to take me to various social functions at Bishopscourt, the lovely home of Archbishop Carter, and I would visit some of his friends occasionally in their beautiful old Cape homesteads. His friends were Christian folk and it was some time before I began to sense the full strength of colour prejudice in South Africa. This would come out in moments of extreme exasperation, or if in the course of polite conversation the "colour question" was inappropriately referred to, or on a rare occasion when a non-European might show signs of being stubborn or "cheeky."

However, at St. Raphael's, as in some other institutions for the sick, a much greater familiarity and friendliness prevailed than is customary in South Africa or thought desirable by many except under exceptional circumstances of misfortune. At the same time there was the double barrier of leprosy as well as colour between the patients at St. Raphael's and the outside world, and this seemed to cut them off from both normal white and black society.

There was actually little danger from contagion, but the ravages of the disease on their disfigured faces and limbs, as well as on their minds, made people shrink away even though they tried not to show their horror. In many cases their relatives would not offer homes to the families of those who were sick, as they would have done under more normal cases of sickness; or it may have been that they were too poor to be able to afford this for so long a time. At any rate some kind of community life had to be provided for them and nursery schools for their children.

The nurses and teachers, both white and black, felt that they were cut off from the world too. Let no one say that the South Africans have not got it in them to overcome racial barriers and prejudices, which so many of them experience as something instinctive and inborn, as part of their natures.

How supremely devoted they were to their work, those young white South Africans, both men and women, at St. Raphael's. There were no claims to heroism or to doing anything spectacular or courageous, but an unassuming satisfaction in a job which needed doing and to be done well. There was nothing much noticeable, other than a quiet devotion day in day out, week in week out, year in year out, to those whose poor minds were often clouded with suspicion and resentment against a world from which all the drama and colour, all the light and love, had gone, a world which had never had any justice in it. The hope and beauty that had gone left them looking like human derelicts at times, like the old hulks of ships on bleak mud flats slowly breaking up under the wind and the weather, especially when you came upon them unawares and they had no time to brighten up for you. Yet these people were infinitely precious in the sight of God. So they were to the archdeacon, whose conventional courtesy, meticulous ways, and strictness, both in the letter and spirit of his religion, seemed like something hard and clean and firm in the midst of so much that seemed to be undergoing a process of slow rot and moral and physical disintegration.

Most moral problems tended to become intensified, and personal relations were severely tested in this small and isolated community where nerves were stretched very taut and where very small, unimportant things seemed to loom very large. We had to make the effort to rise above pettiness and meanness.

There were some in whom an "arrested cure" had been effected at an early stage in the disease, others to whom it had come too late to save them from terrible disfigurements. Some were quite young and still had all the love of life and beauty in them, yet they had to see strangers, and even fellow lepers, shrink away from them in horror. Half their face was beautiful and sensitive and appeared to have the soft bloom of pristine sex upon it; the other half was repellent, with the flesh eaten away or the features fixed in a permanent sneer or grin. Some would have only one or two fingers left on one hand; the other would be just a stump. They would use what fingers or stump they had to sew or make baskets and mats. Some were lame, some blind. But each would have some faculty which could still discern or extract from life some quality of sound or sense which they valued. Some had primitive musical instruments they had made themselves and could still play. Often it happened that whatever remained to them of life, so full of variety and possibilities to those of us who were whole, became a source of fiercely jealous competition among them.

This used to distress me a great deal, making me realize that I had a mind which could think, had been schooled to reason coherently, and I was too lazy to use it except when I had to apply myself to a particular task requiring concentration. I had eyes to see with, but so much of the beauty all around me and over my head and under my feet went unnoticed. What would one of these unfortunates shut up in a dark cell of a prison give for five minutes with my eyes? What delight that brief five minutes would give to that desolate creature staring blindly into the sun's warm blackness. Or that one peering up questioningly as I approached him. Were they ever jealous of me with my sight, these poor dispossessed? Or perhaps mercifully could they not remember?

How could God be so cruel? If He had a mind to create such beauty, why must these minds be closed, their eyes dimmed, and their whole personalities so warped? Why must their lives be such travesties of human life? Did Jesus see such people? He must have seen them often. Only some of them got healed and glorified God. What of the others? When they did not return to give thanks to God perhaps they felt too enraptured and were carried away by their delight. Could they be blamed? Could Jesus have healed all the other lepers there were? Did it require something from them? Apparently not, only the desire and the will to be healed. Perhaps we could all heal them if only we had enough faith. Once I felt so moved to pity by the sight of a leper that I went up and touched him and, under my breath in case he should be disappointed, I asked God to give him back his sight. But nothing happened. I felt very foolish and blamed my pride for thinking anything would happen and then for feeling foolish when it did not.

But supposing what I had once dreamt were possible, would I be prepared to change places with one of these unfortunates whom this dread disease had left only half alive? In my dream I had fled in blind panic from the hellish abyss, but unless I would be prepared to face that and embrace it, what was the worth and sincerity of my pity?

Deep down within me I felt the beginnings of a revolt which I could not understand. It began with an instinctive revulsion, though not against these pitiful, defeated creatures, hideous in their misfortune and lacking the will or the desire to fight, unaware of the injustice of their lot or of any means to resist the oppression which was crushing them, an oppression not only man-made but of the whole natural order of things. I felt for them, because I could not bring myself to accept the possibility of exchanging their lot for mine, an instinctive feeling of revolt as though I were one of them, having my comparatively whole body, mind, and soul with which to rebel against their oppression. Almost it seemed, while I could not express it at the time, as though in the hierarchy of things, beauty, truth, and goodness, truth itself was ranged against beauty and goodness. How could love, if it could be identified with goodness and beauty, acquiesce in the cruel processes of nature devouring people's bodies, minds and souls while they were still alive?

I was afraid of this feeling, yet I could never get away from it. Perhaps it could have been traced back as part of the same experience in the cobbler's shop in Northam, or the furtive reading of a forbidden book, or the thought of homework neglected and the physically frightening consequences.

After breakfast in the morning I used to ride off across the sandy flats covered with wattle and heath as high as the horse's head to study with my tutor. He was an old man who was so bent when he walked that his body was almost at right angles to his legs and he would point out that the action of his sticks in relation to his legs was the same as the action of a galloping horse, only not so fast.

The old man had been a Cambridge don, and had come back to sing his *Nunc Dimittis* in the land he loved. The plan was that he should take me in Latin and Greek and a little history and philosophy. It was the nearest I ever got to a University education. But there were other things that made up for some of the difference. Though his old body was gnarled and bent, his mind was more alert than mine. He had a much greater power of concentration, though there were times when I was so enthralled by his thoughts and the new worlds he was trying to get me to glimpse in his off-hand manner that I wanted to tell him to hurry, hurry, because it all seemed so important. To him it was all just commonplace, almost a routine lecture course. I suppose he had, in fact, delivered these perorations time and time again. Yet he enjoyed this last fling of his wit and scholarship. I think he taught me how to doubt the very foundations of my faith and yet to keep faith. And for that, and for all the effort it cost him, I shall be eternally grateful. For he taught me in such a way that the more I learned from him the more I came to know I did not know.

It was to me a new adventure into the unknown, though not the sort of adventure I had associated with Africa and had looked forward to with such excitement. I felt rather uneasy and fearful about it, for it was not easy to fit these ideas into the rigid doctrinal system of my father and the archdeacon. I had an idea that it belonged to a forbidden territory across an uncharted sea. How much of my own inward trouble had come upon me already through venturing into uncharted waters. I was afraid. I wanted to live, to feel healthy and strong again with that exuberant love of life I had felt sometimes as a small boy when I was able to get away from the overshadowing gloom of city streets, the noise of traffic and the worries of school. I was frightened of death. For a time I had thought I might be going to die. The pain had been a good deal worse than could be conveyed to doctors and nurses who expected cheerfulness, courage, and daily improvement in their patients.

Now I wanted to escape from the shadow of all that into the fresh air and sunshine of Africa. And here I was entering into another sphere of doubt and shadow and uncertainty with the possibility of not being able to turn back, and not knowing what the consequences would be of going on. Thus torn between the desire for adventure and the longing for certainty and a sure sense of direction, I tended to evade questions which would lead me into conflict and controversy.

One of these was the native question which included the question of the coloured people, or people of mixed race, who are in the much greater proportion in the Cape. At St. Raphael's, perhaps because it was their physical afflictions that I first experienced, I was first of all conscious of their oppression by the natural order of things rather than the political or man-made social order. It was akin to my own problem, and I sought to evade it or postpone coming to grips with it.

I was fascinated by the beauty of the Cape and could always escape my inward doubts and dreads by going off for a walk by myself to somewhere where I could lie stripped in the sun and see the rugged mountains dropping sheer down into the sea, and listen to the cicadas in the tall eucalyptus trees, and smell the sweet scent of heath and wild flowers. I could watch the long Atlantic rollers, driven by the south-east trade winds, breaking majestically far out from the shore. It all had a spectacular and dramatic beauty which may have been misleading, but, like the feel of the hot sun on my body, it effectively drew me away from the dark underworld of my doubts and dreads.

I would come back to Compline in the chapel and to the reassuring belief that God had entered into the difficulties and sufferings of humanity by Himself becoming man and living a human life and dying a human death. Whatever the Church made of the doctrine of the Incarnation and Redemption, there was a great beauty, of its own order of beauty, in the truth of the story of God entering so unobtrusively into a world of poverty and ignorance, the human kindness of a harassed innkeeper, and the wonder of shepherds huddled round their fire. It came to me as it has to so many others in times of darkness, pain, or uncertainty, as an inner conviction, that "in Him was life and the life was the light of men; and the light shineth in darkness and the darkness comprehended it not . . . but that was the true light which lighteth every man that cometh into the world . . . born not of blood nor of the will of the flesh nor of the will of man, but of God. . . . He was in the world and the world was made by Him and the world knew Him not. He came unto His own and His own received Him not . . . but as many as received Him to them gave He power to become the sons of God, even to them that believe on His name. . . . And the word was made flesh and dwelt among us, and we beheld His glory, the glory as of the only begotten of the Father full of grace and truth." Always this has come back in times of darkness and despair as a recurring theme.

After a year at St. Raphael's Faure I went to study theology at St. Paul's College, Grahamstown, in the eastern province of the Cape. This is the theological college of the Anglican Church in South Africa for the training of white candidates for ordination.

It was a strange life at Grahamstown. In some ways it was rather like a small English cathedral city set down in Africa, and it prided itself on being so. There were tennis and tea parties and polite conversation at social functions which were as remote from the processes of real life going on all around us as anything could be. This feeling was heightened by the fact that we were studying Christian theology in a segregated college. At times I felt nearer to real life in the library of the college listening to a lecture by the warden than when trying to keep up with the artificial social pursuits of Grahamstown. The people, for all their genuine kindness and hospitality, gave one a feeling of being more British than the British, and I soon learned that it was more diplomatic not to draw even the most innocuous comparisons between life in South Africa and life in Britain, there being a strong streak of South African nationalism in even the most diehard descendants of the 1820 Settlers and the Sons of England.

Bishop Cullen, then the warden, had a good scientific mind and was a scholar well-versed in Greek and Hebrew, as well as in the rival schools of Higher Criticism of the Bible from the humanists of Loisy, Tyrell, and Albert Schweitzer to the neo-Calvinists of Germany. The warden had something of the Hebrew in his appearance, as well as in his feeling for literature. On a sultry afternoon, with his class listless and sleepy, to hear him suddenly break into a recitation in Hebrew of the Song of Deborah was an electrifying experience. With all his scholarly caution and Anglican moderation he could penetrate beneath the hard crust of stylized literary expressions and archaic doctrinal and liturgical forms of words to the reality of the experience which they sought to enshrine.

Through the skill of his interpretation and his love of the material of his craft the whole gospel story became a vivid present experience; so that one almost felt oneself to be with him as one of the company following round the shores of Lake Galilee or walking through the corn fields on the Sabbath day.

There seemed to be an indisputable logic in the doctrine of the Word becoming Flesh. The creative intelligence in the Universe assumed its highest form in the beauty, truth, and goodness of a human personality; appealing to the reason in man, not by words but by a life lived perfectly, true to principle in a particular period of history; captivating the mind and soul of man, not by might or by power but by a spirit of respect for his freedom and intelligence. In the working out there was the tense, but inexorable, logic of the progress of the drama: Eternity entered into time in human form in the poverty and obscurity of an Eastern market town, overcrowded at the time of the census, during the reign of Augustus Caesar, an ironic symbol of the highest form of law and order the world had ever known, since at the same time it harboured within itself the seeds of a divine disorder that was destined to break with non-violence the hard heart of Roman civilization.

The implications of all this in terms of life in our own time, in contemporary social and political terms, I did not then begin to see. The theological implications were worked out for us in terms of the Christian creeds, the doctrine of the Church and the Sacraments, Grace and the Apostolic Succession, and the Thirty-Nine Articles of the Book of Common Prayer. We knew very little about the kind of world we lived in. Our minds were directed and became more and more preoccupied with the effort to understand the meaning of past heresies and their effect on the history of the Church: the great schism between East and West in the fourth century, the Reformation, and some of the modern forms of ancient heresies such as Christian Science, Spiritualism, and the like. We were taught little of comparative religion or the new science of psychology. Liturgics was more important than pastoral religion or ethics. No discussion on the origin of evil was permitted by the warden.

Among the students at Grahamstown I found a particular friend in Ned Paterson, an artist who had won a scholarship from South Africa to the London School of Art and had studied under Epstein. He later founded a flourishing art school at Cyrene in Rhodesia, where Africans are still experimenting to find forms truly expressive of their own art in the context of the present day. He had a very positive, and often pugnacious, personality. He was very original and formed his own artist's conception of other people which was usually highly dramatized, and everyone was expected to conform to this conception. It will be interesting to see how much of the art which he taught Africans at Cyrene will prove capable of reproduction on African soil, without his influence, and in what forms.

The sub-warden at Grahamstown was Alexander Sargent. Sargent was more typically Oxford and academic than the warden. He had been chaplain of Cuddesdon Theological College at Oxford and, like me, had come to South Africa on account of ill-health. He had not been with us very long when he was recalled to be chaplain to the Archbishop of Canterbury, and he returned to England to a very different sort of life at Lambeth Palace. Among the others in that small community there was the son of a Natal farmer, a customs officer, a tailor, and a Jewish cockney from the Mile End Road who had already spent several years as a missionary in Lebombo. So although it was a small community, it encompassed a wider range of outlooks on life than many a larger one whose members are drawn from the same class or country, as one might find in a hostel or college in England or the wardroom of a ship, for example.

In between college terms I visited different parts of the country and stayed at various missions or at the homes of friends of friends. I visited the Society of the Sacred Mission on the borders of Basutoland. The foundation of the life of the community there at Moddepoort was the Mass, the Office, and their Rule of Life. Most of the fathers were from Kelham in England. They were middle-class, middle-aged Englishmen and very set in their monastic and bachelor habits, which seemed to me to erect an insuperable barrier between them and the African people they were there to serve.

One morning, while sitting on the stoep of the mission, and looking out over eighty miles of veld to the rugged tips of the Maluti Mountains of Basutoland, I idly turned the pages of *Punch* and some other respectable journals of English country life which were lying on a table. My attention was caught by the fact that pieces of brown paper had been carefully pasted over the advertisements for ladies' corsets and underwear. I was told by an aged priest that this had been done by an old spinster supporter in England who sent them these journals and did not want the dear fathers to have temptation placed in their way.

One of the younger fathers used to take me for long walks in the direction of the Maluti Mountains which, however far we walked, never seemed to get any nearer. He would talk in a very frank and, I thought then, rebellious way about the handicaps imposed on them by being members of a seemingly wealthy institution and living according to a rigid community rule. I recalled these rebellious statements by one who became a senior and respected member of the community when, many years later, I did eventually visit Basutoland in connection with a terrible outbreak of ritual murders in which parts of the human body were eaten and the blood drunk in order to acquire power. I visited in gaol some of the senior Christian chiefs who were under sentence of death for this reversion to paganism after twenty years of devoted service to the Church. Many of them were the products of many years of missionary training in our schools and colleges, one who was executed was a graduate of Fort Hare University.

I had the same feeling that a great gulf separated the missionaries from the life of the African people when I visited the mission of the Society of St. John the Evangelist at St. Cuthbert's T'Solo in the Transkeian native reserves. But here there were the very saintly Father Calloway, whom no gulf could separate from the love of God and his people, and Father Romsey, with whom I used to ride on visits to his outstations on a trippling pony to which I was not accustomed and which I found very uncomfortable.

What made me feel even more ridiculous was carrying an English 1662 prayer book in my pocket with a Xosa translation and similarly an English hymnal. Did they really express the religion of the African any more than some of the wild and warlike psalms expressed the religions of the dear old nuns there? I had the same feeling about some of my studies at college, particularly liturgiology in which I failed to satisfy the examiners.

Once at the end of a long period of drought I went to stay with a sheep farmer in the eastern province of the Cape not far from King Williamstown. Every day the sun rose full of glory, with the air already shimmering with heat while it was still low over the horizon. Majestically it moved to its full height overhead and then sank down again, leaving red streaks against the deep shadows of flat *kopjes,* frowning as though all nature suffered under the same rule of a tyrant knowing beauty but no mercy.

The sheep and cattle were dying. Every night farmers would go out and shoot those that would not survive until morning. Each morning we would be up early to scan the skies for signs of a rain cloud or a change in the wind. The grass was withered to the roots and the barren earth baked hard as brick in the hot sun. The interminable clear sky looked down with a cruel, pale blueness on the faintly stirring beasts, their swollen tongues protruding from their mouths, who had hardly the strength left to paw the ground. Round some as they lay the vultures wheeled and banked with remorseless patience till the time would come when they could safely alight and pluck out their eyes and tear out their entrails.

Everyone prayed for rain—the churches and the witch doctors—and family prayers were revived on the farms. Then at last it came, and there was madness in the air. Great clouds billowed up dark against the sun. The sky was rent by flash after flash of lightning. The noise split the air and reverberated round the hills like a battle of frenzied giants. The rain came first in big slow drops, then in great cascades of water that swirled and eddied over the hard earth. When the first storm eased there was a steady downpour of slanting silvery streaks. People stood about in it. The women cried and their tears mingled with the rain on their cheeks. The men embraced and congratulated one another. Foaming ruddy-coloured streams coursed and chased one another down the dongas made by other streams before them. A young native on top of a small *kopje* danced practically naked in the rain. He believed his magic had worked the miracle. He feared nothing. His black body was wet and shining as he stamped on the earth and kept leaping into the air and shouting into the wind and the rain with an elemental joyous confidence, exulting in his own unbounded power over the elements, restrained only by the discipline of the rhythm.

Once I went to stay on the diamond diggings at Lichtenburg and Graasfintein with a young lay reader who was carrying on a mission amongst the poor whites there. There were all sorts of people, adventurers from almost every country in the world. Some were farmers who had sold their farms as hopeless and trekked to the diggings as a last resort. Sometimes a whole family, with their house and all their worldly goods on the back of a lorry, would move in from one of the other diggings. Or it might be one of the younger sons of an old Afrikaner of the back veld whose farm had been split up amongst his large family, the younger sons finding their fragments too small to be able to support them. There were a good many "black sheep" from county families and the aristocracy of England and others with weird titles and a grand manner. All would jostle one another in excellent good humour at the dances in the little diggers' hall with an orchestra of squeeze boxes jigging out catchy little Afrikaner folk songs rather like the hill-billy songs of Kentucky. There were no class distinctions, and no one worried about where anyone came from unless they volunteered the information. For some were refugees from justice, others from injustice or just perhaps bad luck. All were there to get rich quick with the diamond fever running in their blood. Once this infection is caught nothing matters—even life itself is of small account. There was certainly no lack of drama. The life, like nature itself, was exuberant with no half measures.

The climate, too, at an altitude of six thousand feet, was exhilarating. The air sparkled. The nights were crisp and cold, and the stars glittered like diamonds. But the stars had no value in terms of buying and selling. Everyone, though very poor, was on the verge of becoming very rich. There was excitement each time a sieve was brought in. After the earth and rock had been sifted by centrifugal force the final process consisted of hand-sifting the contents of a small sieve in the centre of which were crystals and small carbon pellets called "Kaffir corn," in the midst of which the diamonds, if any, would be found.

These tense moments when the sieve was turned on the table were the spice of life to the diggers. For these moments men would live or die. One digger had something in the form of sleeping sickness, but he refused to be sent away to a hospital. He had just enough spark of life left in him to respond to this final process and to rivet his eyes on the small stones and crystals and comb them through with a sweep of his hand.

I had no digger's licence and did not try my luck. In the days before they drew lots there was more than luck involved in staking out a claim. For this purpose rushes would be staged on newly proclaimed ground. Some would hire professional runners and prize fighters, and often there would be free fights with their iron pegs when half-way over the course.

At that time an epidemic of enteric was raging amongst the diggers and, as there was no hospital, tents and shelters had to be put up. Few nurses were obtainable from the cities. The men were too weak to wash or shave themselves and I had this job assigned to me by the lay reader, whose energy was inexhaustible and who never once seemed to think of his own comfort or safety. Most of his time was taken up in attending to the spiritual needs of the white people, and he roared over the veld in an ancient Trojan car which had had its silencer knocked off by a boulder. Sometimes the African or coloured people would ask him for his help and once my sense of Church order was greatly non-plussed when he heard the confession of an old Xosa woman who was dying of enteric and even celebrated the Holy Communion for her before she died. He remarked that there was no priest within a hundred miles. I do not believe that in any case either of them understood anything very much of the other's language.

In these ways I came to understand something of the problems confronting the Church in the dramatically changing and conflicting African scene. One of my holidays while at college I spent in Johannesburg at Doornfontein and Sophiatown in 1928, where I was to return to work many years later. There was at that time a small band of missionaries led by Dorothy Maud and Dr. Tugman, who had begun to wage the ceaseless, losing battle against disease and disorder which the Church is still waging today.

At that time the problem of the influx of population into the gold-mining area of the Reef was still at its early stage. The gold mines acted as a huge magnet, attracting people of all races into the Transvaal. The mines used native labour drawn from all parts of South and Central Africa, but secondary industries were beginning to grow up where there was labour and a ready market. These attracted both the landless Africans from the overcrowded reserves and the poor whites, who thus found themselves competing with low-paid coloured and African labour. Hence the colour bar in industry was imposed to try and preserve the skilled and semi-skilled occupations for white labour. This form of protection can prove as demoralizing to those whom it seeks to protect for arbitrary reasons of race as it can for those whom it discriminates against for similarly arbitrary reasons.

Sophiatown was one of the places on the outskirts of Johannesburg where poor whites from the country met and mingled with the non-Europeans, who were trying to establish themselves in some sort of permanent homes in one of the few areas where they were permitted to own and occupy freehold property. It was not for another twenty years that I was destined to be caught up in the acute social and political crisis which the ever-increasing influx of black and white into the towns was bound to bring about, a problem which eluded practical-minded politicians in the government and purposeful planning by the municipalities.

These problems were a good deal beyond my comprehension, since my mind was preoccupied with theology and Church order. There were not only the problems of Church history and the controversies of the early Church, but those more closely affecting the Church of the Province of South Africa. In particular there was the bitter quarrel between Bishop Colenso of Natal, the staunch champion of the Zulus, who believed in the Higher Criticism of the Bible and the theory of evolution before these had become generally accepted on the one hand, and, on the other hand, the strong-minded High Church statesman and pioneer bishop of the South African Church, Bishop Gray. These early controversies between rival sections of the Anglican Church in South Africa were exceedingly bitter and have left their mark in a schism which still exists between the Church of the Province of South Africa and the small remnant of the "Church of England in South Africa," which periodically lays claim through legal actions to properties which it claims are its rightful heritage. These legal actions are a more orderly and seemly way of settling differences than some of the older methods, which on one occasion, for example, led the bishop and the dean of Grahamstown to compete with one another as to who was going to preach the sermon. They were unable to settle their differences until both actually began to preach at the same time, the one from the pulpit and the other from the lectern.

At that time, more than twenty years ago, the bishops of the Church of the Province were carrying on a valiant rearguard action on behalf of liberal Christianity against an already advancing political theory and practice of segregation later to be known as "apartheid." Generals Smuts and Hertzog had formed a coalition to remove the African people from the common roll (though, unlike Mr. Strijdom with the coloured people, they did this without packing the senate to secure a two-thirds majority) and they passed colour-bar legislation for industry such as the Mines and Works Act prohibiting "pass-bearing natives" from becoming skilled machine operators. The Church was making repeated declarations against the colour bar by means of strongly-worded resolutions and through the mouths of its bishops, several of whom were threatened with deportation at that time if they did not curb their utterances.

In addition to such stalwart characters as Bishop Neville Talbot, Walter Carey of Bloemfontein, and Bishop Carnie and Dean Palmer of Johannesburg, there were two other people whose words made a deep impression on me then. One was the soft-spoken and gentle-mannered Charlie Andrews, who was a strong disciple of Mahatma Gandhi and whom I was later to meet in India. The other was the cultured and statesmanlike representative of the Government of India, Sprinivasa Sastri, who spoke with most moving and convincing oratory to white audiences in South Africa on the problems of the Indian minority. Through the breaking of the Cape Town agreement and the repeated promises made to Gandhi and to the Government of India, the matter was eventually brought to the attention of the United Nations, where it has been debated year after year since 1946. The promise had been given that Indians who had been brought as indentured labourers to South Africa to work on the sugar plantations should, after fulfilling their contracts, be given their freedom and enjoy the rights of civilized citizens of the Union of South Africa, though, at the same time, they were to be encouraged by repatriation allowances to return to India if they wished, or to improve their standards of living and education if they remained in South Africa. I was very deeply moved by a speech by Sastri at Rhodes University. I had not made up my mind on these matters at that time, being preoccupied with many other questions.

In fact my attitude of mind was perhaps well summed up by the warden of the college when eventually the time came for me to leave there to return to England to see my family and resume my training at Chichester Theological College. "You have never been able to make up your mind, dear man, and I don't think you ever will," he said. He had a friendly and sincere way of making the most acid comments and rebuffs. No one ever resented them because it seemed as though he liked us all the better for our faults and weaknesses.

3 Ordination and Communism

I returned to England in 1929 to continue my studies at Chichester Theological College. Though the tradition here was strongly Anglo-Catholic, there was a good deal more encouragement of free discussion. The principal, Canon Leonard Pass, who was a Dante scholar as well as a theologian, preferred his lectures on Christian doctrine to take the form of discussions rather than discourses by himself. In fact some of his greatest discourses seemed to be stimulated by an exchange of ideas rather than to be previously prepared perorations.

Nevertheless, I had a feeling, which I tried strongly to resist, that my thought was being subtly and gently directed, as a skilful trainer can break in a horse almost without the animal knowing it. It has always been one of my greatest regrets that I never enjoyed the freedom and spaciousness and tolerance of Cambridge, my old tutor's university. Perhaps this regret, amounting almost to resentment, strengthened my resistance to allowing my thought to be cast into a mould and shaped by the confines of a logical doctrinal scheme or system of salvation, culminating in a strict interpretation of the doctrine of the Church and the Apostolic Succession. Such would have dictated my relationships with the world and the rest of my fellow Christians. Perhaps if I had stayed at Chichester for the full course of three years my resistance would have been overcome, and perhaps, some would say, it would have been better if it had. But my time at Grahamstown was taken into account and I was ordained by the Bishop of Chichester, Dr. Bell, on the feast of St. Thomas, 1930.

We stayed at the bishop's palace for a few days for our retreat, an American friend and myself having already spent a few days at Nashdom Abbey. At the last moment he received a message from the American Embassy warning him that if he took the oath of allegiance to the King of England at his ordination, as we all had to do, he would lose his American citizenship. So he had to fly to Gibraltar and be ordained by the bishop there with "letters dimissory" from Dr. Bell.

At our retreat was none other than Dr. Bicknell, author of the standard work on the Thirty-Nine Articles of Religion, whose plausible interpretations of some of these articles of belief had so often exasperated me—for example, his exposition of belief in the resurrection of the body "with flesh and bones" and everything that appertaineth intact. I was astonished to find that in real life he had such a delightful sense of humour and sincere devotion.

At the retreat, and on the day of my ordination, I suppressed all my doubts and misgivings. In retrospect it seemed to be improbable that we could all be so far wrong, and that this great cathedral, and scores of others like it going back to Norman and even Saxon times, should not have been built. The Liturgy, however far from our present-day idiom its terminology might be, seemed to consummate in one dramatic act of worship the deepest experience and the highest aspirations of humanity. I felt the continuity with the early Christian disciples when the bishop laid his hands on my head and said, "Receive ye the Holy Ghost. . . ." and afterwards as I walked out in procession, feeling very self-conscious and absurd in my clerical collar.

The strains of Bach on the organ permeated that whole great cathedral, mingled with the beauty of its ancient craftsmanship in stone and wood, and overflowed the walls and roof till it became merged above and beyond in the cold air of winter and in a silence that was so neutral and so receptive that it seemed equally to register the harmony and the discord, the true and the false, the good and the evil. Altogether, I had the feeling that either we were against the Universe or the Universe was on our side. The music and the worship and the sturdy strength of the stone pillars, frail and feeble as these are in terms of history, seemed to partake of the quality of eternity and invincibility, of something that would endure. The waves of sound would go on diminishing, the colour would fade, and the shape and form disintegrate. Yet all the effort and the artistry would not be wasted or lost, but, like the flesh and bones and all that appertaineth, would surely undergo some metamorphosis and continue somehow their striving to create in the face of negation and the imponderable weight of the forces of destruction.

After my ordination I was licenced to a large country parish in Sussex called Slaugham, not many miles from where I was born. It had three district churches attached to it: Handcross, Warninglid, and Peas Pottage on the main road from London to Brighton. There I lived the most conventional form of life I have ever lived. I rode several times a week on horses loaned by one or other of the manor houses in the parish. My spiritual duties were combined with tennis and cricket, dinner and tea parties, endless visits to both rich and poor, concerts, dances, and interminable polite conversation.

Many of the big estates had been broken up and there were now many small-scale manors, which sometimes competed for social prestige, and an increasing number of smaller country houses and week-end cottages. These created an extremely complicated system of social relationships which only a few of the women in the place seemed to understand, possibly because it was they who had devised this social order and who kept it under their control.

After two years in Sussex I went to a fashionable parish in the West End of London, but after less than a year there I moved to an unfashionable parish in the East End. While this signified an increasing restlessness, I find it difficult to understand my complacency during that period of my life in Sussex and the West End of London. How immune I seemed to have become to the influences which were shaping the history of our time. Catastrophic events had succeeded one another from the beginnings of the depression to the Roosevelt New Deal and the rise and triumph of Hitler in Germany.

I think I was becoming aware gradually that my theological training had almost succeeded in innuring me to these influences. I thought of myself as twice removed from the world of events. I was set apart in the sense that as part of the Church I was in the world but not of the world, and I was also set apart within the Church as a priest. But perhaps it was also a sense of unreality in my religion that drove me to search for reality in the East End of London. There at least the evils of the world were being fought or endured, rather than enjoyed with arrogant pride and hypocrisy in a combination of venial comfort and mortal pride, of heartless complacency and overfeeding. I went for my Confession to a priest who had been very fashionable and much sought after as a retreat conductor. He himself forsook everything, including his wife and two sons who were at Eton, and went to live near the docks. Sometimes I would find him in a damp hovel, coughing and exhausted on a bed covered with ragged bed clothes. Whatever his personal dilemma—and that was something which I could never see how he could resolve—he seemed to speak words of truth and life such as I suppose the disciples must have experienced. They impetuously forsook everything, including their wives or parents and even their nets and gear of their trade, and followed Christ, some for the three years of his public life and some even to their deaths. Whatever the objections to his course, there was something about the recklessness of his spirit which seemed to have a spark of the divine in its contradiction of complacency. That complacency seemed to be totally unaware of the desperate struggles of so many at that time to keep themselves alive with less than the bare necessities of life.

This was the period when millions of people in the great industrial areas of Britain, including London of course, lived under a shadow of fear and the dread of unemployment. It was the period of the Means Test, the Unemployment Act, and the Hunger Marches on London from Scotland and the north of England. Something was needed to jolt people out of the comfortable complacency of Kensington Christianity. It was all very well to follow the good vicar on his pilgrimage round the Stations of the Cross in a well-heated church with sweet-smelling incense, but what were these people prepared to do to help the poor, let alone to bring about a change in a system which produced such unemployment in a world of plenty?

On the other hand there was something which aroused more pity than anger towards the old ladies who followed the Way of the Cross. The depression was having its effect on them too. Many of them seemed very defenceless and inarticulate. They had spent their youth in a more expansive age in the security of Victorian homes, in the heyday of Britain's economic prosperity and political ascendancy. Their lives had been restricted and sheltered and lacked all the varied opportunities that are open to the youth of today in occupation, travel, and enjoyment. But their very restrictions ensured that what they did at all, they did with a greater zest and inner enjoyment than we have today. Narrow as their lives may have been they were lived against the background of a great era of ex-

pansion and progress. The dramatic results of this "march of civilization" were everywhere to be seen. No one questioned that it was a march
forward towards the greatest possible happiness of the greatest number.
The purpose and direction, the end of all these increasingly complicated
social, economic, and technical processes, however, were not a matter for
speculation. They were taken for granted.

Now these old ladies, who had known and felt so secure in the kind
of life I had known in Sussex, were inhabiting single rooms in dingy, but
by no means cheap, little Kensington hotels, surrounded by trinkets and
bric à brac and treasured miniatures or photographs reminding them of
a glory that was past. Their stay in India, a hunt ball, their coming out,
or their wedding day. Now there were few who loved or even admired
them, or to whom they could turn in their anxiety and fear for the future. Their pensions dwindled, and their little unearned incomes were
precarious. The hotels were interested only in what could be got out of
them. They were forced into their own society, living in the past or in
a world of make-believe of preposterous social competition, and assumed
hauteur towards others in the hotel of even slightly inferior caste.

Life for so many of them, even with religion, was cruel and lonely
and stark. Without religion it was inexpressibly dreary and false. Bridge
meant more than anything else to many of them. It would begin at eleven
in the morning and continue until eleven at night.

Gradually I was becoming aware that over and above the recognized
denominations of Christianity, and apart from the innumerable little sects
into which Christendom had become divided, there were two kinds of
Christianity: There was the religion which was the divine sanction of the
status quo, and there was the religion which was the divine instrument
of change. No doubt all the truth was not to be found in either exclusively.
There was the conception of the salt as the preservative of all that had
been accomplished by the human spirit in the past and which also gave
it savour, and there was also the idea of the leaven which slowly, im-
perceptibly, but dramatically, transformed the whole lump. Some of the
great persecutions of the Christian era were no doubt due to the deep
resentment and resistance of the lump to the process of being leavened
and its seeking blindly and ruthlessly to extirpate the cause of change at
whatever cost to itself.

There was one incident that brought home very vividly to me the gulf
that separated the East and West Ends of London. A well-to-do young

woman in Kensington had told me when I went to live in the East End
of London that if I ever came up against a really desperate situation, and
there was anything she could do to help, to be sure and let her know.

Late one night after I had gone to bed, I was roused by a knocking
on the door. A young man who appeared very distraught asked me if
he could talk to me in confidence about something very important to
him. I made him some tea and told him to go ahead. He said he was a
driver by trade. He was married, with two small children. He had had
an accident with his truck, had knocked down an old man, and had been
convicted of manslaughter, unjustly he believed. While he was in gaol his
wife was taken ill and was unable to go to work. A relative had brought
his children to see him one day at his insistence and he was horrified to
see how thin and physically neglected they were. He made up his mind
to escape from prison, and he succeeded. He drove off in a car he found
parked and made for London. On the way he thought he was being pursued, and while speeding along a main road knocked a man down, causing the following car to stop and attend to him. He had driven on without
stopping and had just parked the car in someone's back yard. He asked
for the Church's sanctuary. I explained that that was a thing of the past.
The Church no longer had the power to protect people from the law.
What he had told me he had said in confidence, and I should respect
that. Whatever he did, he must do of his own free will. But I talked to
him for a long time and tried to get him to see that it might be better
for the children and himself if he gave himself up and told the authorities
everything. I would see what could be done about the children. I gave
him a meal and said he could stay under my roof for the night and think
it over and get some sleep. The decision as to what he would do in the
morning must be his own. If he decided to give himself up, the young
woman whose phone number I gave him might be able to help with the
children.

In the morning when I awoke he had already left. It was not long before I received a frightened and indignant message from the young woman
in Kensington. I had abused her friendship; she never intended herself
to be used as an accomplice of the underworld. I said I was giving her
the sort of opportunity I thought she might like to have of helping to
undo a wrong that was becoming very complicated and causing more
and more suffering to many innocent people. But she could not see it in
that way, and I never heard from her again.

So often the practical problems to which Christian morality had to be applied were complicated by conflicting loyalties and family responsibilities. These made it difficult for a man who might be a salesman, for instance, to place his own soul's integrity before the job he had been able to secure and on which his wife and children depended. The job often depended on his ability to tell the tale, to persuade some other probably impecunious housewife that a cheap and shoddy article was really worth the investment of some of her husband's hard-earned wages. All too often these matters became too complicated for people, and they would shrug their shoulders and steel themselves against any considerations of morality or religion.

In some ways the parish of All Souls, Lower Clapton, was similar to my father's parish in Southampton. However, it was not so overcrowded and the river Lea seldom overflowed its banks. Also the neighbouring Hackney Marshes were a great asset to the gangs of youngsters and courting couples which frequented them. These gangs of boys and girls were the precursors of the Teddy Boys and Girls of the post-war period. They were not vicious. Since there were not many dance-halls in those days, and cinemas were expensive, they would go out on to the marshes with accordions and mouth-organs over week-ends. They had a code of behaviour of their own, and the force of collective disapproval was usually strong enough to enforce broad adherence to it. These youngsters lacked imaginative leaders, but the churches had insufficient imagination to captivate them, and their efforts were very much hampered by their own strict and negative rules of Sunday observance. These boys and girls had a lightness and gaiety and a highly developed nonchalant sense of humour which was very appealing against the sombre background of their daily lives—the insecurity, the lack of hope for anything better in the future, and the already rumbling undertones of the great convulsion of their world that lay ahead.

Their frivolity was not shared or approved by the politicians of that time, who showed little more understanding of the young or capacity to lead them than did the churches. Rival left-wing groups were engaged in grim and furiously factional competition for supremacy in the fight for socialism and against fascism and war, the Labour party, the Independent Labour party, the Socialist League of Great Britain, the Communist party, the National Union of Unemployed Workers. In opposition to them all, the British Union of Fascists organized marches and demonstrations throughout the East End of London, inflaming opinion against the Jews and acclaiming Hitler and Mussolini.

I found myself being drawn into what proved to be the preliminary skirmishes preluding a great world conflict by the arrival in the parish of the Hunger Marchers from the Tyneside and Scotland. Poverty and fear on the one hand, and the Means Test and the new and much execrated Unemployment Assistance Act on the other, had combined to prepare the ground for the Hunger Marchers. The counter-propaganda that was often resorted to was crude and not very far-seeing. It was rumoured that the Hunger Marchers were coming to take the local people's jobs away. They would stay in London when they had got jobs for themselves. It was put about that they were crooks or irresponsible people escaping from their own wives and families; and the people of the East End were warned to lock everything up, to nail their windows if the catches were broken, and to keep a close eye on their womenfolk.

Such counter-propaganda failed to take account of the real poverty and fear that was rife in the slums of London at that time, and the consequences of the unemployment measures which, both in fact and in fancy, were breaking up family life and causing real resentment. Youngsters were going off and living away from their parents because they could thus draw more money. Sometimes this would lead to dishonest practices, intended to deceive the inspectors. Many feared that the Means Test would be applied to their few precious possessions, possibly a gramophone or wireless set or even their wedding presents, which they might have to sell before they could draw the dole.

Inevitably, therefore, the arrival of the Hunger Marchers created many issues in the parish, or rather it forced them to the surface, for they were already latent. Not only were there immediate political issues, but more fundamental ones as between religion and politics, as between different interpretations of religion in its implications for everyday life, and as between communism and Christianity.

Some of these issues became very confused by the fact that we were all being precipitated into situations which demanded immediate practical decisions. The Hunger Marchers wanted to hire the parish hall which was normally used for dances on Saturday nights and was the only suitable hall in Lower Clapton. The vicar, Father Nottage, who was a very fair, and by no means narrow-minded, man, had felt he must refuse to continue letting the hall for dances other than those sponsored by a church guild or club, on account of the rather loose behaviour that had taken place at some of them.

Now the local reception committee wanted to hire the hall to billet the Hunger Marchers. The advance guard was beginning to arrive, and such was the division of opinion as to what the parish should do about it that a meeting of the parochial church council had to be hurriedly summoned. At this meeting, and outside it, discussion roamed far and wide over the unfamiliar ground of philosophy, political economy, theology, the Thirty-Nine Articles of Religion, the Oath of Allegiance, and the meaning of such phrases as "God and Mammon," the "things that are Caesar's," as applied to "the crisis confronting us in Lower Clapton at the present time." I remember that one saying of Christ that became very freely debated at little street corner meetings was, "Make to yourselves friends of the Mammon of unrighteousness that if ye fail they may receive you into their everlasting habitations." This was given many varied interpretations by those who were for or against a united front, as well as by those who were for staying out of it and not taking sides. One could not help wondering whether the disciples, who were themselves in their time very divided in their minds concerning the earthly and heavenly character of the coming Messianic Kingdom, did not find themselves in a similar dilemma. One could hardly avoid speculating whether the divine author of the remark was not without a sense of humour even in His reference to a matter of such serious and catastrophic significance as the fate of those "everlasting habitations" which later caused the disciples' exclamations of wonder—"Lord, what manner of stones and what manner of buildings." And He had then pronounced the doom of Jerusalem, not in hatred but in anguish, it being the only occasion on which it is recorded that "Jesus wept."

The argument in the parochial church council was eventually summed up by the vicar, who supported the hall being let for the purpose of billeting the Hunger Marchers, it being understood that the Church was not thereby either for or against those who had hired the hall.

There followed days and nights of feverish activity and discussion of every subject in heaven and earth. The hall had to be prepared, cooking, washing and other facilities arranged, and supplies bought and stored in safe places.

Before all this was properly completed the marchers arrived, singing down the street with their banners and a band in front of them. Watching them, weary and ragged and ill-nourished, I could not help recalling something similar to—but also different from—the men marching to the front at the end of the First World War. The Hunger Marchers, too, had a cause that was their own, one they believed in, and whatever sinister rumours had been circulated about them, they appeared to be ordinary working people with the Lancashire or Scots accents usually associated with comedians. This seemed to belie anything very sinister. When they spoke to the people they spoke about things which were of common knowledge and everyday experience. In this way the rumours only re-coiled against those more "respectable" and conservative members of the congregation who had been beguiled into using them as weapons against communism.

A contingent of women arrived, many of them with very badly blis-tered feet, who were obviously devoted to the cause of their menfolk and ridiculed stories about their intentions towards the local women.

In Hackney itself a United Front Committee was formed with local Communists and members of other left-wing groups very much to the fore, and supported by a number of town councillors and clergy includ-ing myself. I was much too shy and unsure of myself to do any public speaking for them as they requested; but in my sermons in church I talked a great deal about the sterility of a faith that was not expressed in work as well as worship, and the inseparability of prayer and action.

I had not begun to realize the implications of joint action with those whose means and ends differed from my own. Nor was I well-equipped, academically, to work out the problems that presented themselves day by day as immediate questions calling for urgent practical decisions. My re-ligion and my theological training served to inflame my moral indignation at the contrast between the real world as the politicians had made it and the world that might have been, that God intended should be, if the natu-ral resources and the scientific intelligence He had given us were used aright. Technologically we were already entering an age when it was no longer necessary for people to starve, yet all over Europe, let alone in the more backward countries, millions of people went in daily hunger, so that it became a mockery, worse than that a profanity, to say, "Give us our daily bread."

The Church, as I had been brought up to think of it, seemed to have little to offer, little to say or to do, about this. My own beliefs seemed far removed from the everyday experience of the people of Lower Clapton, and the forces and motives that shaped their lives and inspired their thoughts and actions. Everywhere one saw the symptoms and results of overproduction, unemployment, and the competition for markets and raw materials which was driving the nations towards war.

Against this background of the thirties, and in the East End in particular, the spectre of nazism was beginning to appear, and strident voices were proclaiming the doctrine of racialism at street corners in Hackney, Stepney, and Whitechapel. I felt repelled by the brutality of their behaviour, and drawn towards those who appeared to oppose this menace with reasoned argument and no little courage. For the Communists had to face, not only their own poverty and unfavourable circumstances but also physical intimidation from the Fascists and the police as well, or so it appeared to me. I was impressed by the courage and self-sacrifice of both leaders and rank and file. They had their own views of the world and of their role in its remaking, which made them capable of great endurance and initiative and often heroic conduct. Indeed this seemed to belie their doctrine of economic self-interest, since often they were the last people who stood to gain by victimization, whether by law or by force.

Without my realizing it at the time, a form of dualism was developing in my own mind and soul, which perhaps could be traced back to the unhappy days in my father's slum parish. On the one hand there was the gospel of God's love for the world and Christ's redemption of it; on the other hand the real world of poverty, violence, filth, and fear. Perhaps the seeds of an emotional revulsion, and even a revolt of reason, had been sown by barely remembered thoughts and feelings—the forbidden book, *Vive la Commune,* and the legendary tales of rebels the cobbler told me as he mended my shoes.

It all began to take on a more articulate and organized form in my contacts with the leaders of the Hunger Marchers, and we had discussions far into the night on economics, politics, and philosophy. I read avidly on these subjects, books such as Engles's *Anti Duhrung,* a manuscript translation of which was lent to me and which made a deep impression on my mind at that time, the Feuerbach correspondence, *Lenin's State and Revolution, The ABC of Communism,* which was then considered slightly off-tune, and Read's *Ten Days That Shook the World.* I was taken to see a number of films about the Russian Revolution and plays like *The Age of Plenty.*

Thus in my mind at this time there were growing up two separate doctrinal systems, with different sets of belief and standards of ethics and conduct, and with different explanations of human motives and behaviour. I struggled to find some means of reconciling such widely different conceptions of the meaning and purpose of life and found myself in a perpetual state of conflict between these two rival explanations of our situation, and I vacillated between two conflicting codes of conduct. My Christian belief elevated the ends above the means and necessarily qualified them; but communism taught the complete subordination of the means to the end. As for social and economic conditions, there was much in what I saw around me to support the Marxian analysis.

We were all caught up in Lower Clapton. There was little time or opportunity for anyone to detach himself and meditate or think, uninfluenced by the events which rapidly succeeded one another. One had a sense of being carried along on a flood tide of history against which it was impossible to turn and struggle or to assert any beliefs or values that placed one above the battle.

I was given a ticket for one of Mosley's meetings at Olympia. I was horrified at the brutality used against the questioners and could not help admiring those who even chained themselves to their seats and called out until they were silenced by his bodyguard. One young stevedore climbed up to the roof above the platform and called down caustic comments on Mosley's remarks. It could hardly be said that they were inspired by a love of freedom; but they hated all that fascism stood for and expressed their opposition in the only way they knew. There were wild scenes of rioting afterwards outside Olympia, and even in all the excitement and shame of finding myself in such a disorderly scene, I could not help being as much amused as shocked at the blaspheming frustration of an old cockney friend, a Covent Garden porter, who was with me. He was searching frenziedly about to find something to throw, which fortunately in the paved streets of our cities is not very easy. His flow of expletive was caused by discovering that some ornamental stones he was trying to pick up were imbedded in concrete.

Comrade Jim had been sent to me by the local United Front committee organizing the hunger march. He was too old to work at Covent Garden any more, but could not live on his pension or allowance. So I gave him two rooms in the house lent me by the parish, and he did the sweeping and dusting. His favourite form of recreation was not to go to a football match or dog racing, but to attend a good political meeting or "demo" in Hyde Park or Victoria Park. He would put on his best clothes for this on Sunday afternoons and would always take the precaution of stuffing the crown of his cloth cap with little balls of paper, in case a policeman's truncheon should happen to descend on him.

Another person who was sent to see me, and who was also in his way symbolic of our time, was a young seaman who came from a refugee committee that had been set up in London to deal with the stream of refugees that was coming out of Germany. He only spoke German and said he had come from Austria, where he had been a member of the *Schutzbund* which had tried to resist Dollfuss. He described how, after the shooting in Vienna, many of his friends had lived in sewers and eventually escaped into the forests. I gave him a room and when I went away for my summer holiday I asked Comrade Jim to look after him, which he was very ready to do. When I returned he had disappeared and the refugee committee was very worried as he had come into the country illegally, though I had not been told this. A girl at the refugee office, to whom he had professed his affection, became suspicious and opened a locked case he had left with her for safekeeping. In this was found a Nazi party credential and several other credentials for Nazi newspapers. He had, it seems, used the machinery of the refugee organization to spy on the people who had succeeded in leaving Germany and Austria. Until then I think the committee half suspected that I had discovered he was in England illegally and had compromised them by trying to clear up his position with the authorities. I bitterly reproached the committee for the fact that many of the unfortunate refugees who came to my house to spend the evening, and had talked unsuspectingly to him, had probably unknowingly betrayed their relatives in Germany. While at the time it seemed like gross irresponsibility, the fact was that the machinery for dealing with the problem of refugees from nazism at that time was totally inadequate and amateurish and there was little opportunity for organizing a system for checking the bona fides of people arriving from Germany.

The stories they told of what was happening in Germany, and especially in the newly established concentration camps, made one despair of democracy and parliamentary and judicial procedures. Almost one despaired of humanity. It seemed as though the very foundations of our world were quivering beneath us and that these tremors we could feel must surely prelude some great convulsion of our European civilization.

For myself, I was not very happy about my relations with the Communists. I admired their courage and self-sacrificing discipline and their all-consuming devotion to their cause, yet, even if one discounted much of what was reported of Russia as mere propaganda, there was still a quality of ruthlessness even in the Communists I knew. They were strongly opposed to Christianity and considered religion in any form as a way of escape from reality at best and at worst as the opium of the people, though they respected Christianity in action in the person of Father Groser and others like him.

It seemed to me that I must try to understand the innermost thoughts of the Communists and to join with them in action as well, whenever I conscientiously could, perhaps so as to show them in the process the true nature of my own values and beliefs. Also I wanted to see from the inside something of their methods and organization. For this purpose I accepted their suggestion that I become attached to a cell consisting of bus drivers and conductors, which met once a week to discuss their problems and their activities in trade union branches and political organizations.

To me this was very much like a church guild except that the men were concerned with their conditions of work, wages, hours and overtime, as well as occasional political questions such as how to organize a United Front Committee. There was the same type of humour, the same alternating bursts of enthusiasm and slackness, a not very different strict code of behaviour and respectability. One found it very difficult to believe in Moscow gold or sinister subversive plots directed from abroad.

My religion at that time seemed to be beckoning towards the religious life. I felt I must try out my faith as a great experiment in living, and that the submission of everything to a life of faith lived in the community was perhaps the answer to communism. However, we had not the organization, and there was no community whose rule of obedience would allow me to follow my own conscience in the matter of politics, where I would be allowed to join in action with others who did not share my faith.

I sought to escape this dilemma by a compromise which only resulted in a further development of the dualism that already existed in my mind between religion and politics, between believing and thinking, praying and acting. Although I was not regarded as a Communist, but rather as a close sympathizer, I found the mental and physical strain of life there in Lower Clapton heavier than I could bear. Eventually I determined to try and resolve my dilemma by going abroad, possibly back to Africa or to India or the Far East, and there to try and make a fresh attempt in a new environment away from Europe. I was twice turned down by a medical board of the Universities Mission to Central Africa. In turn I was also rejected by a medical board for India, but was accepted for Korea though this attracted me much less than India.

I told the Communists that I would be prepared to do anything I could to help their cause there, provided it did not positively conflict with my conscience. I reserved my own right to believe in my religion, while accepting the methods and conclusions of the dialectical materialist analysis of the way the world works when it is not, so to speak, consciously inspired by a true faith in its own Creator.

I was not given any very onerous tasks to perform for the Communists, nor was I taken into their confidence to any degree about the state of the parties there. My name would be sent forward, and I was asked to send back reports on what I found there and on my discussions with those whom I would meet. I was given a very crude form of code to be used for anything that might be thought confidential. I was also asked to deliver at given addresses in India and Japan a sum of one hundred pounds to help towards the travelling expenses of delegates to the Seventh World Congress of the Communist International in Moscow. At least that is what I subsequently concluded the money was for, though it was not specified at the time. Thus it was that my double life began to grow deeper and more divergent than ever it had been in Lower Clapton, E.5.

I did not feel that there was anything very wrong in this, certainly it was not worse than many of the tasks which priests of the Church are expected to perform for the state or local government or for charity or business on the side of the status quo. There was a certain excitement in the carrying out of my commission in India and Japan, where the parties were semi-underground and subject to very close police surveillance through their own agents in the party, and where a close watch was kept on all the activities of the members.

I left England for India and the Far East with a feeling that, though I was committed to assisting the Communists within the limits imposed by my own conscience and religion, I was still in search of the answer to my question. Thus I sailed from London docks as chaplain to an army transport on February 5th, 1935.

4 India and the Far East

I was not altogether at ease in the role of chaplain. As I conducted divine service at a table covered with the Union Jack, the hymns reminded me of John Newton, who conducted services aboard a slave ship. He wrote that he had never known sweeter or more pleasant hours of divine communion than on his last two voyages from Guinea. A high proportion of his human cargo died in the noisome cavities below deck, yet he could write:

> How sweet the name of Jesus sounds
> In a believer's ear!
> It soothes his sorrows, heals his wounds,
> And drives away his fear.

This was not a slave ship, and such conditions no longer existed. But was I so very much more conscious of what I was doing in terms of the present day? Was I really any more conscientious? It was easy to look back and wonder at the blindness of Christians who tolerated slavery for so many centuries without a protest. What were we going to India for? One part of me acquiesced in our imperial rule in India, another and more secret part of me revolted against it. The ambivalence of my thought and action only deepened, instead of resolving itself as I had hoped it would when I got away from Europe. The issues became more and more complicated.

In Bombay my contacts with the Communist and Socialist underground movement had been pre-arranged. I had been given a password and when I left the ship I called on a certain photographer in the Hornby Road and asked to have my photograph taken. While preparations were being made, I inquired after the health of one whose name I had been given. There was a tensing of the atmosphere, and I was told that although he had not been there lately inquiries would be made before I called back for my photographs. This was to enable my picture to be compared with one already sent out independently.

What I learnt, once I was accepted, opened up a new world of tyranny and injustice. It confirmed my revulsion against imperialism and my determination to oppose it even in secret. My duplicity at that time did not appear to matter so much as did the need to fight the twin evils of my own country's imperialism and the Nazi tyranny in Germany.

Only my religion gave any meaning and wholeness to my life. It could hardly be spoken about to anyone, since orthodox churchmen would not understand it and others were not interested or were frankly contemptuous of its ineffectuality. It had to be hidden because only God could be expected to understand all the conflicting pressures and demands that were made on my loyalties and capacities for action. Only in God would these conflicts be reconciled if one tried to serve Him objectively, above all outside influence. Probably this position was not a whit less hypocritical because it was conscious than the seemingly unconscious self-deception of John Newton on his slave ship. But I must set it down as an account of the position I, and possibly others, found myself being forced into at that time. It may help to explain the deepening dilemma and the somewhat equivocal position in which I was to find myself.

I had many discussions in Bombay on the question of ethics and Marxism. I felt drawn to accept the dialectical materialist explanation of imperialism as monopoly capitalism and of nazism as a more highly developed form of it; but I could not bring myself to accept the materialist view of ethics. As in Hackney, I saw that everywhere the behaviour of individuals gave the lie to the Communist teaching. I sought to refute the theory of Kautsky that ethical values were relative to historical circumstances. While accepting the concept that economic motive and group self-interest offered a broad explanation of the behaviour of classes and institutions in history, I felt that it broke down as an explanation of the conduct of individuals, particularly some of the more disinterested and devoted members of the Communist party. I greatly admired their readiness for sacrifice in their cause, while deploring their materialism and contempt for the beliefs and values which I cherished.

I resisted the suspicion that communism might be leading towards yet another form of organized tyranny. It seemed to me that such an eventuality would spell the end of hope for mankind. So I accepted the suggestion that the evidence of compulsion and liquidation was either exaggerated by imperialist propaganda or that these measures were made necessary by ruthless attempts at intervention and sabotage.

From what I had seen in London as sympathizer to the busmen's cell, it seemed that one hope of preventing communism from degenerating into tyranny was if honest people and disinterested Christians identified themselves with their struggle, shared their sufferings and sacrifices and even perhaps their sins and their guilt. By standing above the battle the Church only hardened resistance to Christianity. Amongst the Communists there were good, bad, and indifferent. The question was who would emerge in control, what standards would prevail, and what restraints or advice would they accept in the event of their achieving power?

One challenge which I never really faced while I was in India was Gandhi's philosophy of non-violent resistance, which was to mean so much to me in later years. It was born in Natal, that cockpit of South African racialism; and it was here in Durban, I afterwards learned, that Gandhi had been asked to leave a Christian church where he was meditating because he was an Indian. I have often wondered since whether the history of Christianity would have been different if this and all that it signifies had not happened. Might India not have accepted the faith of Christianity and found new meanings in it, perhaps giving it new expression as well?

In India I felt the reproach to my conscience of Gandhi's frequent imprisonment and fasts; and I learnt from Charles Andrews, who used to attend the cathedral at Calcutta when I was chaplain there, something of the beauty of Gandhi's non-violent approach to the problems of life. But I was younger then, and it was an age of growing crisis and impatience, of violence and intolerance, an age threatened with even more violence from the German, Italian, and Japanese axis. At that time the philosophy of non-violent resistance seemed very ineffectual.

Andrews was so diffident and so torn by internal doubts and uncertainties about his faith that for many years he refused to exercise his ministry. He was very much abused by his own English community, both in India and Britain, for his defence of Gandhi and his attempts to interpret him. There were even demands in Parliament that he should be brought to England and charged with treason. Yet even Andrews was doubtful about the ethics of fasting as a method of coercion. (His thought-provoking letter is quoted in Appendix 1.)

This hesitance, and the inconsistencies which I found in Gandhi's own writings, only deepened—or perhaps were used by me as the pretext for deepening—my own dilemma between thought and action and action and moral values.

Soon after I arrived in India I was offered the post of domestic chaplain to the Bishop of Bombay and accepted this. Before taking it up, however, I continued my journey towards Korea to explain my change of plans to the bishop, who was at that time on a visit to Japan, and also to fulfil one or two assignments for the Communists. As mentioned earlier, one of these was to convey a sum of one hundred pounds to assist the journey of one of the Indian delegates to the Seventh World Congress of the Communist International which was due to convene at that time in Moscow. My advice in India was that he had already left for Russia, but that he was held up for lack of funds in Singapore, en route for China and Japan. When I made inquiries at the little shop whose address I had been given I found that he had already been apprehended by the police and returned to India. The very mention of his name caused considerable agitation and disclaimers of any responsibility for his activities. After leaving the shop I had a distinct impression of being followed, but by various subterfuges I succeeded in eluding the follower, whoever he was.

The thought of being involved in this conspiracy gave me some pleasurable excitement. I derived some satisfaction from devising ways to escape detection, to establish contact and maintain it without betraying my own or other people's identity. I knew enough to realize that, not only were the forces of law and order extremely efficient, but the Communists themselves could become very vindictive and suspicious in the event of failure to fulfil any commission they had assigned—though I really had no conception of the ramifications of all that I was becoming involved in and for which I was accepting moral responsibility. The full extent of this responsibility has only been brought home to me as the whole tragic history of communism in the world has been unfolded. The personal factors, as well as the historical events of our time, need to be studied in order to understand how people can become willing instruments of forces which they can hardly influence, much less control.

After Singapore the ship called at Penang, Hong Kong, and Shanghai before crossing to Japan and calling at Kobe and Yokohama. In Japan I experienced great difficulty in establishing contact with what was then an illegal underground movement. The censorship was very strict and made it impossible to use postal or telegraph services. The police system was efficient and seemingly almost omniscient. There was universal fear of the ill-treatment which the police used to extract information from those against whom there existed even the flimsiest grounds for suspicion. My task was made all the more difficult by the fact that the names of my contacts had been given to me only in English script. I could speak no Japanese and had no means of establishing contact with anyone who did, to whom I could confide the names of those I wanted to meet. As a European unable to make myself understood or to find my way about, I was very conspicuous. And I had to think both of my own safety and the safety of those with whom I was trying to make contact, for whom the consequences of any mistake would be more serious than they might be for me. Somehow the very inefficiency of the whole enterprise reassured me that I was on the side of the weak and oppressed rather than of any sinister conspiracy.

The names and addresses had first to be transcribed into Japanese, if I were to make contact without arousing suspicion. For even if I could find one of the addresses it would be too conspicuous to call there in person. It occurred to me that the only way to get the material transcribed was to do it piecemeal, in such a way that no one person was asked to give the whole name and address. The only places where casual visitors could go without incurring suspicion were the cafés and night clubs, where many of the geisha girls spoke a little English. So I went from one to another and, after a dance or a drink, would start a discussion on how to learn English or Japanese. Slowly I would work the conversation round till I had this word or that written down for me. By this laborious process I hoped to build up the complete name and address in Japanese script. I could then copy it on to an envelope which I proposed to send by a messenger whom I would pay to deliver it. When I had collected the words for one address, and it came to copying the separate pieces of Japanese script on to an envelope, I was convinced that no one would be deceived into thinking it had ever been written by even a half-educated

Japanese. Unfortunately it seemed that there were subtle changes in the form of a word according to whether it was a noun or a proper name.

I lived at this time in a state of continuous nervous apprehension; and indeed some of the geisha girls looked at me very suspiciously when I persisted in playing the game too long and began to take my leave without trying the other forms of amusement they had to offer. I decided to try one other method before I would give up the attempt in Japan, partly in fear and partly in disgust at the inefficiency of those who had expected me to fulfil a mission with such inadequate information and equipment. I bought two tickets for the Japanese opera in Tokyo. I then delivered one of these, with the nickname I had been given, to a place which I believed to be at an address I wanted in Yamachita Cho, Yokohama. When I arrived at the opera the other seat was empty; but the performance would go on till the small hours of the morning and I would have to wait until the end to be sure that no one had come. It was one of the most tense and exciting theatrical performances I have ever experienced, the great beauty and drama of the opera competing with the strong tension within me. To the Japanese the opera and ballet are very much more than a mere means of entertainment. They are the consummation of their art, their poetry and music, their history, their folklore, and their religion. With the elements of romance, heroism, and tragedy, they express also the religious conceptions of sin and expiation and various problems of social conscience. The theatre is part of their religion, a living tradition of hundreds of years; to share their appreciation and emotion one would have to understand not only the Japanese language, but the nation's whole way of life and thought and belief. The performances have a sacred quality, protected by an elaborate ritual applying both to audience and players.

Covering, as it does, the whole of life, there is no element of prudishness even in religious dances, such as the one I saw about light overcoming darkness. A central factor of the whole theme is sexual curiosity and here the element of humour certainly borders on what we should call the bawdy. The goddess of light, Amaterasu O-Mikami, has withdrawn to a cave and is sulking there after being teased by her small brother. The world is plunged into darkness and gloom on account of her concealment. The other gods try to induce her to come out, by dancing in front of the cave. One of them dances in a way no British Lord Chamberlain would countenance for a moment. The dance causes laughter among the other deities, and eventually the hidden goddess can control her curiosity no longer and peers out from her cave to see what is causing all the uproar. Thus she becomes interested and finally appeased and returns to her place in the heavens, to the joy and gratitude of all heaven and earth.

As I sat enthralled, I was also conscious of my fear, with the empty seat beside me somehow betokening not only my own subterfuge and duplicity, but also the feeling that there was another reality beneath this artistry. Beneath it all was a modern tyranny, in which flourished many of the evils of our own industrial revolution; a ruthless challenge to the West, from whom these people were learning modern techniques, was in preparation.

In the peculiar circumstances of my visit to Japan, and especially to the Japanese opera in Tokyo, I was aware of the vast gulf of my misunderstanding of the East. I felt this to be true, with rare exceptions, of all my fellow-countrymen. In India we ruled with arrogant superiority and abysmal ignorance of their centuries of thought, artistic development, and religious and philosophical speculation; though doubtless we have other virtues which compensate in part for this insularity. May not these very deficiencies have contributed to some of those positive advantages, which will weigh in the scales of history against all that India suffered under our rule, advantages such as the indifference, objectivity, and comparative incorruption of our civil service and judicial system?

I returned to India without ever establishing contact in Japan and with a sense of futility and impotence in face of the forces which were already moving towards a powerful combination against both Western imperialism and Christian religion, as presented by white missionaries throughout China, Japan, and the whole Far East.

In China, from what little I saw, it seemed that the missionaries from the West were for the most part very remote from the realities of Chinese political life. Their preconceptions and manner of life created an iron curtain between them and an understanding of what was happening in China, an understanding of the depth and magnitude of the forces at work beneath the surface. Imperialism, at that time, was a stern reality, both economically and politically, and it was inevitable that it should be made both the real and the imaginary scapegoat for all the evils from which the great poverty-stricken masses of China suffered. One could not even pass through the ports of Hong Kong and Shanghai without seeing and sensing the great gulf that was fixed between the European and

Asian way of life, a distance that must have been a continuous reminder to the Chinese of the great discrepancy between precept and practice in institutional Christianity.

Perhaps it is easy to be wise after the event; but I must confess that I felt instinctively aware of the danger, though not of the magnitude of the coming debacle of the West and of institutional Christianity as conceived by the West in China. The uncertain standards and values in my own life and experience inhibited any real clarity of thought and action in facing these same problems in India.

I returned to Bombay and took up my duties as domestic chaplain to the Bishop of Bombay at his house on Malabar Hill, the most fashionable part of Bombay, overlooking the Indian Ocean, the gateway of India, and beyond it the Colaba Fort. Directly beneath us were the Chowpatti sands where Gandhi, Nehru, and other Nationalist leaders held their mass meetings under the banners of Swaraj, Suadeshi, and the Indian National Congress. At night the lights along the waterfront would glitter like diamonds and the night air would be heavy with the scent of flowering trees in the bishop's garden. I would sit alone in the stillness, hearing only the cool breezes from the sea which would sometimes bring the sounds, muffled by distance, of the sad songs of a people yearning for their freedom.

It was not long before I began to feel the strain of the double code of ethics and ideas which I was trying to sustain, while maintaining the unity of my own identity. Living in the fashionable quarter of Bombay, I was confronted continuously with the contrast between the wealth of the European community and its supporters amongst the Indians, some of the wealthy merchants and princes, the small Parsee community and Indian members of the Indian Civil Service, and the appalling poverty and squalor of the Indian masses in the towns and villages. I was the conscious and unconscious recipient of the official point of view, both in season and out of season. On official occasions at Government House, and elsewhere in clubs and "dak" bungalows where I stayed while on tour, there was always the same withering contempt for the Indian Nationalist leaders. Congress was dismissed as a bunch of intellectuals and agitators, in no way representing the starving and illiterate masses whom they wanted to exploit themselves. Mr. Gandhi was seen as a bowler-hatted lawyer who resorted to Indian dress to deceive the masses into thinking he was one of them. This distorted view was very generally held amongst the British community, both civil and military; amongst the missionaries and commercial people only occasionally did one find any deeper insight into what was really happening politically in India, or any long-range view of Britain's own position. It was this attitude that must be held largely responsible for Britain's somewhat ignominious withdrawal from India and the confusion and terrible bloodshed which resulted from the logical conclusion of British policy and the partitioning of India and Pakistan.

This feeling of remoteness from the people of the country belonged not only to the sphere of politics but to religion and social life as well. The Christian religion, so far as the bishop and the Indian Ecclesiastical Establishment were concerned, was really a department of the State. As a chaplain of the Establishment I was regarded by the Indians as a civil servant, and I made out my monthly salary sheet just as any other civil servant and was subject to the same rules regarding pay and leave. The Ecclesiastical Establishment, a sub-department of the educational division, was transferred from one jurisdiction to another to suit the convenience of senior officials or the central government.

Our liturgy and forms of service, appropriate enough perhaps to post-Reformation England, seemed singularly unsuited to the period of India's growing struggle for self-government and self-conscious pride in her own religious and cultural achievements.

This was brought home to me very forcibly in many different ways— once, especially, when I had the task of devising a form of service suitable for the dedication by the bishop of colours and drums for the newly re-constituted Royal Indian Navy. The officers were for the most part British, and therefore Christians, while the crew were both Hindu and Muslim. It was not easy to combine the conflicting martial elements to be found in each religious tradition. To make it even more difficult, the ceremony was to be attended by the Governor, Lord Brabourne, and was to be broadcast over the All India radio. This meant that the timing must be a good deal more exact than the Hindu priest and the Muslim *moulvi* were accustomed to be asked to observe. Each, of course, had to be given an important function to perform in the ceremony, and a part had to be assigned to each in the actual blessing of the colours. There was no question of being able to rehearse the service, and I was in a highly nervous state by the time the parade was assembled and the service due to begin.

My carefully worked out timing for the parts I had assigned to the bishop, the Hindu priest, and the *moulvi* was completely disorganized when the *moulvi* was carried away by the emotion of the occasion; he extended his chanting of the Koran far beyond the passage I had thought appropriate. The governor, who was standing at attention with his very heavy sword at the salute, began to perspire very visibly, his hand trembled, and his sword began to wave. Fortunately it was before the days of television and appropriate cuts were made in the newsreel.

I had several outstations, namely Bulsar, Surat, Dohad, and Baroda, which I visited at week-ends to minister to Christians, including the Anglo Indians and a small sprinkling of Indian Christians. The clubs at these outstations had by this time begun to admit Indian civil servants and army officers, though the atmosphere always felt strained and Indian women hardly ever appeared, which made social life seem rather unequal to the British women.

As bishop's chaplain my most difficult task during the week was interviewing deputations. These often consisted of congress officials who wanted the bishop to intervene in such questions as ill-treatment in the prisons. I found it very difficult to understand the bishop's attitude towards this particular question, and it was often a source of disagreement.

One deputation which asked to see the bishop, led I think by the Congree Mayor of Bombay, sent in the particulars of many cases of ill-treatment in the gaols, where political prisoners had been mercilessly beaten with long canes and had had various other forms of torture inflicted on them. It seemed to me that a strong *prima facie* case had been made out for the bishop to request the intervention of the governor and I told him so. In summarizing the case for him, I decided to reinforce the complaint with another I had received from a member of the League of Mercy, that the police in a neighbouring compound practised their corporal punishment on sacks in full view of their hostel windows.

Without giving any answer, the bishop said that he would like to go for a long walk and talk one or two matters over with me. In the course of a long and exhausting climb up a near-by hill-top, he put a number of searching questions to me, all of which were directed towards making me "face realities." In the end it came down to the question of whether it was not better that comparatively few agitators should suffer in the gaols than that whole tracts of country and innocent villages should have to be laid waste.

This attitude was not uncommon amongst the military and civil servants and even among many missionaries, though there were conspicuous exceptions, such as the Chresta Seva Sengh and its Superior, Bill Lash, who after independence became Bishop of Bombay. The effect of this attitude on me was only to cause a deeper division of mind, and I found refuge in re-establishing my contacts with the underground.

Some of them were under-cover men or leaders on the run, in which case elaborate precautions had to be taken to ensure that no one was being followed. A place would be chosen on the sea-shore or at some lonely spot where, if necessary, our meeting could be explained as a casual encounter. One method of communication I had was to make a certain mark on a pillar outside a certain shop. This was a sign to my contact, who passed that way on his way to work, that there was a note to be picked up at the end of a certain railing made of hollow iron tubes. On one occasion I arrived for a reply just at the moment when a crow pecked it out and flew away with it to make its nest. It was by such means of communication that I maintained my controversy on the question of Marxism and ethics with one or two leading Communists.

When I was transferred to Calcutta to act as chaplain of the Anglican cathedral there, I kept in touch with the underground. There was an added risk in that the Communists were trying to disentangle themselves from the Bengal terrorists, each group wanting to swallow up the other.

I found an amusing friend, and one with a delightfully carefree mind in that oppressive atmosphere, in Humphrey House, who at that time was lecturing in English at Calcutta University. When he first arrived at the railway station and was met by the head of the department and other officials, he was told that arrangements had been made for him to stay at the United Services Club till he had found himself his own bungalow. He shocked and horrified all present by announcing that he preferred to go and stay on Dharamtalla Street with his friend Mr. Sudhir Dutt, whom he had known at Oxford, and who had kindly invited him to be his guest until he had made his own arrangements. From that time onward, Humphrey House was a marked man and suspected at best of communism, whereas actually he was just a normally free and independent Englishman who honestly detested the role his country was playing in India. His movements were closely watched and when he did move into his own bungalow there were C.I.D. men sitting on his wall day and night and padding along after him when he went out. He wrote a very

amusing satire on Calcutta society at that time called "I spy," which his
executors really ought to publish.

It was there too that I came to know the metropolitan, Bishop Foss
Westcott. He was a grand old man, tough and pious, and greatly attracted to the "young idea" which he thought he had found in moral re-
armament. He had much more sympathy with Gandhi than many of the
other bishops, who saw him only as an astute politician and a dangerous
challenger of law and order who would let loose forces he could not
control. I remember being given a long lecture on this subject by another
bishop when I tried to organize a joint letter of protest in connection
with the use of British troops and planes against defenceless villages and
in support of certain cruel and effete tyrants in the Indian states.

In due course I returned to England for two months' leave. I took
with me voluminous reports, which I was to leave in Paris, on the situation in India. It was during this voyage that the Fascist armies entered
Madrid in triumph; not long after we had landed at Brindisi (where I
had an uneasy time at the Customs with my documents), Mussolini
marched into Albania.

After delivering these papers in Paris I attended an enormous Popular
Front demonstration. It seemed to me that these people had faith and
the courage of their convictions in a way that I did not, for my convictions were in conflict with one another. When I saw the comradeship that
existed between people of all nationalities at this demonstration, I felt
the pull of communism as something in which one could lose oneself;
and when I heard the great surging shouts of "Les Soviets Partout" I lost,
for the time, any consciousness of danger in my desire to become sub-
merged in something greater than myself, which would challenge the evil
that I knew in the world even better than I knew the evil in myself.

On my return to Calcutta I sought relief from the strain and inner
conflict of my life there in the study—a very superficial study—of Indian
mysticism. Another method I found more satisfying was to join the Bengal Flying Club and learn to fly. I found an irresistible attraction in flying
and shall never forget the exhilaration, mixed with dread, of my first solo
flight. On a calm morning I flew over the delta of the mighty Ganges and
the Brahmaputra, the great life-giving rivers of India. Looking down on
these great sprawling rivers in flood, so careless it seemed of human life
and habitation, yet not so in reality, I had an illusory sense of power, as
though by touching the stick I could go almost anywhere. Actually I was

just as dependent on my fellow men in the air as on the ground, and on the laws and forces of nature, the wind and gravity, and the position of the earth in relation to the rest of the Universe, as well. Yet the illusion gave me a great sense of satisfaction and escape from my dilemmas at that time.

The situation in Bengal was threatening to result in a large-scale famine. The appalling poverty of the people of India and the heavy burden of the zemindari system of land tenure made one despair of our statesmen at home and of the type of Indian politician which had come to the surface under this system in Bengal. Elsewhere the congress had taken office under the new provincial constitutions and some much needed reforms had already been set in motion. It was regarded as an experiment by both British and Indian politicians and there were many, on both sides, who expected, and even hoped, that the experiment would break down.

The threatened famine in Bengal seemed likely to lead to large-scale community strife between Muslims and Hindus, especially where landlords and peasants were of different religions. Among the British officials there were some who looked with equanimity upon the prospect of such strife, as calculated to provide an outlet for the people's anger and discontent, which would otherwise be concentrated against British rule. The dangerous folly of this way of thinking, and of the community system of political representation in such circumstances, was only to be realized too late, when there were large-scale massacres of Muslims and Hindus and the division of India and Pakistan became inevitable. The fatal error of communalism (i.e., political representation by reference to racial or religious groups) has been repeated almost everywhere where different races had to live side by side, the outstanding examples being South Africa and Central and East Africa.

I sometimes discussed South Africa with Charles Andrews in Calcutta. I used to envy him his inward serenity, though now he was desperately unhappy about his own country. He had had a very unhappy time in South Africa and the attempts he was making in India to arrange for Indians to be repatriated from Natal were not working out well. These Indians, especially the poorer ones, had lost contact with their own families and villages. Having used his influence to persuade them to accept the South African Government's bonus and passage to India, Andrews found he was unable to secure their reception back into their own communities. They sat huddled miserably outside their temporary shelters along the banks of the Hoogly River, a mute reproach to the ineptitude of statesmen and a foretaste of the great refugee camps for displaced persons which were to be set up in India and Pakistan after independence, and indeed in Europe and the Middle East as well. Andrews understood the double difficulty that existed in Bengal, with the impotence of the Provincial Government to carry out even the land reforms suggested by the Floud Commission. But there was also the bad faith of South African politicians and the resentment they were stirring up even then against the Indian community in South Africa. On top of this there were the personal difficulties of his own relationship, both with the Government of India and with the Church, which for political and intellectual reasons had become acute.

He used to come to the cathedral in the early morning. He never made his Communion, but would sit in a dark corner by himself and continue to sit there meditating after the service, when I would be going off to get my breakfast. Sometimes when I stopped to speak to him I saw that the poor old man was weeping, so I waved and went on. I wanted to help, and I think he knew it. But I could do nothing and I hoped he knew that too, and would not think me unfriendly. In any case anything would have been an intrusion. He was so timid in so many ways, yet quite fearless where the principles which he really believed in were involved.

For myself I found refuge from thought and feeling in flight and would hurry off after breakfast for my instruction. I found the strain of preaching in the cathedral increasingly unbearable. Then one night, after I had come down from a particularly exhilarating flight above the damp heat and squalor of Calcutta, I was travelling at a good pace when an oncoming bus, which was travelling at equal speed, had as much difficulty as I in rounding a bend. I remember hearing my skidding wheels scream, thinking that I would not be able to clear the bus swinging in towards me, and that it was Saturday evening and my sermon for tomorrow was still unprepared. My small sports car was spun round like a twig in a fast-running stream, and when I awoke the steering wheel had been broken by my chest and I felt weak and giddy from loss of blood and began to shiver. A car pulled up and an Indian doctor at the hospital gave me an injection, which seemed miraculously to stop my pain and shivering within a few moments.

For several days I cared nothing for whether I lived or died. Then the bishop came and he said some prayers and some lines of Clough:

> *Say not the struggle naught availeth,*
> *The labour and the wounds are vain. . . .*

> *For while the tired waves, vainly breaking,*
> *Seem here no painful inch to gain,*
> *Far back, through creeks and inlets making,*
> *Comes silent, flooding in, the main.*

He said there was still some work for me that needed doing, and I longed to tell him everything; but I felt too weak. Still I did not know what the work that needed doing was, nor did I understand the meaning of the main that came "silent, flooding in." Was it communism? Was it the Kingdom of God? Or was it all just an old man's early Victorian sentiment? For three months of the summer of 1938 I lay in hospital not knowing why I seemed to want to go on living.

In Europe the farce of Munich had weakened the lingering links of faith and any hope that there was something in the old order of things that could survive the rampant surge of Hitlerism. I found myself slipping into the conviction that the only force capable of resisting Hitler and Mussolini was communism. If I survived, I should have to think it all out and I should have to devote myself more whole-heartedly to the cause.

Meanwhile the bishop sent me up to a hill station for the winter months, to Kasauli in the foothills of the Himalayas, where the work would be light and the climate would help me to recuperate.

While in Kasauli I wrote furiously and indignantly, incorporating a good deal of material I had received from the underground, on the political movements of the Eastern States agency, for instance, where women and children were beaten and raped by our soldiers on their punitive expeditions to suppress the people's revolt against their decadent rulers. In face of this, all that we did was dreadfully and pathetically inadequate as an expression of the Christian religion. My own double mode of life was an even more despicable evasion than that of many of the higher ecclesiastics. What I was pretending to myself that I was doing with the underground was quite ineffectual, and it effectively prevented me from throwing myself whole-heartedly into the movement for Indian freedom.

Responsibilities could not be evaded, for inevitably one was for or against the existing order—no one could really be neutral. Andrews and Agatha Harrison, who tried desperately to keep a foot in both camps, performed an invaluable service to the cause by keeping the lines of communication open and making it possible for something of each side to be understood by the other. Indeed without them the rift between Britain and India might have widened into such a deep contradiction and enmity that no reconciliation would have been possible, and the outcome would have been more disastrous for India's unity and friendship with Britain than it was. The flexibility of British institutions would not of itself have availed had it not been for the devoted labours of a handful of people like Andrews and Agatha Harrison, who at the time enjoyed little more than patronizing indulgence at best in Britain and who have now been forgotten in the oft-repeated speeches of politicians on the nature of the Commonwealth and the profound wisdom of "our statesmanship."

When passions are running high the role of mediator is apt to incur the dislike and contempt of the most fervent and radical elements on either side. But it nevertheless requires a strength of character, knowledge of technical procedures, and a delicacy of touch which is a rare enough combination at times when history is running at full flood.

In Europe on the other hand there was reconciliation of a different order, inspired by a different spirit, of which L. S. Amery was saying at that time after Munich:

I doubt whether anyone can really dare to describe this as a peace based on negotiation, on reason or justice. Will it figure in history as anything else than the greatest—and the cheapest—victory ever won by aggressive militarism? . . . We have been reduced from a position of safety and power—power to do good, power to be generous to a beaten foe, power to make terms with Germany, power to give her proper redress for her grievances, power to stop her arming if we choose, power to take any step in strength or mercy or justice which we thought right—reduced in five years from a position safe and unchallenged to where we stand now.

If we had lost the virtues of a great martial nation and had become powerless to challenge the evil of nazism spreading over Europe, and if our own rule in India and Africa had ceased to be an instrument of justice and for the protection of those "who were unable to stand on their own in the strenuous conditions of the modern world," what then had we to offer to India, China, the Middle East, and Africa?

We had corrupted Christianity, a religion which had come from the East, and we were offering it to Asia as a vindication of our own national conception of ourselves and our role in the world as the instrument of law and order. Instead, in India it had become an instrument of draconian oppression in which even the worst local princes could count on our armed intervention to support them on their thrones. What would they say in Britain if they knew what was being done in their name?

"It is better that a few people should suffer in the gaols," the bishop had said, "than that whole villages should have to be laid waste." But they were being laid waste. Their little mud huts were being burned, their pots and pans and their few possessions destroyed. "I was all the time saying 'Namaste' with folded hands," said an Indian peasant woman of her belabouring by one of our soldiers, and somehow her cry seemed to express that of all India under our rule. I took it as a title when I began to formulate my writings into a book.

After I had recovered from the effects of my accident I felt I should return to England. I could no longer even pretend to myself that my presence in India was of any assistance to the Communists, since in Kasauli I was entirely cut off.

I felt humiliated at my duplicity and my impotence in face of the challenge to everything that I had brought myself to believe was worth living for and had been taught to believe was worth dying for. My impotence was partly a failure of courage and partly a failure of intellect. I had no surely grounded philosophy of life capable of inspiring me to stand up and fight boldly against what I knew to be oppression and wrong. I was unsure of the very grounds of my opposition to oppression. I could only half accept the philosophy of communism, and my Christianity was so full of emotional and intellectual contradictions that it was incapable of unifying my interior and exterior life.

I was, like many of my generation, in a state of spiritual and ethical disintegration. And it was this disintegration that we were offering to the East as a Weltanschauung or "world view."

5   War Breaks Out—England

I returned to England shortly before the outbreak of war, determined to try to get published some of the material I had been working on. I worked hard to get it finished and submitted it to a publisher who said, on the basis of the draft he had seen, that he would be prepared to add it to his list. However, it was not long before the imminence of war overshadowed everything else. Reluctantly he said he had come to the conclusion that a book like *Namaste* would not be able to achieve anything in the state of tension which then prevailed, and that it would only be used as grist to the mill of Dr. Goebbels's propaganda machine.

I was still harried by my own internal conflicts and by the sense of being forced to choose between two evils. I felt myself being driven towards the acceptance of communism as the only alternative to the evils of imperialism and nazism. I studied communism further and, urged on by my friends and my own conscience, I decided that I would try a period of mutual probation, during which I would fulfil the functions of a party organizer. I would thus gain some experience of the working out of their theories in practice and see what my reaction would be to the party's organization and discipline.

The stress and worry leading up to this decision seriously affected my health, and I spent many weeks in the Hospital for Tropical Diseases, undergoing X-ray and other tests, all of which were inconclusive. Despite the severe pains I experienced, I was told that my illness was nothing more than nervous in origin, and I left the hospital determined to go forward with my decision. I offered my services to the Party with the understanding that if I found my work incompatible with those Christian beliefs which I still retained I should withdraw.

Meanwhile I organized a joint open letter to the archbishop, signed by Edward Garrett, a former Indian civil servant, Agatha Harrison, and one or two others from the Fellowship of Reconciliation, warning of the consequences of procrastination in India and the danger of serious famine in Bengal.

The work allocated to me by the Communists was that of organizing factory groups in a new factory area, part of which included aircraft and other vital war industries. I lived in a basement near Park Royal and threw myself into the task. Under the new programme these factory groups were to be regarded as basic units of the Party's organization, which hitherto had been based upon street cells and district groups.

The announcement of the Soviet-German treaty did not at first distress me. In a way I felt elated, as it seemed to me then that this was Russia's way of forcing the West to decide where it stood. The long negotiations which had been going on in Moscow showed no signs of producing any results, and it seemed as though this might be a Soviet device to force the Western powers to take the initiative in opposing any further aggression. It was only gradually that I began to realize the implications of Stalin's pact with Germany.

Even before I began work with the Communists, I was experiencing a good deal of pain, though I tried to make myself believe the doctors' opinion that it had no physiological cause. I spent much time at the rectory my father now had at Addington in Buckinghamshire. It was a very small village, enclosed in a park which had been Lord Addington's estate in the heyday of the Hubbard family. He was still the patron of the parish, but after the Russian Revolution, and the loss of their timber estates, they had moved to a small modern house outside the park. Hidden by the oaks and chestnuts was a beautiful little thirteenth-century church.

Bordering on my father's glebe were some woods. In these woods, just before the outbreak of war, I spent many hours thinking about India, about the great conflict of ideologies throughout the world, and of my own internal conflict and pain—hours followed by long periods of darkness, when thinking brought no relief from a pain which seemed to defy all diagnosis.

All hope of reform, whether in India or in Europe, seemed to grow smaller before the mounting menace of barbarous neo-paganism. A period of wrath was upon us and, so far as we could see, a reversion to the dark ages of tyranny. To me it seemed that the ideal of achieving a Christian civilization developed from democracy was more and more unlikely. We had failed. Especially had we failed to carry forward those ideals, for which our own forbears had suffered so many and such frightful casualties, into our dealings with India and other subject peoples. The social reforms which had been achieved in Britain seemed to be dwarfed by the magnitude of our failure in India. Now we were faced with a mighty, ruthless, and cunning power against which our declared principles were of no avail. I hated nazism, its cruelty, cunning, and the bland logicality of its propaganda, which always contained that element of truth which made some of its deductions seem plausible enough. We had failed in our historic mission to build a rational, let alone a Christian, civilization. Nevertheless, it would be preferable to die fighting nazism than to submit to it.

The way of wrath and hatred seemed inevitable to me now. Any further doubt and hesitation meant evading the issues to seek refuge in a private conscience, as Arjuma was told in the *Bhagavad Gita* when the two armies of his kith and kin were ranged against one another. The age of conscience was past. We had neglected all our opportunities to bring the Kingdom of God closer to an earthly reality. Now the opportunity would be gone till the issues had been fought out. But what were we fighting for, and how would our methods of fighting affect the issues and the aims for which we fought?

Inevitably some of these inner disquisitions overflowed into conversations with my father, whose parish work amounted to little more than a means of retirement for him. We both felt we were reaching the end of an age. To him it meant the eclipse of so much for which he had struggled all his life. There was to be a repetition and a worsening of the misery which 1914 had brought to the people in the slums, where his heart was still. He would go on, for to him his Faith was the only foundation on which a new age could be built, whatever the outcome of the war. But he was outside the currents of the social and political thought of those days, and I was deeply involved. I was frustrated spiritually and thoroughly confused intellectually, and any discussions with my parents only caused them much anxiety.

It was on a Sunday morning, the third of September, that the world awaited Mr. Chamberlain's announcement over the B.B.C. My father was putting on his vestments in the church, I remember, just before the announcement was due. I thought he ought to postpone the service to enable people to listen in, but he refused. He began the Sung Eucharist punctually, and I said I would wait and come in late.

There was a tension to be felt everywhere as I looked out on the eternally green English fields and listened to Mr. Chamberlain's voice coming over the air. As I scribbled a little note I thought foolishly of the piece of paper Mr. Chamberlain had waved when he returned from Munich. Then I went through the vestry to the sanctuary to hand it to my father. He was singing the Creed as he glanced down at it, but characteristically there was no faltering in his voice.

At the end of the Creed he turned round to the old men and women and the Sunday school children with my mother and said: "Mr. Chamberlain has announced that England is now at war with Germany. We must pray for our statesmen, for our navy, army and air force and for all whom we know and love." He then continued in the form of the liturgy, "Let us pray for the whole state of Christ's Church militant here in earth."

I returned to London that afternoon, partly to get away from my home and the necessity of any talk or discussion about anything, and also to resume in London the experiment with the factory groups. An endless stream of traffic was coming out of London, every type of vehicle being laden with evacuated families and all their portable possessions.

At the beginning of the war the Communist party line was that Britain should fight nazism, even though the Russians were keeping out. I chafed at the idea of organizing these groups, when I had some flying experience and pilots and air crews were so badly needed, but I had promised to try my hand and I continued. It was not until the war had been going on for some weeks that I realized that all my feverish activity, and the twenty or more groups that I had got started, would be used by the Party for a policy which was gradually shifting away from the aims that I could conscientiously agree with. I began to sense that I was a mere tool, a cog in the political apparatus. However voluntary my actions seemed to me, they were in fact joined to the actions of innumerable others and formed part of a chain which—no matter what my own motives were—would contribute to "an end which was no part of my intention"—though Adam Smith used the words in a very different setting.

This realization did not come suddenly, for the process of becoming an active sympathizer with communism had itself been a long and complicated process, which I had tried hard to resist. It almost seemed as though any action that I chose to take at that time became part of a chain in a social process, leading to consequences which I could not foresee or control. I felt the urge to merge myself in the action and conscience of a group, since whatever I did as an individual had implications of which I was unaware in any case. It was only very gradually that I understood the contradiction within communism itself and the implications of the Party line. Before the war it had seemed to me that I must submit myself to one or other side in the great controversy of our time between capitalism and communism; since I could not preserve my identity in action I must choose which cause I should merge with. I could not remain neutral or rise above the battle, for that would be an illusion.

> *As one betwixt two fires we stand*
> *Whom neutrality cannot save*
> *Nor occupation cheer.*
> *Private stars fade in the blood red dawn*
> *Where two worlds strive.*

I had chosen to try to work with Communists. I was useful to them and, as I have said, we got more than twenty factory groups organized in the Park Royal area, but I felt that there was little room for personal judgement on any fundamental matters. I should be used as long as I was useful and then discarded without any question of personal value. No doubt that was also true of many other undertakings, including the armed forces, but here it seemed to be a consciously thought-out and a frighteningly inhuman philosophy. I could not yet deny much of the truth that I had found in communism and I persisted in this act of submission until I realized also that there was a contradiction within communism itself. There was the action of Russia, if I had judged her motives correctly, in joining with Hitler and there was the necessity for those under threat of occupation to resist nazism; but there was confusion within the ranks of the Communist party with regard to England. There was a growing anti-war policy which was being forced on those leaders who were at first against it.

It was not long before the Party organization was being used to undermine people's confidence in fighting the war against Hitler. Men and women, who had spent years working and striving to build up anti-Fascist popular fronts, were now expected to about-face. Men in the armed forces, after volunteering because of their determination to fight nazism, were now asking what they should do if Britain were invaded. As they mounted guard at the defence works along the south coast they really did not know whether they ought to pull the trigger or not.

Outwardly there was still comparative peace and calm, although war had been declared several months previously, but by the Christmas of 1939 I found the internal strain of the dilemma insupportable. I was taken very ill with acute pains and on Christmas Eve I managed to reach St. Luke's Hostel, where I was found to have an acute obstruction and an operation revealed ileitis or Crohn's disease.

For my convalescence I went down to my parents' home in Buckinghamshire. I had given up the experiment of working with the Communists and had decided I should never be able to work as one of their functionaries, accepting their thought and disciplines in the way that was expected. I still had sympathy with some of their aims and with some of them as individuals, whose courage and devotion to the cause I respected as something greater than I had ever been able to put into any cause myself. In truth I really did not know what I believed in. If I could get fit I should enlist and fight, but while I was convalescing my inner disquisitions continued.

The age of faith had given way to an age of doubt and uncertainty about all the fundamental meanings and values of life. We were lost now in a sea of relativities. Hence it was better to die fighting the greater evil in nazism than the evils we had brought upon ourselves. The other alternative of appeasement was worse, because there would be no possibility of resisting once nazism was victorious, with its power to organize the perversion of men's minds and to goad them on by monstrous untruths to perform acts of cruelty and barbarism without mercy. Having abandoned communism as a creed and a party, as well as a guide to action, any further hesitation seemed contemptible.

The actions and methods used by the R.A.F. seemed quite incompatible with the methods of Christ, and the idea of becoming a chaplain in the armed forces, and exhorting others to fight, seemed wholly abhorrent. Nevertheless, I joined the Home Guard while I was recuperating from my operation at Addington and made up my mind that I would enlist in the R.A.F. when I had recovered.

I felt that I should have to confide some of my difficulties to my parents. My problems were so far removed from their way of thinking that

I had never thought of trying to explain them, and now I also seemed so far from the sure grounds of my father's faith. I tried to explain some of my difficulties in cold reason, and they were greatly bewildered by my state of mind.

One evening in the early summer of 1940, when the chestnuts were in bloom and the smell of mown grass came through the rectory windows, my mother gave way to her anxiety to the extent of imploring my father to have a "heart to heart" talk with me. Despite all that she had been through in her lifetime, it was the first time I had ever known her to give way to tears. He took me for a walk, but we did not walk very far as his leg troubled him a little. We went past the paddock he had ploughed up to grow vegetables and down to some ponds in the wood. While we sat by the still water and talked, a flight of wild duck would circle round us; as they were about to alight on the water, they would catch sight of us and, as with a single mind, would take off again, still in formation.

We had always talked openly and frankly except about my hidden life, and now I tried to tell him about the doubts and difficulties which had brought me to such an unhappy state of confusion and distress. We were trying not to hurt each other in our discussion. The futile arguments went on until dusk, and then we walked slowly back. There had been no heat between us at all. We had wanted to understand each other. He, father-like, wanted to protect me from unaccustomed ideas, which he feared were estranging my mind and soul from the faith which had been the faith of our childhood, and of the generations which had gone before us, the faith which had built his little church in the trees. It was as much a part of the countryside, of the history and the very life of England, as the breath of this summer breeze off the new-mown hay, the billowing green banks of foliage of the elms and chestnuts. The white flag with the red cross of St. George floated above them. That symbol had flown there ever since the stone church was built in the thirteenth century; someone or other had kept putting it up and taking it down. It was there still that night when we came back after I had told my father what I felt I must about my difficulties.

We both felt defeated as we lit our oil lamps for bed. For nothing had really been accomplished, and I knew he was wondering what he would say to my mother. "You must follow your conscience, dear boy. Have some cake and a glass of beer before you go to bed." That night, as I lay awake, I knew I should inevitably enlist in the R.A.F. There were bombers droning high overhead. I had my training as an amateur pilot, and it would help to ease the pain of thought in action.

I cursed the owl which began hooting inanely from a near-by tree. Then there was a sound outside in the passage; it was a jangling sound and it was not easy to think what it could be. When it persisted I got up and went out into the passage. I could see my father standing there in the dim light of a night light which was always kept burning in the passage. He was trying to fit the glass funnel of his lamp into its socket. I went up to him and said, "It's very late, whatever are you doing?" He did not say anything, but went on trying to adjust the lamp glass. So I took hold of it and said, "Let me have a try." It was then, when I came to look more closely into his face, that I saw one side of it was drawn down and he could not speak. He tried to smile and pointed at the lamp.

I struggled to keep calm. I must get him back to bed. But he was unable to walk properly. I tried to lead him by the arm to my bedroom. He would not go and pointed to his own room. I tried to force him into mine, but he resisted. I must keep calm. I must get to the telephone. But he might fall. I must shout for help. But that might frighten my mother. Then the door opened and she came out of her room. I said, "Father is not feeling very well, dear. Give me a hand will you? Just a little giddy." Yes, giddy was the word, giddy.

We got him back to his own bed, and I sat with him while my mother went to telephone the doctor. The maid appeared at the door looking very frightened, and for some reason or other my mother told her to go and boil a kettle. His mind appeared to be quite gone and he could only fiddle nervously with one of his hands. My own mind went racing round in little circles. What had I done to him? How could I undo it? How could I take back all the things I had been telling him? I did silly little things like straightening his bedclothes and tidying the wisps of grey hair over his forehead with my fingers. What a self-centred conceited fool I was. What in the name of heaven or hell did it matter what I thought or what smart-aleck notions I held, what half-baked ideas I had half understood? Even if I did think these things, why inflict them on him like a self-assertive prig.

There seemed to be no end to, or relief from, the agony of self-recrimination. My mind went back over my father's life; it had been so selfless, whatever his shortcomings. And even the shortcomings came from his singleness of mind and purpose, his dedication to the things in which he had so passionately believed. And I, all the time I had been arguing with him, must have been tearing at the very fibres of his mind and soul with my confused and clumsy fingers.

My father lived for nine more years, his body a worn-out frame which was his prison. His mind cleared a little so that he was able to stumble through short simple sentences and to read simple prayers. My mother gave all her time to being with him and nursing him, and, when he could walk a little, helped him as far as the church, where he would be able to read his familiar Office to himself. I was never able to carry on a connected conversation with him on any of the matters we had discussed, though I did all I could to reassure him that I was still holding on to the fundamentals. He would use one of his old phrases that he had learned from one of his old seafaring parishioners at Northam, "Keep on a-going on then."

The doctors told me that his illness had nothing to do with me. I wished I could believe that all the medical technicalities were the whole truth of the matter. In my effort to reassure him and my mother I took on some temporary parish work in London at the parish church of Fulham. I found the parish work a great intellectual and emotional strain. I still felt that I ought to enlist in the R.A.F., but I dreaded the effect of this decision on my parents. Meanwhile I became an air raid warden.

The blitz went on night after night, the bombers seeming to drone overhead in circles waiting for their moment of death. However, the physical danger and fear it aroused was easier to cope with than was the mental conflict of what to think and how to act in the confusion of loyalties and all that was expected of me.

During the first few nights of the blitz it seemed as though all the East End of London must be afire. The dome of St. Paul's Cathedral was red-suffused by the light of the fires in the London docks and in the city. The blood and fire of London was the prophecy with which, for our own reasons, we had failed to prophesy, with all our respectability and our bowler-hatted little money values. Now the poor people were being driven through the streets with fire and hate raining down on them, and the blood was literally flowing down the gutters of Europe. There were flames lighting up the sky to consume us because we had been lukewarm. Neither hot nor cold, God was spewing us out of His mouth.

Each of us had a soul, though. Each could only act in accordance with his own conscience. There was, after all, no other light to steer by but the light of one's own inner reason. I thought of Gandhi and I thought of Charles Andrews in the midst of all that confusion and noise and pain. Andrews was nearer to the mind of Christ than anyone I had ever known. This poor, gentle soul, with his straggling beard and his shuffling gait, had been the object of so much ridicule in South Africa and amongst the young pukka sahibs of India. When the war broke out and the famine came in Bengal, and when the government again imprisoned Gandhi, Nehru, and the other congress leaders, his full heart must have burst; he died, technically, of dysentery.

We were all such small people, but we were made greater by the greatness of the events in which we participated. One night during the blitz on the East End of London, the Auxiliary Fire Service had been called in from all around and they were up all night and day, fed by emergency rations on the spot and unable to get home. One man heard that his wife, hardly more than a schoolgirl, had had her first baby prematurely during the raid. Before he could get back to her, another bomb had dropped and killed both wife and child. He arrived, exhausted and begrimed, to find that his little world had been destroyed while he was away saving a warehouse. They had been such a delightfully healthy and happy young couple, intelligent, without great expectations of life, but accepting the best in people and things. To Air Raid Precautions this was merely an "incident," but it was one that was multiplied hundreds of thousands of times on our own and our enemies' fronts.

That night, I wrote a few lines for the young father, to express my feelings:

> *There is no illumination in these stars,*
> *Their light deceives for space divides the actual from the image.*
> *A thousand years in Thy sight are but as yesterday.*
> *But in these streets*
> *Each moment is significant in time fraught with pain*
> *Where the word is made flesh and the labour is vain.*
> *There is no comprehension in the alert and knowing gaze*
> *Of navigators at these stars:*
> *Cold space divides sight from reason*
> *In the eyes beholding these enactments*
> *For whose unholy entertainment.*
> *There is a roar of engines versus angels*

Above this needless and unsung nativity.
Gloria in Excelsis Deo—Per Ardua ad Astra
For God cannot quicken this time fraught with pain
Where the word is made flesh and labour is vain.

It was then that I finally decided to enlist as a combatant in the R.A.F.

I remember calling to mind a passage from the *Bhagavad Gita:* "Cast all thy acts on Me, with thy mind fixed on the indwelling Atmen, and without any thought of fruit, or sense of 'mine.' Shake off thy fever and fight Arjuma. Not seeking gain, Arjuma, there is a task of holiness to do. Unlike world-binding toil which bindeth not the faithful soul; such earthly duty do, free from desire, and thou shalt perform thy heavenly purpose."

I was advised that there was a better chance of passing the medical tests for the R.A.F. if one enlisted as an A.C.2, and it was as such that I reported in the autumn of 1940 at the Ealing depot, after having been passed as A.1 at the medical examination and classified for training as air crew. There followed many weeks of square bashing at Bridgnorth, followed by several months of further drilling and some technical training at Blackpool. The R.A.F. was short of training equipment and instructors during and after the Battle of Britain. Therefore, though the training and the life were strenuous, I felt a strong sense of anticlimax— as did many others who had come from Australia, Canada, Rhodesia, and South America—to find that we were removed from the blitz to places of safety in the country, where we engaged in futile cleaning, polishing, and drilling for hours and weeks on end.

Not having fully recovered from my operation the previous year, I found the physical training and cross-country runs a great strain. My feeling of frustration added increasingly to this strain and it began to be noticed by my flight-sergeant. One day he expressed his feelings at a P.T. parade in a string of unprintable epithets, finishing with the injunction: "A little less reverence and a little more zip."

After only twelve months in the air force, I began to develop a recurrence of ileitis. I was operated on for this again and subsequently discharged.

6   Civilization on Trial

After my discharge, and a further operation for a resection, I was advised
to return to South Africa. While waiting for a passage to the Cape, I
acted as chaplain to a convent in Bournemouth, with an orphanage
which was run by the Sisters of Bethany. There I was able to think again
about my religion. Also, after the anticlimax of my attempts to become a
combatant, I resumed my duties as an air raid warden.

I began to feel increasingly that, having been spared the kind of fate
that had been the lot of all too many of my friends and contemporaries,
I must use the life that had been given back to me by the skill of doctors
and nurses to fight the evils of oppression and injustice which I knew I
should find in South Africa—and to fight them with new weapons which
were not inspired by the hatred and fanaticism which nazism had let loose
in the world. A way must be found of breaking through the vicious circle
of hate and counter-hate. So far I had evaded this vital issue; my whole
attitude towards life and its problems had been governed by my indecision
and dallying with communism. I foresaw that there would be a great deal
of opposition from the official exponents of the Christian religion in the
Church and I realized this might be even more difficult to deal with than
the declared enemy. As for the Communists, I had not lost hope of convincing some of them of the error of their whole philosophy and their
methods and therefore did not sever all connection, though I was determined not to be merely used by them as I had been in the past. I determined that I would try and convince them, not so much in words as in
action.

Early in 1943 I went to Liverpool, and on a cold rainy morning while it was still dark we sailed down the Mersey to join the rest of the convoy and its escort for Cape Town.

In the R.A.F. and during that voyage to Cape Town my admiration grew for the youngsters in the services. Very often their seeming carelessness about the ultimate reasons and justifications for their actions was by no means due to lack of sensitivity, but to an agnostic bewilderment. This did not hinder them from becoming trained, disciplined, and proficient at the technicalities of their jobs and from carrying them out at times under conditions of extreme danger and hardship, in the face of all the demoralizing discouragement of life in the vast war machine.

There was something very great in the spirit which could endure such regimentation and hardship, in such submission to the complicated and exasperating business of becoming trained and skilled for purposes of death and destruction, in a cause which so many knew so little about. There was a finer quality in this courage than in the piety of those who claimed to be above the battle. Yet there were many whose moral courage in refusing to fight was in a different way as great, and who endured hardships no less difficult to bear with fortitude. I was ashamed of my own physical weakness and inability to stand the strain, which seemed to place me in neither of the categories I admired.

> *—But there is no competition—*
> *There is only the fight to recover what has been lost*
> *And found and lost again and again: and now, under conditions*
> *That seem unpropitious. But perhaps neither gain nor loss.*
> *For us, there is only the trying. The rest is not our business.*

East Coker

The convoy assembled at the mouth of the Mersey in a drizzle of rain and the half-light of morning. I thought I found a good omen to a new venture in finding that a fellow-passenger, whose name was Emmanuel Abrahams, was an African. He was returning via the Cape to Abyssinia, which had been freed and restored to the Emperor by the allied armies. The Emperor was returning by air, but Mr. Abrahams was returning by sea with packing cases of the Emperor's documents. During his exile in England, after his escape from the Italian army of occupation, he had come to have a great respect and love for the British people, both high and low. As a member of Haile Selassie's entourage, he had been well received by English society and treated as an equal on both formal and informal occasions and similarly in academic circles. Travelling on the same ship was Lady Barton, wife of the British minister in Abyssinia, also returning to Addis Ababa. She insisted on Mr. Abrahams sitting next to her at the captain's table and some of the South Africans on board were appalled at her habit of addressing him, as she did her other friends, as "my dear."

The convoy broke up after passing the Bay of Biscay, only a few ships remaining to continue the journey to the Cape. The male passengers took it in turns to keep a look-out and man a quick-firing gun, but there were no incidents except false alarms until we reached the coast of South West Africa, where we put in at Walvis Bay. Enemy submarines were reported between Walvis Bay and the Cape. The German population in South West Africa were strongly pro-nazi and there was said to be a secret radio station on the South West Africa coast signalling the arrival and departure of convoys from Walvis Bay.

We stayed there for several days waiting for the all-clear, and I organized an expedition among the passengers to see the sights of Walvis Bay and the surrounding desert, including the native location outside the town. The expedition included Lady Barton and Mr. Abrahams, the former being almost reduced to tears that such conditions of squalor and oppression as those evident in the Walvis Bay location could exist under the British flag. The impression was not improved by a curt order to Mr. Abrahams, when we returned, to use the crew's gangway on to the ship.

Lady Barton wished to travel overland to Durban, but was rather apprehensive about Emmanuel Abrahams, whom she had promised to protect as far as possible from any embarrassment. It would be a pity if his good impression of Britain and the Commonwealth were to be marred in any way by any untoward incidents in South Africa; and he was under an obligation to accompany the ship all the way round the Cape, since he was in charge of the Emperor's papers. I promised to see what I could do in Cape Town, where I was due to disembark.

Though neat and unostentatious in appearance, his colour and his demeanour, which was not sufficiently servile, seemed to provoke contempt and abuse. It was difficult to get a taxi from the docks, and the hotels seemed to have no accommodation available. That it is very short-sighted on the part of the South African Government not to make some provision for visiting non-European diplomats, is evident from the fact that Emmanuel Abrahams became minister of education in Addis Ababa, was one of Ethiopia's representatives to the United Nations, and subsequently their ambassador in London. In the end I took him to stay at the Society of St. John the Evangelist's Mission in District Six, the slum coloured quarter of Cape Town, where he was very kindly received by Father Bull, the superior.

These difficulties in trying to find accommodation for an African diplomat in Cape Town, in trying to protect him from the insulting behaviour of people who hardly knew such a person existed and who lived in a state of permanent intoxication from the heady brew of white superiority, preoccupied my thoughts during this, my second arrival at the Cape. There was no time to brood on the Africa that lay beyond, though I felt this experience was symptomatic of a vast change in the whole context in which African problems had to be thought out or fought out. The South African armies had helped in the liberation of Abyssinia, but here in South Africa no political considerations carried any force against the dead weight of colour prejudice which prevailed in almost every walk of life.

Preoccupied with the practical difficulties of protecting Emmanuel Abrahams from insults and obtaining some hospitality for him, I had little time to think of much else, though in my mind I contrasted my first arrival in Table Bay with my present position. Then I had been leaving all the unsolved problems of living in my father's slum parish, of the aftermath of war in Europe, and of the General Strike in England that year, 1926. Now I was leaving the problems of Britain and Europe convulsed in the Second World War. The agonies of conscience in the R.A.F. had reduced me to physical incapacity, for Crohn's disease, I was told, probably had its origin in mental or emotional disorder. So I had lain in bed during the storming of one citadel of Europe after another. The Communists had at last fought back and had withstood the German onslaught at Stalingrad while I lay in hospital awaiting an operation. Now I had come away from it all and was going to be brought face to face again with the problems of Africa, problems that I had neglected before or been insensitive about or unaware of.

I made contact with some of the South African Communists on an introduction from Communists in England, but I found them very suspicious of my views and of the fact that I had enlisted during 1940, when

Communists were opposed to the war, and had left Europe to come to South Africa after the second front had been opened. They were also suspicious of my religion. These differences were later to be revealed in a fundamentally different conception of policy to be followed in opposition to the colour bar, the purpose and the methods of struggle that were to be used against it, and the values that might be substituted for the doctrines of self-interest on which it was based. It was of course these same doctrines to which the Communists in their turn appealed as the basis of their conception of social change.

I found great inspiration in discussions with Father Bull at the Mission of the Society of St. John the Evangelist. He was a Socialist of the old school and had a great deal in common with William Morris. I could not help contrasting the character of the old man with that of some of the other Socialists and Communists that I knew, courageous as they were in fighting for their convictions. With the Communists I could not find the unity of thought and action, which was needed to attain a sense of unity and wholeness, a sense of purpose and harmony with the creative forces of the universe, which I seemed to find in Father Bull, for all the monotonous psalm-singing and liturgical dullness through which his religion seemed to find so much of its expression.

Emmanuel Abrahams continued on his way to Ethiopia by sea while I went north by rail to take up the appointment the South African Church Institute in London had asked me to fill, that of assistant priest at the Pretoria Native Mission. When we next met it was in the delegates' lounge at the United Nations, and subsequently, when he became ambassador in London, we met in connection with the case of some Somalis, whom his government had condemned to death for resisting payment of taxes and had hanged in the presence of their wives and families.

As I travelled up through the beautiful fruit-growing area of Paarl and Worcester, with their sunlit vineyards on the lower slopes of the valleys and the towering mauve-misted mountains, old memories of my younger days in South Africa crowded back. Then the world had seemed young, both living and thinking were a great adventure, and my very questions were exciting, though painful, and an enticement to adventure.

When I arrived at Pretoria by some mischance a senior priest of the mission missed me at the station and I took a taxi. He arrived at his house slightly annoyed to find me sitting on the stoep talking to the African priest and drinking a cup of tea which had been brought me. In the conversation which followed, and during the subsequent days, I felt increasingly that it would be impossible for us to work harmoniously together. He was a typical South African patriarchal liberal, who believed Africans to be incapable of doing anything by themselves to help themselves. Trade unionism to him was anathema and there was very soon a clash of opinion on that point between us. One of the African trade unions asked me for some assistance and he expressed the view that they were materialist in outlook, that they were subverting the youth from their loyalty to the Church and were setting themselves up as a rival moral authority and claiming their members' time, energies, and money. Often their meetings took place on Sundays, which was the only day they had free. Another point of difference between us was the fact, which I noticed with great despondency, that the African priests always came to the back door when they came to the house and were never shown in to the room in which Europeans were entertained.

After a few days we had an exchange of views and agreed that it would be to our own and everyone else's advantage if I found work elsewhere. It was thus that I asked the Bishop of Johannesburg for work in his diocese. After seeing him I decided to take up work as assistant priest in the St. Alban's Coloured Mission under Maurice Clack, and I became chaplain to the sisters and orphanage at St. Joseph's Home in Sophiatown, on the outskirts of Johannesburg.

After I had seen the bishop, and we had talked until very late at night, I found I was too late to catch the last train back to Pretoria and had not enough money to stay at a hotel. So I slept the night on a bench at the railway station. On the next bench was a poor white in a lugubrious state of intoxication. Normally he would perhaps have inveighed against parsons as "kaffir boeties"; but tonight he told of how, deep down inside himself, he was sorry for the niggers and thought they got a rotten bad deal from the government, their employers, the foremen, and everyone. "We know they could do as well as us at the job if they were given the same chances. That's what really makes us hate the nigger," said my companion. By some strange twisted code that exists amongst "poor whites" he was entitled to speak more truthfully about the native question when drunk than sober, just as amongst the upper strata of South African society it was in order to speak more frankly on the subject in a private conversation or when abroad than in any public expression of views.

About a month later I left Pretoria and went to live in a rondavel belonging to the sisters of St. Margaret at St. Joseph's Home for Coloured Children at the end of Good Street, Sophiatown, which was to be the scene of much human drama and of much tears and laughter by day and night. The orphanage was a war memorial founded by the coloured people in memory of the men of the Cape corps who died in the First World War. The children were not all orphans in the literal sense, but had been made so in effect by the breaking up of homes through parents separating or being divorced, or through fathers or mothers deserting their homes or serving prison sentences. Some had been committed by the courts on account of cruelty at home or because they needed protection for moral reasons. Some were orphans because the rest of the family did not want them at home: the others were fair enough to pass as white and the one who was too dark would be a handicap. One girl of fifteen had had no education because her family had kept her in the kitchen and treated her as their servant so that the others could attend a white school.

The good sisters of St. Margaret were English and treated them all as children, irrespective of their shade of colour, which was often a matter of intense jealousy and antagonism amongst themselves. Yet this tolerance made for some problems of adaptation when these children left St. Joseph's and went out into a world which was blind to the values they had been taught and unreasoningly cruel in its prejudices against them.

I wrote home, about this time, giving some account of Sophiatown, and I reproduce the letter here to illustrate the impression that the people and the place made on me at that time.

I have a very neat little rondavel here, two thirds of which is a sitting-room and the rest divided between a bathroom and bedroom, quite comfortably furnished. Sophiatown is a native township, housing people of all races and colours; African, Indian, Chinese and Coloured who work in various industries in Johannesburg. The most astonishing mixture I have ever seen, more so than Port Said, which certainly takes some beating. They are all desperately poor with their little houses or huts patched up with flattened out paraffin tins and old bits of rusty corrugated iron which blow about and make an awful din when there is a wind, which is often, and it blows the dust all over everything in great swirling clouds. It mixes with the smoke from the braziers which are lit outside in the evening to do the cooking on. But it blows away the smells! There are these huge, great mine dumps all around, too—great pyramids of pul-

verized rock—all that is left, after the gold has been crushed out of the ore, and when the wind is strong, it blows the dust off them as though they were steaming.

The Mission—officially it is called "St. Alban's Coloured Mission"—covers all the Johannesburg slum areas where the coloured people live (coloured means half caste); the poor white quarters on the fringes of the native townships, and some of the townships themselves. The people are mostly too poor to bother much about race differences; when these arise, it is either as a result of drink, or a purely economic question—competition for jobs.

All the same, it is a queer mix-up. The natives have all become detribalized. There are still some traces of magic, and they dance wild war dances in the streets while others beat drums on old tin cans, anything that will make a noise, and there may be an odd jazz instrument of sorts but it's a weird mixture of primitive jungle stuff and the modern hot swing music. Down here in my corner of the location, they are just getting under way; being Saturday night it will go on till the small hours with plenty of illicit beer coming from somewhere, no one bothers to track it down, and the police don't dare shew themselves unless they decide to make a raid. At least I have never seen any patrolling in the streets.

There is quite a fair sprinkling of Christians. But many of them belong to queer little African sects which have split off from the parent body, very often on account of heavy dues they are expected to pay. They have their own little tin church where they dress up in strange but quite colourful garments, and dance and sing, and pray for hours on end. It is so strange to hear their very lovely singing in harmony coming out of the most dilapidated old corrugated iron building. They have an almost pathetically fervent faith that God will one day come down and put everything to rights for all the oppressed peoples in the land. I say pathetic, because so much of it is deliberate man-made evil. Also it is very pathetic to see these poor little bedraggled processions of Christians wending their way through these unbelievably squalid streets, picking their way through all the muck that collects there, with all the dogs barking at them—a crooked little home-made cross going on ahead of them—and singing with all that pathos in their harmonies which is so characteristic.

Coming back through the location from the place where I go for my supper (the C.R. Fathers' place at Ekutuleni), Johannesburg—with its vast wealth and luxurious modern life—seems very far away though the *lights are blazing all along the range of hills that forms the Witwatersrand. Here there is poverty, and stench and noise, and all that is bred out of these filthy conditions; malnutrition of the children, drunkenness, gambling, venereal disease—over a third of the population has it—and wholesale promiscuity is undermining the basis of family life for the African in the urban areas, and sometimes one feels overwhelmed by the sum total of havoc and misery that our so-called civilization has brought upon the African people.*

Here there are three hundred and fifty thousand of them, miners mostly, separated from their families in the native territories for nine months in the year, to work underground for three pounds a month.

So one is brought back to the pressing problem of the age—poverty in the midst of plenty. And all this under the brilliant sunshine and blue sky and the crisp mountain air of the High Veld in the Transvaal. As one looks towards the luxury blocks of Johannesburg, one is reminded by these little bands of African Christians, of Christ's disciples, when they saw Jerusalem all white and gleaming in the sun on the hills—"Lord, what manner of buildings," and Christ weeping over the city—"If thou hadst but known the things that belong to thy peace, but now they are hid from thine eyes."

It is all that aspect of Christianity which the African seems to understand and love, and perhaps that is why he tends to split off from what he feels are the European-dominated churches and start his own little sect. He doesn't mind how poor and shabby it is, he would rather have it like that and feel that it is his own. I am afraid that is where we are making a big mistake. I had to resign from Pretoria before I had been there a month because I felt so strongly about it, and felt compelled to say something of the sort at the Missionary Conference. I suppose it was awful cheek really, but it was an impossible position I found myself in there. I couldn't have been loyal to the director of the Mission—a European— and to my own convictions, so I thought it best to say so straight away. However, I hope some good will come of it.

In any case I couldn't have stood for all these compulsory levies—12 shillings a year is a lot to these impoverished people with all the taxes and other dues they have to pay—a quarter of their wages goes in rent alone very often, and I don't see how any man can be expected to charge half a crown fee for baptizing a little wizened and half-starved baby. I suppose that all sounds pretty self-righteous but somehow it seems in-

tolerable that we should be turning Christ's gospel into a vast profit-making institution with the poor, the maimed, the halt and the blind forced out into the cold.

Things are better here because the "coloured" people don't come under the same rules and regulations as the natives, also one is more free to speak one's mind. It must have been really very exasperating for the Head of the Mission, poor chap, but I don't think it ever occurred to him that it might be exasperating for me too! But I hadn't come out from England to be dictated to on such matters of principle. I don't think there is any virtue in the sort of humility which always bows to the authority one usually respects.

The churches were all more than half empty, and this was blamed on the younger generation, who think more about increasing their wages than increasing their piety. Are the two things necessarily incompatible? It is not only for themselves that they want higher wages. They have old people dependent on them and some have wives and families of their own. But to some ecclesiastics all that sort of thing is just "agitation." Whatever it is, it seems to me we want a lot more of it!

To be fair though, many of the clergy are very ready to denounce anything which they consider unjust from the pulpit or elsewhere, but any idea that people should get together in trade unions and do something about it themselves is the wrong sort of approach altogether in their view.

I expect the people at home who brought me out here are being told what a self-opinionated young cub they had picked on! And probably this is so, but if one hasn't got some pretty strong convictions in all this physical, moral and social mess, I think one would go right off one's rocker. Even so, I haven't that strong sense of evil that some people seem to feel when they come here slumming. They commit murders when they are desperate or drunk and sometimes even children of six are drunk in the streets on this filthy muck they call beer (yeast, pineapple juice, a dash of methyl to give it a kick, and a dollop of boot blacking to add a little tang)—but there is nothing evil about poverty, ignorance, disease and underfeeding. The evil lies over there where the beauty parlours are, and everything is so nice and hygienic, and people buy and sell to one another with little bits of paper, the products which all these people have created with their hands or dug out of the earth.

Have you any rich people round your way who could raise fifty pounds for this work? We have seven churches covering an area twenty miles long, and are hoping to put up another. The churches are used for plenty of other purposes as well as praying in, in case anyone thinks this a waste! And we really must have a car if the work is to be even a quarter done. They won't allow me to use the native trams and trains that serve these locations and townships, and the roads in many places are too bad for a motor bike. This is not a personal appeal, but. . . .

At the present moment we are having a battle with the authorities who have ordered the eviction of 500 families, coloured and Indian people, invoking the Gold Act of 1908, which lays down that no coloured people may live on "proclaimed" areas, i.e. gold bearing. The Act had long been ignored, and the people have been living there for twenty five years alongside the mines. There are literally no houses for them to go to, on account of the acute housing shortage, so I have threatened to use the churches (which are also church halls) to house the people in, until they are provided with homes. Let's hope this may wake the authorities up a bit. They think they can push these people around just how they like because they are coloured. And it's terrible to see them packing up all their belongings on to carts, and trundling off in search of some temporary shelter.

It was there in the non-European slum districts and shantytowns of that great gold-mining city that I again found all those values that I had tried by so many conflicting means to cherish. They were ranged against all of South Africa's problems of race and creed, of over-concentration of industry and population, problems of migrant labour and land use, of the use of the law as an instrument of justice or an instrument of oppression—and the problem of finding methods that could be used to resist injustice, methods compatible with the creative purpose and not themselves destroying the very grounds of that resistance.

The great South African hypocrisy of segregation or apartheid has been too long supported by those well-meaning optimists who confuse the issues by defending the alleged intention of the colour bar "to preserve the purity of the races," whilst at the same time they deplore its consequences in the reduction of the African people to a state of servitude.

We are told that to the white man has belonged the initiative, the intelligence, the skill, and the capital wealth for the building of civilization in Africa. We are told he must hold that initiative. He must make secure his political ascendancy and preserve his social and racial integrity, while simultaneously allowing the native peoples to live their own life in their reserves and build on the foundations of their own tribal culture. And very plausible that sounds when accompanied by appeals to racial prejudice and the fears of a submergence of white civilization by a rising tide of colour.

Given the opportunity, there is no sphere in which the African cannot prove himself the equal of the white man. Despite the great colour barrier which operates throughout our social, economic, and political life, and the initial disadvantage of learning through the medium of a strange language, there are many Africans who have in fact proved their equal competence with white men in the spheres of science, medicine, and the arts. There are vast development projects waiting for all the pent-up human energy and skill of the Bantu.

But it must be remembered that while the colour bar remains rigidly static, its consequences in terms of human life are by no means static. It not only demoralizes both races, it sets up a chain reaction in ignorance, disease, and hatred which must inevitably lead to an explosion if injustice remains irremediable by constitutional means.

Sooner or later the United Nations will have to face the question of colour or race discrimination as one of the fundamental issues for the future of our civilization. Preoccupation with other matters is tending to divert the attention of Western nations from the related long-term problems of industrial development and soil conservation. These cannot be separated from the problem of finding a harmonious way of life and co-operation in a civilization which has never been exclusively white on any continent, and can never be so.

Let us take a quick look at some of the real facts and economic forces which have been at work in breaking up the tribal culture and the social and family life of the African people. If land is the basis of a people's social and economic stability, the fact is that the African people have been deprived of their lands in the most merciless fashion so that now in South Africa four-fifths of the whole population own less than one-tenth of the land. Look at a map of South Africa showing the areas open to African ownership and settlement and they appear as a few scattered blotches and pimples. These are the native reserves and trust farms. The over-population and over-stocking with cattle has become so intense, and the soil erosion so devastating, that the people are forced out of the reserves to work on the white man's farms and mines. There is also the glamour of town life and the prosperity much advertised by the mines' recruiting agents, in one instance by a poster showing a cow being milked with golden sovereigns flowing from its udders.

At any given time up to 70 per cent of the able-bodied male population of a reserve may be away at the mines, where the wage is 2s. 8d. a day, plus food and a cabin which they share with twenty other men. On the farms their wages are a good deal less and the cry goes up from the farmers for more and more convict labour.

This is possible because South Africa's pass laws and other legislation designed to control the movements of the African population result in the incrimination of vast sections of the community. Almost one in ten is convicted of some "crime" every year, and this is itself contributing to hastening the process of the demoralization of a once-proud race in South Africa.

The consequence of this ruthless breaking-up of the traditional life of the African people, whilst at the same time preventing their entrance into skilled occupations in industry, as well as into the coveted sphere of political and human rights of our system, should be studied very closely before it is too late to repair the ravages and to prevent a state of affairs in the south which would act as a festering sore, poisoning the whole blood stream of African life.

A few brief facts and figures may be mentioned which the reader must interpret for himself in terms of human suffering and demoralization consequent upon the migratory labour system. In a town such as Johannesburg, at a minimum estimate, 30 per cent of the African children born are illegitimate. Among the Cape coloured a 1937 sample showed 36 per cent illegitimacy. In Durban, out of 5,465 native couples living together, only 1,923 were legally married.

Dr. C. W. Gale, venereal diseases officer for the Union, stated that sample surveys among natives showed that between 25 per cent and 30 per cent had syphilis. In 1946 on the Rand, routine examinations showed that 28 per cent of all native males, and 40 per cent of the coloured and native females, had a positive Wasserman blood test.

Dr. B. A. Dormer, chief tuberculosis officer of the Union, told a conference in 1947: "The Union has the dubious distinction of holding the world's record for the tuberculosis death rate among its non-European industrial workers. The Union has 40,000 active cases walking around, yet in Britain if there are more than 200 tuberculotics on the waiting list there are questions in Parliament." In Durban, as in Cape Town, three a day are said to be dying of tuberculosis. This is not surprising when we consider that the Bantu Nutrition Survey before the war showed an average of more than 70 per cent with obvious signs of ill-health and/or malnutrition, and the cost of living has been rising ever since out of all proportion to wage increases, though hospital accommodation has greatly improved.

With these figures on the debit side, must be compared the figure of £2,000,000,000 extracted from the bowels of the Transvaal by African miners whose real wages have hardly increased in a period of thirty-five years. True it is the white man's machines that bring these miners from all parts of the southern continent, though they trek for hundreds of miles on foot. They are brought by trucks across the Kalahari from Ovamboland and Portuguese Angola. They trek from Nyasaland and the Rhodesias, from the Transkei and the Ciskei and the British Protectorates of Swaziland, Basutoland, and Bechuanaland, lured by the white man's gold and the prospect of making a little money on which to live in their denuded reserves.

And it is the white man's machines which lower them nine thousand feet beneath the sun-scorched plateau of the Transvaal. Again it is the white man's hammers that crush the mountains of ore they have laboured to bring forth into a fine powder from which the gold is minutely sifted. The gold is then made into bricks and buried again in the vaults of the white man's banks to stabilize the white man's finances.

Describing this migrant labour force used on the mines, a former South African senator, representing the natives, said:

When one turns the matter over in one's mind, one gets the picture that here we have the position that 350,000 people are completely shut up and shut away from the outside world. . . . It is not only a social position, but a legal position that has been deliberately created by the mining industry itself. When an African goes to a recruiting agent or to one of the recruiting depots to sign his contract to join the mines, one of the clauses in that contract is that during the period of employment he cannot go off the employer's property without permission of the employer. In other words, the moment an African miner puts his signature or thumb print to the contract of employment, he is virtually a prisoner of the gold mining industry. That is a fact. The 350,000 people who work in the

gold mining industry are prisoners in the same legal sense that they are
going to jail for the next 9 to 12 months. . . .

And Mr. D. B. Molteno, a native representative, explained that a similar
system is being applied in the case of farm labour because:

> *. . . The local industrial revolution has not been matched by a revolu-*
> *tion in agricultural technique. Hence productivity in agriculture has*
> *lagged far behind industrial productivity.*
>
> *The results . . . have been a steady process of urbanization and in-*
> *dustrialization of an increasing proportion of the African population and*
> *ever louder complaints from rural employers of a shortage of labour.*
>
> *In the face of this situation government policy has been not to assist*
> *with the reorganization and higher capitalization of agriculture, for the*
> *purpose of enabling it to economize labour and to meet industrial com-*
> *petition, but to attempt by law to ensure the availability to the farmer of*
> *a labour force sufficient to meet their requirements on the traditional level*
> *of technique. . . . The method of indirect compulsion having broken*
> *down, the Government resorted to authorizing and assisting agricultural*
> *organizations to obtain recruited indentured labour from beyond the*
> *borders of the Union. In other words, it sought to encourage the exten-*
> *sion of the compound, indentured system of the mines, with all its waste*
> *of human resources, its destruction of family life, its possibilities of*
> *abuses, to the isolated and more primitive conditions of the farms. . . .*

The pattern of civilization that has grown up in southern Africa is
that of an increasing mass of Africans uprooted from the reserves, mi-
grating to the towns or the white man's farms, and back again to the
reserves in a constant state of flux and instability. Erected on the basis
of this landless, voiceless mass of disease-ridden black people, whose
own culture and social life is being destroyed with only a pathetic travesty
of the white man's city culture to take its place, is the superstructure of
the white man's political system. In this, farmers, mine-owners, and white
labour combine to legislate against black. It is absurd to speak of South
Africa as a self-governing dominion, since four-fifths of her population
have no effective franchise. In the House of Assembly there are three
white members of Parliament elected to represent the whole native population of ten millions—three, that is to say, out of a total of 163. The claim
that the two and a half million whites in South Africa are capable of

using their votes beneficially for everybody is best answered by some of the above facts.

The question of the extension of the franchise must be faced. Inevitably any kind of extension on the basis of communal representation will increase the fears and inter-racial conflicts prevailing in South Africa; but it may be that the constitution-makers could help us to devise a political economy adapted to the peculiar social composition of a country in which many of the people live a tribal life on socially-owned land, others work in industry, and some few are in the professions.

Invariably any reforms directed at improving the lot of the non-European peoples meet with the objection that the white race will thereby be endangered. Of course the cry of universal suffrage does not automatically provide the answer to the racial problems or to the social and economic ills. Electorates separated on racial lines, whilst still a prey to ignorance and gerrymandering prejudice, might make confusion all the more confounded. A system must therefore be found which will overcome the fissiparous tendencies inevitable in such a political system.

A way must be found to draw together people with common interests regardless of their racial groupings—whether they be farmers or industrial workers, black or white. Perhaps some provision could be made for professional and occupational qualifications and the motivating forces of civilization protected, whilst affording a form of representative government which would respond to the needs and interests which all races have in common, instead of driving them apart.

The fact that the majority of the Africans may not yet be educationally qualified to use the vote does not mean that their interests could not be directly represented by those Africans who are qualified. It should not be beyond the wit of the constitution-makers to devise, as a next step, a means whereby Africans in their own tribal organization could be given their proper place and weight in the political system, thereby establishing a more balanced political economy than one which has failed to provide the answers to the problems of a multi-racial society.

When all is said that ought to be said of the missionaries and government servants in South Africa who give such ungrudging service in the sphere of social welfare, education, and health, the fact remains that their labour is being overborne by the consequences of generations of artificially-induced poverty and of spiritual and economic frustration. They do not ask or receive much recognition, these devoted people, and their voices are all too seldom heard or heeded by the policy-makers.

South Africa has no dearth of able advisers. Few countries in fact can have produced such excellent and detailed reports of commissions dealing with every aspect of social and economic reform. The difficulty does not lie in not knowing how the basis of the whole economy can be broadened and full use made of human and material resources. The obstacle has been the irresponsibility and prejudice of the white voters and (failing representation for the four-fifths of the population) the lack of political and constitutional means to carry out these reforms.

The tragedy of South Africa is that her problem is not a colour problem but a white problem. Those who have the political power do not know how to use it. Or they are using it to erect what they think is a barrier to the black man's advance, but what in reality is preventing the progress of the country as an economic whole and is in danger of undermining and eventually crushing the human basis on which the whole economic structure rests.

Oliver Walker, in his book *Kaffirs Are Lively,* writes of South Africa's problem that "It is not a problem of whether black people can become civilized, but how to make an under-civilized white people accept the emergence of black people who may be as good as themselves. It is not a problem of *how* to civilize black people—as is often pretended—but how to regularize their civilization so that their numerical superiority of four to one does not deprive the white minority of an effective voice in the State's affairs. All other versions of the situation are traffickings with the truth. 'Trusteeship,' 'segregation,' 'the preservation of white or Western civilization,' 'guardianship'—these are passing clichés to obscure the inevitable issue which the country *has* to face—the absorption and acceptance into fullest citizenship of civilized non-whites."

The answer of the unreasoning to all this is the question which in South Africa settles all argument—"Would you like your sister to marry a Kaffir?" Ironically enough there has been a one hundred thousand increase in members of the mixed race for every generation during the period of the white man's absolute rule and his segregation policy, apartheid and immorality laws notwithstanding. Miscegenation has come about mainly through illicit unions between white males and females of other races.

The same South African writer, Oliver Walker, challenged the latest version of the segregation fallacy, put forward by a minister of the Dutch Reformed Church, as follows:

The Rev. J. G. Strydom, as all segregationists, would like to have the best of two worlds. He wants to have cheap native labour available to wash his clothes, look after his children, deliver his groceries, dig the gold that balances the national budget, mend the roads he drives his car along, and dig his grave when he is gathered to his fathers. But he wishes, at the same time, to avoid all the responsibilities of handling a working-class population and seeing it progress by creating for it an ordered structure of opportunity such as is normal in a democratic society.

And the evidence of this can be found in a hundred dreadful slum locations and shantytowns outside every city and dorp in South Africa. Yet of 40,000 who were "screened" in the camp known as "Tobruk," where they squatted illegally on municipal land, only 4¼ per cent were found to be without legitimate employment in the factories, shops, and homes of the white people. They cooked their food, nursed their children, and waited on them at table. But they themselves must not acquire civilized standards. Sooner or later South Africa must realize that disease knows no colour bar.

There is little time to lose. It is time for South Africa to abandon some of those wicked travesties of Christ's gospel and apply its divinely given intelligence to the use of all the resources of that country in knowledge, human skill, and labour—and of good will too, so far as it still exists. But there is needed a vision commensurate with the magnitude of the task of building a multi-racial civilization in Africa to which all will contribute and from it take their full share.

Perhaps the time has come for the government in South Africa to call a national convention in which the representatives of all races would take part, so that with the aid of constitutional and technical experts the problems of evolving a political economy adapted to the basic needs of all communities, and the provision of urban and rural stability, could be worked out whilst we have time. There still remains sufficient confidence and good will to work together for a more excellent way than that into which growing fear and hatred are driving us, as those whom the daemons destroy after they have first made mad. For, as William Pitt wrote one hundred fifty years ago in support of the liberation of the slaves:

Let no one say that Africa labours under a natural incapacity for civilization . . . we were once as savage in our manners, as degraded in our misunderstandings. Some of us may live to behold the natives of Africa engaged in the calm occupation of industry, in the pursuit of a just and legitimate commerce. We may behold the beams of science and philosophy breaking in upon their land . . . and joining their influence with that of pure religion. . . . Then may we hope that even Africa though last of all the quarters of the globe shall enjoy at length . . . those blessings which have descended so plentifully on us."

7 Campaign for Right and Justice

In an attempt to cope with some of these mounting problems as World War II drew to a close, I formed a committee in Johannesburg in 1944 which grew into a movement called the Campaign for Right and Justice. Its president was Mr. Justice Krause, an able judge and a liberal-minded Afrikaner nationalist who fought courageously against inhuman prison conditions and the effects of the pass laws, which he knew from experience were manufacturing delinquents in the lower courts whom he would eventually deal with as criminals in the High Court. As secretary of its executive committee I found that it was taking up more and more of my time so that it was really only by the sympathy and indulgence of the Reverend Maurice Clack, my superior, that I was able to continue as assistant priest of the St. Alban's Coloured Mission.

The campaign took up many issues, both detailed cases of injustice and also broad questions of policy. It was never intended to be party-political and appealed to people of all parties and races to support it. It was essentially an extra-parliamentary movement, since we realized that parties were inhibited in dealing with some of South Africa's major problems by the very fact that only a very small section of the population and that of one race had any effective vote. We issued a manifesto and adopted both a negative and positive programme which was later to find expression in the calling of a national conference on regional development, at which the four cabinet ministers most concerned, the ministers of justice, of health and housing, of agriculture, and of economic development were to preside at different sessions. The purpose of this conference is explained in another chapter. Inevitably, however, the negative side of its programme occupied an increasing proportion of our attention and resources.

I drafted a manifesto for the inaugural conference in 1944 and sent this out to a large number of churches, social service organizations, and trade unions with an invitation to send delegates. A number of bishops were invited, and five of them wrote encouragingly about the aims of the conference but regretted they could not attend. In my over-anxiety to have the official support of my church I made the mistake of prematurely announcing this at the conference, only to find the following day that this had been repudiated through a news agency.

The manifesto, which was signed by the president and chairman of the Campaign for Right and Justice, by the acting secretary of the national executive of the S.A. Trades and Labour Council, and by the secretary of the Transvaal Teachers' Association, called on all the people in the land to stand together in their determination to establish what is right and just: on the churches, the universities and schools, and the trade unions to face all the implications of racialism; on the government and medical services to face the problem of malnutrition and preventable diseases; on the law that it should be impartial and dispense justice with equity without reference to colour, race, or creed. It ended by declaring that the Campaign would undertake to mobilize the widest possible alliance of the popular and progressive forces in the country in order to secure:

1. Drastic measures against profiteering, particularly in the production and distribution of food and clothing.

2. Plans for the full-scale development of the industrial and human resources of the country.

3. The provision of social services for all races, particularly in the matter of health, housing, education, and insurance against unemployment.

4. The fulfilment of our obligations to our armed forces and their dependents.

At the end of the conference a committee was elected which issued a more detailed statement of policy and aims, on the basis of which the campaign had been organized. The main points of the statement were:

That there was an urgent need for change in the conditions of life of the overwhelming majority of the people; that poverty, disease, and ignorance were evil in themselves, wasteful of human life and resources, and a growing cause of bitterness between the peoples of the Union; that those who desired to change these conditions, in order to succeed, must speak with one voice, concentrating for the present on those aims which they all shared; that in view of the slowness of public opinion and Parliament to recognize the necessity for change, a nation-wide campaign should be launched calling for:

1. The full and direct representation of all sections of the community.

2. The abolition of all legislation discriminatory on grounds of colour, race, or sex.

3. The provision of land for the landless peoples of South Africa, and assistance in making the best use of it.

In slightly more detail, the conference was unanimously in favour of a minimum working wage of two pounds (six dollars) a week.

The Communist party was divided in its attitude towards the Campaign for Right and Justice. Some regarded it as harmless enough in its aims, but were clearly jealous of the public response it received and suspicious of the religion of people like myself and Archdeacon Wraige, the chairman of its executive. There were also on the committee one or two strong opponents of the Communist party, men who had been members of the Party at one time, but had left it and made no secret of their contempt for its dictatorial methods and lack of scruple. On the other hand there were one or two close sympathizers with communism who may or may not have been members of the Party themselves, and there were left-wing trade-unionists who supported us in the Trades and Labour Council. The African and Indian congresses supported us, as did the more militant section of the "Cape Coloured" organization and the African Mine Workers' Union which I in turn supported through membership in a committee set up to try and protect it from the relentless attacks of the all-powerful Chamber of Mines and its subsidiaries.

I had a furious controversy with Dr. Dadoo, president of the Indian congress and a leading member of the Communist party at that time, at the very beginning of the campaign which helped to reveal to me my own profound differences with official communism, religiously and philosophically as well as in the matter of political strategy. He saw our movement as competing with, and possibly undermining, his own non-

European United Front which seemed to have no moral or religious basis and, granted the underlying Marxian doctrine of self-interest, contained within it many internal contradictions without any cohesive force or strong positive vision for the future. I admired Dr. Dadoo's great personal courage and his trenchant and vigorous denunciation of all the forms of oppression which bore so heavily on the different non-European communities. To him the role of liberal whites, if any, was only to lend their support to non-European leadership. His uncompromising opposition to all attempts to reach agreement on a common basis of action which could include liberal Europeans in the same organization as non-Europeans was, however, a powerful negative influence against the building up of any united movement against the rapidly rising power of Afrikaner nationalism. At that time, with the introduction of anti-Asiatic legislation, there was the beginning of disillusionment with General Smuts and his United party.

The United party was becoming increasingly restive under our mounting criticism of its failure to face the problems to which its own commissions kept on directing urgent attention. Our frequent meetings and deputations to the ministers of justice, health, and native affairs were a source of embarrassment to the United party propaganda chiefs. The rising tempo and pressure of our work brought the resignation of Archdeacon Wraige as chairman—not unjustifiably, for as Archdeacon of Kimberly he had his hands very full and felt remote from the scene of our activities in Johannesburg and Pretoria. I accordingly accepted the chairmanship.

There was a strike of Africans on the gold mines at the end of World War II which precipitated a slump in the price of "Kaffirs" (gold-mining shares) and brought all the resources of government and the Chamber of Mines to bear against the struggling Union of the African Mine Workers. The strike was broken within three days, the strikers being driven up to the surface by the police from thousands of feet below ground. Some of them who were in the compounds were even pursued to the top of the mine dumps and there batoned by the police. Even the financially powerful Jewish community which supported General Smuts and was, generally speaking, the most liberal section of the European community, was divided in its attitude. Apart from the gold-mining interests, some wealthy Jewish farmers were involved in the scandalous treatment of African labourers at Bethal and the Eastern Transvaal. The appointment of a commission of inquiry after our exposures there drove into opposition, and into the camp of Dr. Malan, a great deal of Afrikaner support in the towns of the Transvaal which was indispensable to a United party government at the first post-war election. In the event the United party lost heavily to Dr. Malan in these areas, and General Smuts lost his own seat at Standerton in the Eastern Transvaal and some of his international prestige.

There was, however, an influential section of the Jewish community which was dissatisfied with General Smuts and the United party and had, it seems, decided to try and found a new party. I was unaware of this and of any intention to use the Campaign for Right and Justice as the nucleus of a new party. I had given assurances to the United party, and especially to the four cabinet ministers who had agreed to preside at our Conference on Regional Planning, that we had no intention of forming a new party.

Our aim was to form a vigorous and realistic movement in opposition to the growth of Dr. Malan's form of Afrikaner nationalism and "apart-heid" and to uncover the menacing ramifications of the Afrikaner Broederbond, which was stretching its tentacles into all forms of economic social and political life and was becoming so powerful as to be almost a state within a state. But at the same time we had to focus on the immediate problems of poverty and disease if we were to overcome inter-racial competition and antagonisms. It was not enough to use fine phrases about building a nation. If these urgent problems were neglected, fanaticism would inevitably grow, and the most effectively organized fanaticism would gain control.

There was no doubt that the most effectively organized fanaticism was not communism but Afrikaner nationalism and the Broederbond. We had access to a great deal of inside information about the Broederbond and we had decided to publish this in the form of a pamphlet. The gravamen of our charge was stated on the cover of the pamphlet:

In this pamphlet the true character of the Broederbond is revealed. It is, the author contends, an organization that is rapidly assuming the character of A STATE WITHIN A STATE. Unwittingly perhaps, but nevertheless surely, it is diverting the loyalty of the nationalistically-

minded Afrikaner from the legal government of the Union and thus creating a dangerous economic and political situation for all other sections of the community. The Author is a well known Afrikaner, deeply convinced of the danger of the Broederbond both to the Union and to Afrikanerdom itself.

The facts that it set out may be summarized as follows:

The Broederbond was founded in 1918 with the aims of unifying the Afrikaner nation (the *Volk*), of awakening its national feelings, and promoting its interests. By reason of the historical circumstances through which the Afrikaners have lived ever since their first settlers came to the Cape, the idea of the nation of South Africa has never since its inception appealed to them. They are however a people of strong loyalties, and often of deep religious conviction. The Bond has attracted these loyalties to itself, as the symbol or embodiment of the Afrikaner people, and it has used this religious conviction to justify and strengthen its purposes. Its general secretary could say, in 1944, "The Broederbond is born from a deep conviction that the Afrikaner nation has been planted in this country by God's hand."

The Bond (the Nationalists being then in opposition) claimed that the parliamentary government of the Union is not in accord with Afrikaner traditions, and, deciding for itself what is best for the *Volk,* attempted to ignore or circumvent the established government. Originally, perhaps, an organization with the very proper aim of arousing the Afrikaner to better use of his own latent powers, it had by 1945 become a menace to the continued existence of the Union.

It numbered at that time about twenty-seven hundred, grouped in many small units scattered throughout the country, each a cross-section of the *Volk* in its vicinity. New members, carefully chosen for their usefulness to the organization and their devotion to the Afrikaner nation, enter only by invitation. Numbers are kept down, for the Broederbond is more interested in efficiency than in mass discussion.

The work of the Bond originates in these groups; plans there formulated are discussed among all other groups, studied and reported on by individual members, experts in their fields, and finally submitted to the central council, or *Raad,* for approval, all this naturally in complete secret. The finished scheme is then entrusted to individuals to put into effect, or to lay before the *Volk,* as if spontaneously originating from them.

One of the chief methods by which the Bond has gone to work has been by setting up Afrikaner financial, cultural, commercial, and industrial organizations, and also newspapers and trade unions; it remains the co-ordinating body of practically all of these. In politics it works through the Nationalist party, but it is concerned with much more than party politics alone, and with more than the co-ordination of all pro-Afrikaner activities. "It is the deepest expression of Afrikaner nationalist feeling and religious aspirations; not a thing of today, but the result of a long evolutionary process. . . ." To many Afrikaners the Bond is the State, and evokes in them the same loyalties a State would, often without their consciously realizing it.

Although by its constitution the Bond is not organized as a political party, it is undoubtedly designed to produce political effects, as its "credo" shows:

1. The elimination of everything that conflicts with the fullest international independence of South Africa.

2. The abolition of the inferior position of the Afrikaans-speaking section and language in the state.

3. Segregation of all non-white races in South Africa while allowing their independent development under the leadership of the whites.

4. The prohibition of the exploitation of the natural resources of the people of South Africa by "strangers."

5. The rehabilitation of the farming class and the guarantee of a civilized standard of life for all white citizens.

6. The nationalization of finance and the planned organization of economic policy.

7. The Afrikanerization of our public life and our education in the direction of Christian-Nationalism while leaving unhindered the internal development of all sections of the population in so far as this is not dangerous to the state.

The primary object of the Bond is contained in article 7, which provides for the establishment of complete Afrikaner domination in South Africa, other races to exist on sufferance only. The doctrine of white supremacy expressed in articles 3 and 5, similar to the detested Nazi concept of *"Herrenvolk,"* shows the reactionary policy that would be followed when the Afrikaners came to power. The implication of these aims, and the attitude of contempt and hostility to the legal government with which they are pursued, has led to many attacks on the Bond. The progress of the power and influence of the Bond, however, has persisted in spite of these warnings, and in 1945 it was already, in the opinion of competent observers, the main political reality in the Union of South Africa.

So ran the contents of our pamphlet. As events will show, this was in fact never issued; but more recently, in 1957, much was made public when on May 12th the *South African Sunday Express* published an account of a secret inquiry set on foot by General Smuts, extracts from which are given in Appendix 2. The following week they printed sensational details of a new member's application form (1957), also quoted.

Even if some of the more sensational descriptions of the Broederbond ritual are discounted, the fact remains that as a secret organization it is a great deal more powerful and sinister than an organization such as the Free Masons, on account of its policy and aim to secure Afrikaner domination over all other sections. If it can no longer be described as a state within a state this is because the nationalist government is the State, or is well on the way to becoming synonymous with the State. This is being brought out in the treason trials, where propagation of a freedom charter and the organization of opposition to the government's policies are being identified by the prosecution with treason against the State. Since it is a secret organization, it is impossible to estimate the influence of the Broederbond over the judiciary. By 1958 it was politically supreme.

To return to our earlier pamphlet: Inside the cover it was stated what I had been persuaded was the truth, and for which I ultimately had to accept responsibility: "For personal and political reasons the author of this pamphlet must remain anonymous, but the publishers consider the results of the investigation of sufficient public importance to justify its publication, based as it is on an analysis of statements emanating from the Bond itself."

The pamphlets were printed and were about to go into circulation when I received a letter signed by an official of a powerful, but non-Communist, Jewish organization claiming that the information contained in this pamphlet had been stolen from him and was being published without his consent as the work of an Afrikaner and former member of the Broederbond. He concluded, "I would say that the overall impression is that of yet another step in the direction of constituting the Campaign for Right and Justice as the 'nucleus of a new (progressive) political party.'"

At the same time I was unhappy about the position in the executive of the Campaign. I suspected that the Communist attitude towards it was changing from one of laissez faire to a determination to make use of it also through their sympathizers for its own purpose. Then a day or two before the date of publication I received a visit from two prominent members of the United Party who told me that they supported what I had been told by the official claiming authorship of the pamphlet, that in point of fact a decision had been taken by a strong group within the organization to which he belonged to use the campaign for the formation of a new party, and that very serious consequences would follow from its publication, especially since the information had been obtained through the work of military intelligence. There seemed no disputing their pledged word, and comparison with the original manuscript, which I was shown, seemed clearly to indicate extensive plagiarism.

Under the circumstances I had no option but to cancel publication of the pamphlet, since I was ultimately responsible, not the anonymous "author." Also, since my own pledged word to the four members of the government was involved, I had no option but to suspend the convening of the Conference on Regional Planning. I determined to test whether members of the executive were under the influence that was claimed, and also to put my own position and influence as chairman to the test. When accordingly I forced a show-down on the executive I found that I and those supporting me, including the strongest anti-Communist on the executive, were outvoted. In a mood of black despair I resigned from the Campaign I had struggled day and night for two years to build up.

All this happened against the background of mounting disillusionment and racial tension in Johannesburg and in the country. I felt overcome by a sense of betrayal and frustration in face of what seemed the overwhelming forces of oppression both on the government side and in the opposition. Against these our efforts seemed puny and were made even more ineffectual by the intriguing methods and cynicism of the Communists towards everything that was not controlled by them or harnessed to their own cause. Their support, though, was in a sense a kiss of death. I felt instinctively from that time that there was no recourse left open to me but the path of passive resistance.

I felt betrayed by my own Church. Though, admittedly, my tactics had been at fault, I felt they had not been so much at fault as to give the hierarchy any justifiable pretext for their lack of support, if not open opposition to what we were trying to do. I lived closer to the scene of these incipient conflicts in my little rondavel in Sophiatown than the bishops, and had some sense of the dangers that lay ahead. Two incidents occurred which acted as straws in the wind at that time.

Dr. Malan, while General Smuts was still in power, staged a triumphal march of his Nationalist party and Afrikaner youth organizations through the streets of Johannesburg, a United Party stronghold, to a rally at the city hall. I was invited by a left-wing servicemen's organization to address a mass meeting they were sponsoring as a counter-demonstration. Many thousands, including servicemen, turned out. Feelings were running very high for Dr. Malan, and his leaders had shown themselves to be fundamentally more in sympathy with the Nazis than with the United Nations. I was asked to open the proceedings with prayer and afterwards gave a short, but not inflammatory, address.

But the speaker who followed me spoke as though he was in a paroxysm of rage, and before he had finished the crowd had started throwing empty beer bottles at the city hall. Very soon there was a riot in which the police had to protect the Nationalists, to the fury of the servicemen.

The meeting broke up in wild disorder with the organizers of the meeting nowhere to be found. With the aid of some technicians I set up a loudspeaker in an open window above the crowd and tried vainly to appeal to our people to show some sense of order and discipline in their opposition to Malan. But the police were making repeated charges by this time and they eventually succeeded in dispersing the crowds, leaving everyone with a feeling that Dr. Malan and his Nationalists had triumphed over democracy.

The other incident was occasioned by an accident in which an African boy was knocked down by a tram and pinned underneath it in Sophiatown. His relatives were naturally in a panic at being unable to extricate him. Nobody, apparently, explained that a crane had been sent for and they were awaiting its arrival. The driver and conductor stood about smoking cigarettes and one is alleged to have inquired why they were getting so excited, even if it did mean one less Kaffir. Eventually the Africans took up stones from beside the road and pelted the tram and the white driver, who ran away. Then they took to stoning passing motor cars which refused to stop and help.

When I arrived on the scene I asked the police commissioner to allow one of his native police to explain to the crowds, which were pouring out of their houses, exactly what had happened and what was being done. He irritably told me to do it myself, but I had not the command of their language. Before I could say anything to an interpreter, he ordered tear gas to be thrown and a baton charge; all that we could then do was to try and rescue some of the injured from the fury of the police. I was dressed in my white cassock and it is worth recording that I never experienced any hostility in Sophiatown despite all the provocation and racial propaganda and the frequent excitement of faction-fighting and drunken brawls in the streets.

The rumour spread into a neighbouring European township that there was a native rising in Sophiatown and the men armed themselves with anything they could find, including bicycle chains, to protect their women-folk. Indiscriminate assaults were committed against passing Africans who knew nothing of what had happened. Some were tied up and beaten. Some white hooligans organized themselves into a gang and set fire to the Bantu Press, which printed most of the vernacular newspapers, and twenty thousand pounds' worth of damage was done. Scores of Africans were arrested by the police, some of them as they lay unconscious on the ground, but no white men were arrested. Several weeks later two white men were charged and given suspended sentences.

It was against this background that the Campaign for Right and Justice was struggling and in which it was betrayed, perhaps by me as much as by anyone else, since I had had the experience which others connected with it lacked. I myself was weak and lacked the inner integrity, the clarity of thought, and strength of purpose necessary to withstand the powerful pressures and hostile forces that are at work in that great gold-mining city and cockpit of racialism which is Johannesburg. Concentrated there are all the problems of South Africa, and perhaps of the world of the future, unless G. M. Trevelyan's saying that "the only lesson we learn from history is that we never learn anything from history" can be proved untrue.

It seemed to me that the problems of post-war South Africa were all exemplified in the problems of Johannesburg's slums—some of the worst slums in the world exist there in one of its wealthiest and most modern cities. Failure to face these problems would inevitably bring a dangerous wave of disillusionment with the policies of General Smuts, despite his part in the victory over nazism and despite the discredit of many nationalist leaders who had professed neutrality and even friendship towards Hitler's Germany.

The rapidly mounting problem of Johannesburg's slums was a problem of over-concentration of industry and population and of the total failure of the State and the local authorities, elected by an exclusively white electorate, to make provision for a stable urban African population in place of the migrant labour system which the mining industry and agriculture had come to regard as indispensable. Industrial development had been accelerated during the war on account of the dual stimulus of defence needs and the necessity for temporary protection of South African industry, brought about by the German submarine campaign and the war in North Africa.

A more rational alternative to the Nationalist doctrine of apartheid seemed to me to lie in the regional planning advocated by Lewis Mumford and the architects of the Tennessee Valley Authority in America. Apartheid, it is true, in theory sought to decentralize industry and to control the influx of Africans into the towns. But it is primarily a racial theory designed to secure the political dominance of the white race and its protection from competition by non-European labour. It was a notion of planning erected on a wholly unscientific foundation of racialism, the basic concept being the necessary political hegemony of one race over every consideration of the natural economic and social aspirations of the other races.

Regional planning seemed to offer a more rational possibility of easing the mounting pressure of population on a city like Johannesburg by gradually building up other centres of industrial development in association with the beneficiation of agricultural products *in situ* and the need of agriculture for both irrigation and electrical power.

In the long run, also, the increasing prosperity of African producers and cultivators would result in an expanding economy which would benefit all. The greater distribution of purchasing power, far from undermining European standards, would stimulate greater demands on secondary industries which in turn would increase the employment of whites as well as blacks.

I still think regional development offers a more promising prospect of solving the pressing problems of South Africa than the artificially contrived "planned economy" of apartheid. The impatient reader may prefer to resume the story at Chapter 8. But I have included in this chapter the bare outline of the proposals then made to General Smuts in the hope that these may still be taken seriously, though the United party could not be so persuaded even by General Smuts's own planning commissions in the vital years when he held power before the landslide of 1948 towards the nationalism of Malan and Strydom. Clearly such a programme could now be carried out only by means of far-reaching political and constitutional changes, which would require a powerful combination of people of all races in South Africa.

The concentration of more than 75 per cent of South African industry into 2.6 per cent of her total area has brought about a concentration of social and racial problems within the industrialized areas. This now raises, as a matter of civil urgency, the whole question of the form and pattern of South Africa's future development in relation to her natural resources and national security.

The steady flow of population, both black and white, from the agricultural areas into the towns is likely to increase rather than diminish. Moreover, the housing problem and threatened food shortages resulting from the failure to solve the internal problems of food production and skilled-training and employment in industry, are likely to be felt more severely. In the urban areas an incipient social disorder is already manifested in an alarming increase of crime, vagrancy, and deficiency disease. The African infantile mortality rate was estimated by Dr. Gale, the chief health officer, to be never less than one hundred fifty per thousand and in some areas as high as six hundred per thousand. Often as many as two thousand arrests are made in one week-end in the Rand area. Oliver Walker reported as long ago as 1942, 861,000 convictions in one year out of a total population of less than eleven millions. In 1956 the minister of justice reported that 14,000 non-Europeans received flogging sentences.

These are problems which must be faced in an objective and scientific spirit. For otherwise, in a land torn by political party rivalries, by racialistic propaganda, and sectarian pressure groups, these very circumstances may have only the effect of sharpening antagonisms, rather than uniting the people in a common effort to set a course through this critical period of our history to a more creative and harmonious future.

The war undoubtedly stimulated industrial development in South Africa. However, such development has not taken place on the basis of any co-ordinated plan such as will be required, both by industry and agriculture, to check the flow of population from the countryside to the urban areas and to enable South Africa to develop her own resources *in situ* within the general framework of African development and world reconstruction.

The haphazard manner in which the great industrial areas have grown up or agglomerated in the past is a striking contradiction of the principle enunciated by Adam Smith, whereby man, in the pursuit of "his own interests," is supposedly led by an invisible hand "to promote an end which was no part of his intention." The Johannesburg area, viewed from the air, illustrates the folly of man's refusal to exercise the God-given faculty of conscious thought and rational capacity to plan his environment.

There are, therefore, many and urgent reasons why we should set out to discover how far the thought which is being devoted to the subject of regional planning in other countries is applicable to South Africa.

To what degree would such a conception of planning be acceptable to the various sections of the community, excluding those professional malcontents and advocates of the pick handle for whom the wants and grievances of the people are but grist for their own party political mill?

In this connection a passage apposite to this situation may be quoted from Lewis Mumford's work, *The Culture of Cities:*

We must continually remind ourselves that the period of urban expansion is over, and that the great urban masses created by that period are, in the nature of things, bankrupt: this war [1939–45] is the last declaration of insolvency. The mere massing of population and wealth no longer gives an indication of urban greatness; just the contrary. We have the task of giving form and character to a new period in the world's history: we must provide the stage and the setting for a fresh drama. Good planning in the post war period will rest on the solid foundations of the family and the region. It will emphasize the biological and social needs of the people. . . . Our biggest towns should in future be country towns, that is towns which would maintain the vital link between the soil and the city, between agriculture and industry. . . . The coalescing of urban communities into one vast manhive . . . is a sign of that lack of political discipline which precedes and announces decay. The countryside is not only a producer of food but a breeder of men.

The rift between town and country, between industry and agriculture, has already reached an advanced stage with large areas of our land denuded of soil and people. Practical plans will be required whereby the initiative of industrialists could be encouraged, and the enthusiasm of the people evoked, in undertaking nation-building enterprises such as land settlement and rural housing schemes, rural industries, power and irrigation projects. All of these would fall within the framework of natural regional growth and afford the people of respective groups new opportunities of furthering their own social progress.

In such constructive ways the foundations could gradually be laid for a real renascence of the social, cultural, and economic life of the respective communities. Failure to lay these foundations in this transition period will inevitably mean that those varieties of race, culture, and tradition which go to make up our national life will lead to internal stresses and strains which, in their social and political consequences, might constitute a denial of all that millions of mankind have laboured and fought to preserve in our generation.

The source of racialism and the fear on which it feeds is often found in economic competition. Inevitably, for example, the establishment of rural industries in the native territories employing African operatives or craftsmen would raise the question of competition between white and black labour. But it is possible that the fear and antagonism which this has brought about in the past could be overcome by the establishment of marketing schemes through which the products of such industries would be sold at non-competitive prices.

The surplus between the lower productive cost in such native areas and the distribution prices need not necessarily be expended in the form of an abnormally increased wage, above the present capacity for wise spending; but it could take the form of a collective wage used for the building of community centres, the establishment of co-operative chain stores in the native areas for the distribution of their own products, and the provision of social and cultural amenities at present conspicuously lacking in the native areas.

A gradual increase in purchasing power would, however, greatly stimulate the growth of a home market for the products of industry generally and, in this sense, improve the prospects of industrial expansion upon which adequate employment for European labour will inevitably depend in the future.

For a definition of regionalism the reader may again be referred to Mumford's *The Culture of Cities:*

The region is the unit area formed by common aboriginal conditions of geological structure, soil, surface-relief, drainage, climate, vegetation and animal life, reformed and partly re-defined through the settlement of man, the domestication of communities in villages and cities, the re-working of the landscape and the control over land, power, climate and movement provided by the state of technics. The human region in brief is a complex of geographic, economic and cultural elements.

His perspective of a more virile social life in the "unit areas" of regional development is expressed as follows:

In every region people should be created who will be accustomed from school onwards to humanist attitudes, co-operative methods, and rational controls. These people will be united by a common feeling for their own landscape, their literature and language, and local ways; and out of their own self-respect they will have a sympathetic understanding with other regions and different local peculiarities. They will be actively interested in the form and culture of their locality which means their community and their own personalities. Such people will contribute to our land planning, our industry planning, and our community planning the authority of their own understanding and the pressure of their own desires. Without these planning is a barren externalism. . . . A scientific re-mapping of the country is not enough. . . . Once this spirit triumphs in individual countries it will lead the way to a more co-operative and serviceable civilization.

A provisional delineation of "regions" in South Africa, on the basis of the definition referred to in the preceding quotation, has been made by Dr. Bruwer, former economic adviser to the Industrial Development Corporation:

1. The Lowveld Region,
2. Eastern Cape and Natal Coastal Region,
3. Central Grain Region,
4. The Wool Region or Great Karroo,
5. Eastern Cape, Natal and Inland Region,
6. The South West or Winter Rainfall Region,
7. The Mineral Region.

Before proceeding to outline some of the future possibilities of development for these regions with reference to soil, climate, population, mineral resources, agricultural products, and available industrial capital, it may be necessary to meet the argument that regional development in South Africa would adversely affect our existing economy, orientated around the gold-mining industry, from which a very large proportion of State revenue (70 per cent) is ultimately derived and upon which many subsidiary industries are dependent.

Clearly no drastic changes can be contemplated in the immediate future which would bring about a reduction in state revenue at a time when the extension of the social services needs to be planned and is imperative in order to combat the spread of disease and to check the erosive effects of ignorance on both land and people. The fact remains, however, that the gold-mining industry cannot forever be expected to carry the main burden of taxation, nor can it be relied upon indefinitely as the major source of revenue for the State.

Various government commissions and competent authorities, such as the government mining engineer, have emphasized that the life of the gold-mining industry is limited, and there are many who urge that some remission in taxation is already due if certain mines are to continue in operation.

The stage has now been reached in our history when we must face the fact that we cannot continue to live or thrive, as in the past, on wasting capital resources whether these be in the form of gold, of virgin soil and vegetation, or of labour power.

Ignorance and poverty have already increased the incidence of deficiency diseases to an alarming extent. And again every expert opinion has emphasized the fact that social security in South Africa will depend upon the extent to which we are able to increase the productivity per head of the population and, hence, the total national income.

As contrasted with industry, agriculture in South Africa contributes at present an extremely small proportion to the national income (12½ per cent), and so long as agricultural policy continues in the direction of subsidizing uneconomic production this is unlikely to increase. On the contrary, the now widespread wear and tear of the soil by this uneconomic agricultural production will involve the expenditure of large sums from State revenue to repair the ravages of erosion in those areas, for example, where animal husbandry has been neglected in favour of grain production, and in others where the land is correspondingly over-stocked.

Under circumstances in which the taxable capacity of the people is low, therefore, it would seem as though our only prospect of social and economic advance will lie in the direction of building up fresh sources of revenue, stimulating consumption on the home market, and increasing the variety of industrial enterprises in association with agricultural production.

Planned co-operation between industry and agriculture would in fact offer the reasonable prospect of a real renascence of the countryside, and would enable South Africa to plan her food production on the basis of the increasing physical needs of her people. It would provide the means and the organization necessary for a more fundamental solution of the soil erosion problem than that envisaged by a patchwork policy of subsidizing temporary anti-soil erosion measures.

On the whole the development of secondary industries in South Africa has hitherto been influenced more by the desire to utilize ready-made markets and labour supplies than the desire to develop the country's raw material resources *in situ,* and this tendency has been strengthened rather than discouraged by the rating policy of our railways. (The Rural Industries Commission found that of 4,938 factories in the Union only 1,715 were located in rural areas.)

While no attempt can be made to "map" our available resources according to their respective "regions" in this book, it may be mentioned here that the following unexploited raw materials are of immediate practical interest, from the point of view of building up enterprises which would in the course of time relieve the burden of taxation on the gold-mining industry:

Animal fibres; base metals for ferrous and non-ferrous alloys; clay, salt, and sand (refractories, pottery, glass, etc.); coal (power and plastics); timber (paper, compressed board, packing cases, plastics, artificial fabrics); fruit (canned, preserved, and dehydrated); vegetables and fish (fish oil, fish meal, etc.). Of mineral resources the most important are iron ore, limestone, dolomite, manganese ore, chrome ore, copper ore, asbestos, fluorspar, barytes, corundum, gypsum, tungsten, and tin ore.

While detailed surveys have now been made for the future social and economic life of all communities and ethnic groups, it might well prove disastrous if such development were to take place on the basis of unplanned speculation with a "quick profit" motive, or on the basis of a form of "racial capital investment."

Some time ago it was pointed out in a paper read to the South African Institute of Engineers that:

Instead of building up enormous surpluses which incidentally will simply result in lower prices for our own exports due to the appreciating effects on our currency, it seems to be very much more desirable to utilize these surpluses by investing them in our own nation and building up permanent values in the country.

Can it not therefore be said, both on sound economic and moral grounds, that this is part of the debt which we owe to those who sacrificed their security, and even their lives in some cases, for the land they loved and in whose future they believed?

It would almost seem to be an obligation placed upon us to provide the scope for a scientifically planned investment of a proportion of this available capital in nation-building enterprises which, in addition to developing all resources, would, in practical ways, help us to check those fissiparous tendencies and antagonisms which are now at work amongst the respective racial groups in the country.

Would it not be feasible to found a national trust fund, open to subscription by the general public and by established institutions and administered by a regional planning corporation, for the purpose of financing such nation-building enterprises? In such a way we could begin now to lay the material foundations for a more virile future and a happier relationship between the respective races and communities in South Africa.

A new form of patriotism should begin to take shape in South Africa. It should have nothing in common with those varieties of jingoism which have flourished in the confusion of our political life. It should have its roots in a deeper understanding of the country's real tasks—of the problems and incongruities, the tragedies and hatreds of the past, the prejudices which have been engendered by political party strife. We shall come to see that the varieties of tradition and modes of life in the land are not mutually inimical but are parts of a composite whole. They should serve as sources of strength by their very diversity. They should be cherished rather than treated with mutual contempt and hostility.

Inevitably this development of Africa will presuppose an African charter or "Bill of Rights," the aim of which will be the realization of

Rhodes's ideal—equal opportunity for all civilized human beings and a firm resistance to all policies of race supremacy which impose legal or artificial handicaps on the African people on the grounds of their race. But inevitably this will also presuppose a cultivation of tolerance as a positive, rather than a negative, virtue. Tolerance is not a natural instinct, nor is it an easily acquired virtue in a multi-racial society such as South Africa. It cannot be imposed by external discipline or legislation. It proceeds rather from within, from an inward consciousness and appreciation of the value, inherent in a social structure and a culture different from one's own. Under the form of nationalism of the Nationalist Party, returned to power for another term in 1958, to hold such beliefs and to translate them into practical action in a Freedom Charter appear to lay one open to the charge of treason against the state.

Stephen Alexis, Ambassador of Haiti and great-grandson of General Dessaline, speaking out of the social background of an enslaved people, told the Fourth Committee of the United Nations: "Gentlemen, human understanding is not the natural feeling of man. Understanding, tolerance, benevolence, are all cultured sentiments, which can only be acquired and are not spontaneous in man. Culture and civilization proceed from the soul, not from matter."

8   Durban Nights

On June 13th, 1946, the Passive Resistance Movement, originally initiated by Gandhi, was resumed in opposition to the Asiatic Land Tenure and Indian Representation Act. This was an omnibus measure consolidating all the Anti-Asiatic Laws that have been passed since Indian labour was first imported into Natal, in all some sixty enactments.

When Gandhi as a young lawyer came to practise in Durban, he was soon moved by the injustices against the Indians who had been brought from India in the nineteenth century, by agreement between the British and South African governments, to work on the sugar plantations, the Zulus at that time proving "unadaptable." He began to formulate, before the First World War, the principles of *satyagraha,* commonly known as the Passive Resistance Movement, though in fact it signifies far more, for the word expresses the spirit of truth and love as a power to resist evil.

In the Second World War, the Indian army played a valiant part which won great admiration—grudging admiration sometimes—from the Union defence forces. For smartness, efficiency, and courage in the field, the Indian army could certainly hold its own with any other. Yet in South Africa, after the war, Indians continued to be treated as members of an inferior race and referred to as "coolies."

The Pegging Act during the war had been directed against any further penetration of Indians into the commercial and residential monopolies of the Europeans. Now it was sought to limit and define once and for all the spheres in which Indians could live and transact business. The Indian community saw this as a threat to the very foundations of its social and economic life, for all that political representation was offered it for the first time, in the form of three white representatives in a House of more than a hundred and fifty members.

The residential provisions of the Act were seen as a Hitlerite move to relegate the community to ghettos. Since the Indian community in Durban is numerically about equal to the European, the land prices in these restricted areas, about one-tenth of the whole, quickly mounted out of reach of the average poorer class of Indian.

Passive resistance took the form of occupying in tents a triangular stretch of waste land, which was owned by the municipality, in the centre of Durban. Its resumption was the signal for a revival of racial hysteria in Natal. The colour question began to be raised by Nationalist politicians on their platforms, and by preachers in their pulpits. The more-British-than-the-British raised the slogan "Menace of Asia—the Threat to Africa of an Indian Invasion", and the Indian community was branded as the advance guard of a projected Indian domination of the African continent. This last was seriously put forward in a pamphlet for the United Nations by the Durban Joint Wards Association.

The press was not lagging in its racial incitement against the Indians, and especially the passive-resisters, and very soon mobs of white hooligans began to collect around the resistance camp at the corner of Umbilo Road and Gale Street. It was not long before the tents were pulled down and, after they had been re-erected, set on fire. The authorities seemed indifferent and took no notice when the passivity of the Indian resisters aroused their attackers to physical assault. In conversation the authorities are reported to have said in effect that the Indians deserved what they got, that they had deliberately broken the law and should be treated as outlaws.

Father Satchell (head of the Anglican Indian Mission) and a few other friends of the Indian community did what they could to stem the rising tide of racialism and to secure the intervention of the police to prevent hooliganism, but there were pitifully few of them and their efforts were of no avail.

After this had gone on for about ten days, I was approached by a newly-formed and not very strong "Council for Human Rights" (consisting of European members) and asked to go down to Durban to report on what was happening, and, if possible, to secure action from the authorities. Dr. Dadoo was going to give medical assistance, and the others were Betty du Toit, secretary of a labour union of Europeans and Indians, and Yusuf Cachalia, a cultured young Indian merchant.

Each of us must remember the long drive down to Durban that night. We were all rather nervous, for each had a reputation which was inimical to the mobs at work in Durban, and no one had the least idea how it was going to turn out. En route we slept for a few hours at the back of a little Indian store, and we got up in the chill half-light of morning feeling rather like a section of paratroops going down behind the enemy lines.

When we arrived at Durban everything was peaceful enough as we drove into the city. The great expanse of sea shimmering in the sun looked very inviting. The gaiety of the bathers, the bright contrasts of beach umbrellas, dark palms, and the gleaming white buildings, all seemed to accentuate the folly of man's hates and jealousies.

Only in the offices of the Passive Resistance Council did one sense the tension. Dr. Naicker and the other leaders were looking tired and strained, and immediately began consultation with Dr. Dadoo. Dr. Goonam, the first Indian woman in South Africa to qualify as a doctor, seemed cheerful and unconcerned, however, and others were methodically busy with the task of organizing the scores of volunteers who thronged the offices, and for whom classes of instruction had to be arranged.

Nothing would happen until the evening, when the appointed batch of resisters would be escorted to the "resistance camp" and would there await developments.

It seemed that there were now organized gangs of white youths who planned concerted attacks on the resisters, the operations being directed by a certain individual who was said to be a sort of underhand dealer in second-hand property, known to the police as a "fence," and who had a large number of ne'er-do-wells at his beck and call.

As dusk began to fall the volunteers for the evening were lined up in a hall used for instruction purposes and were addressed by Reddy, their O.C. They were told that they were the custodians of the honour of the Indian people, that the racial persecution and oppression to which all the non-white races in South Africa were subjected were being challenged by the methods of non-violence, of *satyagraha*. That if any single one of them did not feel strong enough in his spirit to go on with it, he should withdraw. No one must be weak enough to allow himself to be provoked or to hit back, no matter how cowardly and brutal the attacks might be, no matter even if the women volunteers were attacked. And no one must be weak enough to allow himself or herself to resort to self-defence, much less to run away. If they were not sufficiently sure of themselves, they should wait and go through a period of further training.

No one relented and after short, matter-of-fact speeches they all marched out. I went to the site of the camp with the intention of observing and reporting on what happened. By now it was dark, and the sea air seemed chilly. At first all was quiet. There were a few catcalls from passers-by in cars, as the Indians marched in file to the centre of the "resistance plot." By this time they had given up trying to erect tents and they stood there in a group with only a lantern.

After about half an hour of waiting groups of European youths, dressed in sports kit—running shorts and gym shoes, or football boots—gathered in twos and threes on the opposite side of the plot. After a while they formed into a group and began singing patriotic songs. Then we heard them being addressed by somebody. When the speaker had finished there was silence while they assembled in some sort of formation.

Suddenly a whistle blew, and with shouts and catcalls the whole formation charged and bore down upon the little group of resisters who were standing back-to-back so as to face in all directions. The attackers were mainly youths, with a few girls bringing up the rear. Some of them were fine-looking youngsters, and perhaps they thought they were doing something brave. With their fists they struck the Indians in the face and about the body. No one retaliated, but some tried to duck or ward off the blows before falling down. On the ground they were kicked. Some lay still; some were groaning. I did not see any of the Indian girls attacked, but I believe one or two were struck. It was all over very quickly, and the attackers thereupon dispersed into the general crowd, while the other Indians went forward to give first aid.

Further attempts were made to persuade the authorities to intervene, but they refused to listen to arguments or to take any action either against the Indians or the gangs of youths.

Inevitably this confronted us all with critical decisions. No one could foresee where the sort of exhibition we had witnessed would end. The Indian community was incensed at the cowardice and brutality of the white mob, and was convinced that the authorities, if not responsible for organizing the attacks in some indirect way, had connived at them in order to break the movement.

Some of us who were European had encouraged the Passive Resistance

Movement by speaking at their meetings and joining in their prayers. We had warned the government that the passage of the Asiatic Land Tenure and Indian Representation Act would have serious consequences for South Africa, both at home and abroad. As Christians we felt it to be part of the whole vast superstructure of racial discrimination in South Africa, whereby it was the law itself which made criminals of the people.

What was to be done? The assaults were becoming more severe. An Indian plain-clothes policeman was pursued by a white crowd armed with sticks and died as a result of his injuries. Tens of thousands of Indians thronged the streets of Durban in procession, and a Hindu priest, a Muslim *moulvi*, Mr. Rustomjee (a Parsee), Father Satchell, and myself went before the coffin to the Indian cemetery. We conducted a service there and, after lowering the coffin into the grave, addressed the enormous, but orderly, crowds, appealing for discipline and restraint. Other Indians, not *satyagrahis*, were also being assaulted.

Should another batch of volunteers be sent in, or should there be a respite to let feelings cool down? As so often happens a vital decision had to be made quickly, and the responsible leaders had to make it. They stood there, on the corner of West Street, considering whether they should not take the responsibility of suspending activities for a few days and call the committees together to explain their reasons for doing so. I was asked by Dr. Naicker and Dr. Dadoo what I thought should be done. I was non-committal, feeling that it was the Indian people who were being tested, not me, and that the decision lay with them since they would have to bear the brunt of that decision. I told him that they must decide, but that I would stand by them whatever their decision.

They determined to go on with it. Probably there are innumerable such sudden strains that test a movement. Any one of a hundred or more could break it if it were not strong enough in all its vital links. But that was one which I happened to witness and which has remained in my memory, for I feel convinced that had the decision been other than it was at that moment, the movement might have been irretrievably broken, or at least interrupted for a long time to come.

That night the attacks were even more violent. I drew up a hurried report on the position, and Mr. Sorabjee Rustomjee cabled extracts from it to General Smuts and to Gandhi and Wehni in India. He thought that the Indian Government would intervene and have the controversy placed on a higher level. For my own part the only possible course seemed to be to throw in my lot with the resisters.

And so that night I found myself one of a nervous little band, standing in the dark in the middle of an open space in that very modern city, with two separate crowds opposing each other—one European and the other Indian, with some Africans.

In the same way as before the attacks began with a charge and a sort of high-pitched hunting cry. The men volunteers were very soon knocked down and were lying huddled on the ground. The girls were not seriously assaulted. I was dressed in my cassock and they recoiled from assaulting me, just as they were about to do so. Having learned something of the spirit of the *satyagrahis* by this time, I spoke to them without heat. Two girls came up and started shouting "Coolie guts" and "Curry guts." "Are you an Anglican? You ought to be ashamed of yourself, you renegade. If I had known what your religion teaches, I'd never have been confirmed." "God would never have had me," said one. "He's had me," said the other. Two men came up and started pushing, expecting I would hit back, but they were bullies and had a frightened look in their eyes for all that they physically had the mastery of us.

It was during this episode that I remember one of the Indian girls, a Muslim, saying to me, after many of the men had been knocked unconscious in front of her, "It's not their fault, they don't know what they are doing." I don't suppose she had ever read the story of the Crucifixion, but her religion had taught her more than those other two girls had found in ours, it seemed.

I felt so sick and helpless, and ashamed, and yet her remark seemed strangely to reassure me in the knowledge that simply by standing still there on that particular piece of ground one was enabling something to be done—yes, enabling God to do something—against the dreadful evil power which was manifest in that sadistic mob. I knew that Zenab Asvat was right, they did not understand. Far more responsible were the religious leaders who preached the colour bar under the sign of the Cross in South Africa and the statesmen and politicians who in season and out of season played upon the racial prejudices of the people.

How dare they do it in the name of Christ! All things are possible in the name of Christ and Christian civilization, it seems, from Torquemada to the organized robbery and subjection of the Coloured races.

Meanwhile, although our protests in South Africa had had no effect, the matter was taken up vigorously in India and General Smuts was asked by Gandhi to use the power of the State to stop hooliganism against Indians. Thus it came about that we were arrested, not under the Asiatic Land Tenure and Indian Representation Act but, ironically, under the law of trespass. Altogether some two thousand or more were sent to prison.

Each time the resisters were arrested and released, pending the hearing of the case, they would return to take up their stand on the same plot of ground, until they were again arrested. When the cases came on there were enormous crowds about the Durban court house and in the court itself. The leader of each group made a statement on behalf of his group. Some of them had served in the war with distinction. Now they stood to attention on prohibited ground as their only means of fighting the same doctrine of race that had threatened the whole world.

There was some irony in the fact that the first magistrate who heard our charges was a Jew. The Jews, with few exceptions, are on the side of political liberalism, such as it is, in South Africa.

My own charges were four of trespassing and one of riotous assembly. I was dressed in my cassock, but having spent the night in it, with no facilities to wash and shave, I looked even less presentable than usual.

After conviction, I was driven to gaol in a police van. The driver said it was dirty inside and the seats were hard, so I had better come and sit next to the driver's seat. This he did partly out of kindness and partly out of curiosity, I think. He asked intelligent questions on the way and seemed to be driving slowly in order to spin out the time of discussion.

9   Durban Days

On arrival at Durban gaol in June 1946 I went again through the formalities of recording my fingerprints and other particulars, as when we had been arrested.

The Afrikaner warders were very astonished to see me arrive in my cassock, but were quite courteous, though studiously off-hand, shewing neither ridicule nor resentment. I was not made to undress in public as were other prisoners, and was given a khaki shirt and trousers, the prison uniform for first offenders, and allowed to undress on a closed-in staircase.

There were only about thirty European convicts in the gaol but the number of non-Europeans was in the region of nine hundred, if I remember rightly, about twice or three times its proper capacity. Being a European and a first offender, I was given a cell to myself. It was about ten feet by seven feet and had a bed, a rope mat which I took up and used as an extra blanket, a small cupboard, and a mirror. High up there was an opening for ventilation which had iron bars and sloping slots, but which had no glass in it. By standing on the cupboard and peering through the slots, I could see part of the sky, part of a Durban street with cars and people walking past, and some shops. At night I could hear the sea, the long rollers of the Indian Ocean breaking on the beach. It was only a murmur, and I doubt if I should have recognized it if another prisoner in the next cell had not told me what it was. I was glad he did.

We were given an allowance of tobacco if we wanted it, and a period each day for smoking and exercise in the prison yard. But there was a long stretch between 4 P.M., when we were locked in, till 6 A.M. For breakfast and supper we had a mug of porridge with a spoonful of sugar and two slices of bread and cold or hot water. In the middle of the day we had a vegetable stew which every other day contained meat. After breakfast at 6 A.M. the open latrine buckets from the cells were emptied, then each prisoner polished his own cell floor, made the bed, and washed. Shaving was allowed twice a week only, razors having to be handed in after use.

For Europeans there was a library from which a book could be borrowed twice a week. It had a fair selection and I improved my knowledge of Victorian literature, Egyptian history, Dryden and Cowper's poetry, together with some plays and novels. I had been allowed to bring with me a Bible given to me by Father Satchell. The day that I was discharged, he came into gaol himself for a term, and was followed in his turn by a Quaker lady, Mary Barr, and a white trade union leader.

I had also been allowed to bring a copy of Gerald Heard's *The Lord's Prayer and Beatitudes,* which I read three times. However, I had to surrender a book by Mr. J. H. Hofmeyr, Minister of Education at the time, entitled *Christianity and the Race Problem,* which amused one of the warders and the other prisoners.

Attended by the visiting Anglican chaplain I was allowed to celebrate Holy Communion in my cell on Sundays, while a warder stood at the open door of the cell. I think it was a hard contrast for that priest from his fashionable Durban parish church. There were usually three separate services for European prisoners, one by the Salvation Army and two others by different denominations. The addresses were simple and brought a breath of human kindness into a hard and sordid existence, in which petty irritations—the theft of some little precious possession such as a stub of pencil—sometimes assumed enormous proportions, and would rankle for hours unless brought under control.

Apart from official punishment, I did not actually see any physical ill-treatment, either of European or non-European prisoners, though I did hear sounds which could have been caused by it. Sometimes in the long silent period prisoners would start raving and beating on the doors and shouting to be let out. Sometimes they were so mad or violent that they were put in strait jackets. Once when I was in hospital I questioned a Zulu prisoner about his face, which was bleeding and battered, and he told me he had been punched by a warder and his head had been knocked sideways against an electric light switch on the wall, but he would not agree to make an official complaint and certainly seemed very much afraid.

The warders were overworked, and there was almost incessant swearing at the non-Europeans who were overcrowded in their cells—there were sometimes twelve or fourteen in one cell larger than ours. The new ones did not understand prison routine and the warders would easily lose their tempers. "Bloody bastard" were the two commonest words one seemed to hear in Durban gaol, except on Sundays when there were more and longer sermons than most of the men had ever been accustomed to in all their lives. The Zulus at their separate service in the yard sang beautifully, but never with their hearts in it as they do outside.

For my own part, in Durban gaol I experienced most deeply the contradiction in my religion between the elements of submission and resistance. I felt the consolation of belief even at the little services conducted in the corridor of the European section. Though I could sympathize with some fellow-prisoners who muttered blasphemously under their breath at the hypocrisy of it all, and sang ribald or obscene words to the sentimental hymns extolling sweetness and light and pleading the sufferings of Christ and the "Blood of the Lamb" in expiation of our sins. The Africans singing in their part of the prison, even in a minor key, seemed to give to the words a quality and meaning which they hardly otherwise possessed.

The cells of the non-European section of the gaol were so crowded that at night the floor space was entirely covered with the forms of prisoners lying alternately head to foot with room only for a pail of drinking water and a latrine bucket. The parades for washing, work-hours, and meal-times were an ordeal both for the prisoners and the harassed warders. Many of the warders took an obscene delight in the searches that were made at each parade for tobacco or anything else that could be concealed on the person. The non-European prisoners were made to strip naked in view of all of us and perform the most grotesque antics so that the warder could satisfy himself that nothing was concealed between the legs or toes or anywhere else on the prisoner's body.

Worst of all were the days when corporal punishment was inflicted. In fact the worst form of cruelty that I came across in gaol was the carrying out of these forms of punishment sanctioned by the law and prison regulations. Those due for this barbaric treatment were made to undress and stand naked beside their heap of clothes in the yard in front of the hospital to await a farcical medical examination. The white prisoners were dealt with separately and more privately, though their punishment was also severe, as witnessed by the marks on their buttocks for weeks to follow.

After one touch each of the stethoscope and a cursory examination of previous weals the non-European prisoners were marched to the other side of the courtyard leaving their clothes in heaps on the ground outside the hospital, and were made to wait in line along the wall of a shed on the opposite side of the prison courtyard. The warders who were to inflict the punishment would pass the time of waiting by practising their strokes, in view of the waiting prisoners, with a cane about four feet in length.

Then one by one the prisoners would enter the shed to be tied to a triangular frame and undergo their sentence. Sometimes there were screams, sometimes there were not; but always, when the victim emerged from the shed, he would hardly be able to stand and could only very slowly place one foot in front of the other and thus make his way back to the hospital for another medical examination. Their buttocks, swollen with livid weals and oozing blood, were then treated by an orderly with some kind of astringent lotion. The whole sadistic ritual that attended this process of the law, the long nerve-racking waiting about, the cold and nakedness and the fear of physical pain were calculated to induce in the victim a sense of shame and dread and of being without protection or means of escape, all of which would reduce their morale and self-respect to the lowest possible ebb and induce in them a sense of the futility of any resistance to the law or society as legally constituted.

In South Africa, according to *The Times* of January 21st, 1956, corporal punishment is being resorted to on an ever-increasing scale. In 1950 a total of 4,400 lashes were administered for various statutory offences, and of these 4,329 were imposed on coloured and African prisoners. In 1954 the total number of lashes administered in prisons for such statutory offences was 78,573, and of these 76,337 were administered to coloured and African prisoners. Since the above date an enactment has empowered African chiefs in the reserves to impose corporal punishment through their native courts; and in carrying out these punishments there is no medical supervision. The recently enacted Public Safety Act further provides for penalties of up to a £500 fine, or five years imprisonment and/or fifteen lashes, for passively resisting or encouraging others to passively resist any South African law.

I tried hard in my prayers to penetrate the mystery of so much needless and deliberately-imposed suffering in the world, but only a mocking echo seemed to come back as from some dark and empty void at the centre of the universe, or worse, perhaps some hideous contradiction of beauty and cruelty in the very heart of the creative purpose itself.

After only a few weeks in gaol I could feel that the strain was bringing on a return of the Crohn's disease which I hoped had been surgically eradicated. Eventually, following an attack of pain and vomiting, I was admitted to the prison hospital and remained there for two weeks. I tried at first to avoid thinking about anything and especially about what had brought me there. It seemed as though the bright sunlight striking the iron bars of the windows made crosses everywhere with their shadows until they became almost an obsession which I could never escape noticing.

While I was in hospital, I asked to be allowed to write a memorandum for the Penal Reform Commission; and permission to use a typewriter was obtained from the Minister of Justice, Mr. Harry Lawrence, with whom I next had dealings at the United Nations.

Periodically an opportunity was given for prisoners to make complaints to a visiting magistrate, though few thought it worth while to do so, believing that it would lead to their being singled out for stricter treatment. When the inspector of prisons came to visit the gaol after allegations of ill-treatment had appeared in the press, and in the proceedings of the Penal Reform Commission, I asked if he would read my memorandum.

In this I had set out some of the more barbaric survivals from old penal codes and the inconsistency between motives of reform and intimidation which one noticed living under this regime. There was, for example, no distinction made between types of offences, so that different types of offenders would learn from one another's crimes. Youngsters would be mixed with hardened criminals. In all, the penal code seemed to be a strange mixture of intentions to punish on the one hand, and to retrieve on the other, the one often defeating the other. Could not half the sentence express society's disapproval and the second half be aimed at reintegration, with more attention given to the individual, his background, and future possibilities? I might add, incidentally, that in Durban, which was a short-term gaol, I was the only white prisoner as far as I could discover who ever had a private talk with the chaplain as long as I was there, and there was, in fact, no provision for individual treatment except as a punishment.

For non-Europeans, the problem of penal reform is so overwhelming that it is hardly possible to discuss it here. The gaols even then were overcrowded with thousands of Africans who were not criminals in any moral sense. When the chief warder heard that I had asked permission to write a memorandum on prison reform he came to see me in hospital. He told me first of the difficulties of carrying out a proper penal administration at all with the low-grade personnel that found their way into warders' jobs. He then went on to say: "The vast majority of these natives are not criminals at all. They are perfectly law-abiding natives really, but they happen to have infringed some regulations under the network of pass laws, the Urban Areas Act, and the Master and Servants Act. By these laws natives are made to carry one or more of up to ten or twelve different passes[1] for different objects—passes which, being illiterate, they may not themselves be able to read. It is not the prisons that you want to reform, but the laws."

Even before the increasingly severe application of the pass laws under Dr. Malan's government, more than 100,000 Africans were convicted every year. Oliver Walker, in his book *Kaffirs Are Lively,* gives the figures for all crimes as 861,269 convictions in one year (1945). With a population of less than twelve million, and with the great majority of these convictions being of non-Europeans, this means that nearly one in ten of the non-European population of South Africa is convicted in one year. Since that time the incidence of crime has greatly increased under the apartheid laws.

Under the Masters and Servants Act an African may be convicted for

---

[1] The following are some of the passes, one or many of which an African may have to carry in accordance with what he is doing:
1. a residential or site permit
2. a lodger's permit
3. a night pass after 11 P.M.
4. a permit to seek work out of the reserve
5. a permit to be in a proclaimed area for purposes other than seeking work, e.g. domestic reasons
6. a copy of his contract with his employer
7. a casual labourer's licence (if that is his work)
8. a registration certificate for those not under a contract of service
9. a temporary visitor's permit
10. an exemption certificate to the effect that he is not required to carry a pass, viz. he is over twenty-five years of age, has been in employment for over three years, has a clean police record, a fair standard of education, and is recommended by his present employer.

such offences as neglecting to do his work or performing it carelessly or negligently, rendering himself unfit through intoxication, or using insulting language to his master or his family.

Such is the meaning of segregation in South Africa. Apartheid, as Mr. Schoeman, the South African minister of labour, is reported as defining it, means:

That Non-Europeans will never have the same political rights as Europeans: that there will never be social equality: and that the Europeans will always be baas (boss) in South Africa. At United Nations meetings General Smuts had explained the position of Non-Europeans by saying that they had not yet reached the same level of civilization as Europeans. This was wrong because logically it meant that when the Non-Europeans were on the same level as the Europeans they would have equal rights. The Nationalist Party said that they would never have those rights. [*Johannesburg* Star, *March 2, 1949.*]

The machine-like regularity of our existence in prison, and the unhumanness of our relations with those who controlled us, would sometimes produce internal storms in people. In the middle of a deep silence someone would suddenly start hammering with his fists on the steel door and concrete walls until, exhausted, his shouts would turn to mutterings and then cease. There would be no response from the other prisoners as a rule. There would be punishment for the culprit of five days' solitary confinement on a low diet which would reduce his vitality to a mere existence. Occasionally another prisoner would respond, as one might on a lifeboat at sea, and try to reason with one who could no longer bear the strain of it. And to that a warder would often turn a deaf ear.

There was a young painter who could only get a job as a sign writer. Sometimes I would find myself sitting next to him on the floor, leaning against the wall of the prison yard during smoking time. He would talk in quick, clipped-off sentences about the hopes he used to have of his career and what he intended to do in the future. Now he was utterly disillusioned. The only thing that had any importance for him was the satisfaction of his own desires, and above all the fulfilment of the rage that welled up inside him.

He had been flogged and still carried the marks of it and sometimes, if the head warder who had administered the flogging was on duty and out of earshot, he would suddenly start a torrent of foul vituperation, looking down between his feet, with a casual expression on his face as though he were merely talking to me. He would say everything that in those long silences he had been wanting to say to the head warder himself and thinking he would like to do to him.

There was also an "old lag" of nineteen who had had four previous convictions. He was an orphan—an illegitimate child—and had been sent to a reformatory at the age of sixteen. He was arrested two days after leaving jail. He almost seemed to believe his story himself—that he had gone mistakenly to the wrong flat in search of someone to whom he was recommended for a job. The door had been open and he went in to see if anyone was at home. The young woman tenant found him there on her return, would not listen to his explanation, called the porter, and had him arrested for "breaking and entering." It was kinder not to ask him the obvious questions since he wanted to be believed innocent, and that was a stage better than boasting of his crimes as some did, or wasn't it? He had a great zest for life and a jaunty way of wearing his old lag's hat which annoyed the warders because it was something indefinable that they could not correct, like the "manner" of some convicts which used to infuriate them.

Usually, though, the warders got the better of anyone, and this youngster presented a sorry spectacle on the occasions when he was on low diet and solitary confinement for some breach of prison discipline. Sometimes I would watch him when I was working in the yard. (I had complained about the rust on the buckets used for drinking water and I now had the impossible task of cleaning them with sand and water.) He would be brought into the yard alone for his exercise. His vitality was at a low ebb and he hardly bothered to look up as he tramped wearily up and down. Sometimes I would flick a friendly pebble at him as he went by and he would rouse himself sufficiently to smile back, his eyes momentarily losing their apathy in a little flicker of pleasure at being noticed. As I watched him slouching backwards and forwards while I ineffectually rubbed sand into the rust deeply encrusting the inside of the buckets, I would be filled with alternating pity and rage: annoyance with myself for not being able to think the thing right through to its end or beginning, rage at my own futile little action and at the inanity of a regime that could drum the humanity out of men to try and make them conform to the inhumanity of its own system. Then my mind would go back over the years to my own youth, the comparative advantages I had enjoyed, unlike this youngster. Perhaps otherwise I might have been in the same position as he.

I never doubted for a moment the rightness and logic of what I had done, even if it was a futile protest against injustice. It was better than continuing to acquiesce. My thoughts took me back to the time I had returned to England from the Cape. I had been ordained by the Bishop of Chichester. The service then, old Conway on the organ afterwards, had made it sound as though all heaven and earth were on our side. The very stones cried out to one of the beauty and integrity of the universe.

But now scrubbing this bucket, and there in that miserable youngster drearily pacing up and down, there was the "question" again. Unless my religion could fight this out it was worthless, meaningless—humbug. In that case the young artist muttering his vituperation against the warder who had flogged him was right, or no more wrong than anyone else.

If the creative power in the universe which we call love could not be brought to bear on this world situation in some more effective way than by interminable sermons, and ambulance work for what we are pleased to call our civilization, then the forces of hate were going to take charge. Wrath and more wrath was, after all, the inevitable next development from a world which believed in nothing but the economic motive of self-interest. Money values and material motives must inevitably produce a similar material reaction at the hate level unless . . . ah, unless what? Perhaps Gandhi had found it . . . a way of breaking the vicious circle of hate—counter-hate. I was getting out of the way of talking about God because somehow He was either everywhere or nowhere, and to mention Him too much seemed like keeping the outside of the platter clean while the inside was like my bucket.

There were moments when I felt a much-longed-for assurance, a certain conviction about the inner rightness of things and the tremendous power of God's love. If only we could find some way of losing our petty little egoisms and let that power use us to act upon events in time, even to the lengths of trying to resist—trying to stem the power of evil that one felt so strongly in that place. Was it absurd? Or was it possible that by merely existing there and holding on, while not ignoring the "question," something could be accomplished?

Love could, after all, only operate through free human beings giving themselves to it, surrendering their freedom to it in order to be free. Or was that all make-believe? Was I really in prison now, or was I more free than I had ever been? Was it just a futile gesture of a rather eccentric clergyman, as I was told people were saying outside, or more maliciously, but no less possibly, a piece of self-righteousness and exhibitionism. These were all real doubts. They could not be ignored; they must be thought through. I was being carried forward on a tide of events and must know where I was going for my own "inner" reasons, as well as because there was a fight on. One must choose one's weapons. One could not stand about and argue like Arjuna with his charioteer, the Lord Krishna, on the battlefield. As for Arjuna, the moment for action could not be ignored. Inaction then becomes another form of action.

That sense of the inner rightness of things was very powerful, though it seldom assumed a more positive expression. One morning while I was in hospital, after having a rather restless night in which there had been a good deal of inner disquisition, I had gone to sleep reading a chapter of St. John's Gospel. Some of it had seemed rather trite. It had not answered my mood, though its language was very beautiful. I fell asleep, wishing it were possible to abandon myself more to the love and purpose of God without so many reservations and gnawing doubts. I woke up with a jump, thinking I had heard some of those words I had been reading, but they were not the words of the gospel and I have not been able to find that particular sentence in the Bible at all. They were quite ordinary words and sound rather prosaic when I say them over to myself. But I shall never forget the power with which they came home to me and the inner peace which they brought with them—"I will show thee the light of the gospel and will give thee thy heart's desire" was what I thought I had heard. I remember scrambling out of bed as though I ought to get down on my knees and then, after a while, feeling rather ridiculous and chilly I climbed back into bed. I decided this was probably just wishful thinking, only expressed in the biblical language that had been in my mind when I went to sleep. But inwardly I knew it wasn't the words that mattered at all. It was the assurance that had come to me. I had not jumped out of bed like that for nothing. And I had that assurance that it was *all all right*. I must go on, even if I felt ridiculous and self-righteous and all the things analytical people said about me. There was something infinitely greater than myself in what was being worked out and if it made me look ridiculous that didn't matter.

That didn't mean to say that everything was all clear and straightforward. On the contrary, only a very little was clear. It did not mean that I had some solid ground to stand on. On the contrary, I was adrift on an ocean. It was an ocean of infinity and I did not know what course was being steered. But it was all right. In the inner core of things was known what the logic of these events was and where they were all leading. It was a great adventure, not knowing. The "question" still remained. One might never know the ultimate answer in this life. The immediate answer came only in the act of taking the next blind step forward.

I hesitate to write this down, as it is so intimate a thing and will sound very shocking to those who expect one to be a kind of monolith of orthodoxy in an uncertain world. But there may be some who are hesitating for security reasons to "enter the path," as the Buddhists call it, and who may feel some little encouragement that it is worth while trying to make a start. Without this inwardness, outward forms and ceremonies can avail little and may, some think, hinder us. But there are others who have gone much farther along the path and who find these forms to be of use and beauty, so it ill behoves anyone to destroy them because they are misused by some as substitutes for the reality they enshrine.

Most of our actions are unco-ordinated because the greater part of our existence, both physical and social, is lived at a level at which higher ethical motives cannot, or at least do not, operate. Our system of economic and social relationships does not permit the exercise of moral judgement beyond certain narrow limits. The individual, whether a managing director or a typist, a politician or a scientist, is caught up in a system of processes beyond his control. Only by a deliberate act of moral judgement and choice can he dissociate himself from those relationships in which he is an accomplice in robbery and murder.

How can the Christian resist the organized evil of which he is himself a part and partner?

The Church of God cannot be content with defining attitudes, preaching sermons, and passing resolutions. The Church must be an instrument of change and of redemption of the world. If it ceases to be an instrument of God's creative purpose and becomes an institution preoccupied with doctrine, church order, and discipline, and identified with prevailing systems, the salt will have lost its savour and be fit only for the dung heap. Then would come the deluge unless God could find some other way to overcome the perversity of man and intractability of matter. Certainly today the Church faces another of the great challenges of history.

The way of wrath and force becomes almost overpoweringly tempting when we are confronted with the sufferings of the persecuted and oppressed. It may be better for them to die resisting oppression than forever to acquiesce in injustice.

But another way can and must be found to break the dilemma of mankind and to resolve the controversies of history, time, and space, by means consistent with civilization and culture. And the inspiration for this can only come from people who believe in something other than self-interest or self-assertion (whether of the ego or a group).

Those of us who belong, not so much to the oppressed as the oppressor group in South Africa have especially laid upon us the obligation of finding another way—a way of dissociating ourselves by civil disobedience if necessary, from oppression of our peoples. A third force may be from beyond space-time.

10 Dark Laughter—Tobruk

Tied to the leg of the table with a yard of string was a brown and white hen, who chuckled to herself and gurgled contentedly, save when angrily flicking her foot or pecking at the cow-dung floor.

In this all-purpose living-room the brown and white hen lived with the family. During divine service the minister's wife could be heard behind the ragged cloth at the back of the altar, alternately spanking, soothing, and dressing her babies. The family of the Reverend Theophilus numbered seven, their living quarters being a part of the Church of Christ, separated from the chancel by a partition made of sackcloth and wood.

But I mention the brown and white hen because she was later to figure prominently in the evidence when Theophilus's church and dwelling was attacked and burned to the ground by a gang which seemingly was visible to everyone except the law and the agents of the law.

The learned counsel for the defence argued that it was highly improbable that such a responsible person as the accused, with seventeen thousand persons under his care, would have led or initiated the attack on the Church in the first place. Even supposing he had done so for the reasons that were so unworthily alleged, it was highly improbable that he would have seized the brown and white hen in one hand and the cross in the other and gone dancing through the streets shouting "Alleluia," as had been alleged. Furthermore, the accused protested that he was suffering from a bad leg at the time.

This whole story is, of course, highly improbable. Yet the court record shows that the Church of Christ was in fact attacked with sticks and knives, that the faithful few who remained inside it, including the minister and his children, were assaulted, and that the walls which were made of sackcloth were ripped to shreds before the whole was burned to the ground, so that nothing remained of it but a scar on the earth and some scattered smouldering ashes.

All the more strange was the fact commented upon in a leading article in the *Rand Daily Mail* that, although the occurrence was witnessed by many hundreds of people, there were no independent witnesses for the Crown or for the defence. Nor were there any police, ambulances, or fire engines available until it was all over. A few sparks fanned by a gust of wind and the whole township, comprising seventeen thousand souls living in houses made of sackcloth, would have been destroyed in a few moments.

Now I must go back a little and explain, so that the facts about the highly improbable hen, the Congregational Church of Christ, the gangsters, and Theophilus, may be known to the reader and may be seen against the extraordinary—many may think incredible—setting in which these events occurred ten miles from Johannesburg in darkest Africa.

Ten miles from Africa's El Dorado, the great gold-mining city of Johannesburg, the overcrowded slum quarters of this industrial centre broke their bounds. From the first trek of a few score families in 1944, the Africans moved in a long procession, like the displaced persons of Europe. And, displaced by our civilization, they set about constructing their own townships on the hills outside the city. They took possession of waste land belonging to the municipality and built themselves shacks and shanties from sackcloth and old tin cans because they were forbidden by law to build for themselves in their own locations. Neither the Johannesburg municipality, nor the police, nor the central government dared challenge them; and the shantytowns grew apace.

A number of us from the churches, trade unions, and other bodies waited in a deputation on the minister of native affairs, Major Piet Van der Byl. We were politely received, but he could not be brought to treat the matter very seriously. This quaint little shantytown that had sprung up on the veld was to him rather a joke, though we were probably too earnest to appreciate it.

Truly it was a joke, the first shantytown. With typical African humour they named it Tobruk, from the experiences of many as prisoners of war;

and a laugh went all round the native townships when it happened. It was a joke that caught on. Daily the numbers of squatters swelled. Lorries and carts were piled up with luggage and furniture. Off they trekked from the slums to the veld.

They set up their own committees. They paid for their own social services, such as they were. They employed their own police, their own magistrates, their own doctors and nurses. They dug their own latrines. They bought their own disinfectants. They disposed of their own rubbish. They appropriated water from the municipality's taps. They licenced their own shops. They brewed their own beer and even licenced their own hotels, all in defiance of the law. But in course of time corruption grew. Frustration bred disillusionment till the self-appointed chiefs and their committees became little more than gangsters, who collected enormous sums in the form of dues, licences, fines, and special levies from the inhabitants, with no proper accounts rendered. The joke grew to such proportions that by 1946 about a hundred thousand Africans were living in these shantytowns.

It was in response to a request from some ex-soldiers who had asked me to go there and investigate their conditions, that I finally went to live there in Tobruk shantytown, not long after my release from Durban gaol. They hoped that I might help them to straighten things out and maintain the peace. I, for my part, felt it was the vocation of the Church, not only to try to understand the problems and difficulties in the life of her people, but to enter into them and share that life.

I was asked to convey a demand for a constitution and a proper system of accounting. This demand was at first met with sullen acquiescence, but the same night an ominous sound was heard. The Zulu war-cry, with its rhythmic cadences, is unmistakable. It grew louder as motor lorries containing bands of Zulu braves approached the camp. They were uncontested by the camp guards and, stamping the ground and beating their drums and clashing sticks with one another, they danced down the main street and took up their positions in the square, challenging all who were disloyal to the chief to fight it out.

No one took up the challenge. But the next night, when the visitors had retired to their own camp again, the chief's hut was surrounded and only my last-minute intervention saved him from a severe thrashing. A message sent to the mission fathers brought them down in their truck and they took the chief and his wife away for the night, promising to bring him back next morning to face the committee which had been formed. When he came no satisfaction could be obtained regarding the funds and next day he left the camp.

Meanwhile we had drafted a constitution, which I read to a public meeting. This was received with great acclamation by thousands of people present, and a committee was elected to carry it out. I eventually agreed to act as a temporary chairman until agreement could be reached regarding the chief's successor.

The committee set about at once to try to establish order and reorganize some of the lapsed social services. The guards and the burial and sanitary officials demanded their pay arrears, which I was able to pay from a sum accumulated on my account at the diocesan office during my three months' gaol sentence.

It was not long, however, before the guards grew restless under the scruples of the new regime and reinstated the old chief. There was no effective force to resist this; and he promptly inaugurated a reign of terror against the leaders of the opposition faction.

It was at this stage that I moved from the chief's yard and went to live with the Reverend Theophilus at the Congregational Church of Christ. There I wrote an article in a Johannesburg paper in an attempt to rouse Johannesburg public opinion with regard to the conditions which were rapidly deteriorating, not only in Tobruk but also in the other shanty-towns which had grown up on the perimeter of the city.

So life went on in Tobruk, and as you walked up and down the little zigzag lanes at night you could see the fires burning low in the braziers, a candle flickering through the sacking walls of the huts, and there was music for every need and every mood. Here the slow, mournful rhythm where a child has died, and further on the quick clapping rhythm of a Zulu dance. Over there were an old harmonium, a guitar, and an accordion at "Mabel's Cabin." On the top of a long pole was the totem, new-style, Mickey Mouse with arms akimbo. The band was jiving away, and bodies were shuffling and shrugging ecstatically. It seemed to be jiving its way into the future, whatever that held for the African in these vast agglomerations that we call towns.

I got into the habit of going along to one particular shack late in the evenings sometimes, to listen to an old man whose harmonium was the delight of his life. He had apparently learned some of the words of his songs from his old wife who had been a nanny to some English children and had perhaps been taught them by their mother. They sounded rather incongruous, set to African music in that shantytown:

> *Stars shine bright and the moon gives light,*
> *I'm going to marry tomorrow.*
> *I'll invite you all to come.*
> *Little birds are singing in the brown corn fields.*

Usually he would finish with a hymn, his favourite being:

> *Like as a Father pitieth his children*
> *So the Lord pitieth them that fear him.*
> *Like as a Father he knoweth our sins*
> *And remembereth that we are but dust.*

Sometimes, incongruously, little snatches of bawdy drinking songs would come sandwiched in between the hymns:

> *My name's A. W. Corbett.*
> *But I don't give a damn.*
> *I've got something in the bottle*
> *For the morning.*

Mabel's Cabin was a few "streets" away from the old man's shack. There they danced till four o'clock in the morning at week-ends, jigging and swaying tirelessly to the rhythm of the improvised, but spirited, jazz band. You could get tea and fry there, and the band would sing:

> *There's a rag time restaurant,*
> *With a rag time dinner time band.*
> *It's all sublime*
> *If you eat your chop you can eat in time*
> *To the rag time dinner time band.*
>
> *The band plays everybody's doing it*
> *While you eat your chop*
> *You feel suffocated*
> *But they will not stop*
> *The grand rag time dinner time band.*

I remember one summer evening when, in a violent storm, Theophilus and I looked out of the door of his shack as his children came scurrying in from the pouring rain. He waited there, for the storm suited his mood, and watched the forked flashes of lightning. A group of women with paraffin cans full of water on their heads were running with long gliding strides, balancing themselves with their waving arms and hands. Winding its way up the valley was a long stream of men and women returning from work, having come off the Johannesburg train at Nancefield Station.

Everywhere the cooking was being done indoors, and smoke could be seen seeping through the sackcloth walls of the huts. The whole appearance of the place with its long stretches of zigzag lanes between the rows of shacks, the earth-coloured sackcloth hanging with their totems or symbols of their trade—a dressmaker's model, an aeroplane, an old boot, a bundle of sticks, a bicycle wheel. Wet and ragged, the battered tins and crooked poles were comical yet strangely sinister.

Theophilus was not conscious of anything comical or sinister. He rejoiced in his comparative freedom, though of course he knew he was a lawbreaker, a trespasser, like all the other thousands of shack dwellers. The rain lashed down and was dripping fast through the leaky roof. It would not last long, but he told the children to roll up the bedclothes and put them under the table. Then they squatted round the fire, and his wife ladled out mealie samp and vegetables for them.

Hannah was plump and had rather lost her shape with much child bearing. Like many of the women of her race, she still more than half believed in the folklore of her people. As a young girl she had heard the call of the *Abantubomlambo*. Once she had only just been rescued in time from throwing herself into the river when they had called her. Even now she believed in the *Tikoloshe,* though she would not admit it to her husband of course, and when people laughed about it she always joined in the laughter. But then so did many of her people—they laughed at things they were really frightened of because the white men laughed, and because at school and in church they were taught to despise everything that belonged to the old life.

This was even true of her husband too. As she watched him sitting there by the fire she remembered the time she had caught him unawares, bathing his face in the smoke he had made with a magic herb, calling her name in that finely modulated voice of his.

Once I took Theophilus in a borrowed car to see the African Blind School at Exenzeleni where we were taking one of his "parishioners."

As we bowled along towards Roodepoort, with the empty veld stretching away to the distant hills, he laughed, and the sound of his laughter with his deep bass Zulu voice will always live in my memory. "Why you put us all in the sacks when there is all this empty space?"

Going back to the church one night, I lay down on the bed in the section partitioned off behind the altar for my use, but it was too early and too noisy to sleep. The children came in for evening prayers, and a few people were gathering outside. Theophilus "rang the bell," i.e., a piece of railway line hanging from a nail and lit the candles.

The children finished their part with the hymn they sang every night:

> *Jesus loves me, this I know*
> *Because the Bible tells me so.*
> *Little ones to Him belong*
> *We are weak but He is strong.*
> *Yes, Jesus loves me, this I know*
> *The Holy Bible tells me so.*

And then in Zulu:

> *The star of the United Church*
> *Is lighting very far*
> *The light of the Church of Christ*
> *Is lighting very far.*

Soon the deep booming voice of Theophilus could be heard expounding the parable of the guest with no wedding garment. He ended:

> *God is the greatest. And the day is coming when the Lord will receive us. This thing what we do it now we must really believe. . . .*
> *The same is in this shantytown. Some people drink. Some enjoy themselves. But there is many people who is dead.*

The opposition to the gangsters who ruled Tobruk had tended to become centred in the Congregational Church of Christ. Every device of intimidation that the gang could invent was used to prevent people from attending the church. Some even had their huts destroyed over their heads. But the booming Zulu voice of Theophilus could not be quieted and was heard for an area of hundreds of square yards addressing a sometimes non-existent congregation.

Meanwhile disorder increased and the growing lack of confidence in the "administration" was met with more violence and intimidation. In vain the co-operation of the South African police was sought. The chief native commissioner shrugged his shoulders and reiterated the phrase, *"pari delicti."*

Then I was prosecuted for living in a native urban area, but when the case came on I sent a note to the magistrate by George Norton asking him if it could be postponed on account of the perilous situation that existed in the camp. There was an outbreak of smallpox which found the health authorities totally unprepared and at first unwilling to face the fact. I isolated nine cases and took them to hospital, but within a few days the number of cases had risen to forty-five. Many of those whom the health authorities were eventually persuaded to vaccinate were treated too late. When the pox broke out on them the witch doctors and semi-pagan sects which flourished sought to persuade the people that this was another device of the white man for doing away with the blacks. The vaccination squads refused to enter Tobruk at week-ends without police protection, and this the police refused to give on the plea that if anything happened they would not have enough men to get their people out. There was also an outbreak of typhoid which by the mercy of God was limited to only a few cases.

When my case eventually came on the magistrate adjourned it in order that expert evidence might be taken as to whether the site of the Church of Christ was actually within the geographical area delimited or set apart for a native location, within the meaning of the Urban Areas Act. This entailed a surveyor taking a bearing on the cross which stood on top of the church and drawing appropriate lines on a map converging on the spot marked X.

The location superintendent was called in evidence at the case, and in Appendix 3 I quote an extract from the court record, together with my appeal against conviction, the judgement, and suspended sentence. I returned to Tobruk and no further action was taken.

It was some time after this that early one morning a young ex-soldier came to me and said he wanted to make a complaint against the gang leader and his guards. He had returned to his house, he said, to find two thieves there making a pile of his belongings. He set up the alarm and with the aid of his neighbours arrested the thieves and took them to the guard room.

The so-called magistrate heard the complaint and imposed a fine of ten shillings, whereupon the complainant said he was not satisfied; he would prefer the case to be taken to a proper court as there had been too much thieving in the camp. For this he received a slash across the eyes with a *sjambok*. Both he and his wife, who was pregnant, were jumped on and kicked and punched till they were senseless. On regaining consciousness they were allowed to go, only to find that meanwhile all their belongings had been removed, leaving them with not so much as a saucepan or a blanket.

We took the young wife to hospital, informed the police and asked that a record be prepared for the court. Within a few days she had an abortion, but when the case came before the magistrate the police said there was no medical evidence that the abortion was due to the assault. The doctor maintained that he had not been informed that it was a police case until after the operation, otherwise certain tests would have been carried out.

Such was one of innumerable cases wherein all efforts to secure redress by proper constitutional means were deliberately frustrated by the authorities. Let it rip was the attitude. If violence does break out, we shall know how to deal with it.

However, an inquiry was held by the representatives of the Native Affairs Department, the municipality, the police, and the chief magistrate, before which many of us gave detailed evidence. At the conclusion the chairman said that a complete record had been taken of the evidence. He stated that he, "with his colleagues from the Police and the Native Affairs, whose presence here indicated that both the Government and the Police are interested in the happenings at 'Tobruk' camp, had listened to the statements. It would be studied by them and in due course the representatives would hear further."

Meanwhile the social services, such as they were, had long since ceased to function. Enormous mounds of rubbish accumulated. The sanitary squads refused to work since they received no pay. When the latrine ditches overflowed, they were filled in and the site built over by incoming squatters.

Children were dying at the rate of one a day and we had to bury them without coffins or in rough wooden boxes carried on the parents' laps in a jolting cart or motor lorry, if one could be commandeered from a driver off duty. Usually Theophilus would ask me to give an address and "offer a prayer." Such moments will always be numbered amongst the most difficult in my life.

The Anglicans in Tobruk liked to preserve their identity and used to hold little prayer meetings in one or another of their shacks. The white missionary in whose district Tobruk lay, would not give me permission to celebrate Holy Communion for them, however, lest it should encourage a sectarian spirit amongst them.

From among these faithful few not only did a resistance movement grow up against the enormities of the gang, but willing helpers were found to perform such acts of charity as those which preoccupied the early Christians. They delivered babies; they visited and prayed with the sick in their spare time; they sang hymns and interpreted scripture to one another. During the smallpox outbreak they helped to encourage the people to come forward for vaccination. When the mothers were too terrified even to handle their own babies, they would come and help carry them to the ambulances.

In them the spirit of God seemed to burn as it had burned in the catacombs, spreading invisibly so that Nero with all the might of imperial Rome could not quench it. Visible only to those who had eyes to see, it was comprehended in the darkness and shone amongst the ragged, tattered houses and the stench of decay and filth.

Then came the day on which the King of England was to visit the native townships of Johannesburg. Sixpence per head was the price of a ticket, which everyone who wanted to see the King must purchase from the "chief."

The guard formed fours and drilled before the great day. They sang the song which had been sung by the native military corps at the defence of Tobruk, "Tobruk Never Shall Fall." On *the* day the Union Jack preceded them, and the chief brought up the rear. It was on that day, whilst the chief and the guards were away, that one of the "magistrates" asked me to come and see him and made a confession, which he asked me to write down and take to the government, i.e., the South African police. It took me several hours to do, but it was impossible to move the authorities even with that atrocious account.

Among the acts of intimidation was one in which a strange semi-Christian semi-pagan sect played an unworthy part. One night whilst Theophilus and I were talking matters over round a coke brazier and drinking tea, a weird sound was heard approaching which brought an unusually startled look into his good-humoured face.

It came nearer, until the voices could be distinguished as chanting

Zulu voices. Round and round the church they danced and sang, finally bursting in and continuing to dance round and round the central supporting pole in front of the altar. Dressed in white, with multicoloured girdles and headdresses, they made a fearsome spectacle, heightened by the imprecations which they called down upon Theophilus and myself and all who followed us in our "wicked wizardry" against the chief and "those in authority." The family were, I think, more terrified than I have ever seen anybody before.

Theophilus was in the grip of a titanic struggle with the whole barbaric past of all his forbears, but occasionally he would throw out a remark that was intended to be reassuring. I admired him for that because it did reassure me, though not his family.

As suddenly as they had come they went. And soon we heard them encircling the chief's hut. The singing and dancing continued there for nearly an hour, one of the faithful reporting breathlessly to us that they were digging under the floor of his hut and were finding many things buried there, bones and entrails, with which we were being accused of attempting to bewitch the chief.

Surprisingly nothing further was heard about this. An expurgation rite was carried out, but I had expected it would have proved the occasion for a final démarche against us. Theophilus afterwards explained it as an attempt to create feeling against us amongst the people.

It was after this that the school which Theophilus and I had started with a blackboard, a register, and a few pieces of chalk was literally stolen from us by the chief. He announced in the public square that only the chief, not the clergymen, could be responsible for a school. He descended on the school with a squad of men armed with sticks and demanded that the register be handed over to him and that in future the teachers be responsible to him alone. He arrested one teacher, placed handcuffs on him, and even went through the farce of sending him to the South African police station several miles away on some trumped-up charge. It must be admitted that this had the desired effect on the other teachers who felt they must put their wives and families first.

Then one night when Theophilus and I were talking over plans for the new school, which had already thirty pupils after being open only two days, we heard surreptitious sounds outside the church and what sounded like orders being given in a hoarse whisper. We stopped talking and listened intently. Presently there was a long blast on a whistle and I heard my name being called in a loud voice of assumed solemnity. Theophilus looked extremely worried and seized a long iron spike used for drilling holes for pegs in the hard earth. I hurriedly implored him to remember some of the things we had spoken about while we had known one another and made for the door. The voice repeated my name in the same monotonous tone, adding the observation, "We are coming for you."

I appeared at the doorway and asked, as nonchalantly as possible, who wanted me and what for. I had no sooner stood erect in the doorway than Theophilus shouted to me to come back, grabbed me by the arm, and pulled me downwards. I had had only a fleeting glimpse of an evil face, full of hatred, but unrecognizable. Had it not been for Theophilus the blow would have hit me squarely on the head. As it was, it glanced off my shoulder in the act of stooping, and hit the doorpost with a resounding crack. The gang thereupon fled, and Theophilus made some derogatory remarks about non-violence.

Despite my own feelings, a fearless, quick-tempered Xosa named Spearman appointed himself my guard after my tent had been torn down one night when I was out. At night, there being no street lights of course, he insisted on my wearing a blanket and a woollen cap such as the Basuto wear. He himself had no work and used to spend all his time in the camp attending to the domestic needs of his many relations.

There was no one in the camp whom the gang feared physically more than Spearman. This was partly because he had a strong following of Xosas who were ruthless in pursuing a vendetta once their enemy had declared himself; but mainly it was on account of his indomitable physical courage, which showed a total disregard for the consequences once his temper or his intuition had prompted a certain course of action.

Eventually Spearman raised the question of remuneration, explaining the difficulties in which he found himself. I told him I could not afford to pay him and keep myself and that frankly I preferred to take my own chances unarmed, since my methods were different from his. I preferred to rely on moral force, and that alone, to resist our enemies, and I believed God was on our side in fighting all these evils around us.

This was not a difficult conception for Spearman, for he himself was an incurable romantic at heart. In imagination he lived as one of his warrior forbears, always on the look-out for danger from an enemy tribe or creature and ready to defend his honour and his life, though now it was clear to him that the enemies he had to fight were of a different kind.

He had no passes and, not having paid his poll tax for three years, was liable to arrest every time he went to town. Like thousands of his fellow-Africans, he completely failed to understand the white man who could prosecute innocent people by the thousand in his courts of law, and at the same time leave thousands of Africans of every tribe all mixed up to be ruled by this gang of crooks, some of them half-breeds.

As for me, "the father" had his own gods and his own spirits who ordered his world and his life for him. The only surprising thing was that the difference between right and wrong, he said, led him to fight against his own people on the side of the Africans. Undoubtedly his own people were against him. The police had been to the camp and issued a summons against him. They had found him guilty in the court in spite of all he was trying to do for the people. But he defied the law and continued living there and the authorities did nothing more about it. It was all very inexplicable. The father's people were accustomed to law and order. They were accustomed to an orderly procedure whereby people could plead their case and were given a fair hearing. Yet they were making the Africans outlaws in their own land.

Spearman was not of course able to read or write, but he puzzled over these things which he would express in his own inimitable way with his brow all puckered up, half puzzled, half indignant.

Amongst the gang leaders, I cannot recall one who would be commonly regarded as a criminal type. The "magistrate" whose lurid confession I took down in writing was an honest and decent-minded family man with a good record for quite responsible work in the mines. A lay reader in the American Methodist Church, he had drifted into the shantytown, leaving most of his furniture stored in a garage (whence it was stolen) because he could not find a house to live in and had had to give up his work in the mines for that reason.

The chief had served in the Union Defence Force as chief interpreter to one of the generals. As the magistrate pointed out, "the whole trouble with him is money, drink, and power." There would have been few men, even with all the resources of the State behind them, who could have administered the affairs of a whole camp of seventeen thousand persons. Without any of the resources of the State behind him, with no trained personnel, there was only one probable conclusion to his career.

The climax came one night after one of the Sunday newspapers' reporters had been assaulted, and the paper had carried front page pictures and headlines about conditions in the camp.

Returning from a visit to the hospital in the Orlando native township, I was met by Theophilus, wild-eyed and breathless and wielding a large iron spike. Scarcely coherent, he declared the church was on fire. They had all been surrounded inside the church. The gang attacked first with sticks and knives, ripping the sackcloth walls to shreds.

Unarmed and taken unawares, those inside defended themselves by pelting their attackers with lumps of coal. Then it was seen that fires were being lit at several different points so, seizing any weapon that came to hand, they fought their way out and scattered to seek refuge in the houses of friends living near by. If their attackers had been fully sober this might not have been so easy.

It was subsequently alleged by Hannah that the leader of the gang had seized the cross off the roof and had executed a triumphal dance, with the brown and white hen under one arm and waving the cross with the other. Nothing, however, was proved against the thirty or forty accused who appeared in the dock, and they were all discharged. The *Rand Daily Mail's* extremely caustic leading article on the trial was ignored by the minister of justice and the police department.

After the fire it seemed clear to all our friends that our cause was defeated, but worse than their physical fear was their abandonment to a terrifying sense of the strength of evil and its triumph over the puny efforts of the good.

Meanwhile under the taunt of the daily newspapers that the police were unable to afford protection to the ambulances summoned to Tobruk, and that criminals from all over the country were seeking refuge in this vast maze of nameless streets and numberless houses, the police department decided to act.

They acted without reference to the Johannesburg municipality, a police officer told me. For months there had been mutual recriminations between the two authorities as to who was responsible for the deplorable situation which was growing up all round the city. The municipality in its turn had placed the blame upon the central government and had sent several deputations to Cape Town. The viewpoint of the government was that Johannesburg had brought this situation upon itself by refusing, over a period of years, to avail itself of the 90 per cent free-of-interest grants which the government had offered to local authorities for housing schemes.

The police department cut the Gordian knot two days after the burning of the church by sending more than a thousand policemen to Tobruk to arrest the inhabitants. Early in the morning of April twenty-ninth, 1947, an enormous cavalcade of armed police and military lorries stretched for miles along the Main Reef Road. They swiftly surrounded the camp and rounded up all the women who could not give an account of themselves and all the men who were without passes, though the majority of the menfolk had already left the camp for their work. Illicit beer from scores of petrol cans was poured into the "streets" so that the air was heavy with the fumes of *skokiaan,* a deadly drink into which certain parts of the human body are sometimes put to increase the potency of its spell, as well as carbide to hasten the process of fermentation.

Many hundreds of people were arrested, but the leaders of the gang were allowed to go free. Somebody is believed to have tipped off the chief, who was not present when the raid took place. In the afternoon he gave an interview to the Johannesburg *Star* and was arrested and released a few days later.

The department of justice left a detachment of their own police in charge of Tobruk and a few days later the municipality's officials proclaimed the site of a new camp which it named Moroka. They issued orders that the inhabitants of all the squatters' camps, numbering about eighty thousand, would be screened, and those who could prove they had contracts under the Masters and Servants Act and could show their tax passes and tax receipts were to be given—or, rather, rented—a plot of ground twenty feet by twenty feet where they could build up their own shacks again with their own materials. Ditches were to be dug for latrines, water taps would be placed at a number of points in the new camp, and eventually it was hoped to make a school, a cemetery, and a recreation ground for the inhabitants. Meanwhile they were to pay fifteen shillings per month for these privileges. Since this sum was a great deal more than that charged by the Tobruk gang, and only half a crown less than that charged for a small house and garden in the municipal native township of Orlando, there was considerable discontent. Many paid for the first month in order to escape from the horrors of Tobruk, but many refused. A vast slum camp, planned to eventually hold 120,000 Africans, was therefore created outside Johannesburg.

Here it should be noted that when this scheme of the Johannesburg municipality was submitted to the Minister of Health and Housing, he absolutely refused to sanction it. On March 4th the Minister received a deputation from the Johannesburg municipality and told them what he thought of their scheme in no uncertain terms.

"In the opinion of the department," he said, "an arrangement which contemplates, for a period of possibly five years, a density of seventy dwellings plus latrine accommodation to the acre, cannot be defended on the grounds of urgency or the exigencies of the land situation or by any comparison with the shocking conditions in the uncontrolled squatting camps [viz. Tobruk] or on the grounds that there will be strict sanitary control. Apart from purely health considerations it does not appear possible that the elementary decencies and privacy of family life can be maintained for five years on and by families living on contiguous plots, only twenty feet by twenty feet, for each family except the four at the end of the blocks, being hemmed in by three other families within earshot and close eyesight, and in many cases with only hessian partitions for even the outer walls."

Nevertheless this warning was disregarded and the scheme was put into operation.

It was not long before there was a serious outbreak of violence in which two European policemen were killed. A commission of inquiry was instituted, or rather one of eight commissions which have been sitting during the last few years was diverted to inquire into the Moroka situation. Evidence given on behalf of the local authorities claimed that the "younger natives in the city and along the Reef are becoming very undisciplined." In the course of his evidence the native commissioner of Johannesburg said, "The lack of parental control in urban areas is having a very bad effect on the behaviour of the younger natives."

It is clear that there are some sections opposed to native education and progress who will point to the experience of the squatters' camp as evidence that the African is unfit to have any say in the organization or administration of his own affairs, that the "native is the worst exploiter of his people," that the urban natives are increasingly lawless and unprincipled.

Having lived for some months in one of these shantytowns, I do not think experience points to these conclusions.

Considering the innumerable difficulties of organizing so large a camp, and considering the lack of any practical assistance from authority and the many obstacles placed in their way, there has been an extraordinarily high degree of order and discipline maintained by the people themselves. In these breeding grounds of every kind of slum viciousness, there is even a certain African quality, an exuberance of life and music amidst death and pain. As a woman reporter wrote after a visit to Tobruk, "As I skidded and slithered through row after row of hovels, I noticed that every single African woman was smiling—they actually looked happy, and I decided that they must have a peculiar sense of humour. God knows, there was nothing to smile at in what I had seen that day." In my plea for mitigation when charged in court with living in a native area, I said rather pompously:

After living amongst these Africans, I can only say that I received always courtesy, respect and friendship from them despite the efforts of a self-interested group to rouse hatred against me. They were always eager to find a way of co-operating with the proper authorities, though again a self-interested group resented the intrusion of health officials, nurses, etc., for fear of interference with their regime.

I have no regrets for the part I played in this episode in the life of the African people. My admiration for the Africans, their endurance, their patience and good humour in the face of such terrible privations, has been greatly increased by living amongst them. They on their part, or some of them, have learned that some of us Christians really do believe the things which are taught in our churches and schools. God has a great destiny for the African people, and I trust that South Africans will put away their fears of African development and help them to find that destiny. The alternative can only be the continued decline of both races and the increase of mutual antagonism.

If the story of the shantytowns could bring both races face to face with their problem before it is too late to solve it, God will have brought some good out of this evil.

II Bethal—Abode of God

It was only a few weeks after the Tobruk affair that I was asked by some Africans to investigate the conditions of farm labourers in the Bethal district of the Transvaal. Many people in South Africa ascribed the subsequent defeat of General Smuts at the hands of Dr. Malan in 1948, and the loss of his own seat at Standerton, in large part to the happenings at Bethal and its surrounding district. It has been claimed that the drastic action taken by the United party Government antagonized the *platteland* vote and especially that of the farmers in the Eastern Transvaal.

This account of that hectic episode and of events since then should serve to show that the action of the Minister of Justice was by no means drastic enough. It will also illustrate the difficulty of securing remedial action for the African people by means of South Africa's present electoral system. Most of this chapter was written in South Africa at the time, and is drawn from a memorandum published in the *Rand Daily Mail* on the subject of farm labour in Bethal, together with correspondence and extracts from newspaper editorials. I have added to it some of the evidence on which my statements were based and an account of the position that has since developed.

Bethal is a little *platteland* town in the Eastern Transvaal. Its name would give it distinction—so the early settlers thought—as a holy place, like the original, where Jacob rested and dreamed that a ladder stretched from earth to heaven, and he felt himself to be in the presence of God. Or like Bethlehem, where Christ was born in the land of Judah, for the name means the "abode of God."

"Your Heavenly Father knoweth that he have need of all these things" —so read the *oudstryder* and nodded approvingly, sitting by his fire. As surely as the sun would rise, big and red through the mist in the morning, so surely did He know what lay beyond and over the hills, and beyond that further still. God's knowing was all that mattered. He would lead them as He had led those whom He had chosen into the promised land and away from bondage to any man, those who had the courage to go. And when they had decided to settle there, He would abide with them and they would be His people and He would be their God. The Kaffirs and all other devil-worshippers must be subdued like the beasts that crept amongst the shadows; God created them to serve, they must therefore be tamed or slain.

Such was the simple pastoral piety of the early settlers. It is easy for us to discern the hypocrisy in the faith of those of another age whose circumstances and conflicts have become less clearly defined with the lapse of time.

But now speed and efficiency have come to Bethal with the combustion engine. The law of survival, the dominance of the strong, reasserts itself in the economic and social relationships of our age—the townsman has come back to the country and brought with him the standards of commerce, the maximum profit motive.

Perhaps what has been happening in Bethal is significant of a new and dangerous trend in the development of South Africa's economy. It was Mr. Justice Maritz who sounded the first note of warning in 1944 when hearing the case in which Franz Mario (*Rex* v. *Isaac Sotetshi,* Case No. 858–1944, committed 17/5/44), a native agricultural labourer, had been flogged to death for trying to escape. He pointed out that the compound labour system was something quite new to him in our agricultural economy. In the course of the case a member of the jury explained to the judge the system which had come into being at Bethal and the necessity for preventing labourers from escaping from the farms before concluding their contracts. The judge pointed out it was not the accused, an Induna named Isaac Sotetshi, who was to blame for the killing of Franz Mario so much as the system which subjected him, and those in his charge, to such conditions. Accordingly, though guilty, the accused Induna was given only a light suspended sentence.

Only a few months previously Philipp Lebovo (*Rex* v. *Johannes Mahlangu,* Case No. 696–43, sentenced 26/1/44) had been so severely beaten that he died, the defence being that he was attempting to escape and that five Indunas were preventing him.

On October 25th, 1944, the diocesan synod of the Anglican Church warned the Native Affairs Department of what was happening at Bethal in a lengthy memorandum and a resolution which were forwarded to the Native Affairs Department, the Jewish Board of Deputies, and the native representative. The resolution called for the appointment of inspectors "who shall inspect the compounds on the farms and ensure that every compound labourer shall have free access to the Native Commissioner."

The memorandum pointed out that "the contract labourers are shared out among the farmers in lots of ten or twenty according to the size of the farms. They are housed in any farm building which may be available and the area is fenced and policed by Swazi or Basuto Indunas. There they remain and except when they go to work they are never let out unaccompanied by an Induna. Wages vary from 10d. per day for young boys, to 1s. 3d. or 1s. 6d. . . . ."

The memorandum concluded: "Contract labourers move only at the will of the employer weekdays and Sundays alike. They cannot get to the magistrate unless they escape. It must be clear that the extension of the Mine Compound System to the farms without any of the safeguards against exploitation of the labourer which Magistrates, Native Commissioners and Government Inspectors of Mines so constantly provide is leading in the country to the kind of exploitation of the labourer characteristic of the worst periods of the Industrial Revolution in Europe."

The shocking conditions prevailing in this farm compound system as well as the strictures of Mr. Justice Maritz were soon hushed up and forgotten.

The Native Affairs Department seemed reluctant at the time to take any strong action in the matter, to take any action at all in fact, which might alienate the good will of the farmers. In the course of his reply (1944) the minister referred to the fact that the matter was one which had "engaged the attention of the Department for some considerable time." He emphasized the difficulty of keeping in touch with owners and native labourers on widely scattered farms, and the danger of losing the good will of farmers as a whole by taking measures which may prove impracticable in the very varied conditions which obtain throughout South Africa.

After some years' delay, however, inspectors were appointed by the

Native Affairs Department, and inspections were duly carried out to the satisfaction, apparently, of all concerned. Nevertheless such were the "difficulties" in establishing the truth about these compound labour conditions and, despite regular inspections, in keeping in touch with what was happening in the compounds, that cases of flogging and assault had become "very common," to use the words of the public prosecutor.

It is worth quoting one of these cases in detail, for it will be clear from the remarks of both prosecutor and magistrate that it was not an isolated case and that the warnings uttered have by no means proved effective in preventing the indiscriminate flogging and ruthless exploitation to which these recruited labourers are subjected.

It is not the worst case known to the authorities by any means. Moreover, according to the allegations of some of those interviewed by the writer, many cases are concealed by means of burying the bodies of those who have been flogged and giving out that they have run away from the compound.

In the case in question, Balthaser Johannes Brenkman, a farm foreman, appeared before Mr. B. H. Wooler, R.M., in the local magistrates' court. He was charged on several counts with assaulting two native labourers. (See Appendix 4.) To quote briefly from the account in *De Echo* for June 6th, 1947:

In reviewing the evidence the magistrate said that accused had said he carried a sjambok in the lands with him, presumably also for protection, but the accused admitted that he had at times used the sjambok to chastise the labourers, which he had no right to do, the bossboy had on two occasions according to the admissions of the accused in his presence, used his sjambok on the labourers, and some of the boys had complained that accused had set his dog on them, which was borne out by medical evidence.

The conditions disclosed in this case are tantamount to slave driving, the magistrate said. On a farm of 400 morgen 25 native labourers were employed and they were driven to do their work by means of the sjambok. It was akin to slavery to drive the boys in this manner and practices of that type would not be permitted. . . .

"I endorse the remarks of the prosecutor," the magistrate said. "The number of assaults in the district had been prolific."

Mr. Wooler also said that jail would be imposed, without the option of a fine, in any future cases of the sort.

These accounts in the press, it must be remembered, followed repeated warnings to the departments of justice and native affairs.

To me the lands appeared to be well tended and prosperous (1947). The harvest was good, the only complaint being the shortage of native labour and of jute bags to convey the grain and potatoes.

A strongly-worded resolution had been adopted by the farmers' labour recruiting organization. This seemed to cause some of the local inhabitants to smile, and many regarded it as "very unnecessary", though others approved. It read as follows, as published in *De Echo:*

BOERE-ARBEIDSVERENIGING: RE TREATMENT OF NATIVE LABOURERS

The Board of the Boere-Arbeidsvereniging brings to the notice of its members the following resolution taken by the Board on the 29th day of May, 1947, viz: RESOLVED: *Whenever the Board is of opinion that any member of the Boere-Arbeidsvereniging has assaulted locked up or in any other manner whatever ill-treated any native labourer recruited by the Vereniging, or that such member has in any respect failed to carry out the conditions of the labour contract entered into between him and such labourer, then and in such case the membership of such member will be cancelled by the Board and his name will be removed from the register of Members of the Vereniging; no further native labour will be supplied to such expelled member and his name and address, as well as the circumstances and the reasons for his expulsion, will forthwith be communicated to the Department of Native Labour and to the local Native Commissioner. At the same time the said Department will be requested to issue the necessary instructions to all Native Commissioners in order to ensure that no further native labourers are attested for such expelled member.*

In the interest of these members of the Vereniging who faithfully fulfil their obligations to the native labourers and who accord them decent treatment, the Board feels itself obliged to carry the above resolution rigorously into effect.

Phone 104, Box 43   P. L. Du Toit
Bethal, 30th May, 1947   SECRETARY

One of the features of our national life which most people are becoming aware of by slow degrees is the shifting of population which is going on apace. This in general is a drift on the part of both Europeans and natives into the towns. The Dutch Reformed Church has recently become seriously alarmed at the uprooting of the younger generation of country-born Afrikaners from their localities and the substitution of secular and neo-pagan influences for those of the Church and the home. Even more marked is the accelerating influx of native people from the over-populated and overstocked reserves into the concentrated urban centres of the Rand, the new Orange Free State and Vaal industrial area, and the four principal coastal towns.

The problem of the urban squatters is one which is looming larger and larger in South Africa. Apart from the soaring figures in the Johannesburg area, several hundred Africans were recently arrested in Durban for trying to set up a shantytown, while at the same time publication of a report on the native locations of Durban was suppressed by the city council for fear of its effect on world opinion. In Cape Town Africans are trekking into the city on foot all the way from the native reserves, so that the regulations prohibiting travel by train to Cape Town from the Transkei and Ciskei drought areas have proved nugatory. Increasing numbers of them are living in shacks and caves and little *pondokkies* on the Cape Flats.

The pass laws have proved quite ineffective in controlling the influx of Africans; they are presumably retained largely for the revenue they bring in from those fortunate enough to be able to pay "admissions of guilt."

The huge urban agglomerations that we call towns have never been planned to accommodate a permanent African population. Thousands of native servants live without any facilities, close to the fashionable suburbs. It is even forbidden by law for a man to live with his wife in the same servants' quarter, though both may be employed in the same household.

Under the circumstances it is not surprising that both tribal and family life are fast disappearing, though there are pathetic attempts to preserve these by the people in the shantytowns. Neither institutional Christianity nor what is vaguely termed the "West" are providing an alternative culture or social structure. There is growing up a black, neo-pagan, amorphous, and increasingly amoral racial group, whose needs and aspirations are nobody's business. This group, constituting four-fifths of South

Africa's population, is regarded by most white people, including politicians, as a problem almost independent of the general problem of the development of the country and its great resources; for the colour barrier, taken for granted by every important European group, is necessarily a barrier against the economic and social progress of all the non-white groups and will undermine the security of the whites.

Both in the towns and in the country the cry goes up for more drastic measures to control the natives; and there is an ever-increasing demand for compound labour, on the farms as in the mines. The farmers' recruiting organizations have resorted to almost every device to induce natives from Rhodesia, Nyasaland, and other parts of Central Africa to come to the Transvaal. The following is a report from the *Sunday Express,* June 22nd, 1947:

MAGISTRATE APPALLED AT TREATMENT OF WORKERS
"SLAVE GANG" ALLEGATIONS IN TRANSVAAL
FARMERS FEAR NATIVE LABOUR BOYCOTT

Bethal, Saturday

Scenes reminiscent of slave-trading and chain gangs are being reported in the North-Eastern Transvaal as a result of the shortage of Native farm labour.

These reports are being made as a sequel to the revelation that bogus recruiters of Native labour are intercepting Natives crossing the borders of the Bechuanaland Protectorate and Mozambique in search of work, robbing them of their money and personal belongings, and forcing them into the employment of some Transvaal farmers, who are alleged to be no better than slave-drivers.

A good deal of the evidence concerning these practices has come to light in recent trials in the North-Eastern Transvaal, the latest being that of Balthaser Johannes Brenkman. . . .

The police are confident that the activities of bogus labour recruiters will be curtailed soon. Many farmers are worrying about the effects of all this adverse publicity on Native labourers, who may boycott an area which is already finding it difficult to obtain Native farm labourers.

It is estimated that approximately fourteen thousand labourers have been recruited in the Bethal district alone. Those who succeed in escaping can be seen wending their way towards Johannesburg and the Reef towns to swell the problems of the slums and the squatters' camps there.

There is constant interaction and the clamour is likely to grow for more and more drastic control. For crimes, especially crimes of violence, are increasing and it is probable that "more drastic control" will come to mean more and more compound labour for the farms. What the Bethal farmers have begun on their own initiative other farmers are likely to continue to demand of the State. Already, in fact, prison camps are being established in some localities from which labourers are hired out to farmers at the rate of 9d. per day.

Thus there is the danger, failing any alternative plans for a more constructive solution of the problem, of a further consolidation of South Africa's racial oligarchy by the organization of a vast system of native compound labour, not only for industry and agriculture, but even for municipal and other public enterprises.

It was in view of these noticeable trends that I went to Bethal after the strong condemnation which has been expressed to see, at first hand, what some of the actual conditions of recruited or compound farm labour were. First to be visited were two buildings standing a little way outside the town near the station. These formed the depot for receiving newly-arrived recruits. The buildings were made of brick; they had concrete floors and holes with iron bars for windows. When a batch of new recruits arrived they were locked inside. There were no blankets or mattresses, and a group which we questioned told us that these were not provided.

Next I interviewed at the location an African attorney, the chairman of the local branch of the African congress and a member of the location advisory board. He told me that a short while before the white people in Bethal had wanted to hold a meeting in the location to urge the native people to boycott the Indian stores and only trade at the co-operative store which they were going to establish. The African advisory board had objected to this meeting being held and protested to the magistrate, who, under the law, was obliged to prohibit the meeting. As a result of this the attorney had himself been assaulted by a gang of Europeans and severely knocked about.

I then went on to a certain farm where I inspected the compounds or living quarters. It was late in the evening and the labourers had returned from the fields to their quarters. These again were brick barnlike buildings without glass windows, with concrete floors and fires burning in braziers and open hearths. The air was so thick with smoke it was impossible to see more than a few feet. The men were squatting on heaps of sacks which were also their working clothes. There were three or four straw mattresses amongst about fifty men and no blankets, though I was told that the employer had provided each man with an overcoat only a few days previously. Many had no boots and one especially, a herdsman, complained of this. He had to be up at four o'clock in the morning and, coming from Nyasaland, was not used to the cold weather. One group I questioned was sitting round a fire eating the evening meal. This consisted of a large clod of mealie meal and pumpkin wrapped in a piece of sacking, each man taking a handful at a time. They said that enough of this was supplied three times a day, but complained that they only had meat once a week, on Sundays. All of them complained of the length of working hours, some having to rise two hours before light and not finishing until dark, i.e., 4 A.M. until 6 P.M. All maintained that they were very roughly treated by the foremen, both black and white, were always being cursed at, and very frequently beaten with *sjamboks.*

They said that they had made all these same complaints to a magistrate or inspector who had come out to the farm, but there had been no attempt to improve matters except that now the door of the compound was no longer locked at night. Many of the men—they could not say how many—had escaped and gone away and had not been heard of since. But for the most part they were either too frightened to leave, or did not know where to go, or needed their money. One Nyasaland man said he was also afraid to go back to Nyasaland as his family would despise and ill-treat him unless he took back with him money, cooking pots, and other things from the shops.

All complained repeatedly of being abused and cursed at for everything. Many of them had come in contact in one way or another with white missions in their own country. Here the white foreman always swore at them, saying, "Do you think you came down here to be a lot of Jesuses?" Then he would kick or beat one of them.

Their pay was about £2 per month, a month being thirty working days. If a man was sick or injured he received no pay until he recovered. Sundays and holidays did not count towards the contract time, and in order to earn twelve pounds it was probably necessary to stay for about nine months. The fare cost about £3 1s. 0d. from Nyasaland and that had to be refunded; the journey time did not count. Thus, if they were intending to return to Nyasaland it would cost another £3, leaving them at the end of nine months with only £6. (Incidentally why should a single third-class ticket for a native male from Blantyre in Nyasaland to Johannesburg cost £3 1s. 6d. [female £3 5s. 0d.], but a return ticket from the same place £7 13s. 0d.?) One man whom I saw at the depot bought a second-hand overcoat a few days before, which cost him 35/-. It was already frayed at the cuffs and pockets. His toes were sticking through the toecaps of his boots and he also needed a blanket and various other oddments, but he dared not go back to his *kraal* without money. He had boasted of all the things he would bring back at the time he had been persuaded to sign the contract. He now wanted to go to Johannesburg, but had no pass to travel, no money to pay the poll tax, and was told he might be put in prison or sent back to the farms. While he was telling his story there was much nodding and the drawling "ah" with which the Bantu expresses his sympathy.

After seeing another compound similar to the other two, I returned to Bethal, and went straight to the house of the farmer. Here I was surprised to be told by his wife, who opened the door, that she knew who I was; in fact her husband was out looking for me. She gave me coffee and said she would get in touch with him, then went into the next room to telephone. After a few minutes he burst into the room, and I explained that I had just come from his farm and thought he ought to know that some of his native labourers were complaining of being ill-treated. Although they respected him as their boss, they wanted him to know how cruelly they were being treated.

"Before you say any more," he replied, "let me tell you I don't want to know anything from you. The inspector and the magistrate have been round my farm and they are perfectly satisfied. That's good enough for me, and it had better be good enough for you. I may as well inform you that I know who you are. I have just come now from making an appointment with the magistrate. I told him my man has reported you going to my farm without my permission and I have told him I want to ask his advice what to do about it."

On being informed that many of his boys had come from Christian missions where they had been to school, and that some of them had learned to speak English, he replied that religion did not come into it. If his foreman brought religion into it by telling them they were not a "lot of Jesuses" that was the foreman's business. His job was to get the work out of them. And that was all he was concerned with, too. He was only interested in getting the work out of them. And if he didn't get it, so much the worse for them and for anyone who interfered with them.

He finished by warning me to keep away from the place and said he was going to think out what he was going to do. I informed him that he must act in accordance with his own conscience, and that I too reserved the right to do so. And there the matter was left for the time being.

The following morning I visited another farm and inspected six compounds built around a high walled-in courtyard, identical with the slave quarters in the old Cape homesteads. There I observed much the same conditions.

The analogy with slave conditions which the magistrate pointed out will be recalled. I believe that slave conditions were preferable, and, from many considerations, more humane, than a system which ignores the fact that a man is a man. It is not so much that he is a man with any political or religious rights, for that is a very far cry from the present situation on many South African farms, but that he is a man with all the instincts and impulses of a man, that he has a wife and family whom he may love and wish to protect and be with. Under even the most adverse conditions of slavery it was to the economic interest of the owners to ensure the survival, and even the training in some occupation, of the children of their slaves, and to make some provision for their housing and healthy upbringing. The compound labour system on the farms makes no attempt at any such provision. A man's life and the lives of his family are worth nothing. All that he is worth is the work which he can be made to put into his contract. If that undermines his health, or breaks up his family, or destroys his soul, that is not the concern of his employer. Nor should it be the concern of any interfering missionary!

On the other hand, there are increasing signs of an awakening on the part of the non-white sections of the population. The third Great Trek is not that of the *Voortrekkers* but of the non-Europeans. While the majority of them may be unaware of the forces which move them in the direction of the towns and the money-wage economy, there are a growing number for whom this movement of the non-Europeans is becoming a conscious and purposeful search for land and freedom, as were the other great treks. More and more it tends to assume a political, and also a moral, character, for the issues are seen to be both moral and political issues. Probably they are the issues of life and death for the non-European peoples in the country, for the process of physical and social disintegration cannot proceed much further without endangering the whole life and integrity of the race. At least that would apply to the African and Indian people; and there is some indication of this growing awareness in their joint decision to take a political stand in the boycott of the meagre and indirect political representation which has been offered them, and in their demand for the repeal of the Land Act and the Asiatic Land Tenure and Indian Representation Act. The coloured people (in South Africa coloured means those of mixed race) are sharply divided between those who would cultivate friendship with the whites and those who see their future in collaboration with the blacks.

On the whole, then, there are signs of growing resistance on the part of the non-Europeans. In the opinion of the writer these may well prove to be the most hopeful signs there are at present for all the communities. Though inevitably a hard struggle lies ahead, the fact remains that the future of the Union and indeed of the whole continent is bound up with the future of the African.

To South Africa, first among the Western nations, has come the opportunity of showing whether Western or "Christian" civilization can or cannot make provision for the economic development and social and political emancipation of non-white peoples. Her statesmen have not as yet proved equal to (nor perhaps even aware of) the magnitude of the task confronting her. She has vast resources of land, mineral wealth, human energy, and a rich variety of human cultures. She has yet to evolve a plan of national development which will accord with some harmonious pattern of life and discoverable creative purpose for the respective races.

After I had visited Bethal and written the memorandum which I have been quoting, I went to see the editor of the *Rand Daily Mail* and discussed what could possibly be done to bring the matter to the attention of the public and to secure some remedial action. I told him that I had been considering whether the matter ought not to be raised in the overseas press, since we were unable to get any effective action from the government. After a good deal of discussion, and after he had made some investigations through his own staff, he decided to publish my memorandum. An added incentive had been a letter from an irate farmer who complained about my inquiries in Bethal.

The memorandum was followed up by an editorial in the *Rand Daily Mail* of June 28th, 1947, which said:

BETHAL'S BLACK SPOT

The rule of law in some parts of the Union has been impaired of late. In Tobruk native township, a private army ruled by the bludgeon; and in the Bethal district, the rule of the sjambok has apparently been in vogue for years.

Yet, in spite of the fact that conditions at Bethal ought to have been known, there has been no sign, so far, of any vigorous effort to restore order there. In May, 1944, a Judge publicly drew attention to the system which made it possible for labourers to be beaten to death for trying to escape from their employers. In October of that year the Diocesan Synod of the Anglican Church submitted to the Native Affairs Department a full report of what was going on. But neither the Judge's strictures nor the Synod's disclosures has had the slightest effect in galvanizing any-one into action—unless it was the wielders of the sjamboks, who bela-boured their unfortunate victims still more.

The courts, it is true, have to some extent intervened. There was a con-viction recently: the magistrate strongly condemned the practices: and the prosecutor declared that he would prosecute the guilty with all his power. That is very well of course: but it has to be remembered that, when one is up against near-slavery, the court's power is likely to be ex-ercised only on rare occasions. Its protection is denied (by the slave-drivers themselves) to the victims. Almost the only way a complainant can get to the magistrate is by escaping from his captors. And if he tries to escape he knows well enough that he runs the risk of a further flog-ging, which may quite conceivably end in death. That sort of thing has happened in Bethal before. . . .

There was an immediate and prolonged uproar in the Union press, both English and Afrikaaner. There were demands for withdrawal of the allegations or my immediate deportation. There was a demand that Gen-eral Smuts and the Minister of Justice should attend a mass meeting of all the farmers of the district at which I should be present. I received a stiffly worded letter in Afrikaans and simultaneously a telegram from the secretary of the *Boere-Arbeidsvereniging,* asking me to attend a meeting on a certain date to explain my conduct.

I replied that I should be very happy to accept their invitation and spent a good deal of time in preparing an address in which I hoped to point out that we were reaching a turning point in our history; that we in South Africa were called upon to play an increasingly important role in the future of the African continent; and that if we were not to find ourselves an isolated backwater we must begin moving with the times and even take the lead in the matter of native policy and administration.

"We are here to try and face facts," I had written in my prepared statement, "not to spend our time in recriminations." I had a fond hope of introducing a certain amount of reason into the proceedings, though I was warned that there would probably be violence and that the farmers were determined to get even with me.

A journalist told me that the wildest threats were being uttered by some of them, and many said it would serve little purpose to go, as the farmers were in no mood to listen to reason. The police questioned me about my intentions and I received a mysterious note, which I decided to ignore, asking me to go to the native location before the meeting began, on a matter of life and death.

On the day appointed for the meeting I was offered a lift by some friendly journalists in their car. We had to start very early in the morning from Johannesburg. It was winter and extremely cold at an altitude of six thousand feet. And we were all a little nervous about the outcome.

I was well armed with facts and figures, and evidence to substantiate what I had said in my memorandum, and was proposing to say. Both the editor of the *Rand Daily Mail* and I had refused to withdraw any allegations. I had, as a matter of fact, interviewed a Nyasaland government official who had been dealing with the complaints of natives from his territory about their treatment at Bethal and other districts in the Eastern Transvaal. I asked him whether he thought my statements were exaggerated or needed any correction. He advised (unofficially of course) that nothing should be withdrawn and he showed me some of the letters with which he had to deal.

He said that his government had been trying to deal administratively with this flood of complaints of cruelty for a good many years and it had become so serious that they were advising their people not to allow themselves to be recruited, but the draw of the higher wages in South Africa was almost irresistible to these Africans.

I was also told that there had been a succession of magistrates at Bethal who had tried to clean up this scandal. But as soon as they tried they became unpopular, and pressure was brought to bear on Pretoria to have them withdrawn. The present magistrate, whose statements I quoted in my memorandum, was himself posted elsewhere very quickly. The Transvaal farming district is a vitally important political factor for any governing party. Nevertheless, the Minister of Justice had bowed to the storm of protest, and hundreds of police had been drafted into the area and had been making inquiries, on the basis of which a number of prosecutions for ill-treatment were carried out and convictions secured, though usually the convictions were against the foremen rather than the farmers themselves.

When we approached Bethal it was obvious that the meeting was being looked forward to with a good deal of excitement, not only by Bethal itself. Farmers had been trekking in from the surrounding countryside in their speedy little covered carts with pneumatic tyres, and the streets were thronged with cars and police.

The journalists thought it would probably be wiser if I were not seen arriving with them. So I got down from the car and walked into Bethal on foot, dressed in my old khaki overcoat. After a cup of tea at a local café I went towards the town hall, which was thronged with people. Loudspeakers were being erected outside for the benefit of an overflow meeting. The hall was crammed full, and already on the platform was the secretary of the *Boere-Arbeidsvereniging,* a representative of the Native Affairs Department, the native commissioner, and the chief of police.

The opening speech of the chairman, explaining the purpose of the meeting, was listened to with great attention, and (to my shame) not being able to speak Afrikaans, this was interpreted to me after some caustic queries as to whether it shouldn't be translated for me into the "Kaffir" language.

In due course I was called upon to speak. I began by thanking them for the courtesy of being allowed to come and state my case and proceeded with the oration I had prepared, but I had hardly got beyond the first few sentences when the shouting and stamping began. A few journalists at the press table were able to catch something of what I said for a short time, and I had taken the precaution of giving them a copy of what I proposed to say.

I kept resuming my seat, the chairman would appeal for order, and then I would begin again. They had not come to hear a sermon. "Keep that for the pulpit." "What about the 'slavery'?" I said it was their own magistrate who had first talked of near-slavery conditions. I went on to refer to the specifications of the ministry of agriculture for housing cattle and was proposing to describe exactly what I had seen. But the booing and shouting made it impossible to continue and other speakers were called for.

As reported by the *Rand Daily Mail,* the secretary of the *Boere-Arbeidsvereniging* said:

Native recruits for farm labour were obtained in a lawful way by the Organization, and at great cost to the farmers. Many of the natives, when they came to the organization, were almost dead from hunger. They often arrived without even a blanket to cover themselves. . . .

The root of the trouble was that the natives did not want to work on the farms, but merely used the farmers as "stepping stones" to get to the cities. Desertions by native labourers were one of the most serious problems with which the farmers had to contend. . . .

One of the farmers in the audience gave an address, saying: "As a result of the police invasion, farming on the Highveld had virtually ceased during the past few weeks. Two European farmers had been arrested and thrown in gaol as the result of statements made by Kaffirs. Bail had been refused them although some outside farmers had volunteered to stand security for them up to £5,000. They had also had their fingerprints taken, 'like Kaffirs,' and had been subjected to other indignities."

As far as I was concerned the meeting concluded after an Afrikaans woman rose from the audience and insisted that Afrikaner motherhood had been insulted. She was the mother of three sons and strongly resented the insults against her nation. A demand went up from the audience that I should be made to stand while she was standing. The atmosphere was very tense by this time, and the chairman and chief of police were looking very worried and signalled to me to stand. I complied, but said nothing. She resumed her seat. I resumed mine. She rose again, and so did I. There was a shout and I resumed my seat, wondering how long this ludicrous farce could possibly go on. When she had finished some said I should reply, and I rose to do so. But the uproar began again.

It was at this point that the police chief sent one of his men to tell me that I should immediately follow him out of the stage door entrance. I realized that there would probably be a riot if I remained. So I complied. Outside there was a high-powered car with two armed police and a driver.

And before any of the people outside could realize what was happening, the car had accelerated and driven off.

I was taken to the police station and kept there for many hours. I never knew how the meeting had wound up, but was told that a large crowd of Africans had assembled and listened to the proceedings coming over the loudspeaker and had wanted to send a deputation to thank me afterwards. Later they came to Johannesburg, as they had not been allowed to see me, and made their statement to the press instead. There was no doubt that there were people in the audience and in Bethal itself who were sympathetic, but it would not have been a good moment to declare it. In any case, not all the farmers of Bethal are as primitive in their methods and behaviour.

Some time later, at a mass meeting of farmers in the Bethal town hall, the Minister of Justice stated that the Bethal farmers were vindicated. He further explained, according to the report of the *Rand Daily Mail,* that: "Official acts had resulted because of statements made by a former magistrate of Bethal in a court case, and subsequent official reports about farm labour conditions in the district. The allegations by Mr. Scott, whom the farmers appeared to regard as a 'gogga' and a 'spook,' had definitely not been the reason for the police investigation."

That was in 1947. In 1948 complaints were still being received. One from a Nyasaland labourer to the British Government read:

The containts of this dirty letter is a complaint to you. . . . I had come to this place due to the sicking of better employment and I think about in March you received a letter from me applying for work. And that the reply had found me ready for work in S.A. But when I came to the Vaal River they conscripted me therefore came to this place near Bethal.

What I am going to say furthermore is that the system of work at this place is doing too much damage to Africans by making work hard and the most bad thing is that he is too much beating and ration scale is almost that of pigs. The housing is very nasty too where we get packed about fifty in a room with the guard standing at the door. We therefore have no choice of standing out allow but with a sentry standing behind which means to say that we purely taken to captivity for six month. Boys and men have gone out from here while having very heavy scars over their bodies and our ears are now rather deaf wipping is made the daily food.

*We always blead blood. Could our mother Government think over this
please. I am not able to escape but could you please set your people free
from such troubles. The work would be very easy if such would not be
trouble. I am not able to say any further but claim for a freedom from
you the mother Government.*

Yours humbly—

This letter, amongst others, was forwarded by the Nyasaland government representative to whom it was addressed, to the director of native
labour, under a covering letter which mentioned that the writer of the letter "is known to me and applied for employment in this office in March
this year. . . . He served with the King's African Rifles for three and a
half years and subsequently with the labour department in . . . and came
to the Union with the intention of continuing his education with the
Union College. . . .

"I shall be grateful if you will cause an inquiry to be made. . . . I may
add here that despite the public interest which was aroused last year by
disclosures in the press of conditions on certain farms in the Bethal area
and the investigations that resulted with a view to improving these conditions, I still frequently receive complaints of ill-treatment and withhold-
ing of wages from Northern territory Africans employed on the farms in
this part of the Transvaal. Unfortunately due to a natural fear of reprisals
the complainants hardly ever have the courage to sign their names and
as a result it is difficult to take any steps to help them. . . ."

A few months later I wrote to the Minister of Justice, stating that the
abuses in Bethal were still continuing and quoting cases of recruitment
and forced contracts. I concluded:

*It seems as though nothing short of legislation empowering Native Com-
missioners not only to inspect labour conditions, but to withhold labour
from those farmers who refuse to conform to a minimum standard of
decency and humanity, will achieve any lasting results. Such legislation
has been introduced to deal with the problem in other territories in Africa.
Is it not time that the action taken by the Department of Justice a year ago
in the Bethal District was followed up with legislation designed to protect
Native labour from such brutal treatment and inhuman conditions of
living?*

This letter was forwarded by the minister of justice to the minister of native affairs from whom I subsequently had an acknowledgement, with the assurance that an officer had been detailed to carry out investigations in the Bethal district and that his report was awaited. No further reply was ever received.

Perhaps those farmers who complained that desertions by native labourers was one of their most serious problems would find a solution if they experimented along the lines of this farmer, whose letter was published in the *Rand Daily Mail:*

For years South African farmers have complained of "labour shortage." Yet this need not be a problem.

Ten years ago I decided to try an experiment which represents a radical departure from the customary method of employing native labour. I gave my native employees an interest in my farming operations and let them share in the responsibility of running the farm.

The three most obvious needs of farm labourers are suitable housing, sufficient food and reasonable wages. But even if these are satisfactory to the worker, there is no guarantee that he will be completely satisfied by them.

Enthusiasm for the work must also be instilled into them. Thus to create a sense of pride in their work, one must add an incentive. The incentive I have chosen is a bonus system, and a share for the employees in the running of the farm.

For each native family I have erected a well-constructed four-roomed cottage. The children attend school on a neighbouring farm and are to a great extent assisted with free books.

The monthly cash wages of employees range from 14s. to £2, the amount depending on the ability of the worker, the responsibility he bears, and his length of service. For every native who has more than a year's service with me, I also pay the poll tax. . . .

The writer then proceeded to detail the system of feeding and allocating bonuses and concludes:

To provide for the sharing of responsibility I have conceded the right of engaging and dismissing members of the staff. This is done by the staff as a whole. I simply retain the right of veto. The workers are keen on their work and will not tolerate any laziness. If one of their number is not pulling his weight, a meeting is called and the worker in question is warned: should this have no effect he can be sure of being out-voted at the next meeting, resulting in his dismissal by me.

The reward this policy has brought me is a satisfied staff and keenness in work. I have had practically no labour trouble since this scheme was inaugurated. Not only has the scheme proved a financial success, but it has also made my farming a great pleasure.

Printed alongside this letter was another:

. . . I have spent my whole life working with natives in factories, mines and on the farms. . . . The native mind cannot understand kindness. Since time immemorial he has been treated with blood-thirsty brutality by his chiefs and headmen; that is the reason why he regards kindness as a sign of weakness and fear. If you show consideration for the welfare of a native, he immediately becomes insolent and demands more.

Let us face the truth. In the past we have been too liberal in our treatment of the natives, and we are paying for it today in the wave of crime, robbery and assaults. To speak of better wages and housing is nonsense. All the wages and housing schemes will not change the native. He will remain dirty, lazy and thoroughly dishonest. He does not understand decent civilized treatment, but can, and does, understand a good hiding. If we want the natives to be law-abiding, let us speak to them in the language they understand; the language of the sjambok, administered frequently and with vigour. . . .

The language of the *sjambok* is still being spoken at Bethal, though the people of the Bethal district are not the only ones concerned. The *Rand Daily Mail* editorial on November 18th, 1949, said:

They seem to take irrigation very seriously in the Zeerust district. In a case that came before the Circuit Court there on Wednesday three men were found guilty of assaulting an elderly Native who later was taken to hospital and died under an anaesthetic. It was shown that one of the accused became annoyed with the Native because he had not done his job of watering properly. It was therefore decided to punish him.

Apparently the employer was unable to carry out this punishment single-handed; so he called in his son and his son-in-law. What they did to the Native is not fully revealed by the report of the proceedings, but counsel for the defence explained on behalf of one of them that, though he struck the Native with his fist, he had not intended to injure him as much as he did. Be that as it may, the punishment certainly taught this idle labourer a lesson and he will neglect no further watering jobs, for he is dead.

The student of proceedings in our courts will find nothing unusual in this story of the chastisement of a Native employee that was carried too far. The evidence and the verdict are familiar enough. But the sentences surprise us. Having found these men guilty of assault, the Court imposed fines of £15, £30 and £7 10s. 0d. Teaching a Native not to neglect a watering job cost them £52 10s. 0d., but it cost the Native his life, for it is a reasonable supposition that, had it not been thought necessary to punish him, he would not have had to go to hospital and would not have died under an anaesthetic.

These fines compare curiously with a fine of £125 which was recently imposed on two Natives in Pretoria because they had failed to mark the retail selling price on goods they had displayed for sale. In the case of the man who was fined £15, it was pleaded, in mitigation, that he was "elderly." Alas, it is a trifle late now to point out that the Native, too, was elderly.

The cry for more farm labour continues, and the government, in seeking to supply the need, aroused the following comments from the *Rand Daily Mail* on September 2nd, 1949:

WHY NOT PUT THEM ALL IN GAOL?

Two bright ideas for providing the farmer with labour have come to our attention within the past few days.

One is the building of a new gaol at Leslie. This edifice is to be opened today by the Minister of Justice, Mr. Swart, and by the Director of Prisons: and its purpose, as plainly set forth in a statement by the company which built it, is "to supply the local farmers with labour." Not, the reader may note, to punish the criminal: still less to reform him and make him a useful member of society: the object is frankly economic rather than judicial.

Only one difficulty occurs in this connection. Suppose that, by some chance, a serious decrease in crime were to take place. In that event there might not be sufficient prisoners to fill the gaol, the farmers would once again be faced with a shortage of labour, and the new gaol would become something of a white elephant.

We trust that this aspect of the matter has not been overlooked, for once crime and labour become so closely correlated, it will be important to see that a plentiful supply of criminals is always available. Happily, there is no need for apprehension on this score at the moment, since many of our laws are well calculated to make criminals: but it will be obvious that any falling-off in crime would have to be viewed with the gravest disquiet.

Since then several other private gaols have been built for this purpose.

There is no end to the story. In March 1952 the South African magazine *Drum* published an eight-page article about its own investigations into the situation in Bethal. This revealed that the same conditions still prevailed as those reported above. In the wordy warfare which followed, *Die Transvaaler,* controlled by Mr. Strijdom, now prime minister, said, "The article is written to stir up trouble and cause ill feeling." The *Rand Daily Mail,* in an editorial, replied, "We are satisfied that what the magazine *Drum* has said about labour conditions in the Bethal area is substantially correct. The Minister of Native Affairs eventually appointed a small committee to inquire but its report was never published. The Institute of Race Relations which conducted an inquiry on its own initiative reported that 'in twenty per cent of the cases they examined labourers had suffered ill-treatment, sometimes serious.' Enough evidence they considered, had been found to justify an official inquiry."

Writing in 1956, Mr. Anthony Sampson in his book about the magazine *Drum* concluded, "But the root of the trouble, the contract system, remained: and with it remained the abuses. In the next year, the usual court cases came up in Bethal. Two labourers were hung handcuffed from the ceiling as punishment; kicking, flogging and chaining continued without much change."

"There'll always be a Bethal," a veteran South African journalist said. "It's a hardy annual—good for a story once a year." And every year since then there has been some fresh revelation of the ill treatment of African farm labourers in this or some neighbouring district in the Transvaal.

12　Black Magic

One night in Johannesburg after the Tobruk affair I received a mysterious message from a small village in Basutoland. It was scrawled in pencil on a grubby piece of paper, and it enclosed some dirtier looking sheets which were covered with very small writing in Sesuto. In South Africa anyone who makes the smallest gesture of sympathy for the oppressed is almost inundated with appeals or petitions for help in the righting of some wrong. This is one of the most distressing features of South African life for anyone who attempts to live a life consistent with Christian beliefs or liberal principles. I thought this letter which had come to me by hand perhaps would turn out to be an appeal for money, until its bearer told me he had been asked to wait until he knew whether I would come with him or not.

Then I found that he was expecting me to go with him to his village, eight thousand feet up in the mountains of Basutoland, five hundred miles away. I told him that of course it was quite impossible, as I had no car. He said his friends were in great danger and if one of my white friends would lend us a car it might be possible to save them.

It concerned a little political organization known as the *Lekhotla la Bafo*—or Assembly of the People—whose executive members had all been arrested. The sheets of paper covered with minute handwriting had been smuggled out of the gaol at a place called Teyateyaneng.

I was very busy trying to prepare documents on the South West African case for the next U.N. Assembly session and was also feeling exhausted after several months in the Tobruk shantytown. The demands on one's limited spiritual resources were seemingly unlimited, and I felt exasperated by this man who stood humbly twirling his ragged cap and suggesting what I could do and could not do.

There was never any time to do anything properly. The South West African case, which I will write about later, was extremely intricate. One had only to make one major mistake in one's facts or figures, in their presentation, or in the diplomatic finesse which was required to secure the support of those who knew and cared little about these remote African tribesmen, for their cause to be lost in a world racked by many more pressing questions.

"My friend, your people must learn to stand on their own legs," I said. But I knew the flaw in this half-truth before I had finished saying it. Sometimes I felt like just going away and leaving all this misery and confusion. Perhaps the only way to cure it would be by devoting oneself wholly to prayer and meditation. It was like trying to stop the leaks in a boat which was old and worn out. One wore oneself out trying to do all the impossible things that were required. It was all very well for the Good Samaritan, but what if the whole road was littered with victims of a decaying social order?

However, the native's soft-spoken answers to my cowardly jibe against his people's helplessness inevitably made me relent. An offer of a car followed an account of the matter I gave to a European friend. We packed up food and blankets, for it was winter, and set off along the straight roads of the *platteland* and into the Orange Free State, travelling by night and day till the Amaluti mountains poked jaggedly through the mists.

I thought over his description of the contents of the letter he had brought me, which I later had translated in full. It alleged that many people were being arrested for murder and that they were being ill-treated and bribed to bear false witness against each other. There followed some details which read:

ON THE MURDER OF MOCHESELA AT CHIEF BOSHOANE'S PLACE
WHOSE BODY WAS DISCOVERED ON THE 21ST JUNE 1948

This murder was not investigated satisfactorily. Mass arrests were made and they were told that they had murdered the man. This statement was made through Justinus Ratsiu of Mapoteng, who at the time this man was murdered was in jail at Teyateyaneng and how would he know how this man was murdered? Immediately after Justinus wrote the names and gave the list to the police sergeant then he ordered the police to arrest the people on the list.

Justinus advised the police sergeant to get Mashapa to make that false statement which he had made so that the others on the list could be implicated. The results of these arrests were:

1. Raletsukana Posholi was put under torture for 54 days after he had declined the offer by the Police Corporal Michael of £20 if he would state that the deceased Mochesela was killed by the order of Chieftainess Mamakhabane.

2. Mashapha Pokonyane was offered £80 plus an income of £3 per month by the police officer if he would state that Chieftainess Mamakhabane ordered that the deceased should be murdered. When he refused to make the false statement he was taken to the house where they are tortured where he was kept for over two months of sufferings.

3. Steyn Sebajoa was also tortured for over a month after he had declined the offer to implicate Chieftainess Mamakhabane falsely.

4. Mosala Kolotsane was forced for a month and three days to implicate Chieftainess Mamakhabane and was threatened that he would otherwise be killed.

After an account of Chief Gabashane's arrest, the letter continued:

Are we still protected? It has come to that stage where it seems that the Government is no more protecting us but killing us. It seems that the Government is trying means of taking Basutoland solely for itself in the near future. At present there is one fear which is prevalent among the chiefs, the witch doctors and the people together with the Lekhotla la Bafo alike. As I write this Kelebone Rametse is in jail where he is being tortured to say that he and the members of the Lekhotla la Bafo went to burn Roma College. . . .

There is the truth that Ritual Murders are existent in Basutoland, but instead of investigating the matter and catching the culprits it has become the reason for implicating innocent people.

On the way my companion told me something of the life of his people and their fears of being incorporated in the Union of South Africa. He told me about the ritual murders mentioned in the letter. The senior Christian chiefs of Basutoland had been arrested and were in gaol in

Maseru. This had given rise to a great deal of suspicion on the part of his people that the British Government was preparing to appease South Africa by acquiescing in her demand for the incorporation of the three British Protectorates, Basutoland, Swaziland, and Bechuanaland. One of these chiefs, Gabashane, in particular had been to the forefront in opposing a plan to hand over a strip of tribal territory to the government for the purpose of building a road or railway to link up with those of the Union.

In the capital, Maseru, the atmosphere was heavy with suspicion and fear. The officials and their wives could think of little else but the ritual murders that were alleged to be taking place. I spoke to a great many people, both black and white, and there was hardly a single point on which there was not violent difference of opinion.

Below I give a description taken from court records. The leading accused was a Roman Catholic chieftainess and the story, if the allegations were true, forms a terrible commentary on a hundred years of Christian missionary effort in that territory.

The ritual happened one night following a marriage feast in the village. At a pre-arranged place on the mountain slopes outside the village, the participants were assembling. They had been summoned, so the accusations read, by the chieftainess and her witch doctor, the purpose being to secure power for her son who was due to be "placed" in office as a tribal chief. While the marriage feast was in progress a messenger went from one to another of the participants informing them of the place appointed and that they were expected to be there as soon as the moon rose over the horizon.

The appeal quoted the case for the prosecution, as outlined by the attorney general of Basutoland. After describing the alleged movements concerning some nineteen men, it ran on:

They went a distance to a place about 335 paces from the village, m'lord, where, as always happens in these ritual murders, the Accused proceeded to cut up the deceased while he was still alive. The evidence will be from eye-witness accomplices that Nos. 5, 3, 7, 6 and 2 in that order cut pieces of flesh from various parts of the body, calf, groin, breast, the biceps and finally the whole of the skin from the face, and the pieces which were cut were placed before No. 4 Accused on a white cloth. The blood, once again as is usual in these cases of ritual murder, was collected by No. 8 Accused in a receptacle which is described as a "billy can" and finally the tongue, the eyes, and the throat were cut, and only at that stage apparently did the deceased finally end his sufferings and die.

The visibility, m'lord, for what was going on was provided by a lighted lamp which was brought to the scene of the alleged murder by one of the accused. The deceased, having thus been very thoroughly done to death, m'lord, No. 1 (the accused Chieftainess) thanked the party and warned them that they must make no report to the authorities. The flesh which had been taken from the deceased was taken away, a portion of it by No. 3 Accused and the remainder by No. 4. . . .

Such is the general pattern of the ritual murders for which during the past few years some one hundred forty persons have been tried and forty hanged, including three of the senior Catholic chiefs.

Many Basuto refuse to believe that these ritual murders have been as prevalent as has been charged. When I visited them in gaol some, including the accused, alleged that the cases had been framed against them by the police, and the bodies of those who have been assaulted and robbed "planted" on their land. Many of the co-accused whom I interviewed alleged that they had been ill-treated in gaol to force them to give evidence as accomplices and so to save themselves the extreme penalty.

The chieftainess in this particular case, whom I questioned in Maseru gaol during the course of her trial, had a rosary in her lap, and when I said that I hoped the whole truth would be told in court and that justice would be done, she replied enigmatically, "How will it help us to tell the truth in that court? Only if God helps us shall we have justice."

It proved extremely difficult to arrive at any coherent account of the true meaning of these ritual murders. There were heated contradictions, not only about matters of fact, but of their sociological significance. There were differences both amongst the white missionaries and traders who had lived long in the country and amongst the Basuto themselves. One African clergyman, an Anglican priest, well spoken of by the white missionaries, said that in his district there was no such fear and never had been in his memory. He thought the truth of the allegations was extremely unlikely, especially since the evidence was almost always only that of accomplices—"Some of the chiefs have many enemies," he hinted, but would commit himself no further.

If the accounts as given in court are to be believed, it would appear that this form of black magic has gone through a complete cycle. In the most primitive form anthropologists know, the victim was chosen from the tribe—as was the custom amongst the South American Indians—was often a member of the chief's own family, and always chosen with the consent of the whole tribe, and even with the consent of the victim. When the chief needed greater power, for whatever purpose, he sought it by this tribal ritual. When the social conscience began to assert itself in a rudimentary way the victim was taken from another tribe. At an even later stage prisoners of war were used, and then only dead bodies. When murder became contrary to the white man's law the medicine men used parts of animals, lizards, cocks and hens, cats and dogs, and these can still be found on sale in stores and little herbalists' shops in the streets of Johannesburg. It was not in that sense "black" but rather "white" magic, a means of obtaining power over the tribe's or the chief's enemies.

I questioned a young educated Basuto, who had attended the School of Oriental Studies at London University, on some of these points. His comments on their religious and social significance are worth quoting as illustrating the application of the mind of an educated African to this grave problem, which goes deep down to the primitive African consciousness and the roots of Bantu religion and culture:

Although many Basuto hold the view that ritual murder is a practice which was introduced into Basutoland by the amaHlubi and amaNgwane who fled to Basutoland at the time of the Lifaqane wars, it would be difficult to prove that it is not a Sotho practice today. If this could be proved, a certain amount of good might result, namely that the people would not be inclined to cling tenaciously to what was proved to be a foreign custom. But I hardly think that much can be gained in this way.

Superstition is the root problem to be tackled. Until the belief in charms and in the power of the witch doctor to exercise them is removed, there will continue to be such barbaric practices. The medicine horn is only one of the means by which people try to guard and strengthen themselves, their homes, stock, and position against calamity. If ill-luck assails them they believe that it is due to stronger charms than their own, and the only remedy they think of is to get even stronger charms and to employ greater witch doctors. But even if there are no calamities there is always the need to better oneself, to improve one's position and fortune, and this they believe can be done by means of charms: charms to gain favour

with one's employers, to give one prosperity in business, to give one the
luck of finding diamonds on the mines (and the bonuses that go with such
a find). . . .

The witch doctors are all exploiting superstitious belief and their chief
weapon in doing so is mystery. Even the innocent herbalist prefers to dig
his roots at night and to cloud all he does with mystery.

Human flesh is still believed to be the most mysterious, and conse-
quently the most potent, of all ingredients in a medicine. . . .

He said that there was little doubt that recently there had been an unusually large number of cases of this type of murder, and that people were
increasingly nervous about being out late, answering remote calls, and so
on. He insisted that the majority of people took no part in such things
and were very uneasy about the state of affairs in the country.

He urged again the need to eradicate superstition and encourage the
education and social development of the people as a whole. In this connection my informant had some disquieting comments to make on the
way that Christian institutions can be misinterpreted. And he quoted an
instance of a priest blessing seed corn, with the comment: "When it is
considered that the witch doctor's methods are very similar in form to
these, it will be appreciated that there is the possibility of misunderstanding arising about the purpose and function of ritual in the Christian
sense."

Before going on to see the people who had sent for me, in their faraway village, I also interviewed a number of the accused in the case concerning Chief Gabashane, as well as Gabashane himself who vigorously
denied any complicity in the ritual murders. He was a young man, spoke
English, and was a graduate of Fort Hare University. I subsequently received a letter from a retired bishop of the Anglican Church who had
known him as a student, saying that he was prepared to vouch for
Gabashane's character as a young man, and inquiring whether a petition
for his reprieve could not be organized.

The following are samples of the statements I took down from some
of his co-accused:

It was suggested to me that I should say that the chief offered me
money to kill the deceased. For four and a half months the police ham-
mered this into me. By hammering I mean that repeated suggestions were
made. I was also told that if I accepted this suggestion I should not be

charged with murder. My feet suffered from the cold which was in the cell. I had only one blanket.

I was also mentally tortured by being told that the chief had confiscated my lands and my cattle and on another occasion I was told that two of my cattle had been killed and that the police were going over to my place to have a nice time there and to eat up all the meat. On another occasion I was told that my wife had been assaulted with sticks and had many injuries and was in hospital but that I could not go and see her there.

The wife of one of them made the following statement:

I went to see my husband on Monday. . . . I asked him how it was that he said the things he had said in the court about the chief and he said that he found himself compelled to make the statements he had made in the court on account of the treatment he had received at Teyateyaneng and that he had been guilty of cowardice. I tried to find out if the statements he had made in the court were true or whether these statements had been suggested to him. He was very vague in his reply and kept mumbling about his brother being in trouble. He then went on to tell me that he felt quite certain that he would die quite soon and he asked me to bring the child to him so that he might see him before he died.

It was on account of the extreme difficulty of establishing the truth about these allegations and counter-allegations that I wrote then to the secretary of the government and the resident commissioner of Basutoland, appealing for a judicial inquiry to be set up. No such judicial inquiry was appointed, however. There was then no court of criminal appeal in Basutoland, and appeals can only be made to the Privy Council on narrow legal grounds, or if it can be proved that the very foundations of natural justice have been violated.

However, the purpose of my visit to Basutoland had not been in connection with these ritual murders but with certain accusations levelled against the *Lekhotla la Bafo.* After their arrest the executive committee members of this organization had been kept in gaol on a charge of murder and arson. My companion who had come to Johannesburg was a relative of one of the accused. Amongst the accused there was also an Indian, the son of a storekeeper who had taken part in the passive resistance movement in Natal. It was alleged that he had loaned his motor lorry for the purpose of helping in a plot to burn down a Catholic mission school.

There was nothing to be discovered about these accusations in Maseru so we were obliged to take a very rough track into the mountains to the village in which this organization had its headquarters.

Here in a little mud hut, in an atmosphere of extreme nervousness and apprehension, I was told the version of the affair which the relatives of the accused appeared to believe. They maintained that the organization was very unpopular with the police, who were for the most part South Africans, on account of its determination to oppose any move by South Africa to incorporate the territory into the Union.

The present case was being framed against them, they maintained, in order to cripple their organization and discredit them in the eyes of the Basuto people. In the fire which had destroyed one of the dormitories of the Roma Mission College four African children perished, and the mere accusation that the *Lekhotla la Bafo* was responsible brought upon them the odium of the whole population.

It seemed that one of their executive members had been arrested and had turned King's evidence against his fellow members. This crown witness, after his arrest, had been kept in gaol at Teyateyaneng for many weeks, at the end of which he had made a statement incriminating the other members of his executive. He then escaped, or had been allowed to go free, and found his way to their village, where he warned his fellows that he had been tortured in the gaol and had been forced to make a statement incriminating them. The police, so they alleged, on hearing that he had warned them and made a statement about his ill-treatment, rearrested him, and after he had been in their custody again he renounced his second statement and adhered to his first.

The stories contained a good many unlikely elements. The brother of the accused Indian, whom I questioned, claimed that he could prove that his motor lorry was out of commission at the time and unusable. The relatives of the executive committee members maintained that even if their organization had decided to resort to such methods as the burning down of missions, it was preposterous to imagine that they would have chosen one of the children's hostels, in which their own African children were sleeping, rather than one of the other buildings.

The Roman Catholic fathers whom I visited at Roma said the fire had started on the second storey and they had entertained no suspicions that it had been caused by anything more than a short circuit, until many weeks afterwards when the police began to investigate, following some talk overheard by one of them at a beer drink. The arrests had resulted in a good deal of local hostility towards the fathers on account of the charges of murder and arson by Africans against their own children, though elsewhere the hostility tended to be directed either towards the police or towards the *Lekhotla la Bafo,* according to the predilections of various sections of opinion.

Meanwhile the executive committee members were being kept in gaol without trial at Maseru. They made no complaints against their treatment in that gaol when I visited them there, unlike the accused in the ritual murder trials whose complaints I have already quoted. I might add that these complaints were made to me in the presence of an African warder, and where necessary by his interpretation. Only the interview with the two Catholic chiefs, Gabashane and Bereng, took place out of earshot of any prison authority.

The stories which I had taken down sounded in part improbable; but I was not confident that they were any more outlandish than the events which were alleged to be happening in Basutoland at the instigation of the chiefs and others who were leading the opposition to incorporation into South Africa, and who were now accused of these dastardly crimes.

I visited the paramount chieftainess, who had read the Basuto welcome to King George at the Pitso in Maseru. She was very nervous and told me that suspicions were now being directed against herself of charges of ritual murder. The police were spying on her and, although she was the chief constable of Basutoland in name, she was not consulted about what they were doing. She gave me a copy of a petition that she had addressed to the resident commissioner, asking for an inquiry.

It seemed to me that the whole affair was altogether beyond me. All I could do was to comply with the request of the *Lekhotla la Bafo* to try and secure the services of a lawyer to defend them. Accordingly I took one of their number with me and, driving all night, reached Johannesburg in the small hours of the morning. He had no pass and seemed afraid of being out of my sight. After some hot porridge and a bath I took him to His Majesty's building where the lawyers' offices are, and there he negotiated with a young K.C. to defend them. That evening we began the 275-mile journey back to Maseru.

In the morning the attorney called at the gaol and asked permission to see Josiel Lefela and the other members of the *Lekhotla la Bafo*. He was given permission by the chief warder, who seemed obliging enough. Within a few days all the accused were released from the gaol and told to return to their homes and a charge was laid against the prospective Crown witness. As finally reported in the Johannesburg *Star* of January 21st, 1949, Harold Velaphe "was convicted of arson and sentenced to four years' imprisonment with hard labour."

This case gave me many qualms, as I felt convinced that if the attorney from Johannesburg had not appeared on the scene the accusations would not have been so quickly withdrawn. Also I had been handed a confidential circular from government sources, showing great concern about the prevalence of perjury. Two years later, a Basuto association wrote to the high commissioner quoting a number of cases where perjury was proved in court, and asking for better police investigation.

Having made a request through the government secretary, I cabled to the Commonwealth Relations Office, asking that a full inquiry should be instituted.

When I later arrived in England I took the matter up again with the Commonwealth Relations Office and managed to secure two firms of solicitors to represent *in causa pauperis* some of those accused of ritual murders who were unable to afford to employ counsel.

I well remember that it was Christmas Eve when I had managed to get all the documents copied. I went from St. Edward's House, Westminster, where I was staying with the Cowley fathers, to Downing Street with a covering letter addressed to Mr. Noel-Baker. On the way I went into the Abbey. People were kneeling round a crib, and an old lady knelt by the grave of the Unknown Warrior—"For the sacred Cause of Justice and the Freedom of the World." Suddenly the air vibrated with the clanging of the bells proclaiming the unspeakable joy of the birth of the King of Peace.

The African tragedy being enacted in Basutoland seemed almost unbearable on that Christmas Eve—not knowing where the truth lay in all the conflicting allegations by chiefs and people and government. The ritual murders, some believed, were a terrible perversion of the most sacred mystery in our holy religion, the sacrament of the Body and Blood of Christ. Even some Protestant Christians whose advice I had sought had suggested it was an inevitable consequence of teaching "medieval notions" to Africans.

Out in the drizzling mist of Parliament Square the bells sounded less clamorous, and I sheltered in a doorway to read over once more my letter to Mr. Noel-Baker before handing it in, with the fantastic and incredible story which the accompanying documents told of suspicion and hatred and loss of faith. I repeated our request for a commission of inquiry and urged:

This matter seems to be one of some urgency now since there are more than a score, perhaps several score of persons who have been sentenced or are awaiting trial on the charge of ritual murder and because of the far-reaching implications—spiritual as well as social and political implications—which must be faced by the Administration and others concerned with the welfare of the African people in that territory.

. . . Meanwhile, pending such an inquiry, and in view of the large number of death sentences and presumably varying degrees of guilt attributable to those concerned, the question of clemency may be one which could be referred to such a Commission and, if that is so, could not a stay of execution be granted until its findings are known? I understand that in some instances, for example that of the Chieftainess Mamakhabane and her co-accused, there are difficulties about their appeal to the Privy Council and am anxious to discover what these difficulties are.

. . . Hence I felt obliged to act immediately as I am not sure when the next executions are due to take place and whether they might be affected if the request for such a judicial commission were granted.

The season will serve to remind us that this is not only a political and judicial question but a matter of faith and morals and is part of a profound crisis in the whole life of the African people.

It was only many months afterwards, when their appeals to the Privy Council had been dismissed, that an anthropologist was appointed to go to Basutoland to conduct an inquiry. He was sent out without notice being given beforehand, and those of us who knew about it were asked not to make it known. But I heard that on the morning following his arrival at Maseru the chiefs whom I hoped he would be able to question had been summarily executed on the grounds that a plot to release them from gaol had been uncovered.

While at the United Nations, I received a request from the *Lekhotla la Bafo* that I should forward a letter from them to Mr. Trygve Lie. During that session of the United Nations, immediately preceding the question of

South West Africa on the Trusteeship Committee's agenda was the report of the sub-committee on non-self-governing territories. The British Government's report to the Fourth Committee contained no reference whatever to the serious situation in Basutoland and the fact that some forty or more were under sentence of death for ritual murders. However, references were made to the matter by the Brazilian delegation, and attention was also drawn to the demands for the incorporation of Basutoland, Bechuanaland, and Swaziland into the Union which the South African press had reported Dr. Malan as making, for reasons of "defence."

The report of the anthropologist was published after many of the executions had taken place. It dealt more with general causes than particular cases and found a main contributory cause the multiplication of descendants of chiefs and the consequent competition for "places" among them and rivalry in the matter of seniority, prestige, and salary. It was hardly within the anthropologist's terms of reference to deal with the deeper spiritual implications. The Mau Mau had not at that time appeared as a repudiation of the white man's religion and system of justice and law and, as in that case, it is not easy for a ruling people to accept their share of the blame when disillusionment or a break-down of confidence leads to the perpetration of such enormities.

The visit of the paramount chieftainess, Mantsebo Seeiso, and her councillors to London in 1957 to protest against the appointment of a South African resident commissioner in Basutoland was not marked by evidence of cordiality or mutual confidence. There was still considerable resentment over the fact that the anthropologist, Mr. G. I. Jones, who had been sent out on a one-man commission of inquiry into the causes of ritual murder had mentioned the paramount chieftainess as one to whom a good deal of suspicion had pointed on account of dynastic rivalries. On the other hand he had not investigated cases of chiefs who had been executed, but who the Masuto suspected had had evidence planted on them because of their persistent opposition to government policy.

The chieftainess made no request this time to be granted an audience with the Queen, though she requested, and was granted, an audience by the Pope on her way back to Africa through Rome.

To add to the resentment of the deputation, it was announced at the end of their visit to England that consultations had been going on with the South African defence minister in London at the same time, and that agreement had been reached to establish radar stations in Bechuanaland

and Swaziland, and that permission had been given for the South African air force to "fly over" Basutoland. In these days intelligent Africans are well aware that surveys can be carried out by aircraft. A long-standing controversy has been the question of whether South African companies should be granted concessions to prospect for minerals in Basutoland, the Masuto having strong objections to this.

I had been informed that geiger counters had been carried in South African aircraft passing over the high commission territories, and that by flying at a constant height above ground level it was possible to do a quite effective survey for fissionable materials.

As soon as the deputation arrived back in Basutoland I had a request at the Africa Bureau to assist two of them to return to England as they wished to pursue their objections further than had proved possible. Recently reports have come in from Basutoland that good progress is being made with talks on constitutional reforms. Officials maintain that these reforms will give the Masuto considerably more say in their own government on a more representative basis and more control of revenue from their own taxation than they have had since their tribal system came under British protection.

13   Bechuanaland—Foundation for Hope

The High Commission territories of Basutoland, Swaziland, and Bechuanaland are still governed directly by Britain through the Commonwealth Relations Office, which is also responsible through the same high commissioner for Britain's relations with the Union of South Africa. This arrangement would be understandable if both countries were committed to pursuing the same policy towards Africans and their land rights, for Basutoland is entirely encircled by South African territory; Swaziland is surrounded on three sides; and Bechuanaland is sandwiched between the Central African Federation, South Africa, and South West Africa.

In the last century King Khama, the father of Tshekedi Khama sought the protection of Queen Victoria from the Boer republics, whose slave raids into his country were a frequent source of bitter complaint by David Livingstone and other missionaries, and also from the Germans who were beginning to occupy South West Africa.

Livingstone's trenchant letters to the government and missionary societies in England, coupled with the arrival of Khama and his associate chiefs in London (where they sat patiently waiting for many weeks in a Bloomsbury hotel for an audience with Queen Victoria), eventually secured for Bechuanaland the status of a British protectorate.

Today this territory, believed now to contain deposits of copper and other minerals, including uranium, offers Britain a great opportunity with

African co-operation, to demonstrate to the whites of neighbouring territories that Africans are capable of taking part in their own economic, social, and political development in a way that could increase the prosperity of both black and white in that part of Africa. One of the bequests which old King Khama, the first Christian chief of Bechuanaland, made to his son was an idea. Tshekedi Khama, chief at that time, told me about it when I was staying with him in 1948 as we sat on his stoep one evening.

We were talking about Africa past and present and the new forces that were at work changing the face of it and of their effects on the life and soul of his people. The evening became night and the night morning while we were still thinking of the impact of civilization on Africa over the past hundred years.

He spoke of the effects of migrant labour breaking up the tribal and family life of his people and he outlined some of the great hopes he had for the development of his country, which would make his people less dependent on migration to the Union's farms and gold mines.

He believes that the principles of African tribal society are adaptable to changing agricultural needs and methods. "The administrative and judicial work of the tribe start in the family group and are not superimposed by the chief as is commonly supposed," Tshekedi remarked. "The father maintains law and order amongst his sons and he is answerable for the conduct of his family circle or lineage group to the ward headman, who is similarly responsible for the affairs of his ward and answerable to the chief of his tribe. Disputes naturally arise in a family circle, and it is for the headman of the group to try and settle these by arbitration, but, failing settlement, the cases are referred to the ward headman and to the chief of the tribe, if and where necessary.

"The Bechuana society is a peasant community," he said. "Tribal government has no elected members to do the administrative work, but nevertheless this primitive system is truly democratic because it is socialistic in structure, principle, and practice. Individual enterprise is, however, by no means condemned or discouraged.

"A tribal community has immense possibilities for co-operative effort," continued Tshekedi. "The various groups already have their lands in one area for any intensive system of agricultural farming. The cattle of the village groups, similarly, graze in a common area, thus making it convenient for the establishment of cattle improvement schemes, co-operative dairying, etc."

Great efforts have been and still are being made by the Bamangwato people of Bechuanaland to carry old King Khama's ideas into effect. In fact Bechuanaland perhaps provides one of the most hopeful signs in Southern Africa of the development of the African people through their own efforts. We were to see an example of this at Moeng the following day where a real tribal enterprise was developing in the form of a secondary and technical training school, where the people were being trained to become skilled craftsmen and cultivators. In 1948 the Bamangwato were supplying voluntary labour and a regiment to lay a pipeline from a weir in the hills to the site in the valley where five blocks of buildings for the school have been erected.

The aim of Chief Tshekedi in fostering this project was to provide modern educational opportunities for his tribesmen. He wanted to combine the ordinary academic curriculum with practical training and actual work in technical subjects, such as carpentry, building, agriculture, animal husbandry, mechanics, and even commercial subjects, such as typing, stenography, and book-keeping.

All this was being done on the initiative of the Africans themselves, out of their own revenue and without subsidies from the government or the missions. Roads were constructed through Moeng, sixty miles from the railhead. Despite the exceptionally heavy rains, transport of materials was kept going by tribal-owned lorries and teams of oxen. Bricks were made on the spot and baked in a wood-burning kiln. A European contractor, however, inspected these before use.

A stonemason was engaged from Britain. He had been repairing some of England's ancient monuments damaged in the war, including the House of Commons, and was working in a range of hills twenty-five miles away from the school site, hewing and delicately chiselling the pastel-pink sandstone there into pillars for the main educational block.

The road from the village of Moeng runs up a steeply inclined ravine with dense tropical bush on either side. The water rushing down this ravine during the rains turned the road into twisting gullies and scattered loose stones and rocks over it. But the work went on.

As we slithered and bumped over the road in a smart station-wagon belonging to the chief, baboons barked angrily on either side of the ravine—still unreconciled to having their sole occupancy of the place challenged. Enormous spiders' webs were strung like aerials from tree to tree.

The sun glistened on them as it must have done since the morning of earth's time.

There was a fine pioneering spirit about the young Africans engaged on this project. The virgin veld had already been ploughed and Mr. Bokwe, the African agricultural instructor from Fort Hare, was reaping a plentiful crop of corn and vegetables. A large herd of tribal cattle was grazing on the lower slopes of the saucer-like valley.

The school was to be maintained from the revenue of the tribal administration. This is derived partly from money coming from native taxation in the territory, which is made over to it by the protectorate government, and partly from income from tribal lands and property.

The tribal lands which are held in trust by the chief, unlike those which are held individually, are farmed by co-operative methods. At the ploughing season almost the whole population of Serowe, the native capital, of about thirty thousand people, treks off with all their movable property in ox-wagons to the tribal lands, leaving a deserted city. They remain in camp for two weeks or more; and the ploughing, harrowing, and sowing is organized in manageable blocks with a dozen or twenty teams of oxen to each block. I watched a hundred acres ploughed in this way one morning; it was then harrowed by successive teams of oxen all carefully timed so as not to obstruct one another in the act of turning. The sowing was done by a long diagonal line of women stretching up to the skyline, their many-coloured dresses making an unforgettable picture. The whole process took only a few hours.

The harvesting, of course, is also done collectively. Tshekedi Khama has built tribal-owned silos and grain storage tanks. The whole harvest, whether owned individually or collectively, can be safely kept instead of having to be sold to traders and then bought back at a greatly enhanced price later in the year, as used to be the practice, and is still so in many parts of the Union.

My last glimpse of that ploughing scene was of a young South African expert directing the next operation by means of signals with his stick.

In the evening, sitting round a fire under an immense motlha tree, I sensed, and was happy about the new enthusiasm of these young Africans. They knew they were engaged in a worth while job for their people. Tshekedi Khama's optimism and confidence in the project, in any case, was infectious.

There was no racial rancour; no nazified nonsense about *die Volk* was being taught in the churches and schools, or any doctrine of race rule or superiority. Each man looked to his neighbour with respect for the important part each had to play on a practical job.

There was confidence in the British Protectorate Government and a desire to co-operate with all who shew good will towards their work for its own sake. They chose a white man, formerly employed in the Union, as the first principal of this first secondary school to be established by an African tribe in Bechuanaland.

Beside those new white buildings, well spaced, with their gleaming aluminium roofs, there were the round mud huts of the voluntary workers. Beside these again, to complete this picture of Africa past and future, a wild tribal dance was being performed. During the day they had worked for the coming generation of Africans, many of them too old to profit from their work themselves; at night they danced for their own enjoyment, to the whistles and the drums, with simple elemental pleasure of movement in rhythm. Thinking over this night scene in that saucer-like valley, with the dark outline of slumbering hills against the skyline all round it, I had to put firmly back in its place a little shy pride in the knowledge that all this was happening under the protection of British rule.

Old Chief Khama's idea was that the African people's only hope in face of the advance of the white man's civilization in Africa lay in becoming educated, trained, and skilled in the various occupations at all the levels of that civilization. (Booker Washington had a similar idea.)

I do not know whether he foresaw all the cruel consequences of the colour-bar legislation in the Union of South Africa, designed to prevent the development of the African people and their acquisition of skill and knowledge. The fact is that the colour bar is not a result of the white man's disbelief in the capacity of the African to become his equal. It is imposed because he recognizes that thousands of Africans in other territories are yearly becoming skilled doctors, technicians, agricultural experts, and fears competition in spheres which in the past he has been taught to regard as the preserves of the "white race." But was there ever any such thing as a white civilization—can there ever be in the world of the future?

In Africa there is needed the birth of a new emancipatory spirit which will release the enormous resources and pent-up energy of that vast continent. The effort that has been made by this African tribe to stand on its own legs and to adapt its social structure to modern requirements is a most hopeful portent.

There is however a sequel to this particular story, which I cannot fully tell because it is not yet concluded and may have legal implications. But it is part of the whole struggle of the African people for education.

Then the marriage of Tshekedi's nephew, Seretse Khama, the heir to the chieftainship, to a white girl, the misunderstanding among his own people, and the bitter opposition from the Union of South Africa and the Bechuanaland protectorate authorities resulted in endless confusion and recriminations. These placed in jeopardy a great deal that the Bamangwato people have achieved towards the adaptation of their social organization to more modern needs and conditions. Indeed, the threat was made that the whole principle of "indirect rule," or self-rule, by the tribe might be abrogated. Such are some of the consequences of race prejudice on the attempts of these African people to find education and a way of co-operation rather than of conflict.

Differences arose between Tshekedi and Seretse, more on the question of expediency in face of white prejudice than of principle. A division arose in the tribe and between the chiefs and the British Government as the protecting power.

Tshekedi went into voluntary exile and was prohibited from entering tribal territory again. A court case arose over the inheritance of tribal property which involved large expenditure in lawyers' fees. Seretse was summoned to London by air with his legal advisers, and after discussions in Whitehall was prohibited from returning to any part of the Protectorate.

It was Tshekedi Khama who some years before was deposed by the protectorate administration for sentencing a dissolute white man to be flogged. Phineas Macintosh was the son of a white trader in Bechuanaland whose removal had been requested of the protectorate authorities on account of his frequent interference with native women. Finally he was warned that his behaviour was demoralizing to tribal discipline, that the African young men were becoming increasingly resentful, and that if he continued in his ways he would be tried by tribal law and punished by tribal custom. He agreed that if it happened again he would accept tribal punishment, and accordingly on the next occasion he was sentenced to be flogged. This produced such an uproar in the South African press that the

British Government instructed its acting High Commissioner, Admiral Evans, to bring Tshekedi to trial.

Tshekedi once gave me a description of the affair, with the utmost good humour. It seems the admiral had arrived in full dress uniform at Palapye, together with a force of three hundred naval ratings and marines and two field guns. Tshekedi had taken the wise precaution of disarming his whole tribe in order to forestall any possibility of an accident or "incident." Many of their weapons were so rusted that they would never be used again. Some were muskets dating from the slave raids before Livingstone's time. He collected them in an enormous heap before they set off on horseback to welcome the admiral and provide his escort to Serowe, the capital of the tribal administration. On the route over devious sandy tracks the marines and seamen became separated from the ammunition wagons, and the ammunition from the field guns, by many miles. The field guns themselves became fast embedded in the sand and trucks had to be sent for to help tow them out.

In due course they all arrived at Serowe and there Tshekedi was paraded bareheaded between two armed sentries with his tribal council ranged behind him, and the admiral, on a throne erected for him, sat flanked by two field guns, facing Tshekedi and his people.

The case was duly heard and the sentence of deposition duly pronounced. After this Tshekedi was whisked away in a car with an armed guard to a police cell for the night, and then conducted across the border into exile. Before he left, however, some of the European wives of the officials shook him by the hand and assured him that they would not rest until this gross miscarriage of justice was put right. They were true to their word, and it was rectified within a month. Tshekedi's reinstatement was ordered by King George V, and Macintosh was banned from the native territory by order of a British court of inquiry.

Tshekedi told me he was invited, on his reinstatement, by Admiral Evans to visit him on his flagship at the Cape. He was piped on board, I think I remember him saying, and took tea with the admiral, who said he trusted there were no ill-feelings and that from now on bygones would be bygones. Tshekedi said that he bore no ill will on account of any misunderstanding that may have arisen. But he thought he did owe it to his people to explain that his standing and authority could not be quite the same as if the affair had not happened, and he hoped it could be remembered and taken into account if he were ever not able to make things work as smoothly as heretofore.

"If a stranger were to come aboard a ship and summon the ship's company, and then inform them that the captain of their ship was no longer going to be their captain, but that another would be appointed in his place, and then after a time he were to return and say that the former captain would now again take command the position would not be exactly the same as if that had never happened," Tshekedi politely told the admiral.

Sometimes it seems as though our officials go out of their way to weaken the position, or even crush the power, of those who are willing to co-operate. There is unfortunately still the type of official mind which can only think in terms of conqueror and conquered, of exalting the former by debasing the latter, though, in point of historical fact, the British protectorates of Bechuanaland, Basutoland, and Swaziland were never conquered. They were ceded voluntarily to Queen Victoria by their tribal chiefs who sought protection from the Dutch invaders, just as the Hereros, Namas, and others in South West Africa sought British protection from the German invaders. They are still High Commission territories administered directly by the Commonwealth Relations Department of the British Government. South Africa has persistently made attempts to persuade British Governments to let her incorporate these territories, as she sought approval of the U.N. to absorb South West Africa. Her politicians in South Africa today claim that British approval was implicit in the Act of Union.

Britain has a great opportunity to show South Africa a better native policy and at the same time to fulfil her obligations towards the African people who have trusted her. The outcome is being watched intently by Africans all over the continent. The Seretse matrimonial question, now happily settled,[1] has tended to obscure some of the real issues and to intensify others which are more personal.

There remains the task of adapting the African's social organization to present-day requirements, and the changing conditions of a very fine cattle ranching country with considerable other resources. Coal, copper, and fissionable materials have recently been discovered there. The possibilities of subsidiary industries, for hides, skins, timber, furniture, paper

---

[1] See Chapter 17.

manufacture, are well known to the chiefs, as well as the great advantages which have been demonstrated in co-operative methods of agriculture, marketing, and dairying, as described above.

Now that they are both back again, it should be possible for Seretse and Tshekedi to work together with the other Bechuanaland tribes. Given an enlightened British administration, they could get on with the job of showing what possibilities there are in African social organization and land use, where these are not obstructed by myopic colour prejudice and the spitefulness, intrigue, and hypocrisy that grow out of it. Much must depend on the British Government's good will and good faith in the matter, but if that is available there are immense possibilities of showing what Britain and Africa can do together.

Here it may be well to mention a project which I have often discussed with Tshekedi, though it does not fall within his own immediate tribal area but that of another Bechuana tribe. This project is also bound up with the future status of South West Africa and is one of the reasons why importance must be attached to that question.

I had heard of course from the Africans of that strange phenomenon in Bechuanaland where a river which rises away up in the tropical rain belt, flows down through Portuguese Angola and the northern corner of South West Africa, through the Caprivi Zipfel, and empties itself into huge fresh water lakes and marshes in the Kalahari. (The Caprivi Zipfel is a strip of land which the Germans claimed as a corridor to the Zambesi which they then believed to be navigable to the sea, not knowing that the Victoria Falls lay between.)

It was not until I met Professor Wellington, a geographer of the University of the Witwatersrand in Johannesburg, that I realized the enormous possibilities of this region in the middle of the desert. He told me that the Okovango River, rising in the tropical high veld or *planalto* of Angola, has an average flow which his gaugings showed to be about 14,-000 cusecs (cubic feet per second), or the equivalent of an annual discharge of about ten million "acre-feet," i.e., enough water to cover ten million acres a foot deep. The river in flood time rises to a flow of 33,000 cusecs and never falls below about 6,000 cusecs. The river thus empties itself into a depression in the sandveld forming an enormous delta about 5,000 square miles in area.

Here in the middle of the Kalahari Desert, waiting for co-operation between black and white, is a delta as big as the delta of the Nile. Here, with only a comparatively small outlay of capital for a canal at the Popa Falls, are these two million acres of cultivable land on which "crops of rice, sugar, groundnuts, cotton and many other crops could be grown without the risk of insufficient or excessive tropical rainfall," according to Professor Wellington.

Are the soils of the swamps likely to be worth cultivating? Wellington's answer is, "So far as they have been tested they promise well. In the adjacent sandveld there is always the danger of bringing up to the surface the subsurface lime concentration. In the delta there seems to be no brack concentration of this kind: the soils are sandy with a top layer of humus and an underlayer of clay. So far as one can tell they would respond favourably to irrigation."

Summing up the project he says the following facts emerge:

1. The western part of the delta, comprising two million acres of former and present swampland, could be isolated from the eastern part and drained.

2. A canal from the Popa Falls could supply water to this land continuously at the rate of the low flow of the river, viz. 6,000 cubic feet per second, without the necessity of constructing a dam.

3. The soils would probably respond well to irrigation. "It is interesting to notice," he concludes, "that in North Africa the French have had remarkable success in a similar scheme on the Upper Niger, above Timbuktu. Natives trained in agricultural schools at Marseilles, are producing rice, cotton, groundnuts and other crops. The conditions on the Niger appear to be very similar to those of the Okovango swamps which a former Secretary to the Bechuanaland Administration called a 'potential Egypt of Southern Africa.' It is surely time to develop the potentialities of this immense water supply at present of value only to crocodiles, hippos and fish hawks."

What an opportunity here to show what civilization can do if some vision and technical knowledge could be used to evoke the enthusiasm of an African tribe for its own land. Are we so degenerate that there are no young technicians who would volunteer to go out there and take on this pioneering task of helping the Africans to help themselves? When I talked to some young white people, British and American, at the Sevagram peace conference, they said they would be prepared to go if the Africans wanted them and the British Government would allow them in. I spoke to the chief engineer of the Government of India. He said if he could help with advice he would be prepared to fly over and survey the project for them, if only as a gesture to help the Africans on their way. Some of the followers of Gandhi offered to make up a team from some of those trained in the methods of basic education and show the Africans what it could mean for the use of their land, the development of rural industries, and their rural economy.

Have we statesmen who are farseeing enough to help us find the more co-operative way, or is it to be the old story of too little understanding and too late? "I would say that in all their naive confidence, despite the abjection into which they have been thrown, these people are willing to co-operate. They do not wish to hate. . . ." said Stephen Alexis, of Haiti, whose great-grandfather helped his people to free themselves from slavery, when he heard the story of the Hereros in the Trusteeship Committee.

As I write these words in an old Sussex farmhouse in sight of the South Downs, during a brief respite in a rather hectic life, I can understand the feeling of a people for their own land and their own country where they were born. It is beginning to get light and the air is quite still. There is a large pond at the end of the lawn with an island and willow trees on it. The water is shining with the first light of morning and moorhens cleave the surface. As the light strengthens, there on the top of the Downs is Chanctonbury Ring which has gone on through all the ups and downs of England's fortunes.

One is reminded too of a little Bloomsbury hotel in London where a small band of African chiefs, in their best clothes, waited for many months for an audience with Queen Victoria. They sought her protection from the Dutch who were trying to steal their land from them. And their patience was rewarded, despite all the obstacles placed in their way. "We are as the lice in your blanket," they had written to her from Africa. . . . All part of our history and of theirs. . . .

14 The Heritage of Your Father's Orphans

Soon after I was released from gaol in 1946, I was invited by Chief Tshekedi Khama, regent of the Bamangwato, to stay with him in Bechuanaland. I knew that Frederick Mahareru, the paramount chief of the Herero tribe, who lived there in exile with 15,000 of his people, had made a request to see me, and I guessed that he was anxious about the South West African Referendum, upon which the Union of South Africa was basing its claim to incorporate the mandated territory of South West Africa. According to the Union's delegation at the United Nations, the majority of the 300,000 native inhabitants of that territory and the 38,-000 whites were in favour of incorporation, but many of us in South Africa had serious misgivings, which were confirmed by the *New York Times* correspondent's dispatch on the subject.

When I reached Serowe, I had a long interview with Tshekedi Khama and later with Frederick Mahareru. From this quiet, dignified old chief, I learnt that the Hereros in South West Africa had been sending messages of distress to him, their paramount chief, across the Kalahari Desert, imploring him to go with them "with all possible haste." As he was unable to go, he asked me to go on his behalf.

"Chief Frederick," said one of the letters, "the heritage of your father's orphans is about to be taken from them; and because we cannot speak with one voice, as we are scattered all over their country, our heritage may therefore fall to that side for which we have no liking. Let the Chief, despite pressing duties there, come with all haste to us, we pray you, son of the Chiefs of our fathers. Come quickly to us."

And another: "We do not sleep because we are being asked for our land so that it may be made one with the Union; but we say, no, we refuse. We say that the country is ours that we have been robbed of it unjustly. The Government has not paid heed to what we say but continue in their efforts to prevail over us. Indeed we do not sleep. And from whence shall our help come?"

The next day I set off on the long train journey from the Transvaal round the southern edge of the Kalahari. I was impressed as always with the vastness of Africa, but also with the fact that the habitable areas are decreasing. There is an inexorable ruthlessness about Nature there which should command the utmost respect. But man's puny and ignorant defiance is threatening to reduce vast tracts of Southern Africa to desert. After three days of seemingly endless stretches of desert scrub, one arrives quite suddenly at Windhoek. Set in green hills, this capital city with its spires and clean wide streets and brightly flowering shrubs belies the hideous history of that "sunny land." There are abundant signs of prosperity about the former headquarters of the imperial German Government. Only outside, in the native locations, is there the shantytown poverty so familiar in the Transvaal.

An official of the Non-European Affairs Department at the municipal office directed me to the location in which the Windhoek Hereros lived. (It was afterwards said that I had come by stealth.) There was amazement on the faces of the young Hereros when I told them that I had recently been with their paramount chief, and that I wanted truthful answers for him to certain questions. When they had overcome their first suspicion, they were almost overwhelmed with emotion. It was decided that the chiefs must be told of the purpose of my journey, and a meeting was arranged at Aminuis reserve where Chief Hosea Kutako lived.

The native commissioner, Mr. Allen, gave me a one-day permit to visit this reserve, and with several members of the tribe I set off in a borrowed lorry. There was a sort of solemnity about that journey which I only fully appreciated after we had gone some miles along the road to Gobabis. There, at a certain place, the lorry pulled up and I was asked to go with them a little way into the bush. Rather puzzled, I followed these Hereros, dodging thorn bushes, until we reached a certain kind of tree. There all knelt down facing in the same direction and I instinctively followed. After a short silence the leading young man prayed in the Herero language and was translated by one of the interpreters.

I discovered that we were kneeling close to the place where the German war against the Herero people had begun. The prayer asked for a blessing on our journey, which after so many years was being undertaken with the object of restoring the Herero people to the land and the life which they lived before a great wickedness was done to them, a thing which no Herero would ever forget. After asking God to take care of the chiefs and leaders of the people and to bring us back safely along the right road, the leading young man took a handful of earth and gave each of us a little on the palms of our hands. It was taken into the mouth almost like a Communion rite and then spat out.

Then we resumed our journey through Gobabis, and, for nearly sixty miles, jolted along the roughest track I have ever travelled.

It was after midnight when we reached the Aminuis reserve. A man had been sent on to warn Hosea Kutako that a visitor was coming, and when we arrived several women were already preparing a meal. Chief Hosea himself was lying down, having only just been wakened, and he probably thought I was a white trader who had lost his way. I began to explain, through an interpreter, that I had come many hundreds of miles to see him, that letters had been received by Frederick Mahareru regarding the referendum and his people's fears. As this was explained to Hosea his first look of incredulity slowly gave way to an expression which perhaps I will never be privileged to see again. It was twenty-five years since Hosea had seen Frederick Mahareru, and that was under tragic circumstances. Twenty years before that Hosea had escorted his chief, Samuel Mahareru, and his son Frederick after they had given up the struggle against the German army, and had trekked across the Kalahari to Bechuanaland. Hosea had intended being ordained to the ministry, but when a chief was needed to lead those of the Hereros returning to South West Africa and he was chosen, he had accepted the responsibility, had returned in the face of the infamous extermination order of Von Trotha, and has remained faithful to it, almost without hope, ever since.

Hosea had about him the same impressive quality that I had noticed in Frederick Mahareru. In his lined face there was the oppression of a whole people. There was no haste about his movements. Slowly he rose to his feet and began issuing orders with complete self-possession. I was asked not to say anything more for the present and was given porridge and tea. After a while the chief's councillors began to arrive, each carrying his little stool, and sat grouped around a brazier in his hut.

Then the whole matter had to be explained to them. It seemed strange to have travelled all that distance and, after their long separation, to be communicating something which was intimate and personal to these two old African chiefs. And yet, bound up in it was the whole history of their people, and the fate of Germany in two world wars, and now the birth of the United Nations.

There was a curious tenseness about these Africans hearing of the United Nations—they who had been relegated to the edge of the Kalahari Desert, who prayed always for the return of their lands and the reunion of their people. Talking to them in that hut in the early hours of the morning, with the sand outside reflecting the light of a full moon, it almost seemed as though they regarded the United Nations as the answer to their prayers. May the cynics blush for shame, they do regard it as God's instrument of justice and freedom for their people.

On my return journey I considered the referendum (see Appendix 5) in the light of what they had told me. Chief Hosea had described his reactions as follows:

When I got up I said, "I have heard what you said, but I will not answer you at present. I will answer you when the five great powers have sent their representatives, the Americans, the British, the Russians, the Chinese and the French. I should very much like to have the representatives of the five great powers here when I shall give the answer of my people to this question of incorporation.

"Firstly, our fathers made a pact with the Germans when they were in this country. Because there were no witnesses this pact broke down without any witnesses. As you now refer to this question of incorporation I should very much like those impartial witnesses to be present. At this stage we are unable to give you any answer."

After I had made this statement the authorities asked the people, "Are you all on the side of Hosea?" All the Africans present said: "Yes, we are on the side of Hosea."

Festus Kandjo then took up the account and explained that he did most of the speaking on behalf of the hundred leaders present that day.

He had described the history of his people to the administrator and continued:

In the First World War in 1914, the Union troops came to fight against the Germans in South West Africa. The Germans . . . asked the Berg Damaras, the Hottentots and the Hereros to fight against the Union troops and to prevent them from entering the territory. All these African tribes refused to side with the German troops. . . . When the South African troops reached Luderitz Bay our chief Samuel Mahareru, who was then in Bechuanaland, sent a message to the people of South West Africa saying: "I, Samuel, the Chief of the Hereros, inform you that the troops which are coming from South Africa are the enemies of the Germans and you should not fight against them. To clear away all doubts and in order to confirm that these troops are coming with my approval, I am going to send my son Frederick Mahareru and my other son Alfred Mahareru to accompany these South African troops." On account of that, many people were shot and some were hanged by the Germans. Although we had been shot like this we did not fear because we knew it was our duty to obey the chief. . . .

In the Second Great War of 1939 . . . we, the oppressed Africans, thought that it was a golden opportunity to throw in our lot with the English people and to fight so that the English people and their allies may attain their aim of fighting for the freedom of all people irrespective of colour. We gave our sons to the fight and then we gave our money to assist the King of England and the Allies to win the war. Thus we hoped that we, who had been oppressed by the Germans and who were still suffering under the Union Government, may enjoy freedom. . . . Now that war has ended we should like that this country of South West Africa be given back to the African people and that it should not be incorporated into the Union of South Africa.

Their request that a commission from the United Nations be invited to come and conduct the referendum was summarily rejected, and the administrator's reply to Chief Hosea's alternative that four spokesmen from his people should go to the United Nations Assembly, "to speak for me and for my people," was that they had no right to go to the United Nations while they had not got their own government.

It was clear to me that there was no foundation for the Union Government's claim that the annexation of South West Africa was based on "the wish clearly expressed by the overwhelming majority of all the Native races in South West Africa."

Nor was the referendum clearly explained. In one instance, the man who had conducted the referendum, Major Hahn, had been quoted as saying that the government had come to ask the Ovambos who they wanted from among these people of the United Nations to rule them. A Chinese? A Russian? A Portuguese, or an Englishman? He did not mention anything about the incorporation into the Union of South Africa, and the African recounting this episode said, "Taking it for granted that they were being asked if they wanted to be under the British Crown, they said they wanted to be under the British." Apparently no attempt was made in this case to explain the constitutional position, nor the effects on their land rights of being brought within the Union's system of land laws and colour-bar legislation. Nor was any explanation given of the possible alternative, the trusteeship system of the United Nations.

Reporting on the results of the referendum to the United Nations, the Union Government stated (*History of Mandate,* p. 84):

If there was one question that recurred more than others it was whether any change in the administration of the Territory would remove them from under the shadow of the Crown of King George of England. Once assured that the change implied no departure from South Africa's partnership in the British Commonwealth of Nations, the Natives declared themselves fully satisfied on this point.

It was only after this assurance had been given that they consented to vote on the proposal. Yet the officials had no conceivable right to give such assurances, knowing that any South African government has the right to secede from the British Commonwealth and that the then opposition (now the government) had openly declared its republican aims.

Later, when a number of Herero chiefs and other African inhabitants sought an interview with the South African prime minister in Windhoek, the secretary of state for external affairs replied (October 20th, 1948):

The Union Government do not consider themselves accountable to the United Nations Organization, to the Government of the United Kingdom, or to the British Commonwealth in respect of their administration of the Territory of South West Africa, and therefore cannot look with favour upon the Proposal that a delegation of the Herero people should visit Europe for the purpose of making representation along the lines suggested.

I returned to Chief Frederick Mahareru in Bechuanaland, and there, together with Tshekedi Khama and leading Herero chiefs, the future was discussed, and a petition to the United Nations drafted. This petition asked for the return of the lands belonging to the Herero people. It also asked for the return of their paramount chief living in exile with 15,000 of his tribesmen, for the re-establishment of their tribal organization, and the reunion of the Herero people within one tribal area. They claimed that the subdivision of their tribe into eight separate reserves with no freedom of movement between one and another was destroying the integrity of their people.

Under the League of Nations they had the right to petition the Permanent Mandates Commission. But since the Government of the Union of South Africa had twice refused a request from the United Nations to submit a trusteeship agreement for South West Africa, that right had seemingly been lost. "Whose wards are we now?" they asked, and, "Rather than repeat the well known facts and figures concerning the Union's Native policy, we have asked for an impartial commission from the United Nations organization to investigate and report on how far and with what effects this repressive policy is being enforced in South West Africa."

I then returned with the petition to South West Africa and asked the chiefs there if it represented their views and if they were still of one mind about presenting it to the United Nations. The matter was fully discussed by the headmen of the tribe who had already consulted with their people, and the petition was signed at three places, Gobabis, Windhoek, and Okahandja.

The signing at Okahandja coincided with an annual ceremony at the graves of their ancestors who had been slain by the Germans. It was strange to find myself walking in a long procession of Hereros, the women bringing up the rear in their multicoloured dresses.

As the procession passed through the grotto of tall palm trees where the chiefs are buried, every man, woman, and child placed a branch of green leaves on top of some of the graves and placed stones on the others. Their own ministers conducted the service in the Herero language and

I was asked to give an address and say a prayer for the Herero nation. After the signing of the petition, prayers were said and two hymns were sung. Who shall say that a people who have maintained their spirit against all the horrors that have been perpetrated against them—who can sing as they sang, and pray as they prayed—are uncivilized? The prayers of Chief Hosea, as he stood erect in the strong sun with his hat in his hand, were quite unforgettable:

> You are the Great God of all the Earth and the Heavens. We are so insignificant. In us there are many defects. But the Power is yours to make and to do what we cannot do. You know all about us. For coming down to earth you were despised, and mocked, and brutally treated because of those same defects in the men of those days. And for those men you prayed because they did not understand what they were doing, and that you came only for what was right. Give us the courage to struggle in that way for what is right.
>
> O Lord, help us who roam about. Help us who have been placed in Africa and have no dwelling place of our own. Give us back a dwelling place. O God, all power is yours in Heaven and Earth. Amen.

Standing there in that grotto of green palm trees, my soul was sick with shame at the thought of the treatment which this proud people have received at the hands of the white race. I was so impressed by the fine spirit and bearing of these people, that I spent long hours in public libraries at Windhoek and Johannesburg investigating their history, and comparing what some of the chiefs had told me with the British Government's account of their treatment under the German colonial administration. Many of the accounts they had given tallied almost word for word with the verbatim records in the British Government's Blue Book C.D.9146. As a result I was able to piece together the history of the tribe, whom the Germans themselves had spoken of as "a proud, liberty-loving race, jealously guarding their independence, and with very strong family ties." Despite their inhuman treatment at the hands of the Germans, they showed a chivalry which stands in marked contrast to the brutality of their opponents. Gorges, in his report to the British Government, declared, "When the Herero rebellion broke out, the Hereros, under special order from their chiefs, spared the lives of all German women and children and all Missionaries."

Although it was the British who had first sent a German missionary to South West Africa in 1814, he very soon placed himself in direct communication with Berlin and thus began the gradual infiltration of other German missionaries into the territory. "These good missionaries," reported the British Government's Blue Book C.D.9146, "had to support and maintain themselves and their families. They could only do so by combining religion with business. Accordingly it was found necessary to establish a general store in conjunction with each mission station, from the profits of which the missionary could live. . . . Whether this combination of shopkeeper and evangelist was calculated to have the best spiritual results, in so far as concerns the simple savages, it is difficult to say."

In 1876 the Herero people made a petition to Her Majesty Queen Victoria, through the governor of the Cape. Various other tribes also asked for the protection of the British Crown. However, only Walvis Bay and the immediate vicinity were in fact annexed in 1878, and in 1890 the other areas were actively colonized by Germany instead.

Whatever their precious pledges and plans for the native races, as given at the Berlin Conference of Colonial Powers convened by Prince von Bismarck as recently as 1885, German policy at the time of the annexation was enunciated by an official of the German Colonial Office in the following terms:

The decision to colonize in South West Africa could after all mean nothing else but this: namely that the native tribes would have to give up their lands on which they had previously grazed their stock in order that the white man might have the land for the grazing of his stock.

When this attitude is questioned from the moral law standpoint, the answer is that for nations of the "kultur-position" of the South African natives, the loss of their free national barbarism and their development into a class of labourers in service of and dependent on the white people is primarily a law of existence in the highest degree. . . . By no argument whatsoever can it be shown that the preservation of any degree of national independence, national property and political organization by the races of South West Africa, would be of a greater or even of an equal advantage for the development of mankind in general, or of the German people in particular, than the making of such races serviceable in the enjoyment of their former possessions by the white race. (Deutsche Kolonialwirtschaft, *p. 286.*)

Thus was enunciated a policy—a doctrine of race superiority—which in the name of what they were led to believe was a "Christian" civilization, decimated their people and deprived them, by stealth and force, of their lands and herds and homes, of all that was most dear to them. Thus began a war which did not end until, according to the official estimate, the Berg Damara people had been reduced, the Nama people had been halved, and the Herero people, in accordance with the extermination order of von Trotha, had been reduced from 80,000 to 15,000 men, women, and children.

When it came to writing down their case for the United Nations, I felt that I could not do better than to put it in the words of the people themselves, whether it were an Herero, a German, or an Englishman describing what he had seen. I have no room here to tell the whole tragic story in detail, though certain accounts are included in the Appendices. Thus Hendrik Witbooi, a Hottentot chief and the father of one of the present petitioners, had written to the English magistrate at Walvis Bay in 1892. His letter and an account of what followed are given in Appendix 6.

After making his appeal against the ill-treatment his people were receiving from the Germans, he continued steadily in his way of life, despite an ultimatum from the German Governor Leutwein. The Germans decided to make an example of him and made a secret attack. Though he and most of his fighting men escaped, the carnage was terrible among women and children, as even the attackers reported.

Everywhere there was abuse and the seeds of rebellion. One Herero Chief, Daniel Karika of Omaruru, said later in evidence before the British inquiry commission:

Our people were being robbed and deceived right and left by German traders. . . . They were flogged and ill-treated and got no redress. In fact the German police assisted the traders instead of protecting us. Traders would come along and offer goods. Often when we refused to buy goods, even on credit, the trader would simply off-load goods and leave them. But in a few weeks he would come back and demand his money or cattle. . . . He would then go and pick out our very best cows. . . . If we objected or tried to resist, the police would be sent for, and what

*with the flogging and the threats of shooting, it was useless for our poor
people to resist. . . .*

At the same time land owned and occupied by the Africans was being
confiscated in lieu of debts and was then being sold freely between one
European settler and another. Again no redress was open to the Africans
and inevitably this provoked the Hereros—however futile it might be—
into open rebellion.

The British Government concluded its chapter dealing with the cause
of this rebellion with the following words:

*There is something deeply pathetic in this picture of the desperate
Herero warrior with his ancient rifle and half a dozen cartridges deciding to rise and defend his liberties against the might of the German Empire, and despite his worries and anxieties and the terrible future which
faced him, passing resolutions and giving orders to ensure the safety of
the women and children of his oppressors.*

The Herero War, as it came to be known, was begun with deceit and
bad faith and trickery. It ended as a war of extermination, rape, and
robbery against a simple people, the care of whom had been entrusted
to a nation which boasted a superior culture and subsequently twice
brought death and destruction to Europe and to civilization in pursuit of
the same mythology of the *Herrenvolk*.

After the defeat of the Hereros the whole people, men, women, and
children, were driven towards the Kalahari, some to seek refuge in the
desert or to cross it in the hope of British protection in Bechuanaland.
Their defeat and flight can best be told in the words of a German soldier
writing a letter home to his family, reproduced in the British Government's Blue Book. This is quoted in Appendix 7. It is a terrible picture.

Samuel Mahareru managed to cross the Kalahari with his son Frederick who succeeded him as paramount chief in exile and Chief Hosea
Kutako, who later went back to South West Africa. They were received
by King Khama, the father of Tshekedi Khama, who as an infant re-
members his mother telling him of their arrival on the verge of death
from thirst and exhaustion. Khama gave them land in Bamangwato territory and allowed them to settle there. The story can be taken up in the
words of Festus Kandjo:

The Herero people tried by all means to protect their Chief from fall-

ing into the hands of the Germans, until they succeeded in getting their Chief across the border into Bechuanaland Protectorate. These troops protected their Chief armed only with knobkerries until they brought him into a land where they could be sheltered. The aim of the Hereros in trying so hard to protect their Chief was to maintain their claim to the land because, as long as their Chief had not been captured or killed, the Germans could not say that they had conquered the people and that the land was theirs. We know from our law that as long as the Chief of the tribe is not captured or killed it cannot be said that the land has been captured.

Governor Leutwein was then succeeded by the notorious von Trotha. Whilst deploying his troops at strategic posts, he sent messengers of peace to the Herero leaders, saying that the war was over and they would be allowed to return with their cattle to take possession of their lands. When the leaders came to the German garrison to discuss these terms, they were disarmed and they and their followers were shot without warning. Then, says the British Government report:

Von Trotha issued his notorious "Vernichtunge Befehl" or extermination order in terms of which no Herero man, woman, child or suckling babe was to receive mercy or quarter. "Kill every one of them," said von Trotha, to ensure that never again would there be a Herero rebellion.

This order, be it remembered, was made against an already defeated people, ready to come in and surrender on any terms and entirely without ammunition or other means of waging war. . . .

When the spirit in which this order was conceived and given and carried out is understood, and when the real purport and object of the preliminary acts of treachery whereby the Chiefs and leaders were murdered, are borne in mind, it will be easier to understand that the following sad and terrible details as to how the extermination order was carried out are not figments of the imagination, but the sworn description of eye witnesses, and that the ghastly slaughter which took place was approved by von Trotha and the master whom he served.

One of the extracts which followed is given in Appendix 7. This and much more had to be told to the United Nations that they might understand what the Hereros had suffered. The petition takes up the story:[1]

---

[1] U.N. Document. A/C.4/94,95,96,97.

From that time onwards, the Hereros have been a landless, homeless people wandering in search of a place of abode for themselves, their children and their cattle. At the end of the First World War the promise of a return to their native land where they could live as an united people was shamelessly disregarded and their hopes had become frustrated.

The verbal promise was never redeemed. At the end of that war, the League of Nations placed South West Africa under the Union of South Africa as a mandated territory. Germans were allowed to retain their property, and the first act of the German group in the South West African Assembly was to demand and obtain the withdrawal of the British Blue Book C.D.9146—*The Natives of South West Africa and Their Treatment by Germany*—from which so many of the above quotations were taken. The natives of South West Africa were kept in ignorance of the fact that they had the right of appeal to the League of Nations. Hence, though they subsequently appealed frequently to the authorities in Windhoek, their appeals were never carried further.

Sometimes it is argued, as though in defence of the South African Government's administration in South West Africa, that at least the African people are not suffering under the same policy of extermination and brutality as that carried out under the German regime. But it must be pointed out that in so far as the purpose of that policy was to establish a racial oligarchy, to entrench white supremacy, to deprive the African people of the lands and other resources of the earth, and to reduce them to a state of servitude, that purpose had been already achieved by the Germans. The South African Government, when it took over the administration of the territory, was in a real sense the permanent beneficiary of the policy carried out by the Germans.

The history of the oppression of those people was not finished under the mandate, for in 1922 there was an event that became known as the "Bondelswarts Rising." The Bondelswarts are a Hottentot or more correctly Nama tribe, and this was a confused affair in which the administrator at the time, Mr. Hofmeyr, acted like a dictator and aroused much critical newspaper comment. There has never been any satisfactory account, but it was in effect a miniature war, even to the use of aeroplanes, for the first time against a barely armed native tribe.

At the same time, the people of these territories were continually being moved to make way for white people. Much later, after my first visit to the United Nations, I asked Hosea how they came to the Aminuis reserve. This is the story he told me.

In one place they had put down boreholes, which they had paid for with trust money. They were chased away after three years. The government put up a fence and told them "never to dream of Orumbo again." Even though their houses were burned, they stayed for some time, but most of the cattle were outside the fence and they had to go. After a while they were offered new land which Hosea rejected, he told me, in the following terms:

We are a big nation, and as such we shall not develop in country like this where there is only deep borehole water. In fact it is a desert where no human being ever lived before. It is a country only good for wild beasts. On top of that it is not healthy for the people or the cattle. We told Mr. Cope, "We are the original inhabitants of South West Africa and we know the best and worst parts of the whole country. . . . We are human beings. And we do not want to be changed into wild beasts. Only wild beasts can live without water."

Not for long were they left to live at Rehoboth, where they then were. Following some other trouble between the coloured people and the government, the place was surrounded by armed forces. They charged to within a few yards, and many were hurt with knives and bayonets. The leaders, both coloured and Herero, were imprisoned.

After this they were driven out with what they could carry and such cattle as were near their houses. They were told to ask for passes to return for the rest of their cattle, but when they got to Aminuis these were refused and all that stock was lost. This was about 1925.

Many years later a South West African commission investigating conditions among the Herero people concluded its report:

It is to be hoped that some way will be found by the Government to gain the confidence of the Hereros because they are sorely in need of moral and social regeneration. Their racial pride and their distrust of the white man make them a difficult people to help, but it should not be impossible to get them to see the necessity, in their own interests, of measures being taken to save them from ruin. . . .

This followed a detailed analysis of the causes of the death rate being higher than the birth rate in the reserves in the police zone during the years from 1929 to 1946, and the extremely high incidence of venereal disease, unknown before the coming of the white man. The low birth rate was ascribed both to the immorality of the women and to ". . . abject poverty to which they were reduced, and the altered mode of life which they were forced to adopt when they emerged from the 1904–07 rebellion, a shattered and broken people with their numbers reduced by more than one half, with their tribal associations destroyed, and with little or no hope of re-establishing themselves or their tribal customs. . . ."

This much and more had to be conveyed to the United Nations. It was by now August 1947, time to present the petition at Lake Success. Chief Hosea had asked that four of his representatives should be allowed to go, but had been told he had no right as they had not their own government. I was therefore asked to deliver the petition to Lake Success, and to represent their views for them to the British Government and to the United Nations.

I felt that it was a very serious matter indeed to go outside one's own nation in an appeal to the nations of the world. But the situation in South Africa was deteriorating and repeated appeals to the State had on so many occasions produced no more than polite assurances. In the past year alone there had been the repercussions from the Indian passive resistance movement in Natal, the Tobruk shantytown, and Bethal, and it seemed now as if the only hope for the African people was an appeal to the conscience of the world. These great evils, which seemed to be beginning to overshadow the whole continent, were not evils that confined themselves to lines drawn on a map, nor could it be said that one's Christian loyalties were limited by frontiers of a particular nation or state. The United Nations was civilization's second attempt to build a rudimentary world order, and the appeal could therefore legitimately be made to that body as an instrument of international justice. And it is as such that I have attended the United Nations to renew their petition each year for ten years. Each year the United Nations has reported the appeal to South Africa and has now established its own procedure for supervision.

In Johannesburg in October 1947 I was delayed six weeks in attempting to get a visa for the United States. Eventually I left without the visa and flew to London, where the Minister for Commonwealth Relations politely regretted that he could not see me as the matter of the petition was the concern of a Dominion government. There was more delay in London. Then the American Embassy granted me a limited visa, after Sir Maharaj Singh had requested me to go as his personal adviser.

It is difficult to convey a sense of the hectic spirit that prevails at the United Nations where all the post-war problems seem to be too big and too intricate to be dealt with individually, even if there were the will and the faith to do so. Plunging in and out of overheated hotels and telephone booths, buses, and subways, up and down the long corridors of Lake Success, and throughout the long sessions of the United Nations, one watches the real problems of our age being immersed in surging waves of words, of propaganda and counter-propaganda, and one is afflicted at first with a terrifying sense of futility—of tragicomedy.

I felt, when I arrived, that the organization was desperately in need of some spiritual driving force. It needed integrity and faith and it needed the prayers of all the peoples in the world. But it was not getting them. From all sides I was oppressed by a tendency to profound disillusionment, a cynicism, and the absence of any accepted standards of value or of any sense of creative purpose in the scheme of things. Yet the faith of the Hereros, a predominantly Christian tribe, had survived three wars and partial extermination. How could I hope to justify that faith and so place their case before the United Nations that they would attend to their appeal?

I found that a sub-committee had already been appointed to draft a resolution on South West Africa and that it was too late for me to be given a hearing. However, the copy of the petition that I had sent ahead had reached the secretary-general and, thanks to the Indian delegation, had been circulated to all members of the Trusteeship Committee and recorded as Document A/C.4/94,95,96,97.

For the previous two years, the South African Government had refused to submit reports on South West Africa, according to the terms of the Mandate, and at that session the Trusteeship Council were debating a report sent in after the South African Government had been reproved in 1946. When the matter came before the Council, a resolution was passed calling the Union Government's report "incomplete" and, since the government's letter enclosing the report had said that further information would be supplied if required, a series of fifty questions was asked. Answers to these were requested before June 1948, when the Union Government's report would again be considered by the Trusteeship Council and its observations submitted to the General Assembly. This at least was something accomplished by the U.N.

For the moment there was nothing more to do. After the feverish anxiety of those few weeks during the debates it was good to enjoy the hospitality of a young couple who seemed to typify so much of what is best in the New World—its enterprise and love of adventure (in thought, more than in action, today), its combination of idealism and toughness. Sartell Prentice, then the administrative secretary of the Commission of the Churches on International Affairs, and his young wife gave me the run of their home at Port Washington on Long Island. I had barely enough money to return to South Africa and none to spare for office work, printing, and the like, and as New York is ruinously expensive I do not know what would have happened to the work I had come to do if it had not been for their kindness.

I was alone over Christmas and, marooned by snow, I spent a good deal of time thinking about the enormous number of words that had been uttered during those recent debates on the problems of South Africa and of the Hereros who, for me, had become symbolical of all the landless and dispossessed people in the world.

Where can be found the moral force that the world needs so desperately? I thought much of *satyagraha*. Non-violence is much too negative a word to describe it. Yet passive resistance is a description of only one aspect of a movement of the human spirit, rather than a definition of the movement itself. Love, creative purpose, self-sacrifice, non-violence —all these are bound up in the word *satyagraha*. As Gandhi conceived it, it is the Way of Life, rather than a mere political tactic, just as Christ's gospel is a Way of Life—a relationship of the self to the creative purpose, and it performs its function to perfection only when it is completely subordinated to that purpose. That is the profound religious truth which, in God's good time, will unite East and West.

A few days later I was back in Africa, when we heard the news of Gandhi's assassination on January 30, 1948—it seemed as though one of the lights which had offered a bearing to mankind and a hope of peace was extinguished. Amidst all the speeches and display of grief it seemed right that we should go and say our prayers at the passive resistance camp in Fordsburg. Standing there on that plot of ground, there was some incongruity in the broadcast from Delhi, relayed by loudspeakers, which followed the period of almost deathly silence when we had prayed there in the place where his spirit was, in a sense, born—in the turmoil and stress and passion of South Africa's racial conflicts.

The loudspeakers brought us the sounds and description of Gandhiji's last procession, that of his mortal remains to the funeral pyre, borne on a gun carriage and flanked by an Indian regiment of cavalry with the pennants fluttering from their lances.

15 A White Man's Jesus

When I returned to South Africa from the United Nations after my first attempt to secure a hearing for the Hereros on the question of South West Africa, I found that a movement had begun in the Transvaal, aimed at the boycotting of Indian traders in the small *platteland* towns. This was a movement closely analogous to the boycott of Jews and the Nuremberg Laws in Germany. Dr. Malan, in his main statement on apartheid (in April 1948), had said:

The Party holds the view that Indians are a foreign and outlandish element which is unassimilable. They can never become part of the country, and must therefore be treated as an immigrant community.

Another of the Nationalist party candidates for election went further in his manifesto:

The dregs of India came here half a century ago to work on the sugar plantations. . . . The coolie is not an inmate of this country, but a usurper and exploiter. Millions of people have recently been shifted in Europe to solve racial problems. Why can we not shift 250,000 coolies?

The great majority of Indians in South Africa are extremely poor and work as labourers on the sugar plantations, in factories and stores, and as municipal street cleaners and so on, though it is true that a few of them have become very rich indeed, and some of these by unscrupulous methods. Originally they were brought as indentured labourers on con-

tract from India by agreement between South Africa and the British Administration in India at that time.

After the original indentured labourers fulfilled their contracts they
were free to take up other employment. Some of them joined those who
had come with them from India as traders, storekeepers, and craftsmen.
They set up stores in the small country "dorps," as well as the big towns
of the Transvaal and Natal. Some of them have carried on their busi-
nesses for many generations.

In the South African countryside today, however, we have the tragic
if natural result of backward farming communities rearing large families.
The farms become split up and shared amongst the young men until in
the end they cease to be economic holdings. The younger sons are obliged
to look for work in the neighbouring market towns. The more enterpris-
ing set up stores of their own where they found themselves in competition with the already established Indian traders.

Since the Indians have no vote they are powerless to resist the demands of the white community for a government policy of withdrawing
trading licences from Indians. Nor have they any power to protect themselves from a boycott movement such as we were witnessing in the
Transvaal. Some of the worst features of that boycott movement were
challenged by law, such features as the picketing of Indian shops and
the practice of employing loudspeaker vans to go through the streets calling out the names of Europeans who were entering Indian shops. Meetings were held in the native locations in which anti-Asiatic propaganda
was spread by Europeans, and the Africans were urged to boycott their
stores.

I toured a number of these *platteland* towns, interviewing farmers and
trying to express the view that the country was being disgraced by this
movement and that it could only lead to racial friction. (There can be
no doubt that the disastrous riots which took place later in Durban and
elsewhere between Africans and Indians were in part fomented by this
kind of propaganda.)

I was never given a hearing at any public meeting. Some members
of the Anglican Church in one small "dorp" asked me to go there and
requested the Dutch Reformed Predikant, who opened the boycott meeting with prayer, that I might be allowed also to lead them in prayer. This
request was refused. One of my supporters, however, a farmer in the
district, voted against the resolution calling for a boycott, along with six

other farmers who considered the movement very shabby and mean against a defenceless people. They later told me that on the way home they were "ridden off" almost into the ditch by a car which had followed them. Realizing it had been done deliberately, they turned about and reported what had happened to the police.

While in the act of making a statement to the constable on duty, the other car pulled up and my friend was knocked backwards off his chair. A free fight in the police station followed between his son and the farmer who had assaulted him, ending in the latter's defeat. There was no prosecution, however, and a departmental inquiry never gave any satisfaction.

In one district of the Transvaal I was asked to interview an old Afrikaans-speaking farmer. He received me very courteously in the old-fashioned tradition of his people. He had a large farm which had been afflicted by drought, though there was a promise of rain in a changing wind. He sat at the head of a long table. His sons were seated on one side of the room, the eldest nearest him, and the womenfolk, his wife, sisters, and daughters, on the other side. He was tall and well-built, with blue eyes, light hair, and beard, and he motioned me to a seat beside him at the head of the table. By his left side was an enormous family Bible, on which he rested his arm.

He began by saying that he had heard I would like to speak with him and had set apart this time. It was right that white people should discuss their differences, especially when these concerned the native people who were placed under us. He believed that I had taken part in, or attended, some conference abroad about the natives and he would like of course to hear what the representatives of other nations had had to say about our problems. But first he would like to say what he thought about them himself. These were people and problems which had to be lived with, not merely discussed. He and his forefathers had been living with them side by side for many generations now. Therefore it was right that I should also be given an opportunity of listening to him.

The old man thereupon expounded his views at great length and expressed the fears that he and many of his people felt. The natives were getting altogether out of hand. They expected too much. The towns were ruining them. They paid them higher wages than the farmers could afford and taught them a lot of wrong things. The able-bodied native men went away to the towns and left their children and women as squatters on the farmers' land.

Of course some farmers were bad employers. They did flog the natives, especially now that some of them were getting cheeky. He did not flog his natives. Occasionally he had to give one a beating, but it was very rare, and at this his sons nodded in confirmation. I think he was telling the truth. Some of the farmers did not feed their natives properly, he said. They were unhealthy and had not enough energy to work. The Native Farm Labour Commission had found that. Then they flogged the natives to try and get more work out of them. He was all against that and was always saying so in public. They were spoiling the labour market in the Western Transvaal though he had kept many of his "boys" for a long time.

The "coolies" were out of place in the country. They were always making trouble for the government, and it wasn't right that they should have all the trade with the white people in the district. The Farmers Co-operative was the proper trading organization for the farmers to patronize. He would like to see all the coolies sent back to India. The natives and the whites would get on better. The Indians were doing a lot of propaganda in the country about breaking down the colour bar for non-Europeans. That of course was impossible. The Lord in His wisdom had made people of different races and nations. The different peoples He had distinguished by different colours. It was therefore not right to want to mix them all up. And for a people like his own, living in a continent like Africa, it was right that they should cherish what had come down to them and had been preserved by their forbears. He then asked me to tell him what the matters were that had been discussed at the United Nations.

I outlined the course of the United Nations debate on racial discrimination and the treatment of Indians in South Africa. I said this question of race was one which now affected every nation in the world. It was not merely our South African problem. Other peoples were beginning to take a pride in their race and were beginning to ask for freedom as his own forbears, the Voortrekkers, had sought freedom. Some of his own people had suffered from persecution in their own country. Others had crossed the Vaal River to escape from my ancestors. Now the whole world was talking of freedom. The United Nations had come into existence because that freedom had been threatened. It was still threatened. But freedom, like peace, was indivisible. It would grow or die. We could not have it for ourselves and deny it to others indefinitely. We must be-

gin to move forward with the rest of the world. I quoted from a speech
by Mrs. Vijyalakshmi Pandit, ambassador of India, at the United Nations:

*We write a Charter to promote human rights, and then proceed to ask
for a committee to define them, for a Court of Justice to interpret them.
That way lies disaster. . . . Let me therefore state the real issue involved
in this resolution, which affects not only the Indians in the Union of
South Africa but all the people of Asia and Africa. For us, it is not the
mere assertion of certain rights and privileges. We look upon it primarily
as a challenge to our dignity and self-respect. . . .*

The old man listened in a rather puzzled way, his lips pursed dubi-
ously. He had opened the Bible and was turning the pages slowly. It had
become very dark as huge billowing clouds rolled in front of the sun,
casting their shadows over his lands.

He said, "Yes, I have read in the papers some of the things that were
said about my country. Mrs. Pandit said, for instance, that Jesus Christ
could not come to South Africa. That was a very wrong thing to have
said. Of course Jesus Christ is here in our country. Every morning we
have our prayers. All the family is here. I call in the servants and I read
a chapter to them. And we say our prayers here in my house. 'Wherever
two or three are gathered together, there am I,' He said. Of course He
is here in my home. I cannot understand how any white man could sit
and listen to a 'coolie' woman saying such things about his country."

Gently I tried to bring home to the old man a truth which he had
never really faced, and which would be quite abhorrent to him. I explained that what Mrs. Pandit had meant was that under the immigration laws of the country and the Asiatic Land Tenure and Indian Representation Act all Asiatics were prohibited from entry, and those that
were here were discriminated against on the grounds of race, on the
grounds that they were as God had made them to be.

For the purpose of that particular Act, Asiatics were defined as peoples whose national home was in Asia. (Jews had been exempted under
the Act.) But Jesus Christ was born and lived in Asia and was regarded
as an Asiatic by every other nation. That is what Mrs. Pandit had meant
by her remark.

The poor old man seemed utterly taken aback. "Jesus Christ . . . an
Asiatic." His eldest son, who had been sitting forward on his chair with
his hands on his knees and his elbows out, stood up and walked up and

down with his fists clenched. How could any man sit still and listen to another white man saying Jesus Christ was an Asiatic? Clearly to him I was a renegade to my race and my religion. By now it had become quite dark and had actually begun to rain. On the wall was a picture of Jesus Christ with blue eyes and a straw-coloured beard, holding a lamb. It could almost have been the old man himself when he was younger. He followed my eyes to this picture and the rain drops came quicker on the roof. There was suddenly a splitting clap of thunder and the rain descended in full fury on the corrugated iron roof. Speech was impossible because of the noise. And we sat, each preoccupied with his thoughts. The old man was obviously pleased about the rain, but was too preoccupied and too polite to change the subject of conversation to the weather. His eldest son had gone out to see what the prospects were, whether this was a passing thunder shower or whether it might be a long rain.

After we had sat for a while longer the old man rose and went to the window. There were huge puddles forming all over his lands. The hills were obscured by a grey curtain of rain. He raised his arms as I went over and stood beside him. "You see," he said, "the Lord is blessing us today." I had not the heart to make an obvious quotation from scripture which came to mind. Since further conversation was not easy, and his farm track was likely to be impassable if the rain continued, I said goodbye, wished him and his family well, thanked him for his courtesy and restraint, considering how much he differed from my point of view and how strongly he felt on these matters, and took my departure. He promised he would think over what I had said. And I had a feeling that he would when he was alone, and not under any necessity to put up an argument to defend his religion or his race.

16   The General Assembly Decides

When I returned to Windhoek there was a certain amount of comment in the South West African press, and a question was asked in the South African Parliament as to why I had not been prevented from leaving the country. The Administrator sent for me and complained that I had not shown him a copy of the Petition before taking it to the United Nations.

I was anxious to report the progress of their case to the Hereros, but I could not get a permit to visit their reserves. I learned that on February 24th, 1948, the native commissioner had given a report (Appendix 8) on the recent proceedings at the United Nations. This account of the lengthy debate held by all the great nations was the sole statement made to the 300,000 non-Europeans whose fate was involved.

Eventually a meeting took place in the location near Gobabis, to which I was given an entry permit for four hours by the local magistrate after a promise that I would not hold a public meeting. Chief Hosea opened with a prayer:

> *Thou art the Great God. . . . We are only Thy creatures. Thou seest that we have no dwelling place—no resting place that we can call our own. We thank you for bringing back this stranger to us safely. Bless us in all that we are to do, and guide us with Your Wisdom. Forgive those who cause suffering to us as Jesus Christ asked forgiveness on those who crucified Him without understanding. Amen.*

Then I described the United Nations conference and left a verbatim record of the Trusteeship Council proceedings with the interpreters so that they could be studied and discussed. In order to be able to give a full account to the United Nations in the future, I asked Hosea and Festus Kandjo how they came to be placed in the Aminuis reserve, and they told me much of what I have already described.

I asked further questions, and was told by Chief Hosea that once, when cattle began to die by thousands, he took a sample of the grass in the area to Windhoek, to report the number of deaths. "I was told that I had only brought this report because I wanted to leave the country, and to go and live in the British protectorate, and that I should stay where I was. 'Perhaps,' they said, 'the cattle disease will die out,' or 'the cattle will get used to the district,' or I must 'learn to master the disease.' What I am wondering," he added, "is why are the people taxed, since hardly any money is spent on the people."

When I asked why the Herero people in Bechuanaland have been increasing in numbers, while those in South West Africa are decreasing, Festus Kandjo repeated how they had been scattered and divided and often mixed up with other peoples by the Union Government. He also thought that stopping polygamy had helped to cause the falling numbers.

He said that they would like their young men to be trained in agriculture. "But," he added, "the Union Government has never given any encouragement to our young men to learn. The Rhenish Mission schools we have had for a hundred years never took our children beyond the primary stages."

I told them then that it was right that they themselves should present the case of their people to the United Nations, and that I would try to bring it about. Then Hosea concluded with another prayer.

After these discussions I was anxious to go to Epikuru, for I had heard that conditions in that reserve were very bad, and that many of the cattle were dying of anthrax and "*gallamsiekte*." I was refused a permit to the reserve, but fortunately received an invitation from a cattle farmer to stay on his farm in that area. The farmer had served for twenty years in the police in South West Africa. While I was at the United Nations he had written me a very interesting letter describing the pressure which had been put on civil servants to favour incorporation and the ill-treatment of the native people in South West Africa. This had been circularized.

While I was there I took down a statement from him in which he described how the native people in the police zone (the area governed by European law rather than African tribal laws as in Ovamboland), especially the Hereros, had been given the most unhealthy parts of the country to live in, and how they were losing thousands of stock every year through *gallamsiekte* and *lamsiekte:*

The conclusion I have come to after thirty-three years' experience here is that anything is good enough for the Native, and no consideration is due to him in the eyes of the Government. . . . I shall go on trying to defend what I know to be right here, as long as the British flag still flies, but there are things being done here for which the British will one day be held to blame. . . . It is the name of Britain . . . which is being used to cover up the brutal and unjust rule of the Natives which is being carried on here. . . . There are many people both here and in the Union who still believe in Britain, but there are many who cannot reason things out for themselves. They know there is dreadful injustice and corruption of the worst kind in the Administration and they lose faith and give up.

He went on to tell me of the unjust trading regulations; and I also learnt more about the pass laws from a reinstated German whom I met there.

I was further told that even the Ovambo people, whose lands and tribal organization had hitherto remained intact, even during the German period, are today being remorselessly drawn into the Union system whereby the native inhabitants and their lands are treated as "reserves" —that is to say, as reservoirs of cheap labour for the farms and industries of the Europeans. Both the tribal and family life of the Ovambos are being seriously affected by the exodus of thousands of their young men every year to work on the farms and gold mines.

All this information was of value in preparing the case for the General Assembly.

Meetings with the native people had to be held at night. I found that in my absence many tribesmen had been called to the Criminal Investigation Department and questioned regarding their dealings with me. What had I talked to them about? Who had accompanied us? Who lent me a lorry? Even the bishop of Damaraland and other prominent Europeans whom I had interviewed, had been visited by members of the C.I.D. and interrogated regarding my beliefs and opinions and my movements.

For two months I remained in camp in a dry river bed outside the Windhoek location, waiting for permits to hold a meeting in the location and visit the reserves to explain how their petition had been received at the United Nations. During that time I came to learn something of the fears that overshadow the whole life of the African people—not the old fear of magic and devilry, but the new fear which civilization and the white man's judicial and political system has brought.

Awakened by the sound of a low whistle, I would lift up a flap of the tent and find there half a dozen black faces, peering inquiringly through the bush. Holding their sticks and their hats, they would say there was a matter which they would like to speak about. And by the light of a hurricane lamp wrapped in a blanket, under the lee of a bush, I would record their statements.

When it was obvious that no permit was to be granted, I returned to the Transvaal and wrote to General Smuts, asking for his intervention. After three weeks—the day after his party's defeat in the elections—I received a reply stating that "he cannot see his way clear to intervene in a matter which he feels should be left entirely to the discretion of the Administrator of South West Africa." I had also attempted to get permission to show the United Nations film, *The People's Charter* to the Africans, to give them some idea of the purpose of the United Nations organization and the tasks of peace as being the responsibility of all nations and races. This was also refused, probably because the film shows members of the coloured races, from different parts of the world, sitting down at the same conference table as Europeans.

For some months I was busy drawing up documents in preparation for the coming session of the United Nations. These included the Africans' own replies to the fifty questions put to the Union Government on the subject of South West Africa. There was also the need to work out the implications of the whole question being referred to the International Court of Justice, as seemed very probable.

As for further personal representation, I had grave doubts as to whether anything more could be achieved, but I was convinced by the earnestness and certainty of the leaders of the tribe whom I saw in brief meetings outside the reserves. The question of my fare to Paris was solved when Tshekedi Khama and Chief Frederick Mahareru arranged that the tribe in Bechuanaland should sell some of their stock to pay for it. I left Serowe with a bag full of ten shilling and one pound notes, conscious of the depth of their faith, and the warmth of their hopes. With Tshekedi Khama I had gone to see the resident commissioner in Serowe, and Tshekedi told him about the collection of this money. He was friendly and interested and made no objections.

In Johannesburg I decided not to book the air passage in advance, but instead went to the airport one night at the beginning of November 1948, the notes having been carefully counted out earlier in the evening. All went well as I bought my ticket and went through the usual formalities. Then, as the friends who had come to see me off and I were drinking a last cup of coffee, the harsh tones of the loudspeaker called out my name, and directed me to the immigration office. Apprehensive and tired, I complied and was asked by the immigration official if he could see my passport again. Some instinct warned me not to produce it and I maintained that as he had already passed it, I could not see why he should want to re-examine it. My stubbornness wore down his resistance, and he finally revealed that he had just received instructions by telephone from the Department of the Interior that it must be cancelled. I again refused to part with the passport—he had no written authority to support his demand, and if he wanted it, he would have to get it by law or by force. My luggage was removed from the plane, and it took off for London. I was left to meditate on the new barriers that grow up to take the place of the old barriers of space and time.

In the next few days I waited for further action from the minister. Suddenly my host suggested that any cancellation of a passport could only be made on the passport itself, and when two young Indians agreed to drive me across the border into Southern Rhodesia, the journey began again. Arriving too late to achieve anything much at the Paris session in 1948, I waited in England till the following summer for the 1949 session in New York.

I had not a dollar in my pocket when I landed in New York, and I was unable to get any from the South African bank. As I stood on the quayside amongst a mountain of everybody's luggage but my own, I was suddenly overjoyed to hear a shout and the rasping voice of my old friend Sartell Prentice. As he rushed towards me as fast as his lame leg would take him, and clasped my hand in one hand and my shoulder with the other, I thought how much thanks my African friends owed to this

American with such a great heart, and to his gifted wife Agnes. He was pressing a wad of dollar bills into my hand. He was out of a job himself, having been knocked down by a car and broken his legs and resigned from the Commission of the Churches on International Affairs. He offered me hospitality at his home on Long Island for as long as it should be necessary to get the question of South West Africa safely into the hands of the United Nations. It was still doubtful how much supervision could be exercised by the U.N. And he was actually thanking *me*. I knew what he meant—it was for giving him this opportunity of putting right something which he knew and believed to be wrong and which he felt to be an oppression upon himself and his own freedom.

The International League for the Rights of Man had appointed me as their consultant at the United Nations and it was through the intervention of Mr. Roger Baldwin in this matter that I was finally given a visa to attend the U.N., a very restricting transit visa from the U.S.A. He asked me to sit as their observer at the Sub-Committee on Racial Discrimination of the Human Rights Commission.

Even so, the question of my status became something of a problem to the United Nations Secretariat. I had been appointed consultant by an international organization, without the approval of my own government. Were all representatives of such organizations at the United Nations to be subject to the approval of the U. S. State Department or, more indirectly, of their own governments? If so, this might seriously interfere with the freedom of choice and effectiveness of the work of such organizations. This was fully appreciated by many members of the secretariat in the Legal Department and Non-Governmental Organizations Section, and a tribute should be paid here to the integrity of those officials who behaved in a thoroughly principled manner as international civil servants in what seemed to become at times something like a minor cold war.

The question of my accreditation to the United Nations Department of Public Information arose soon after my arrival at Lake Success. No question was raised by the appropriate official at the United Nations when it came to my accreditation as an observer for the International League at the United Nations. However, to my surprise, although no mention had ever been made of any kind of approval by the State Department being necessary for this accreditation, I was told that my application had to be submitted to the State Department.

I found attendance at the Sub-Committee on Racial Discrimination of the Human Rights Commission immensely interesting, though there must be few people who are aware of the great care and attention given to every shade of meaning of each word in the original texts and in the translations. One had a sense that this convention on human rights which was being drafted, however long and wordy the debates, had thousands of years of human history and struggle for justice being written into its content.

The right of petition by individuals and groups over the head of their own governments to the United Nations, which naturally interested me, was exercising the great powers. The anomalous position had arisen of the inhabitants of trusteeship territories having the right of petition to the United Nations, but not the inhabitants of metropolitan powers or of colonial territories.

It seemed to me, however, that the declaration of human rights, and the convention which was now being drawn up, did not fully take into account the position of a country such as South Africa. The underlying preconception of the commission was that all the countries concerned had the ultimate intention, and at least declared purpose, of abolishing inequalities and discrimination in the law, even if this should be variously interpreted and its period of possible realization should differ.

South Africa had declared its disbelief in equality and maintained that there were degrees of dignity in the human race. She defended her whole state system of racial discrimination on the grounds that this provided for a separate differential development of different races having different cultures. Such is the doctrine of apartheid, and it was therefore not surprising that the South African representative had withdrawn from discussions on the Human Rights Commission in Paris, and had not been a signatory to the Declaration of Human Rights.

When the Human Rights Commission concluded I had assumed that as a consultant I should be able to attend any sessions of any organs of the United Nations. But when that commission concluded its session, there arose the question of my continued stay in America for the period of the General Assembly. I was told by an official that I ought to make provision for my departure by the earliest available means.

I had not paid any attention to the technicalities of the matter. I had not of course had any other function in the United States except the practice of my religion. I was invited to preach and to celebrate Holy Communion and was licenced for this purpose by the bishops of New York and Long Island. One authority averred that I ought not to preach any sermon or conduct any service without obtaining the permission of the State Department, specifying the time of service, character of the audience, purport of my remarks, and so forth. The presiding bishop, however, told me that if any difficulties arose through my accepting an invitation to preach, I should refer the matter to him immediately, and I did in fact preach on four or five occasions at churches on Long Island and in Harlem, New York, and no difficulty occurred. Subsequently Dean Pike and the Bishop of New York received an assurance from the Justice and Immigration Departments that none of the restrictions placed upon my speaking and living within certain boundaries in Manhattan should be taken as implying any interference with my spiritual duties. In fact, through the hospitality of Dean Rose of the General Theological Seminary, I reside outside the prescribed area and preach when invited at St. John's Cathedral, which is also outside the area.

As the time of the opening of the fourth session of the General Assembly drew near, amongst all the complex questions confronting the United Nations there were two which inevitably had important bearings upon our South African problems.

President Truman had enunciated his famous "Point Four" proposal on technical aid for the development of backward territories, and this was to be taken up in the Social Committee. Then there was the vitally important conference under the auspices of U.N.S.C.C.U.R. on the conservation of the natural resources of the earth. At this conference it became abundantly clear that there can be no talk of world food and population problems without reference to Africa. The evolution of the whole concept of law and the requirements of long-range planning should make it possible to halt the process of ruthless "mining" of land and human resources. On the other hand, the undertaking of such large-scale projects as those contemplated in Africa would inevitably require the understanding and enthusiastic co-operation of the indigenous population. Hence there could be no effective plans for soil conservation without safeguarding the indigenous populations' rights and title in land.

Several influential Americans, with whom I discussed their country's responsibility in the future development of backward territories, were of the opinion that an international trust fund should be established for the purpose of providing the capital resources as well as the technical assistance necessary to carry out some of the vast projects, which were too

long-range and too closely related to long-term government policy to at-
tract immediate profit-seeking "venture" capital. The alternative is clearly
a rapidly accelerating retrogression of both land and people.[2]

All through that summer the heat continued. I occasionally had a few
hours off for a bathe in Long Island Sound where trim little sailing craft
flecked the sea with white canvas and gay pennants. And there were a
few days' respite in the Episcopal Church Hospital where much kindness was shown by doctors and white and coloured nurses. The same
must be said of the medical staff in the United Nations clinic who
generously interpreted the rules to allow me to be treated there as an
"emergency."

The mental and physical strain of those three months cannot easily be
described. It was clear from the beginning that the colonial powers were
strongly opposed to any precedent being set for direct appeals to the
United Nations over the heads of metropolitan powers. South Africa was
lobbying strenuously against me among those who might be expected to
support the Herero case, and even approached Liberia with the story that
I was a crank and quite unqualified to speak for the native people.

There was a furious round of press conferences and meetings with
non-governmental organizations. The Commission of the Churches on
International Affairs, whom I had approached through the World Council of Churches, was unable to associate itself with what I was doing, but
was not hostile to it. The International League for the Rights of Man
supported me, and Roger Baldwin and Dr. Max Beer put in some valiant
work in the lobbies and in Washington. I addressed, and gave evidence
before, the Commission of Inquiry into Forced Labour and showed them,
as well as some delegations, a documentary film entitled *Civilisation on
Trial in South Africa*. Part of this had been taken in South West Africa
and Johannesburg. I approached non-governmental organizations' con-
sultants at the United Nations and international organizations such as
the Women's International League for Peace and Freedom and also an
advisory committee of the Young Women's Christian Association.

So although it seemed a rather lonely and forlorn fight to many people, including myself, sometimes there were a good many hidden forces

---

[2] S.U.N.F.E.D., the Special United Nations Fund for Economic Development
has now been established by the U.N.

at work, and individuals who were unable to act in a representative capacity did so, nevertheless, on their own personal account.

All this entailed a good many interviews and carefully thought-out approaches to people and organizations holding widely different viewpoints. One false step or serious error in matters of fact, figure, or presentation, could have had disastrous consequences where, in addition to hostile forces seeking grounds of offence, there were naturally those who would have been glad to find some adequate excuse for not taking sides in a matter which for so long had been remote or embarrassed them with a state whose support they perhaps required.

There had already been the three resolutions, passed each year by a two-thirds majority of the General Assembly, calling upon South Africa to bring the mandated territory of South West Africa under the trusteeship system. General Smuts' government had given an undertaking not to proceed with its "incorporation" into the Union. But subsequently an act had been passed in the Union's Parliament "integrating" the territory into the Union. The Act gave the white settlers, numbering one-tenth of the whole population of South West Africa, six seats in the South African House of Assembly, and the non-Europeans, nine-tenths of the population, no representation at all. They were to be represented by one white senator in the Upper House chosen by the government for his "knowledge of Native Affairs." This indicated the progress in self-government after thirty years of the Union's administration of the mandate as a "sacred trust of civilization" in which the well-being of the indigenous inhabitants was to be the first and paramount consideration.

There has seldom been any clearer case of the violation of Christian principles by any Western power. Yet hours and days were to be spent in argument over procedure, precedent and protocol, before the human problem of the native inhabitants, who were being robbed of their lands and rights for an unforeseeable period of history, could be considered.

Sometimes it was difficult in the hectic rush of keeping appointments, writing articles, addressing meetings, and preaching sermons, to keep that tranquillity and confidence in the infinite resources of the creative power of good in the world. So much seemed to depend, for these defenceless people, on the use of my time and energy in opposing the highly-organized political forces which strenuously opposed the just treatment of their case. The very fact that they themselves had been prevented from coming to the U.N. and the whole past record of our white "civilization" in its dealings with them, spurred me on to attempt more than was possible with the limited mental and physical qualities at my command.

I never seemed to be able to free myself from the nervous strain of carrying this burden. Fierce suspicions would take hold of me at the sight of a friendly delegate in close conversation with a member of the South African delegation. At other times, I had a strong but indefinable sense of being supported by the good wishes and prayers of all kinds of people from old ladies and nuns in their convents, to members of trade unions and men like Professor Gilbert Murray, and Mr. Greenidge of the Anti-Slavery Society of England who in his own person carries on the great English liberal tradition; he gives the impression that he values nothing in or out of this world higher than his own personal and intellectual integrity.

How could one compare the value to our cause of the prayers of an aged reverend mother and her community with the gold and prestige or political influence of a state. The contempt for this spirit and for those eternal values which had grown up in a neo-pagan world had been manifest in the regimented hordes of Nazis goose-stepping all over Europe. But what was their endurance value compared to the spirit of the old reverend mother and her kind? Europe had been devastated twice in our generation by this doctrine of arrogant nationalism and racialism. It had really started in Africa, and there it was being revived. Our civilization was being brought to the very brink of its suicide even while, for the first time in history, a convention was being signed against the international crime of genocide and for the establishment of elementary human rights.

On United Nations Day there was a half-holiday, and all the delegations joined in the celebration of laying the corner-stone of the new United Nations building on Manhattan Island. I had omitted to get a pass to the enclosure but a gust of wind brought one of Mr. Truman's phrases—"The United Nations is greater than the sum of its parts" and a reference to the honour which had fallen upon the United States of providing the land and space for this monument and instrument of peace, world order, and freedom. Despite what the cynics had to say, it was, on the whole, an impressive occasion and aroused hopes of a period of sanity for the world and a chance to rebuild the old wastes of our civilization.

After a while I struggled free of the crowds. I found a secluded spot and tried to get my mind back to some of the underlying realities of the matter and of this exhausting episode in my own life. I tried to put some of these thoughts into words and, failing any better expression of gratitude, sent these lines to our supporters:

The spirit of the Lord is nowhere to be seen
Is lost in the night among the stars in their courses.
Is sightless and soundless, but is seen by the hearts desirous of the
        light.
It gleams as a diamond on the dew of the morning.
To the eye of desire of the truth, the spirit of the Lord is visible,
But nowhere to be found and kept.
Nowhere to be held, possessed, but discerned by the heart's desire,
Hidden from the hater, and the lover of his life, the prejudiced,
The knowers of all knowledge and the teachers of all truth.

The spirit of the Lord is voiceless,
Inarticulate as the rushing torrent from the hills.
The spirit of the Lord is not locatable
To the fickle is fitful as the flame on the marshes.
Is frail and easily extinguished
By the wrath of man working not his righteousness.
Is mighty as the mountains, reared up,
Shaped, twisted, and distorted by centuries of slow gigantic move-
        ment
Is hardly accessible as their poised and jagged crags.

The spirit of the Lord possesses those who desire it.
Is unpossessable. Fades as the manna but ever renewable.
More precious than diamonds and rubies,
More abundant than the sands of the shore,
Golden, by the crushing and washing of the sea
(Not by the mines of Mammon destroying land and people).

The spirit of the Lord is unconfined, by bars and prison walls,
By sacred aisles, and choirs and places where they sing.
It blows where it lists
To make music for the shepherds clothed in sackcloth
When the lamb of God is born.
Gloria in Excelsis Deo, et in Terra Pax.

The spirit of the Lord is a sword
Dividing truth from untruth, without hope, fear, or favour,
More exact than the balance, more truthful than the true.
More just than justice.
Forgiving where the law condemns, more exacting than the law.
To the possessors of the law the spirit of the Lord is lawless,
Breaking with non-violence the fetters forged by fear.
Subversive to those who are fearful of the evil.

The spirit of the Lord is unreliable
To those who would, if they could, believe in its purpose.
Too tolerant to those who are intolerant of time.
Is vague and impractical to the apostles of force,
Timid to the regiments of the righteousness of Might.
Weakness to condemners of the Way, the Truth and Life
Next a defiantly dying assassin and a lately penitent thief.

Praise be to Thee O Lord for these mighty mountains
Unpossessed and unpossessable by their possessors.
For these diamonds on the cobwebs in the first light of morning.
For the four winds of heaven and the stars which cannot come down.
Praise be to Thee O Lord for a generous heart in those who are
*   fearful*
And the dispossessed.
For those whom our injustice has left human yet.
Glory be to God for the spirit of the Lord is free.
It opens up new and still untrodden ways
Through the streets of the city and the prison yards,
The paths of the jungle and the desert sands.
Glory be to God for the infinity of his forgiveness
Apportioning no rewards for the evil and the good
For the abundance of his eternal heart, pulsing in the Universe.
Glory be to God for the destiny of equality in his infinity.
For the spirit of the Lord is in the good and the evil, undefeasible,
Creating and re-creating all from our defeats.

To me it seemed as though this spirit was being tested in the struggle to secure a hearing for these Africans above the din and clamour of propaganda and counter-propaganda and the mighty pressures and delicate diplomatic finesse whereby good causes can so easily be deflected from their course. Right and wrong become confused with one another, there is talk of compromise and expediency, and considerations of law and procedure are exalted above justice and honour. In the lobbies, dining rooms, and cocktail bars there were swift exchanges between delegates and complicated bargains with votes by some whose country's self-interest appeared more important than the rights or wrongs of questions remote from the immediate fortunes of their own states.

When the debate began in the Fourth Committee there soon appeared an alignment of forces as between the colonial and non-colonial powers, the United States in this instance being fairly consistently on the side of the non-colonial powers.

On the morning of November 18th the chairman of the Fourth Committee, Mr. Lannung, announced that discussion of the fourth item on the agenda—the question of South West Africa—would begin.

The South African delegate, Mr. Jooste, opened by saying that his government could not ignore indefinitely the unwarranted criticism of its administration of South West Africa, or the effects of that criticism both in the territory and in the Union itself. In the course of his speech he explained that the Union Government was firmly convinced that the policy of encouraging the separate development of the indigenous population in its own environment was to the advantage of that population. Segregation was not a measure against any particular group.

At the conclusion of his defence of the Union's administration, Judge Ingles of the Philippines recounted the history of the South West African case before the United Nations and reminded the committee that the Trusteeship Council, after studying the first annual report transmitted by the Union Government, had observed that the indigenous inhabitants had no franchise, no eligibility to office, and no representation; that only 10 per cent of the total budget expenditure was devoted to the indigenous inhabitants, comprising 90 per cent of the population; that the European inhabitants—10 per cent of the population—owned more than half of all occupied land; and that the facilities for education of the indigenous inhabitants were negligible within the police zone and quite lacking outside it. He remarked that the South African representative had alleged that those observations were unjust, but had not adduced any facts to refute them.

Mr. Ingles felt that the policy of apartheid was designed for the repression of non-European races, and he concluded by saying that his delegation would be content to accept the decision as to whether the issues of the case should be referred to the International Court of Justice or settled by a vote of the members of the United Nations. At the outset of the discussion that followed it seemed that sympathy lay with the tribes of South West Africa and that those delegates who spoke had not been convinced by Mr. Jooste's defence.

However, it was still uncertain whether any state would accept the responsibility of initiating a resolution that I should be given a hearing in the Fourth Committee. Many states had promised to support such a proposal, but it was necessary for one country to make the first move. At the last moment the representative who had given me a verbal promise was unable to take the necessary step because of lack of confirmation from his government. A long silence greeted the chairman's request for speakers, and the meeting was adjourned.

The adjournment gave me an opportunity to mobilize supporters over the week-end, and some feverish lobbying had to be done. On Sunday it was pouring with rain and I finished a round of interviews with a visit to Mr. Stephen Alexis, ambassador of Haiti to the United States, whose ancestor was a leader of the slave armies which liberated his country from Napoleon. I left him a copy of my memorandum with the plea that he help, whether directly or indirectly, and the National Association for the Advancement of Colored People also appealed to him. I was told that a spate of telegrams was being received by the secretary-general, and the Women's International League for Peace and Freedom joined me in lobbying several other smaller powers. One of the South American republics finally raised the question of a hearing in an indirect form which gave the others the opportunity of joining the fray once it had opened up.

There were many tense moments while the discussion centred on the question of procedure, and for days the debate swayed back and forth, plunging me alternately in expectation and despair. However, by twenty-eight votes to six, with nine abstentions, the Fourth Committee finally decided to request the secretary-general to circulate the documents relating to the request for an oral hearing. A sub-committee headed by the U.S. was appointed to examine my credentials. At this point I was greatly upset to receive an air-mail letter from the Bishop of Johannesburg telling me that he was terminating my General License to work in his diocese since I was no longer there. I could understand his difficulty, but it distressed me at the time, being conscious as I was of my weakness under a heavy burden. (Later, when the Bishop of Chichester heard about this, he gave me a General License to work in his diocese.)

There were times throughout that debate when it seemed as though all the efforts that had been made by so many in Africa and Europe to get a hearing for the tribes in South West Africa hung by little more than a hair, and I felt as an almost physical force the immense weight of the opposition of those powerful states which were against a hearing, while their representatives seemed to command unlimited resourcefulness in the use of procedure for obstructing what they disapproved. Furthermore all the committee's time and patience were being taken up in this debate on procedure, which was hardly touching the substance of the matter as it concerned the Africans.

Once or twice when voting on one or another procedural point was imminent, Sartell Prentice, who could hardly bear the suspense of the debate, would go hurrying along the corridors to retrieve one of our supporters who had slipped out to have a drink in the lounge.

As the debate went on for six days I had increasing qualms that, if a hearing were granted, anything I might say would seem like an anticlimax. I was feeling far from fit and dreaded the thought of being too ill to speak, or if I did, of failing to convince such a formidable gathering as the Fourth Committee of the justice of the Africans' cause.

After further delays and discussions my credentials were accepted as being "of good faith and credit." At last, on the morning of November 26th, the chairman asked me to take my place at the committee table. There was a sense of enormous relief as I heard those statements, which I had taken down thousands of miles away by the lantern-light under a thorn bush, being translated into the five United Nations languages by the interpreters in their glassed-in boxes. The Fourth Committee room was crowded to capacity, and one had a sense that everyone, including the United Nations secretariat, reporters, and interpreters, was glad that the substance of the matter was at last being dealt with, and that the words of the Africans themselves could now be heard after the interminable procedural arguments.

I tried to tell the whole story of these Africans within that short space of time. The tragic history of the tribes under German rule had to be briefly described, quoting from the British Blue Book of 1918 (C.D.9146), and their present existence illustrated by their own statements. One I quoted was made by a leading Ovambo agricultural labourer who had spent three years on the farms as a contract labourer:

These Ovambos when they go to the farmers and find that some of them do not treat them well sometimes ask for a permit because they want to go to the police. The masters, of course, refuse them a permit and then they go off on their own to the police. When they arrive there, the first question is, "Where is your pass?" Reply is, "I have no pass." Question, "Why?" Answer is, "I ran away from my master, he treats me badly." Question, "Where are you from?" Answer, "So and so place." Answer, "All right because you got no pass we stick you in jail. You got no right to come here with no pass, no permit, no nothing."

They go to jail for fourteen days to one month. When that time is finished, they give the boy a pass to his master. As I look at it, the boy is perhaps frightened to go back on account of the beatings and because of being away for two weeks in the jail. Then he will come sometimes to Windhoek. Here he is asked in the street, "Where is your pass?" He must answer, "I got no pass." Question, "Why you got no pass?" He must answer, "I ran away from my master because he is bad." They say, "We cannot receive you as a complainer; first of all we got to let you fall under the Pass Law. We got to show you you got to have a pass before you come here to Windhoek." Then he is getting another fourteen days or one month, unless he pay the fine.

I have got no record of this. But this is how it is. He does not serve his sentence in Windhoek. They send him to the place nearest his work. Then in the courts the interpreter does not always understand. Secondly, that man does not understand the law here. So you see these poor men; they get the sjambok from the master, but the law, he cannot make it understand.

I tried to make a case through the Advisory Board but the Chairman of the Board will ask many questions I cannot answer.

Another statement read:

The sheep that I have been speaking of here are karakuls. Each sheep may be worth four pounds. The sun burns this poor fellow looking after the sheep. Sometimes the rain falls and he must take them home before sunset. Sometimes it is cold and he has no clothes or shoes. He works in rags and tatters. If each sheep is worth four pounds, then 700 sheep are worth 2,800 pounds. But what does this poor fellow earn every month?

This shepherd looking after all these sheep earns anything between five shillings and seven and sixpence or eight shillings per month as his salary (1948). And from this he has to help feed his wife and children. He only gets about a sixpence worth of mealie meal per day. During the lambing season this poor shepherd must collect all the lambs from the sheep, tie them around his body and carry them home. He carries them home alive and his master kills them when they get home after separating them from their mothers. Each pelt from a lamb is worth about two pounds. The karakul is the black diamond of South West Africa.

Then I quoted Festus Kandjo:

Do you think, in your own opinion, that such people who are treated as lifeless articles should know anything about incorporation? It is being said that Ovambos favoured incorporation. And yet they are the most ill-treated people in the whole of the territory. A person who does not know his own name, how can he know what incorporation means?

As the Bishop of Damaraland had pointed out, commenting on the Referendum, "to those who know South West Africa the significance of the figures is quite different from what appears on the face of them. The 30,000 who were against annexation by the Union are the only Natives who have any idea of the meaning and significance of the matter at issue. . . ."

I asked that the Africans should be given an opportunity of stating their case before the United Nations, or before a commission appointed for that purpose, and that until they had expressed their views through their own spokesmen no final decision should be reached regarding the disposal of South West Africa. And I asked that their lands should be returned to them and their territory brought under the trusteeship system of the United Nations:

The future of all Africa and of South Africa especially calls for a firm holding to their moral obligations by all civilized nations. Thus they will firmly establish the principle of trusteeship, a principle which South Africa herself in former years had an honoured part in initiating.

Then I concluded with Hosea Kutako's prayer on the day when the petition was signed:

> . . . *Give us the courage to struggle in that way for what is right.*
> *Oh Lord, help us who roam about. Help us who have been placed in*
> *Africa and have no home of our own. Give us back a dwelling*
> *place. . . .*

At last the voices of the Africans had been heard in that forum of the world. The simple reiteration of their thoughts and the cruel facts of their experience proved profoundly moving after the lengthy and tedious procedural debate which might well have prevented their case being heard at all.

As Stanley Burch wrote forcefully in the London *News Chronicle:* "The trumpets should sound in the shantytown of Johannesburg. The angry mutter of Africa has broken through the crust of the United Nations. . . ."

At the United Nations, the oratory was supplied by Stephen Alexis in a torrent of perfect French. Beginning, "After having listened to the statement made by the Reverend Michael Scott I now understand fully why so much was done to prevent his being heard by this Committee," he went on to deliver a scorching indictment which I have no space here to quote.

In the debate that followed, the resolutions to be submitted to the General Assembly were considered and eventually, on December 2nd, 1949, the draft report of the Fourth Committee on the question of South West Africa was adopted and, on the 6th, by an overwhelming vote the General Assembly passed two resolutions (see Appendix 9). The first regretted the cessation of reports from South Africa and asked that they should be resumed. The second resolved to refer the whole matter to the International Court of Justice for an advisory opinion on the legal aspect of South Africa's international obligations and her competence to modify the status of the territory of South West Africa.

At last our cause had been vindicated, and the matter now lay with the legal experts of the world. Opinion was strong on our side. Alas, among the messages and telegrams which came in during those days, there was one telling me of my father's death a few hours after the Fourth Committee hearing. Another was from Tshekedi Khama, regent of Bechuanaland: "With God all things are possible. Silence means no forgetfulness. Thoughts and prayers always with you."

On May 16th, 1950, the International Court of Justice assembled at the Palace of Peace, a large baroque building erected by the Carnegie Foundation at The Hague.

During the six days that the legal implications of the South West African controversy were being argued I was impressed by the cold and abstract formality of the proceedings which had a strength and a dignity of their own, peculiar to the law.

At each session the thirteen judges (one was missing), in their black gowns and white lace bands, filed into their places at the long table facing the courtroom in a slow procession led by the registrar, Edward Hambro, an eminent Norwegian. At each successive session the oral hearing proceeded at the point where it had left off while all the judges sat silent throughout, except for the introductory and closing remarks of the French judge, president of the Court. At their entrance, all in the courtroom would stand to attention as the chief usher announced, "La Cour!"

The history of the subject was first dealt with by Dr. Karno, assistant secretary-general of the United Nations Legal Department, who gave a masterly summary of the whole controversy. The legal arguments which ensued illustrated the confusion that exists in legal theory, especially with regard to the location of sovereignty during this period of evolution of international law towards a higher conception of world order and responsibility.

I, as representative of the International League for the Rights of Man, had intimated to the Court my willingness to be cross-examined on any of the evidence which formed part of the record of the Fourth Committee, submitted by the secretary-general, and to which the Court's attention was called by Dr. Ingles of the Philippines (see Appendix to Summary Record of the Fourth Session of the Fourth Committee, 1949). Those who are interested in the details of the discussion should refer to Dr. Karno's presentation (C.R. 50/5. seq.) and to the written and oral statements submitted to the Court by the governments of the United States, Egypt, the Philippines, India, and South Africa.

The International Court gave its advisory opinion in writing at The Hague on July 11th, 1950, in answer to the questions addressed to it by the U.N. General Assembly. In the operative part of the opinion the Court stated:

That South West Africa is a territory under the International Mandate assumed by the Union of South Africa on December 17th, 1920; that the Union of South Africa continues to have the international obligations stated in Article 22 of the Covenant of the League of Nations and in the Mandate for South West Africa as well as the obligation to transmit petitions from the inhabitants of that Territory, the supervisory functions to be exercised by the United Nations, to which the annual reports and the petitions are to be submitted and the reference to the Permanent Court of International Justice to be replaced by a reference to the International Court of Justice, in accordance with Article 7 of the Mandate and Article 37 of the Statute of the Court.

There is some irony in the position taken up by the South African Government towards its Mandatory obligations. At the end of World War II and at the demise of the League of Nations, South Africa claimed that, the League having died, the Mandate was also dead and that she, as trustee, therefore had the right to inherit the property. When in 1946 the proposal by General Smuts for incorporation was rejected by the General Assembly, South Africa still maintained as she does today that the Mandate had died. During the protracted negotiations with the U.N. Special Committee on South West Africa, South Africa showed that she was not prepared to concede any rights to the United Nations in respect of South West Africa except a recognition of the judicial authority of the International Court of Justice (which could not in any case be abrogated by a unilateral action). She offered to send annual reports to the three remaining Principal Allied and Associated Powers—namely, Britain, France, and the United States—but she declined to make any provision for supervision by the U.N. or to undertake to transmit petitions.

In the event of the Union Government continuing in its refusal to report on South West Africa or to accord "an international status" to the territory compatible with the resolution of the General Assembly, further recourse could be had to the International Court of Justice for its compulsory jurisdiction.

Dealing with compulsory jurisdiction under Article 7 of the Mandate, Sir Arnold McNair, the British Judge at the International Court, in a separate opinion published with the advisory opinion of 1950, called attention to this possible course of action.

The General Assembly accepted this advisory opinion and established (by Resolution 749 A [VIII]) a subsidiary organ which in addition to continuing to try to negotiate an agreement with South Africa was empowered to "examine such information and documentation as may be available in respect of the Territory of South West Africa," to "examine reports and petitions which may be submitted to the Committee or the Secretary General," and to "transmit to the General Assembly a report concerning conditions in the Territory."

The United Nations, thus recognizing that South Africa may have no legal obligation to place South West Africa under the trusteeship system, has nevertheless obligations to transmit reports and petitions to the United Nations, and has sought to meet South Africa by setting up at great expense a special committee. This has now become a permanent subsidiary organ of the United Nations with a membership of nine member states, namely U.S.A., Uruguay, Mexico, Pakistan, Ethiopia, Finland, Brazil, Egypt, and Indonesia. This committee has produced a report each year from all the information accessible to it and it examines petitions concerning South West Africa.

The Court expressed the opinion that "the degree of supervision to be exercised by the General Assembly should not . . . exceed that which applied under the Mandates system and should conform as far as possible to the procedure followed in this respect by the Council of the League of Nations." The General Assembly therefore referred two further questions to the International Court, namely, (1) whether decisions of the General Assembly on questions relating to reports and petitions from South West Africa should be regarded as important questions within the meaning of Article 18 para. 2 of the U.N. charter thus requiring a two-thirds majority vote, and (2) whether it is consistent with its previous advisory opinion to grant oral hearings to petitioners, on matters relating to the territory of South West Africa.

To both of these questions the International Court has given its opinion in the affirmative on June 7th, 1955, and on June 1st, 1956, respectively. Both these advisory opinions were unanimous.

At the hearing at The Hague on the latter question the British Government, having asked for a postponement of the case for a week, requested the opportunity to make a statement. The British Attorney General Sir Manningham Buller accordingly appeared at The Hague and occupied the morning session of the Court with a lengthy argument against the granting of oral hearings to petitioners, as this would exceed the degree of supervision which actually obtained under the League, whatever might then have been permissible. Thus he has by implication accepted the previous advisory opinions of the Court and the establishment of the U.N. Special Committee on South West Africa with the right to receive and examine reports and petitions, though disputing the technical point as to whether they should be written or oral. His argument that the granting of oral petitions would be contrary to the Court's previous opinion was not accepted by the British judge, Sir Herscht Lauterpacht, who gave a lengthy separate opinion, but concurred in its conclusion. Nor was it accepted by the United States Government which had submitted a written statement to the Court favouring the granting of oral hearings to petitioners.

After the Assembly session of 1955, when it was decided to refer the question of granting oral hearings to the International Court, I felt I should return to South West Africa to explain to Chief Hosea and the others why this question was being referred to the Court when I had myself been granted hearings by the Fourth Committee on five different occasions which they had been prevented from attending. I wanted also to give them some first-hand account of all that had transpired at the United Nations and what their own position was, as inhabitants of the territory, in relation to the U.N. Moreover, I wanted to confide in Chief Hosea the truth about my own position, such as I have set out in this book, and the real reasons why I have experienced so many obstructions and restrictions when I have visited the United States to attend the U.N. on their behalf.

However the South African Government had, during the U.N. session of 1951, sent me a written declaration that I was "a prohibited inhabitant of or immigrant to the Union of South Africa" and would not be allowed to land at any of its ports. There appears to be no legal redress against such a fiat of the minister of the interior, and I was unable to get it rescinded. In January 1956 I wrote to the South African High Commissioner in London, asking him to request the appropriate authority in the Union to permit me to visit South West Africa, for the purpose of giving an account of what had transpired at the U.N. to those who had asked me to go there. After four months' delay I received a formal letter, signed "Your obedient servant," telling me that this request had been refused.

It was ten years from the time I had first cabled an appeal to the United Nations on behalf of Chief Frederick Mahareru, after seeing him in Bechuanaland, to the publication of the third advisory opinion of the Court, upholding the right of the inhabitants to make oral petitions and the United Nations to hear them. For ten years South Africa defied two-thirds majority resolutions of the General Assembly, passed each year, and the opinions of the International Court of Justice. On the contrary South Africa has proceeded with its plans to absorb South West Africa in the political, economic, and social system of the Union and to extend there its network of discriminatory legislation against the inhabitants, who are properly wards of the United Nations. True they claim to pay verbal deference to world opinion by not calling this process "incorporation."

If South Africa is to be held to her moral and legal obligations the international community must decide what course can be followed which will bring South Africa back into the comity of nations and to a realization of the importance of the sacred trust bestowed upon her.

As a positive action the United Nations could, as our petitions have repeatedly pointed out, call the attention of the South African Government and people to the many ways in which the United Nations and its specialized agencies, such as the World Health Organization, the World Bank, the Food and Agricultural Organization, and the Children's Emergency Fund, could assist in the solution of the dire problems of poverty, disease and malnutrition amongst the African people of South West Africa. In the course of time such an approach might penetrate even the hard hearts or heads of wealthy diamond merchants and karakul sheep farmers in South West Africa.

Alternatively and simultaneously it would be possible to influence South Africa by establishing in the international community standards of freedom from discriminations on grounds of colour or race or religion in such spheres as sport, in the Olympic games, for example, and in education and entertainment, so that what is feared and dreaded in South Africa may be seen to be not only possible but to have healthy and happy results in the world outside.

In the sphere of international law, Britain, America, and France, or some other former members of the League of Nations, could seek the compulsory jurisdiction of the International Court in the matter of South West Africa through invocation of Article 7 of the Mandate treaty. Any continued defiance would then entail possible recourse to sanctions and even to the Security Council.

Certainly the so-called Western nations cannot afford to see a debacle of democracy in Africa such as may well happen if the political doctrine and practice of "apartheid" is allowed to spread the disease of racial hatred and to poison the blood stream of race relations from the South into

Central and East Africa. Already this cult has created suspicion and dis-like of the white man amongst Africans and other so-called "non-Europeans" far beyond the borders of South Africa. Thus far from being solely a domestic question for the Union it has become an international question affecting Britain and even the functions and person of the Sover-eign. The Crown is inevitably involved in the question of South West Africa since the mandate was entrusted to South Africa "for and on be-half of His Britannic Majesty" and his successors. Today, as far as the United Nations is concerned, the Crown has to be advised by her British ministers on the one hand and by her South African ministers on the other. Hence there was a pointed question by the delegate of Mexico at the U.N. as to how Her Majesty the Queen is advised on this matter and whose advice must prevail.

It would therefore help to resolve this dilemma of loyalties and good faith if the compulsory jurisdiction of the International Court could be sought or its powers of arbitration invoked and its decision then accepted by Her Majesty as head of the Commonwealth.

This compulsory jurisdiction was again requested, as in previous years, in the statement which I made to the Fourth Committee on September 26th, 1957. Once more I had to act as representative, though I was sup-ported at the meeting by Mburumba ua'Kerina Getzen, a student in the United States, the only African from South West Africa then studying abroad. I was also able to include in my account a very able and moving plea from a young Herero man, Jariretundu Kozonguizi, who graduated from Fort Hare University and had the confidence of his chiefs and people and would have been their spokesman in person had he been allowed.

I urged the necessity of turning to other methods of breaking the dead-lock which still persisted after ten years of painstaking negotiation. Dur-ing all this time the situation in South West Africa had been steadily worsening and my statement (sections of which are quoted in Appendix 10) was able to give new information illustrating the shameless exploita-tion on which is based so much mining and agricultural wealth—a system of economy particularly susceptible to the pressures of sanctions and boycott for which I now pressed. Several resolutions were passed at the twelfth (1957) session of the General Assembly, including one calling the attention of former members of the League of Nations and other states concerned to the possibility of seeking the compulsory jurisdiction of the International Court of Justice under the provisions of Article 7 of the mandate. The same resolution requested the Committee on South West Africa to consider the legal implications of legislation affecting the status of South West Africa by according the white population six elected representatives in the Union Parliament and vesting African lands in South West Africa in the South African Native Trust and its trustee, the South African Minister of Native Affairs.

As soon as the resolution referring to the possibility of recourse to the International Court for its judgement was tabled by twelve states, an unusual course was adopted by the chairman of the Fourth Committee for the 1957 session, Mr. Thomat Khoman of Thailand. He introduced a resolution himself from the Chair, proposing that a Good Offices Committee be set up with the United Kingdom and the United States as members and a third member to be nominated by the president of the Assembly. This resolution was strongly supported by the United Kingdom and the United States. The unusual procedure and the speed with which the chairman's resolution was introduced seemed to take many delegates by surprise, and the alacrity with which the United Kingdom delegate spoke in its favour gave rise to certain suspicions having regard to the attitude previously taken by the British Government on this question.

On reflection, however, most delegates, except those of the Communist states, decided it was worth giving mediation another trial since both Britain and America were willing to act, provided South Africa agreed to take part in the discussions. The resolution of the chairman was accordingly passed by fifty votes to nine, with thirteen abstentions, together with four other resolutions dealing with petitions and the work of the Committee on South West Africa. Sir Leslie Munro nominated Brazil as the third member of the Good Offices Committee.

When I returned to England in November 1957 I wrote a letter to the *Times* pointing out the opportunity which the setting up of this Good Offices Committee gave to Britain and America of bringing their great influence to bear on the South African situation. This has become a growing menace in Africa and a reproach to Western standards of civilization which cannot be evaded any longer on the plea of domestic jurisdiction. My letter to the *Times* concluded:

It may be that cooperation between Britain and America in facing this problem with important implications in Africa will pave the way for cooperation between Britain and America with a more long-term vision of economic and social development in Africa. An example might be made of this in the High Commission Territories of Basutoland, Swaziland, and Bechuanaland. Could not a commission be set up for these territories which would be able to draw upon the resources of the Specialized Agencies of the United Nations, especially the World Health Organization, the Food and Agriculture Organization, the Technical Assistance Board, and the International Bank?

South Africa could then perhaps be persuaded by example as well as negotiation to regard the "outside world" as not necessarily hostile and lacking in understanding of African problems and to see how the enthusiastic cooperation of Africans can be won for the conservation and use of their land and human resources.

In Bechuanaland the Okhavango river continues its flow of fresh water into the desert at a rate of 15,000 cubic feet a second. Geographers such as Professors Debenham and Wellington have, for many years, been urging the great possibilities of development in this region. The situation in that part of Africa calls for an inspired effort on the part of some of our economists, technologists, and men and women working in the field with some understanding of human nature as well as nature, and something a little bit more generous than some of the politicians seem to have meant when they have spoken of partnership.

It so happens that this area, the delta of the Okhavango, in the Kalahari, forms part of an area adjacent to that occupied by a section of the Herero people of South-West Africa who sought protection from Britain with their Chief Frederick Maharero during the German massacre of their people in 1904. Here it would be possible to show South Africa the advantages of cooperation with "the outside world" and with Africans, as an alternative to her increasingly dangerous isolationism in Africa.

Nov. 8, 1957

17　The Africa Bureau

Since 1950, when I received a notice from the Union Government while I was attending the U.N. session, declaring me to be a "prohibited inhabitant of or visitor to the Union of South Africa," I have made several attempts to secure the rescinding of this order at least so far as South West Africa is concerned but so far of no avail.

These years have therefore been spent in building up an organization to try and ensure that people in Britain are aware of the magnitude of their responsibilities and the nature of the problems that have to be faced in Africa. In particular it seemed important that Africans who come to Britain should have adequate facilities for stating their case to all sections of opinion in Britain and should not find themselves forced to appeal only to one section, and that perhaps one which espouses their cause for the sake of the partisan use that can be made of it. Inevitably Africans feel attracted in a strange and often seemingly hostile country to those who shout loudest in their favour. But sometimes considerations of party or personal publicity that can be got out of a particular case are inclined to weigh heavier than considerations of the best tactics to be employed in order to get the best results in a particular case, which if tactfully handled may be able to secure support in more than one political party or religious group. There was also the need to keep people in Africa, especially the leaders of the different communities, informed about happenings in Britain and the British Parliament which concern their country. Often these are very inadequately or one-sidedly reported in the African press.

For this purpose we began publishing an *Africa Digest* of news and views on British-African questions.

My own experience of arriving in Britain with a petition from little-known tribesmen in South West Africa had brought home to me something of the difficulties facing Africans who arrive in Britain. I had little knowledge of the intricacies of political party life in Britain, and the little knowledge I had was probably more dangerous than no knowledge at all.

If Africans take the trouble to send a deputation to Britain, which is often done at considerable cost derived from the sixpences and shillings of impoverished people, it is right that they should not only be given a proper hearing but that their case should not be spoiled by being used as the weapon of one faction. Though Africans are becoming aware of this danger now, both effort and organization are needed to circumvent it.

It is in no spirit of contempt or ingratitude that one speaks in this connection of the stage army of the good. In this age of go-getting and paucity of ideals there are all too few who are willing to devote themselves to good causes. The very fact that they are so few, and that they have to keep going off the stage and coming on again for a different scene, renders them less and less effectual. Then again, attracted to every good cause there are the mad the bad and the sad who, when mixed together, are apt to make a motley and undisciplined army to rely on in difficult manoeuvres.

All too often, too, it has happened that a very good case has been taken up by the most extreme or near-lunatic fringe, in whose hands it can either be made into nonsense or become merely a stick with which to attack the governing party or the Archbishop of Canterbury, or the Colonial Office. Then the merits of the case are apt to become of secondary importance, and the result is that support for that particular cause becomes restricted to the support which that particular party doctrine or nostrum is able to command for itself.

How different might have been the history of Kenya if the Kikuyu chiefs, when they came to England in the 1930s to ask for quite modest constitutional reforms, had received the attention in influential circles in Britain which their case deserved. Socially some of them were well received, though no doubt colour prejudice did manifest itself and was not without effect on their own attitude. But politically their main, if not their only, support came from the accustomed loudspeakers on colonial questions. The result was that one of them visited Moscow to hear more about communism, and the rest returned jaded and disillusioned with British justice and also with the white man's religion. Jomo Kenyatta subsequently was sentenced to seven years' imprisonment during the Mau Mau revolt, in a trial that will probably in the eyes of future historians come to be regarded as one of the most significant trials of the century.

The seeds of revolt undoubtedly grew out of their disillusionment and disenchantment. Failing any adequate constitutional means of change, the resistance to injustice took on wilder and more and more irresponsible forms, till the leadership got into the hands of the unscrupulous gangster type of religio-political leaders who were capable of using any and every means to appeal to the hatred and the most base and violent instincts of their people. Moderation thus became something to be scorned and ridiculed by both white and black in Kenya, rather than as something to be determinedly striven for as a *modus vivendi* for all communities in the country.

The Mau Mau revolt began before any of our attempts to build up an organization and a coherent body of public opinion on African questions had had time to take shape.

The first of these tentative moves towards such an organization took the form of the joint publication of a Penguin book called *Attitude to Africa*. The group consisted of its four contributors, Professor Arthur Lewis, Martin Wight, Colin Legum, and myself, with David Astor, Lady Pakenham, Arthur Creech Jones, Margery Perham, and John McCullum Scott. It was about this time too that Mary Benson, who had served in North Africa as aide to one of the South African generals, became our secretary. As a South African she was attracted to our work and to the idea of forming the Africa Bureau and worked for it in the most selfless way in place of the fame and fortune she had attempted to seek in the film world. Later Lord Hemingford returned from Africa and became our chairman.

The group has been held together—more than that—fused into an organization, by their common interest and sense of urgency about Africa in the context of the post-war world. But the tasks of building an organization are slow and complicated and, in our case, beset by a great deal of misunderstanding, petty jealousy, and efforts on the part of other organizations to "co-ordinate" us, on the plea of unity in the common fight. From their point of view this had the laudable aim of extending the scope of their own influence and support; but to us it would have meant limiting our own possibilities of influencing opinion to that which was already enjoyed by them. All the same our refusal to be co-ordinated under the umbrella of the Movement for Colonial Freedom or Christian Action was often interpreted as a form of egotism or superiority.

These complications were in no way diminished by the sudden controversies into which we found ourselves precipitated by developments in Africa at an ever-quickening pace, before our organization was able to get firmly on to its legs.

The first of these events was the arrival in Britain of Tshekedi Khama, who had voluntarily exiled himself from his own tribal territory in Bechuanaland as a protest against the British Government's handling of the delicate question of his nephew Seretse's marriage to a white girl in London.

It was difficult to deal delicately with any aspect of this question in the middle of the uproar that ensued in Parliament and in the press of Britain and South and Central Africa. Tshekedi resolutely refused to be drawn into the uproar, or diverted to a conference in America by M.R.A., but pursued a policy of patient explanation and negotiation with the secretary of state for Commonwealth relations of the Labour Government. He confided in us his hopes and fears for the future of his country, as well as his proposals for dealing with the question of his nephew Seretse's marriage. We arranged introductions for him, as a result of which he was invited to address gatherings of the Commonwealth Parliamentary Association, Chatham House, and various parliamentary groups and missionary societies.

Before his voluntary exile he had asked for a commission of inquiry, not on whether his nephew was "a fit and proper person to be a chief," but on the question of native law and custom which arose when a young chief contracted a Christian marriage or a marriage under Western monogamous law. Under the old tribal law a chief could marry one or more wives of his own choice, but in the case of his marriage to the woman who was to be regarded as the bearer of future chiefs the consent of the tribe was required.

Tshekedi contended that the old tribal laws and precedents were no longer applicable, and that a great deal of the confusion and conflict among his people was due to the constitutional impasse which had been created. It was this that he felt should be the subject of a commission which might recommend an adaptation of the law. There was, however, strong pressure on the British Government from South Africa and Rhodesia. A commission was set up to inquire whether Seretse was a fit and proper person to be chief and, in the course of taking evidence, it inevitably divided the Bamangwato into conflicting factions. Moreover its proceedings were never published, so suspicions could not be allayed.

Tshekedi himself renounced the chieftainship for himself and his heirs and proposed that an agreement should be signed between himself and his nephew, in which they both renounced chieftainship and would return to their country and build up a representative council which would take the place of the chieftainship. It was not until five years later that this proposal was eventually adopted and an agreement signed by them both. In the meantime the matter had been debated back and forth in successive Parliaments and a great deal of heat and anger generated amongst officials, the general public both in Britain and America, and amongst the Bamangwato themselves, to say nothing of other Africans who saw it as only another instance of white superiority.

The composition of the question was persistently bedevilled by well-meaning champions of freedom for colonial peoples and professional public relations experts, who interfered with every attempt to bring about a joint statement by Tshekedi and Seretse on the lines of his proposal. Left-wing Socialists and anti-Imperialists were strongest in urging Seretse not to abdicate or compromise his position as chief, and a deputation from Bechuanaland claiming to be his supporters was welcomed by certain organizations with little consideration being given to the worth of their case, the truth of their claims to be loyal supporters of their chief or their standing in relation to their own people. They were Africans and they were against the government so they must be supported and meetings organized for this purpose.

In all this controversy there was of course the interplay of the strong personalities of the two Khamas, both of them men of character, though of widely different dispositions and upbringing. Ruth Khama was also a strong character herself, though bewildered both by the interplay of the personalities of her two male relatives and of British politics, which she never pretended to understand.

There were indeed few of the participants in that little drama of modern Africa and Britain who did understand all the implications of what they were doing or what was being done to them.

At the end of a long debate in the House of Commons, in which the future of Tshekedi and his people had been strenuously debated, I remember one of the leading protagonists coming up to Tshekedi in the lobby after the division in which the vote had gone against his being allowed to return. He slapped Tshekedi on the back with a good-natured laugh and exclaimed: "Well, Tshekedi, anyhow you have seen how our parliamentary institutions work. You realize of course that a lot of our chaps would have much preferred to be in their lobby just as there are a lot of their chaps who would rather have been in ours."

I can still hear the burst of African laughter ringing through the cloisters of the House of Commons which greeted this remark. There was, I thought I detected, a slight note of hysteria in it as well as amusement, for Africans often laugh when they are hurt. It is so much the thing to do that sometimes even when others are hurt they laugh and it is not by any means always callousness. Tshekedi's laugh finished with his characteristic series of jerky little hisses which can be prolonged if necessary while thinking of a suitable reply. But the gentleman had passed on, so no reply was needed.

The task of lobbying different parties and even competing groups within the same party is a very intricate and delicate one, not easily understood by Africans and others unfamiliar with the devious ways and byways of the English political scene. It cannot be performed by a strongly partisan group, or an organization with a flag-waving name, or one dominated by an individualist personality. This applies as much in the religious as in the political sphere. It is one of the reasons why our advisers, knowledgeable in the ways of the world and human nature, recommended an innocuous-sounding name such as the Africa Bureau.

The negotiations with Tshekedi and the government lasted all through the hot summer months of 1951 and necessitated endless interviews and the drafting and re-drafting of memoranda with Tshekedi and his legal adviser and Mary Benson and myself sitting up far into the night. At first this took place at No. 2 Park Street, the Cripps Arms, where Tshekedi was invited to stay, but after the negotiations with the government broke down he transferred to a quiet little hotel in Bloomsbury. At that time I was the guest of Dr. Fred Irvine, a Quaker in charge of the Friends International Centre, and his wife Dorothy. We owed much to their generous hospitality and encouragement. We had no office and the multiplying files of correspondence were kept under my bed.

Everything done by Tshekedi was done with tremendous gusto and good humour but with punctilious regard for detail and custom, and good form, whether of England or Africa. He was also always very careful to find out, in preparing an address in English, what the exact connotation of a phrase would be for his audience so that it expressed just what he would have wanted to convey in his own tongue. Mary Benson spent herself to the utmost in all this and then typing far into the night, and seriously affecting her own health. Everything had to be done in great haste, without organization or equipment, and in a tense atmosphere of strain due to both the personal and the political tensions involved in the case.

Once, when Tshekedi was due to give an address at Chatham House, the typing of it had only just been finished a few moments before it was due to be delivered. The whole bundle of papers was thrust into Douglas Buchanan's hands to be sorted into consecutive pages by him and Tshekedi as they went along in a taxi. Mary Benson and I arrived later, just as he was beginning his address.

Disaster loomed at the end of page 7. There was no page 8 in the text he had before him. When he turned over the page it obviously made no sense. We looked at one another in acute discomfort, but he was not in the least flustered. "Page 8, where is page 8?" he boomed in the direction of Douglas Buchanan, who dutifully produced out of his pocket three page 8s and handed them to him.

Tshekedi's original proposals for the composition of the whole affair have now been accepted, and he and his nephew and Ruth have returned to Bechuanaland. It is good to read of the patient and painstaking efforts all three of them are making to build up a happier and more prosperous future for their people and their land.

A staff reporter of the Johannesburg *Star* wrote to his paper on July 10th, 1957, from Serowe:

A great change has come over the Bamangwato Reserve. In the seven months since Seretse Khama returned from exile with his English wife, Ruth, the Bamangwato have settled down to a new and peaceful life. Gone are the conflicts in the tribe, the refusal to co-operate with the authorities, and the tribal feuds, family against family. Seretse Khama, 35 years old and now a private citizen but still regarded by his people as their chief, has brought with him a fresh outlook for his people and a spirit of hope. The Royal Khama family is again united for the first time since Seretse's marriage split the tribe. Seretse's uncle Tshekedi Khama,

who opposed the marriage and went into exile with his personal sup-
porters, is the most frequent and the most welcome visitor to Seretse
Khama's home. He and Ruth are the closest friends and Seretse's two
children, seven-year-old Jacqueline and four-year-old Ian, adore their
uncle. . . .

The reporter, a frequent visitor to the Bamangwato country during
the troubles of the past nine years, closed his report from Serowe with
these words: "I have a feeling that when I leave here tonight my job in
Bechuanaland will be finished. The Seretse Khama story has come to a
fairy-tale ending that could easily be 'and they lived happily ever after.' "

While the Bechuanaland controversy was still unresolved we were
precipitated into the question of the Central African Federation. Conferences were held behind closed doors at the Victoria Falls Hotel and in
London, at which representatives of the Labour Government, in the first
instance, and latterly of the Conservative Government, officials of the
Commonwealth Relations Office and the Colonial Office, became more
and more committed both in principle and in detail without either the
British people or the African people knowing exactly what was being
done. Mr. James Griffiths went to a great deal of trouble to consult
African opinion in Central Africa and in doing so won the trust and good
will of the Africans, who had never known a Secretary of State to concern
himself so much about their views or shew them so much sympathy and
personal consideration. Secretaries of State had previously appeared before them as great personages speaking with very authoritative voices
and liable to become very irascible at any sign of criticism or presumption
in the attitude of the governed towards their governors.

It was partly this that to some extent lulled the African leaders into a
belief that the British Government was unlikely to impose federation on
them. However, there was a general election in 1951 and a Conservative
Government came into power in England. Even so, there had never been
any pledge by the Labour Government that consultation implied consent,
or that they were under any obligation to consider African opinion as
decisive.

African chiefs and the congresses of Northern Rhodesia and Nyasaland
protested vigorously against the federation scheme, as an attempt to enforce white domination on the Southern Rhodesian pattern on the two

northern territories which were still protectorates of Britain. They raised funds from the sixpences and shillings of their followers to send deputations to Britain and they presented a petition to the Queen. The Africa Bureau and other organizations arranged meetings for them with members of Parliament, and we organized public meetings for them to address in London and the provinces. It was in this way that there came into existence, in the university and other provincial cities, councils on African affairs which have stimulated interest in their localities in problems of such great importance to Britain and Africa.

Only at Cambridge University was there any vociferous opposition to the chiefs' presentation of their case, and even that was not exactly vocal. It took the form, as soon as the meeting began, of a fusillade of Chinese crackers from outside the Union, and an indeterminable number of hep cats on pianos produced a cacophony the like of which can never have been heard before either in Cambridge or in Africa. There was much recrimination afterwards against the members of the political club responsible; but we were all grateful for the typical African humour of one of the old chiefs, who thanked those responsible for the din for the way in which they had shewn their approval "in a manner according to their custom" even before they had heard what was going to be said.

The chiefs presented a petition to the Queen, but, to the undying shame of the then conservative Colonial Secretary and the officials of the Colonial Office concerned, the chiefs were given a rebuff when they asked if they might be granted an audience with the Queen. She was advised not to grant their request and they were not allowed to see her even in a social capacity. Extracts from their petition, which was published by the Africa Bureau in January 1953, are given in Appendix 11.

Meanwhile, I took them to Westminster Abbey, where nothing impressed them so much as the simple paving stone in the floor of the west nave, inscribed:

> BROUGHT BY FAITHFUL HANDS
> OVER LAND AND SEA
> HERE RESTS
> DAVID LIVINGSTONE . . .
>
> FOR THIRTY YEARS HIS LIFE WAS SPENT
> IN AN UNWEARIED EFFORT
> TO EVANGELISE THE NATIVE RACES,

TO EXPLORE THE UNDISCOVERED SECRETS,
TO ABOLISH THE DESOLATING SLAVE TRADE,
OF CENTRAL AFRICA,
WHERE WITH HIS LAST WORDS HE WROTE:
'ALL I CAN WRITE IN MY SOLITUDE, IS,
MAY HEAVEN'S RICH BLESSING COME DOWN
ON EVERYONE, AMERICAN, ENGLISH OR TURK,
WHO WILL HELP TO HEAL
THIS OPEN SORE OF THE WORLD.'

Inevitably my thoughts went back to the early days of the Universities Mission to Central Africa, the Universities' response to Livingstone's great endurance and faith and passionate campaigning. Their attitude in the great federation controversy seemed to be in marked contrast to the earlier faith which had earned the respect of so many of the African chiefs, which had won them and their people to the Christian religion and their acceptance of the protection of the English Queen.

Now here were these chiefs—some of them Muslims, some Christians —who had come at great expense to appeal to Britain to keep faith with them. Opposed to them, and received in all the best circles, were Roy Welensky and other swashbuckling politicians who spoke honeyed words about British ideals and the Western way of life in one breath and in the next muttered dark hints about a Boston tea party in Central Africa and being forced to look towards South Africa.

In all this the voice of Christian opinion seemed strangely muted. Considered opinions were expressed, confidential memoranda were sent to the government, and even a cable to Sir Winston Churchill by the Bishop of Nyasaland. But there was little positive action. The inequities and dangerous unbalance of the whole federal scheme was not seriously challenged by the Anglican Church, and the opposition of the Scottish Presbyterians seemed to die on the threshold of the passage of the Enabling Bill through Parliament. Yet the churches had more knowledge, more experience of the Africans' and others' views than any other institution, certainly more than the Colonial Office and Parliament, and they had more access to opinion and more opportunity to influence events than existed anywhere else. Some of the utterances of members of Parliament in favour of federation shewed an almost incredible ignorance and failure to grasp the facts or implications of what they were doing. It was as much as some of the African members of the delegations sitting in the strangers' gallery could do to restrain their alternating laughter and anger.

It was a never-to-be-forgotten experience shepherding by subway these aged African chiefs from their little Bloomsbury hotel to the House of Commons and back, and arranging their tour to address audiences in the provincial cities of England, Scotland, and Wales. Perhaps it was worth while, despite the result, for they felt something of the warmth and fairness of British people and their willingness to hear people who had come to them in the conviction of the truth and rightness of their cause. The white settlers after all have many relatives and friends to state their case for them in the press and Parliament in Britain and even in the Royal household.

There was the one contretemps at Cambridge University; but Cambridge has more than made up with good measure for that unusually errant sense of humour by the skills and talents it has sent back in such abundance to all parts of Africa from Ghana to Rhodesia.

Out of their visits to Britain has certainly come a better understanding of Africa and the great awakening that is going on there, on the part of ordinary people in Britain. It seems, however, as though the time has come for the establishment either of a standing committee of members of all parties, or some other recognized forum, before which recognized African leaders can appear to state their case without it being left to the efforts of voluntary organizations to improvise meetings when such crises are precipitated. If the British Parliament is to fulfil its role as mediator in Africa, and cultivator of living constitutional government in the complex conditions that exist in such widely different territories, some more effective vehicle than the present African Affairs Board will have to be found to convey to Parliament true facts and opinions.

There can be no doubt that the chiefs were to some extent deceived by the very fact that the Colonial Secretary in the person of James Griffiths had been prepared to listen with such patience and care to all their objections to federation when he was in Central Africa. They could not bring themselves to believe that Her Majesty's Government would be so untrue to the pledges made when the treaties of protection were agreed on between their forefathers and Queen Victoria, and attested to by the missionaries from whom they had received the Christian faith, as to impose federation.

They spoke of the movement of resistance they would organize if this were to happen. It would, they said, be a non-violent movement of passive resistance or civil disobedience, but they would never be able to acquiesce or persuade their people to accept federation. All I did myself at that time, apart from organizing meetings and interviews and press conferences for them in Britain, was to point out that if they intended to organize opposition to federation as they were everywhere saying they would, the time to do so was before the Enabling Bill was passed by Parliament. They found it difficult to bring themselves to believe that Britain would be so unfaithful to her trust as to allow such a Bill to be passed.

I promised them that if it proved impossible to secure a free vote on the Bill, so that members could act in accordance with their conscience without disobeying the party whips, and if it seemed likely that the Enabling Bill would be passed by Parliament, I would come to Central Africa and let them know. Then would be the time to launch their movement, not after the Bill had become law, since it would then be infinitely more difficult to secure its repeal.

Accordingly when the suggestion of a free vote on the Enabling Bill was rejected, and it was clear that the Labour Party itself was not unanimous in its opposition though Jim Griffiths and other labour leaders were now speaking strongly against the imposition of federation without African consent, I flew to Central Africa and had talks with the chiefs and members of congress who had visited England. They had already passed resolutions to organize a movement of non-violent non-co-operation.

I gave it as a personal opinion both in private and in public in Nyasaland that there was nothing incompatible between such non-violent resistance and Christ's teaching. This was denounced over the radio by the bishop of Nyasaland, who said that it was incompatible with the Christian gospel to teach people to disobey the law and would inevitably lead in the end to violence. My own view was, and still is, that the methods of non-violent resistance are compatible with Christ's teaching about respect for one's opponents and the forgiveness of one's enemies. I told them in Nyasaland that in a matter of conscience we must obey God rather than men and that St. Paul's teaching that the powers that be are ordained of God must be understood in the light of Christ's own words and actions. He did not seek to evade an issue because it might result in violence to Himself and his followers. In fact he did not content himself with teaching generalities about the Fatherhood of God and the brotherhood of man. Hungry and thirsty as the common people were for his message of the creative love of God, he saw that the power of evil had to be challenged, even if it expressed itself through the authority of the State and the hierarchy of the Jewish Church of that time. Accordingly he remained only a short time teaching the crowds that followed Him around the shores of the lake. The full implications of his faith in the creative power of God must be faced. And it was when he set his face to go to Jerusalem that the disciples began to hold back, some to have doubts and some to dispute amongst themselves about what their position was going to be in the future Kingdom. Most of them would have begun to realize where this was all leading.

For Christ the implications of the simple prayer He had taught them: "Our Father who art in Heaven . . . Thy will be done on earth . . . Forgive us as we forgive them. . . ." were worked out in action, as prayer must necessarily be, and culminated in the Garden of Gethsemane in His own prayer: "Father if it be possible let this cup pass from me. Nevertheless not what I will but what Thou wilt." His arrest and conviction on the charges of treason and blasphemy were in accordance with the law of the land. There is surely a sense in which it is true to say that He disregarded the law, and even that He deliberately incurred the penalty of disobeying it.

Believing as I did, and having identified myself with the non-violent resistance movement in South Africa, I felt I must support this in Nyasaland. I did not take part in the making of their decisions, but encouraged them to keep their movement true to the principles of non-violence. After I had been deported from Central Africa it was suggested that I had instigated the civil disobedience movement, which was quite untrue. Though I never made any secret of my views, they did no more than give moral support to those who already felt the need of new methods and techniques of resistance, more compatible than the old methods of violence, with the gospel of Christ and belief in the dignity and worth of the human person.

This was the burden of what I said both in private and in public, though it may not always have been well expressed or well translated or well understood. Unfortunately the same was true of what was being said by the bishop of Nyasaland, and gave rise to a great deal of resentment amongst both Christians and Muslims.

At the time, I wrote an account of an episode in Nyasaland in order to try and convey something of the spirit of the Africans in their opposition to federation and the attempt to lead them by another way than that of violence against injustice and bad faith. Here, in an abbreviated form, is what I wrote.

Much will depend on the response which Britain makes to the efforts of moderate-minded African people to secure by non-violent methods the redress of what they sincerely feel to be grievances. . . . It is important for Britain to understand that the efforts which are being made in Nyasaland to keep their movement non-violent is one of the fruits of generations of Christian effort in that country. To think of it and treat it as incipient Mau Mauism may only be a way of discrediting those Africans who are opposed to a violent movement, and of ensuring that violence will eventually grow and spread there. . . . When all other constitutional means have been tried and have failed, and the penalties of disobedience are voluntarily incurred, these penalties need not be imposed with unnecessary application of force and intimidation, such as that used in the suppression of gangsterism and hooliganism. . . .

With other African chiefs, eighty-two in number, Philip Gomani has expressed his people's opposition to Federation. He was seriously ill in hospital when, without informing him, the district commissioner caused a notice to be posted up at his headquarters, informing his people that Federation had been "decided upon" and that the Queen was in favour of it. (In fact the Enabling Bill had not yet been passed by Parliament.) The chief at once sent out advice to his people on how they should conduct themselves non-violently and terminating certain regulations issued on his authority.

During these days strenuous efforts were being made by officials to persuade the chief to cancel his advice to his people to oppose the imposition of Federation. When he persisted in his refusal to do so, he was finally suspended and ordered to leave his district in 24 hours, and was told that the district commissioner had now been appointed as Native Authority in his place.

I was staying with Chief Gomani as his guest at Lizulu, his home and traditional headquarters, at the time he received his banishment order from the governor. On arrival at his house, he had found that many of his people, hearing of the chief's trouble, had come in from the surround-

ing districts. They remained there, old and young, men and women with children on their backs, sitting quietly in his garden and around his house all that day, and the following night. . . .

The chief sat with his wife and counsellors round one of the fires. . . . The people were all exhorted not to resort to any acts of violence, no matter what happened, or how provocative the police might be if they came. There was no hatred or anger in his voice as he appealed to God, to Jesus Christ and to the Queen to behold the plight of his people and to take pity on them in all their fear and trouble. The police raid was expected at any moment. . . .

Suddenly everybody was alert as a young boy came running with the news that police cars and trucks were arriving. The people cleared a passage for them, and the leading car drew up in front of the chief's house, the others remaining at some distance. . . .

There was much confusion and delay. Then one of the African leaders asked that Chief Gomani should be allowed to address his people and explain what was happening, or that someone else should do so. But the police emphatically refused to allow this.

By coaxing and persuasion the argument was carried on, with the chief moving in the direction of the front door. Eventually the police emerged on to the verandah and tried to force a passage through the crowd to the car.

When the chief had been brought to within a few feet of the car, the police commissioner, apparently thinking it might be impossible to get him into the car, blew his whistle and the police began to launch a tear-gas attack. (It afterwards transpired that the African Askaris refused to make a baton charge.) The tear gas was thrown amongst the crowd, who did not know what it was, and believed it to be poisonous. They scattered and the chief was hustled into the car and driven away. I followed on foot and found that it had been stopped some way down the road, and that about ten Africans were pushing it in the opposite direction to where the driver intended to go. Then someone opened the car doors, and the chief was carried away on their shoulders to a small hut in a near-by village. . . .

It was decided to take the chief into Portuguese territory, where many of the chief's tribe reside. As dusk fell, he was lifted on to one man's shoulders, and the whole party, including his wife and two sons, set off across country to the Mozambique border, which was crossed some time after midnight. . . .

On nearing the Portuguese headquarters, one of the chief's sons was sent on, to inform the authorities and to ask if we could proceed. While waiting, Chief Gomani made a statement, which I took down, stressing how he had hitherto co-operated with the British authorities, and hoping that if possible he might be allowed to go to Britain, to make a last appeal and to get medical treatment there. The chief's son returned with two jeeps and a message that the Portuguese authorities would receive the chief. . . .

Subsequently the chief was returned to British territory in handcuffs, where he went to hospital awaiting trial. I myself was deported to England without any charges being made against me, and without any opportunity of explaining my position to any competent body. . . .

The chief, who had served the Crown faithfully for many years, was suspended from his office and banished from his home and property without trial. For the sake of the future, it must be pointed out to the authorities that much of the violence and ill-feeling engendered by their action could have been avoided if the authorities had been able to bring some statesmanship and imagination to bear on their attempt to deal with the situation. A senior Government official should have accompanied the police, and the chief should have been allowed to explain that courting imprisonment was the method he had chosen of protesting against the imposition of Federation on his people: that this, unlike the old way of fighting and violence, was the new way of expressing opposition in a civilized manner, and that they should follow his example and remain non-violent. A responsible official of the Government could then, without any loss of face, have expressed some appreciation of the character and loyal service of the chief, and confirmed that his imprisonment was something which he was voluntarily courting by way of protest, so that he need not be regarded as a criminal in the usual sense. He could have expressed the hope that a better understanding would eventually prevail between the Government and the chief and his people as always in the past. The Africans would have responded to this.

I could not, at the time the police asked me, "use influence" simply in order to facilitate their task. A greater regard for the African was needed, for his way of thought. . . .

I quote this here because it is still relevant to the situation in Central Africa and because it seems possible that the techniques of resistance used by these Africans are likely to spread. They have their counterpart in the bus boycott movement in South Africa where thousands of Africans walked fourteen miles back and forth to work before light and after dark every day, rather than accept the terms imposed on them. Similar boycott movements have been started in Northern Rhodesia against the colour bar in post offices and public buildings and also in the southern states of America. There is some irony of history in the fact that out of darkest Africa something new is coming which challenges a civilization caught in a mounting conflict of ideas and practices, which presuppose force as the only ultimate weapon of conquest or persuasion, a civilization whose rival doctrines of self-interest assault the citadel of the human soul with all the means of propaganda, selected truth, and brain-washing.

The subsequent history of the Central African federation has served to confirm the fears of the Africans and our own in the Africa Bureau. Sir Roy Welensky's government passed an Act in the winter of 1957 to amend the Constitution and to give even greater preponderance of representation to the white community. Lord Home announced the British Government's decision to reject the reference back to it of this measure by the African Affairs Board before it was debated in the House of Commons. On November 26, 1957 an uninspired debate reached its predetermined end by a vote of 301 votes to 245. The two sides never seemed to come to grips with one another or with the fundamental issues at stake. Throughout the debate no mention was made of the tragic history of the Act of Union of the African Franchise in South Africa and the circumvention of the entrenched clause, designed to protect the coloured people's franchise. The Central African Franchise Bill which followed the Constitution Amendment Bill gives to the white voters the power to influence, and probably to control, with their votes the kind of spokesmen Africans may have to represent them and the power to forestall the possibility of any effective boycott of the federal government by Africans. And all this was done on the plea of "non-racial political representation."

The Reverend Andrew Doig, European M.P. representing African interests, writing at this time said:—"Now we have had what I can only call the disastrous visit of Lord Home. His treatment of the African Members in interview, must have killed any remaining hopes of having their case listened to and their questions answered. They were told that only one thing mattered—economic advancement and that that in itself was the final justification for Federation."

Meanwhile the boycott of shops and beer halls in Northern Rhodesia has been met with attempts at forcible suppression and the deportation of congress leaders. While the secretary of Congress, Kenneth Kaunda, was in England to interview Lord Perth and Lord Home and to make an appeal to organizations in Britain, many arrests were reported to have taken place in his home province, and some ugly allegations were made against the conduct of local authorities and district officers which the Colonial Office appeared to be unwilling or unable to answer.

Seeing the tense faces of Africans in the strangers' gallery during the debate, one could not help sensing the disenchantment of Africans at what was being done at Westminster in Britain's name. I looked across at Sir George McLeod, who was in the strangers' gallery too. It seemed as though Parliament was being used to hoodwink the British people by means of what amounted to a confidence trick. See extract from speech of Arthur Creech Jones in House of Commons, Appendix 11B. Has a nation which boasts such men as Livingstone, McKenzie, Steere, and Lugard the government and farseeing statesmanship we deserve in this more complicated, but no less adventurous, period in our history and that of Africa?

Meanwhile in London increasing demands were being made on the Africa Bureau including many personal requests for help. Some were obviously very urgent, especially those from students. There were some whose parents did not enjoy the favour of the Colonial Office and who found it difficult to get scholarships and even to get into universities at all. There were some from Kenya, one who was nearly through his medical course, whose parents were interned under the emergency and were consequently faced with the ruin of all their hopes. It did not require much imagination to realize how much potential good or evil for the future of Kenya there was bound up in the question of whether they could complete their courses or have to return with their hopes and efforts brought to naught through no fault of theirs. So we set up the African Protectorates Trust and into this Freda Troup (a graduate of Newnham, Cambridge) put all the royalties of the book she had written about South West Africa, *In Face of Fear*. Margery Perham of Nuffield College secured a scholarship at Oxford for Berthold Himumuine, who had been my interpreter in South West Africa. He was the much respected head-master of an Anglican Mission School. But mean-minded authorities refused to give him a passport to leave the country to take it up and they wrote a surly reply to a courteously worded plea from the vice-chancellor appreciating all that the white Rhodes scholars from South Africa had meant to the life of the University.

There were so many anxieties and so many different sorts of things clamouring to be done at once. Despite the generosity of those who had helped to set up the Bureau the machinery was pitifully inadequate to all the tasks. Everyone was being overworked and the health of our secretary, Mary Benson, who gave herself so unstintingly, was being undermined. In addition to the physical strain there was the spiritual and nervous tension for anyone with imagination enough to see the implications of what was being done and not done, and to sense the opportunities that were being lost through lack of means.

One day out of the blue came a letter from a solicitor saying that I had been left the residue of an estate amounting to more than five thousand pounds by someone who admired the work I was trying to do. Behind it lay a tragic story of a woman who had brought up a coloured girl as her ward. The ward had grown up and qualified as a nurse. Then one day she was found dead on a beach; her death was due to poisoning and the coroner's verdict was suicide. Her guardian, a Miss Webster, was so afflicted by grief at her being brought to such a state of despair that she made out a will in which she left the residue of her estate to me, whom she had never known, to use "as he deems best for the betterment of the Coloured peoples' condition materially and spiritually." Within three days of making this will she committed suicide herself.

It seemed as if the poor woman's wishes could be fulfilled if the money were given to the African Protectorates Trust for scholarships for African students, and I wrote to the solicitor to this effect.

The law however decreed that she had not made a "valid charitable bequest" and that her estate must be treated as though she had died intestate. Mr. Justice Upjohn made our disappointment even more difficult to bear by his remarks which were published in *The Times* and the *Manchester Guardian:* "There was no end to the means which Mr. Scott might, acting perfectly bona fide, employ. The use to which he was entitled to put the fund was by no means confined to the betterment of the Coloured people in Africa. He could finance a political party, establish a trade union for Coloured people, run a newspaper, and promote legislation in any number of countries." The judge added that I might argue, and had in fact argued, the case of some coloured people before the United Nations.

The other trust which I had designated as a possible beneficiary under the will was the African Development Trust. This had been set up by the Africa Bureau with Sir Walter Moberly, Lord Noel-Buxton, Canon Raven, and myself as trustees. Its purpose was to assist a pioneering effort in Southern Rhodesia at a farm called St. Faith's in the diocese of Mashonaland. Guy Clutton-Brock had gone out there with his wife Molly and small daughter Sally. He had started an agricultural project on some land owned by the Church on which many African families had squatted and were in danger of being evicted by the government on grounds of their inadequate farming techniques. He was running it on a co-operative principle and on the basis of a true partnership between the races. Molly Clutton-Brock had also started a clinic for undernourished and deformed children which was doing a very good work, but which lacked equipment. The results she was getting were in fact attracting a number of white mothers with their spastic children. It had begun as a real venture of faith by people who knew their job technically and were willing to give everything they had to it.

They were joined by a young farmer, Cedric Widman, who had farmed very successfully in Devonshire. He worked his own passage on a cattle ship to Walvis Bay and was the first white man, as far as I know, to work under an African farm manager and to accept an African farm labourer's wage, living with Africans and sharing their meals. His life and death at twenty-nine has been written about elsewhere, but its effects are still felt in that part of Africa and will always be remembered as part of a great venture of faith at a time when dark storm clouds were gathering on the horizons of Rhodesia and Nyasaland. The politicians were talking cajolingly about partnership and co-operation on the one hand and more menacingly about South Africa on the other. (Commenting on a speech by Sir Roy Welensky on co-operation, one African remarked, "He does all the co-ing and we do all the operating.")

I appealed against the judgement of Mr. Justice Upjohn on the advice of solicitors on behalf of the two trusts, but the appeal failed and those whom Miss Webster had sought by her actions to assist were rendered a hundred pounds the poorer in costs.

It was not long after the Central African federation controversy that I received a mysterious anonymous letter from South Africa, handwritten in block capitals and with a rubber stamp of the Chesa Chesa army. It was accompanied by a typewritten declaration of war by fire. "Chesa Chesa is not Communist nor Mau Mau," it said. "We don't kill. But we will burn and have burnt many places." I felt suspicious about the origin of these documents, and this suspicion was confirmed by African leaders. I did not therefore issue a press statement on the subject, thinking that this might do more harm than good. But the ideas contained in these papers have now been widely publicized through their use by the prosecution in the mass trials in South Africa in which 96 African and other leaders were accused of treason.

These papers are reproduced, in part, in Appendix 12 as revealing a trend of thought which, however irresponsible, is being given currency by the very methods which the government is using in its attempt to suppress African organizations and leadership.

Hard on the heels of the federation controversy came another major crisis in the banishment and deposition of the *Kabaka* of Buganda. H. H. Mutesa II arrived suddenly and unceremoniously in Britain at the end of 1953 in a Royal Air Force plane. Only the previous year he had formed part of the royal procession at the coronation of Queen Elizabeth II. Now he came for some advice to our little office in Westminster, where the Africa Bureau with its sorely overburdened staff tries frantically to deal efficiently and humanely with a score of complicated problems all at the same time.

Fortunately the Kabaka was a very human and understanding young man, despite the disadvantage of having been brought up in the atmosphere first of a traditional African court and then of Magdalene College, Cambridge, and the Grenadier Guards. He was a good shot, played cricket, football, and tennis and he had come to enjoy the life of a young man of wealth in English society. Yet he seemed able to move freely from one world to the other without any loss of his humour or poise.

For the last several weeks he had been engaged in close conversations with the new governor of Uganda, Sir Andrew Cohen. The discussions concerned various reforms designed to secure the future of Uganda as a unitary state with a representative legislative council. One of the problems centred around the difficulty of building up a unitary state and at the same time providing for the continuance and growth of the traditional form of government in the Kabakaship and Lukikko of one kingdom in Uganda, namely the Buganda.

The Buganda were suspicious that the proposed constitutional changes for the legislative council were intended to undermine, or would have the effect of undermining, their own traditional form of self-government, the Kabaka and the Lukikko, which to them meant something a great deal more than local self-government. It was to them the linch-pin of their social system, and bound up with it were not only their political ambitions for their land and people but also their religious life and their culture, their music and dancing, their sport, and all their traditional ceremonies. These even mean more to them than the ceremonies surrounding our own royalty mean to the people of Britain. They were suspicious of government policy both for Uganda as a whole and for East Africa, where it had long been feared that the long-term aim of British policy was not independence but a closer association in some form under the domination of the white settlers of Kenya.

The negotiations held in secret between the governor and the Kabaka were bedevilled by this fear and suspicion, which were not by any means ill-founded. In an after-dinner speech, Oliver Lyttelton, then Colonial Secretary, fresh from his success in bringing about the Central African federation, had forecast the possibility of a similar pattern for East Africa. A storm of protest followed, and the opinion of local officials was not successfully concealed from leading Africans in Buganda that there would be no possibility of a federation with Kenya and Tanganyika as long as the Kabakaship remained intact.

All this combined to produce what was often called the "stubbornness" of the Kabaka in the discussions which took place with the governor over several weeks. When the Kabaka insisted that he could not accept the proposed constitutional changes without being allowed to consult with his Lukikko, the governor insisted that under the 1900 Uganda agreement the Kabaka was bound in the event of dispute to give his support to the policy of the Protectorate Government.

The Kabaka was placed in an impossible position, first because he was expected to be responsible both to the British Government on the one hand and to the Lukikko of his own people on the other, but also because in fact no dispute had yet actually arisen. Nor could it arise until it had been referred to the Lukikko. The Kabaka however did refuse to promise that he would commend the government's proposed changes in advance of the discussion. Rather than agree to this, he said his people would prefer to be independent of the policies that were being proposed by the Protectorate Government for Uganda as a whole. By this the Kabaka claimed that he meant that the Kingdom of Buganda should maintain its old relationship with Britain under the 1900 agreement and not be drawn into schemes the end of which could not be foreseen for Uganda as a whole.

A day came, however, when the governor had previously decided to treat the Kabaka as though he had broken the agreement. When the Kabaka arrived at the governor's residence everything appeared as normal. No one had observed the armed police even in the grounds of the Kabaka's palace or that a Royal Air Force plane was serviced and ready to take off.

After the discussion between the Kabaka and the governor had proceeded for some time, and when the request for permission to consult the Lukikko was again reiterated, the governor drew a paper from beneath the blotting pad on his desk and proceeded to sign an order withdrawing Her Majesty's recognition from him as Kabaka which in effect meant deposition. He drew out another paper and signed it, and it was handed to the chief of police who was now present. When the Kabaka asked incredulously if this meant he was under arrest he was told that that was in fact his position. He was not allowed to return to his palace or to say goodbye to any of his family. He was escorted to the plane and arrived in London the following morning in his tropical suiting. Someone had thoughtfully provided a shaving kit but nothing else.

On hearing the news, the Kabaka's sister, known officially as the *Nalinya,* collapsed and died of shock. It was in a way symbolic of something, though less drastic, which happened to the whole people of Buganda as a result of this tragic attempt to combine arbitrary rule with constitutional law.

The Kabaka came to the Africa Bureau when he arrived in London, bewildered but unshaken in his conviction that to have done anything else would have been a betrayal of his people. We advised attempts by every legal and constitutional means to bring about his restoration and the settlement of controversies by the more civilized means of discussion and negotiation. There were many ugly possibilities, in the period which followed, that the situation might degenerate into brawling and even something in the nature of a Mau Mau movement.

The services of two of the ablest of Britain's constitutional lawyers were secured, and a case which took the government completely by surprise was initiated in the local courts against those who had been appointed by the governor as Regents during the Kabaka's absence, on the grounds that this was done in breach of the agreement of 1900. The decision was taken in great secrecy in Dingle Foot's chambers in consultation with the members of the Lukikko delegation which had followed the Kabaka to London. Secrecy was enjoined in case the government was tempted to regularize the steps it had taken by Order in Council under a different Act. Once proceedings were begun by an African lawyer flying to Entebbe to serve the writ under the 1900 agreement, action under the Foreign Jurisdiction Act was made much more difficult.

There were many flights to and from Uganda by members of delegations, by the two counsel and their clerks, and by Sir Keith Hancock of the Institute of Commonwealth Studies, whom the governor had the wisdom and generosity to appoint to try and unravel the constitutional difficulties in which everyone was floundering. The story culminated in Uganda in a judgement which was greeted with tumultuous applause, although it was only half a legal point in the Lukikko's favour, and cheers for Diplock and Foot.

Perhaps the most unsavoury part of the story, however, was the attempt made by certain officials to destroy the Kabaka's reputation once he was safely out of Uganda. This was done by means of telling stories which denigrated his character, stories which, because they were only repeated in private rooms in the House of Commons, could not be challenged by law on the grounds that they were protected by the rules of parliamentary privilege.

The case concerning the regents, though only one point had been decided in the Kabaka's favour, did not come to the Privy Council; for the decision was made that the Kabaka should be allowed to return to his kingdom under a new form of agreement.

Eventually the day came when the Kabaka and his many guests, which included his learned counsel and their wives, Lord and Lady Hemingford, and three others of us from the Africa Bureau, returned together in his plane. The plane was greeted on arrival by Sir Andrew and Lady Cohen, by the royal drums which had been silent throughout the Kabaka's exile, and by cheering, dancing, and singing crowds, the like of which had never been seen or heard in Buganda within living memory. Some of the constitutional problems however still remain, notably how to maintain the autonomy of the Kingdom of Buganda within the framework of self-government for Uganda as a whole.

It may be that the problem will only ultimately be solved within the general framework of a constitutional solution for the problems of African self-determination, not only in the adjoining kingdoms of Uganda, but in the neighbouring territories of Kenya and Tanganyika also.

For Kenya, a new chapter will begin with the ending of the Mau Mau emergency. Exchanges opened between two African members of the Kenya Legislative Council and the secretary of state in July and August 1957. Mr. Mboya and Mr. Ngala came as a deputation to Britain and asked the Africa Bureau to help them. They asked for increased African representation before they could participate in the Executive Council of the new Constitution,[1] a declaration of the ultimate aims of government in Kenya, and a definition of the general direction of any new constitutional and franchise proposals. They affirmed their readiness to co-operate if more equitable representation were granted, and they were very fairly received in this country. The press statement given in Appendix 13 shows the situation at the time of their return.

In the winter of 1957 the colonial secretary, Mr. Lennox-Boyd, visited Kenya. He recognized the justice of the African claim for more representation in the legislative council to bring them nearer to parity with the combined representation of the immigrant races, since they represent nearly six million Africans as compared with less than sixty thousand white people and two hundred and forty thousand Asian and Arab people. But Mr. Lennox-Boyd rejected their demand for fifteen additional African representatives which would have brought them up to a bare majority over the total elected members for the other races, though not a majority in the event of the official members, nominated by the British Government, siding with the whites and Asians. This the Africans thought would give them the protection they feel that they need.

The Africans insisted that their claim for increased representation should be decided apart from the question of their participation in the

---

[1] Under the Lyttelton constitution there were a total of 16 European members (including 2 corporate members) to 50,000 Europeans, 6 Asians to 250,000 Asians, 1 Arab to 30,000 Arabs, and 8 Africans to 6,000,000 Africans.

Executive Council of Ministers. When they persisted in this attitude and refused to join the Council, the elected European members resigned. The Colonial Secretary declared the Lyttelton constitution at an end and imposed his own constitution in which Africans are given six additional representatives and which provides for a further addition of twelve elected members, four from each racial group, these to be elected by the Legislative Council sitting as an electoral college. But the African members refused to take part in this election.

The elected African members accused the Colonial Secretary of "trickery" in using their refusal to participate as a pretext for imposing his own constitution in place of that of his predecessor. They contended that the impasse was created more by the inability of the elected European members to agree among themselves than by the Africans' refusal to join in the government.

It seems clear that there is the need for a firm declaration of long term aims for Kenya. As the African members put it, "If we are being taken for a bus ride we can only be expected to agree upon the route if we are permitted to know what our ultimate destination is going to be." Until the British Government makes such a declaration of policy the suspicion remains that Britain's protecting power is gradually being surrendered to the local white settlers, and that the plan for a federation of East Africa on the pattern of the Central African "white supremacy" state has not yet been altogether abandoned.

There is therefore still danger in the fact that the constitutional and political alternative to the methods of the Mau Mau revolt among the Kikuyu still elude us in Kenya.

Yet there is something sanely practical and still trustful in Tom Mboya's plea that a "constitutional expert" should be sent out from Britain to help them. In April 1958 Tom Mboya and six other African members of the Kenya Legislative Assembly were charged with malicious libel and conspiracy against other Africans prepared to stand for election, and all this has resulted in more racial bitterness than the "non-racial politics" which the new constitution was intended to promote.

Another great African occasion to which Lord Hemingford as chairman and myself as director of the Africa Bureau were invited was the celebration of Ghana's independence in April 1957. There was a moment in the celebrations which, despite the obviously dangerous trends towards corruption and abuse of power, seemed to bring vividly into focus so much of the history of Britain and Africa.

It was at a thanksgiving parade in the stadium at Accra the day before Independence Day. Just in front of me a Welsh voice could be heard singing "Thy Kingdom come O God." It was Jim Griffiths, former secretary of state for the colonies, now representing Her Majesty's opposition. On the dais was the governor, soon to become Governor General Sir Arden Clarke. It had required some courage and some humility to take a man out of prison and appoint him prime minister of the country. Following an older pattern of colonial rule, the processions demanding his release would have led to measures of repression in the name of "law and order" and the fleet would have steamed into the harbour to shew the flag. Now the British cruisers were there with all their flags flying in honour of the representative of the Queen, the Duchess of Kent, and the birth of a new state in Africa. Sir Arden Clarke was standing next to Prime Minister Kwame Nkrumah, rewarded by the confidence of his prisoner in the hour of his own and his people's triumph. Away to the left the Union Jack was flying for the last time over Christiansborg Castle, where the slaves had been kept, injured and terrified, after the slave raids before being shipped across the Atlantic. Away to the right was the Assembly Hall where Parliament would meet tomorrow to constitute the new sovereign state of Ghana.

I had two talks with Dr. Nkrumah and left with him a memorandum on possible courses of action to deal with South Africa's defiance of world opinion (Appendix 14). I urged on him the special position of his country in this matter, and reminded him of the ever-present danger that South Africa might go on to demand the incorporation of the three high commission territories of Basutoland, Bechuanaland, and Swaziland into the Union as well, if something were not done.

In West Africa it was exhilarating to find Africans doing all the things which are denied them in the Union of South Africa. We are told it will require hundreds of years of tutelage by a self-designated superior race, and subjection to discriminatory laws, before they are capable of doing them there. Thus in West Africa there are African builders and carpenters, engineers and mechanics, Africans trained in all the skilled occupations, African magistrates and judges. It is possible for an African to become anything up to the prime minister of his country, and there are no laws which prevent anyone on any grounds of racial origin from going anywhere or doing anything that his fellow man can do. To a West African this is all taken as a matter of course, and they find it impossible to understand a state of affairs in which people's movements and aspirations are controlled on such arbitrary grounds as membership in a particular race. In hotels, public buildings, transport, and restaurants all races mix freely, and although there are many reasons for anxiety in the matter of corruption, and the tendency towards one-party rule, the atmosphere of freedom from racial conflicts and restraints makes the South African situation seem like a nightmare. There is also an irrepressible quality about the Africans in West Africa, which gives also a basis for hope that they will succeed in overcoming the obstacles to their progress which inevitably crop up in a new state enjoying its first full taste of power and responsibility. There are still all the unwritten laws to be made, which in the case of Britain form so vital a part of its constitution and parliamentary system.

I hardly had time to do more than enjoy the celebrations in Ghana, and hear what people of many different outlooks and occupations had to say about the problems and possibilities of the future, before I had a cable telling me that my mother had been taken seriously ill and that the doctors were unable to give any definite opinion on how long she was likely to live.

18 ". . . For Birth or Death?"

My mother's death did not bear thinking about for any length of time. It was seventeen years before, at the time when the shadow of defeat hung over France, that my father's stroke had seemed to bring the shadow of death over our family for the first time since my childhood. Like many others, I had always put off thinking about death because it was too enormous in its implications and too decisive a fact to be thought about casually or indecisively.

My father's death had happened while I was away from England, in fact on the day after the little momentary triumph when I had been granted a hearing at the United Nations. I had been quite numbed by the news, which arrived soon after Tshekedi Khama's cable with the Bamangwato motto "With God all things are possible." And feeling numbed I had also felt incapable of facing my mother in her loneliness and exhaustion and had callously escaped and flown on to India to attend a conference on peace. I called to see her sitting alone in the room she had tried to make their home. She seemed utterly spent and desolate. Her face was twitching but she shed no tears. She thought it was right for me to go on to India as arranged; that was what father would have wished. Telling her to rest all she could, I had gone with a righteous sense of duty only half aware of the burden I had left her alone to bear.

It was there in India in 1950 after the conference that I first began to write down the story of the little triumph, as it seemed, at the U.N. I was sitting on top of a hill, that in England would be called a mountain, called Mani Kot, in the foothills of the Himalayas.

Some had come to Sevagram to seek solutions for their own internal conflicts, some to find peace in the external struggle for justice for the oppressed people of the world. Perhaps the answer is that neither peace nor justice can be found without the other, that to search for either separately is to render one incapable of finding the truth.

> *Somewhere beyond the railhead*
> *Of reason North and South*
> *There lies a magnetic mountain*
> *Riveting Heaven and Earth.*

All the events in this little drama of human struggle passed through my mind as I sat on the rounded summit of Mani Kot with range upon range of the vast Himalayas stretching away into invisibility. Each action in the story represented a little individual act of choice by a person or a small group of people. We were all quite ordinary people for the most part, who only wanted an opportunity of doing something to help to put right a certain wrong. Generous-hearted people who gave freely of their time, their energy, their technical knowledge or skill when an opportunity was given them. Measured in terms of size, as things are measured in the world today, it was a comparatively small wrong, dwarfed by events of the magnitude of the Nazi tyranny, the counter-terror of Hiroshima, and the preparations for bigger and better Hiroshimas. Even the tragedy of Mau Mau in Kenya has been dwarfed by the greater tragedy of the French in Algeria. But this wrong that was done to the Hereros, first by the doctrine of the German army that Might is Right and now by the doctrine of the South African state that Law is Right, is basically a wrong of the same order, made of the same stuff as all the other evils that are threatening to convulse our world. Just as there is no beginning to the story, so there is no ending. There is only a continuation of the struggle to affirm what is true, to deny what is untrue, to resist what is evil, and to discover what there is of goodness and beauty in a world where their opposites seem often to be mightier than the forces of creation.

Against the background of that panorama the separate little choices and actions of such ordinary people became transfigured by a sort of glory, as a "negro" poet has expressed it. They became part of a texture, as though they might veritably be part of the pattern of a tapestry whose whole design could not in the very nature of things be known or visible to us. Like figures in a living fresco, they stood out in statuesque simplicity. Hosea Kutako, the aged Herero chief, standing with his hat in his hand in the strong sunlight, uttering his prayer as I left to find my way through the thorn bushes to the airport. There was Frederick Mahareru their paramount chief, patient in exile for fifty years, allowed to return after his stroke to die in his own land. There were Freda and Leon Levson and the Rose-Inneses, unbelievers with a passion for truth and justice and my hosts for so many anxious and impoverished months. There was the mother superior whose kindly gentle soul had a quality stronger than the jack-booted fanatics who goose-stepped over Europe, still believing "Might is Right." There were the Quakers, Fred Irvine and his wife, befriending everyone at the International Centre while Fred wrote his learned treatises on woody plants of West Africa and famine foods. And there was the peal of laughter from another bearded old Quaker, John Fletcher, peering under his bushy eyebrows through the bars of a prison cell. There were the inconspicuous lives of an editor, a doctor, a typist, preferring to play their parts anonymously in causes which have no reward. There was Mary Benson, who had given her health and strength to it.

In the souls of such people is the stuff of life. For all that we have, all of us, time and again betrayed that indefinable "cause," it will be from among such people in all the nations of the world that will be born again and again a new spirit of resistance to evil, which will be the only force that can save our civilization.

Institutional religion, whether Christian, Muslim, or Buddhist, seems inadequate to evoke this spirit in the full measure necessary to deliver us from the evil of hatreds created by racial, national, or religious fanaticism or the tyranny of the modern state over the individual. The positionalism—the wise defining of attitudes by the elders of the World Council of Churches—will not suffice.

It was in these mountains of northern India that the Lord Buddha had sought a way to perfection, and offered it in words which sound so similar to those from the voices of Christian, Muslim, and Hebrew prophets of other times:

> Enter the Path! There is no grief like hate,
> No pains like passions, no deceit like sense.
> Enter the Path. Far hath he gone who

Treads down one fond offence.
Enter the Path. There spring the healing streams
Quenching all thirst. There bloom the immortal flowers.

Swiftest and sweetest hours.
Kill not for pity's sake and lest ye slay
The meanest thing upon its upward way.
Give freely and receive, but take from none,
By greed or force or fraud, what is his own.
Bear not false witness, slander not nor lie.
Truth is the speech of inward purity.

Now death was coming to my mother. I was in West Africa when I received a cable that she had been taken seriously ill. Again I had been vicariously enjoying a momentary feeling of triumph, at the celebrations of Ghana's independence, which I had felt honoured to attend as a guest of Prime Minister Kwame Nkrumah. I was passing through Nigeria on my way home, and had given a talk to the students on my first visit to the great new university and the teaching hospital of Ibadan. There had been great rejoicing in Ghana at the removal of the last human barriers to their freedom and right to determine their own destiny. And now came this cable.

I took the first available plane to Kano and London, the train from Paddington to Devonshire, and stayed at my brother's house in the small hamlet of Crapstone in the parish of Buckland Monachorum. My mother had made a good recovery from her attack, but had aged greatly. She had lost none of her humour, but found it difficult to strike a mean between making light of her condition and indicating that she knew her life was drawing to a close. Between my brother's home and the house where she was being nursed there was a stretch of Dartmoor, which at that time was ablaze with golden gorse. In the sunshine the air was heavy with its scent and the hum of bees. In the early morning when I walked across the moor, one after another the larks would start up and soar into the sky, their exuberant song expressive surely of nothing but the sheer delight of being alive. It was difficult to believe they were not fully conscious of this feeling.

On Easter morning I took her Communion to her and, just as I was about to enter the house, the first cuckoo that I had heard that year sounded an authentic note of assurance of spring. It seemed to charge the whole air with the sound of Beethoven's *Pastoral Symphony*.

"The Blood of our Lord Jesus Christ, which was shed for thee, preserve thy body and soul unto everlasting life." It was hard to say the words strongly and confidently and with all the assurance that was needed.

It was the loneliness of her approaching death that my mother seemed to feel most. She had always dreaded having to do anything alone. She seemed to derive some comfort from having one of us there during those days of her gradually declining strength. I came and went in between visits to London to speak at meetings and to attend to work at the Africa Bureau concerning the impending visit to Britain of two African members of the Kenya legislature, Tom Mboya and Ronald Ngala, and members of the African Congress of Northern Rhodesia.

During these visits my mother used to like to talk about old times—she was not very interested in the present—and to hold hands occasionally without the necessity of saying anything. She would like to tell long-remembered stories, often told and retold, and little intimate recollections would pass through her mind like keynotes of her past life.

With so many urgent matters waiting to be dealt with at the office and so many problems pressing for some solution, and knowing how much depended on finding a new approach in Kenya and Rhodesia, it was difficult not to convey a sense of preoccupation and restlessness.

I visited Germany on a lecture tour for a few days for the Ecumenical Church Movement, and while there I saw the competition between East and West in the reconstruction of a great ruined city. I also met the Countess Von Moltke and the wives of other German resistance leaders who were executed in the last days of Hitler's terror, and the chaplain who had smuggled their letters out of gaol.

While I was away my mother was stricken with a very painful attack of shingles and this was followed by a stroke.

The spring was passing into summer when I got back to Devonshire, but the larks were still singing in the early mornings when I walked across the moor, and once, for the last time, I heard the cuckoo. When I first went in to her after her stroke she was quite conscious and recognized me at once with a look of pleased surprise. Her hair was quite white now and the nurse had tied it back on one side with a piece of light blue ribbon like a child's, and it exactly matched her eyes. They were no longer heavy and tired but wide open, and there was still a sparkle of humour in them.

Yet they were sad and solemn when she focused them on the Crucifix which my brother Nigel held towards her with a piece of honeysuckle twined round it. But she was not ready to die yet. She clung to my hand, as though drawing some assurance from it and only relaxed her hold as she went to sleep to the sound of the rhythmic cadences of the psalm I recited: "He will not suffer thy foot to be moved and he that keepeth thee shall neither slumber nor sleep. . . ." "Ye shall not be afraid for any evil tidings for the Lord Himself is thy keeper."

There was little strength in her hands and fingers. Day by day it was slowly ebbing from her worn-out body. Each morning after a restless night I woke with a start, thinking that this might be her last day of life. Almost it was like waking up on the morning of one's execution. There was the same feeling of inevitability that one shared with others in gaol, where there was no power that could intervene to prevent the law from taking its course. Every human device was employed to ensure that a condemned man could not escape the penalty of the law, even by death at his own hand.

Before light I would wake up with a feeling of dread. Perhaps she needed something. Once during the night I walked across the moor; the night nurse appeared to be asleep, and I was afraid to waken her. Supposing the nurse did go to sleep and there was no one to hold her hand when death came to take her? So with the skies greying and the stars fading I would follow twisting sheep tracks through the gorse and heather and tall bracken till I found myself outside her window. Sometimes the nurse would be sitting with her eyes closed, though probably not asleep, and I would stand with my face close to the window and hold my breath to enable me to see if my mother's hands moved or if the bedclothes on her bed were still moving with her breathing.

As the skies lightened, another day would begin. Another day of nightmare in the face of remorselessly approaching death, and with it a sense of impotence and futility. I could only repeat the same prayers. I was too tired to think. There was nothing fresh I could say: "Don't worry. . . . You are quite safe. . . . Don't feel lonely. I am still here. . . ."—till by repetition it was made to sound absurd. Life ebbs away so slowly that one is amazed at its persistence, and the returning flickers of consciousness give one moments of illusory hope and make more marked the final transition from life to death. Yet not even the horrifying physical symptoms of the onset of death deprive the cessation of life of its majestic drama.

To what end? To what purpose? That is the question that remains. "The Lord gave, the Lord hath taken away." "We brought nothing into this world. It is certain we can carry nothing out." She was like a small baby at the end, but without the joy and expectancy of a new thing born with such great possibilities. All her possibilities had been realized or had been frustrated. Yet though she had brought nothing in and could carry nothing out of this life she had contributed so much to the life we and many others had known.

When I left her for the last time to go to a meeting in London, which she would not have wanted me to miss, the caress of her fingers was so weak it could hardly have depressed the last note of the Chopin *Nocturne* she had played so tenderly at Northam. Yet it seemed to symbolize the gentleness of a life of service and submission to the will of those whom she loved, or those whom she feared because of the strength of their personality or their determination to get what they wanted. But there was also her submission to her Creator, whom she both loved and feared, and this, as so many came to find out, was often the most decisive factor in her thoughts and actions.

As I watched her dying it seemed to me that such is the perennial struggle within the human spirit until, and perhaps beyond, death. Expressed externally in the world of events, this is now reaching the stage of an apocalyptic trial of strength. Violence calls forth violence, and hate, counter-hate. It always has, and many say it always will. If that be so, we may as well reconcile ourselves to the inevitable doom of man and of his attempts to build a rational civilization. The scientific discoveries of our age, culminating in atomic energy, have heightened all the irrationalities, indisciplines, and areas of lack of self-control of our human nature and our human systems.

Says Lewis Mumford in his *Programme for Survival:*

The most complete transformation of the self must take place among those who have been least concerned with the psychological and moral nature of man. If our leaders remain fossilized and fixed, if they remain unimaginative, limited, brutish, if they continue automatically along the path on which they have been going, they will bring on catastrophe. This is not an idle threat nor is it the panicky reaction of mere laymen: it has come first from those whose theoretic and practical knowledge of atomic energy gives them the fullest authority to predict the consequences of its misuse. In the course of an atomic war, the planet itself may be made permanently uninhabitable. . . . Unless we can arouse our imagination sufficiently to picture the consequences of our acts and to appraise rigorously their actual character, there is no further enormity that we might not as a people be ready to commit. For mark this, if we can use one atomic bomb we can use two, and have done so. If two then twenty: if twenty then enough to wreck the world. . . .

Nevertheless Mumford is not without hope of a thorough-going revolution of thought and attitudes, proceeding from within the soul of man and powerful enough to challenge the degeneracy of morals and culture. He says:

Even under the limitations of his present development modern man possesses enough life furthering impulses and life directed goals to save himself. But only on one condition: that a change in attitude overcomes his inertia and makes these impulses and goals operative. Man cannot save himself without first healing his split personality, without giving up his current habit of pursuing at the same time two different and incompatible goals. Power must become the willing servant of love. . . .

When I had arrived in India for the Quaker peace conference I had received a message asking me to visit a prominent ecclesiastic, an Englishman of the old school, who was still living in India. He told me he had seen a statement to the effect that I was in sympathy with Gandhi's principles and that I believed them to be compatible with the Christian spirit. He did not know Africa, but after a lifetime's experience in India he himself had reached the conclusion that Gandhi must be held mainly responsible for the prevailing indiscipline and corruption that were rife in India. Teach people to disrespect the law and disobey the law, as Gandhi had done in India with his *satyagraha* and civil disobedience campaigns, and inevitably it led to anarchy, so that the Nationalists were themselves responsible for the disorders they were faced with when they came to power. He hoped that I should not go back to Africa and teach the black people the same principles.

I replied that in South Africa the disorders were the consequence of a long period of misrule. Was it not better that resistance to these evils should assume the higher and stronger form of non-violence than violence? Had he any other means by which these long-standing injustices could be remedied? He said he was not in a position to advise about that, though he was prepared to believe that there was a great deal of injustice going on. I concluded by suggesting that it was, after all, some tribute to Gandhi's work and spirit that two Englishmen could sit in peace and safety debating it after the political convulsion that had shaken India.

The whole discussion seemed very remote from reality, though there is no doubt that he was an able and amiable person whose experience of life through this whole period of India's history had never brought him to the point of re-examining his social traditions or his intellectual presuppositions. And now at the end of his life he was an angry old man, lonely in his bitterness and the knowledge that life was passing him by.

The hooliganism which follows from our failure to undertake the real tasks of peace, the feeding of the hungry and clothing of the naked, and which flourishes wherever ignorance, poverty, and fear exist, is but the symptom of a schizophrenic condition which may ultimately lead to the apostasy of science, an abandonment of moral responsibility, and the physical disintegration of the civilized world by atomic and other weapons corresponding to the moral disintegration which Lewis Mumford describes. The millions of landless and homeless refugees fleeing from the victims of fanatical delusions, which unscrupulous politicians have used to provide a catharsis for their own frustrations, are but the forerunners of worse things to come. The destruction of the equivalent of a hundred cities with one hydrogen bomb is but the political corollary of the destruction of our forests and soil, and moronic neglect of the divine intelligence in man in favour of the scaling down of all life to money values and the crowning of Heaven and Earth with a bowler hat.

I remember how when I arrived at Sevagram from the United Nations I saw for the first time Gandhi's ashram, which to many millions has come to be associated almost as much with man's hope of peace on earth and good will amongst men as Bethlehem has for Christendom.

I had come straight from New York, the colossus of the West. I had followed intently the course of the debate on "the condemnation of the preparations for a new war." I landed on the *Queen Elizabeth* in time to catch the K.L.M. plane to Karachi and Calcutta via Amsterdam, and arrived at Sevagram just before Christmas. There the first thing I saw was a well with a blindfolded bullock harnessed to a shaft, interminably walking round and round in circles with a young boy walking behind it with a switch.

I was afflicted with a sense of futility which nothing could allay. It remained with me, this dreadful sense of futility, mounting towards panic, with the fuller realization of what I had come to find, of what millions in the world were anxiously looking for. Even on Christmas Eve it persisted as we all stood round while some Indian peasants played the part of the shepherds and some young Tibetans acted as the Three Wise Men. And we sang, led by a German delegate, *Stille Nacht, Heilige Nacht*.

As we stood in the darkness among the cowsheds somebody chanted from the *Swetaswatara Upanishad*:

> *Him I have known, the Great Spirit*
> *Him who is Light, who is beyond all darkness.*
> *To know Him, and Him alone, is to pass beyond death.*
> *There is no other way.*
> *He is the Whole, other than He is naught,*
> *Greater or smaller there is nothing other.*
> *Still as a tree, unshaken in the heavens,*
> *His Living being fills the Universe.*

The Indians knew their sacred songs by heart. We Christians had to sing our hymns from typewritten papers. We had to hold them up to the light of a lantern and look through the paper, as whoever had typed them had put the carbon sheets the wrong way round. Even when we sang one we knew by heart—"He was little, weak and gentle, joys and tears like us he knew"—our voices sounded very cracked and discordant, compared with the beautiful lilting rhythm of the *Ramayan* which is like the sound of the swiftly flowing Ganges, tumbling and twirling over its rocky bed. "Raghupati Raghava Raja Ram"—all their voices follow closely with such expert ease the checks, twirls, and cadences of the rhythm.

Then some others chanted from the *Quran Sharif*, words which few Christians know:

> *In the name of God the merciful and compassionate:*
>
> *Behold the Angels said:*
> *O Mary,*
> *God hath chosen thee and purified thee—*
> *Chosen thee above the women of all nations,*

God giveth thee glad tidings of a Word from Him.

His Name will be Christ Jesus the son of Mary
Held in Honour in this world and the Hereafter,
And of the company of those nearest to God.
He shall speak to the people
In childhood and in maturity
And he shall be of the company of the righteous.

And God will teach him the book and Wisdom
The Law and the Gospel,
There is no God except God. And God he is indeed.
The exalted in power, the wise.

Which was the reality? My mind recalled the long rows of shanties in Karachi. In Calcutta my friend Sudhindranath Datta, a Bengali, had sat far into the night telling me of the tragedy of Bengal divided between India and Pakistan. He had been in charge of a relief squad. His mother had been saved by a kindly Englishman extricating her in his car. The trains had been coming into Calcutta from Pakistan with mangled bodies hanging from the doors and windows. In the streets of both dominions children had been crucified on doorways. Women had been flogged to death and disembowelled while still alive.

The Muslim chant changed into a Buddhist hymn called the *Vision of Peace* from the *Mahayana Sutra:*

Where tread the feet of the Lord Buddha,
Village and city are full of grace.
The people live in harmony,
The climate is soft and gentle,
And there is never too much rain or wind,
The crops are ample, the folk are free from care.
Weapons and soldiers have no place there.

Near me was standing Dr. Tomiko Kora, a woman delegate from Japan. She had given an account of Hiroshima which was even more terrible than that published in an entire issue of the *New Yorker*. She told us also of Japan's population problem following the loss of her colonies. An energetic birth control campaign by the American occupation authorities had now even reached the stage of practising abortion on grounds of poverty, she told us.

My attention was brought back by the singing of the *Metti Sutta:*

> *Let the noble disciple bear no ill-will towards any living being.*
> *Let him cultivate loves towards all, seen or unseen, far or near, born*
>   *or yet to be born.*
> *Just as a mother would protect her only child, at the risk of her*
>   *own life,*
> *Even so let him cultivate a boundless heart towards all beings.*

Standing over there was Mordecai Johnson, Negro president of Howard University in America; and there was Yrgo Kallinen, defence minister of Finland, whose strong face, looking as it did now, I had noticed when at a pathetic little reception given in our honour by one of the villages, an old peasant woman had knelt down and touched his feet. He had been speechless, with a tear coursing down his red cheek.

The stars glittered down on us with a light that was thousands of years old, as old as this human message—"Gloria in Excelsis Deo: et in terra Pax hominibus voluntatis boni."

But was it cold or kindly—this glittering light? How many others have wondered or are still wondering?

My mind went back to the war years before I had wrestled with my conscience and compromised by enlisting in the R.A.F. against the advice of a bishop who wanted me to be a chaplain. Now I was reminded of a night during one of the first raids of the London blitz when I was an air raid warden. There was a big fire at the Surrey docks, and the dome of St. Paul's was suffused with red, the windows too were glittering red from the reflection of the flames.

My mind returned to Sevagram. The chanting went on, a never-ending river, telling of the perennial struggle of the human spirit striving towards perfection. It was from the *Dhammapada* now:

> *Wakefulness is the way to immortality;*
> *Heedlessness is the way to death:*
> *Those who are wakeful die not,*
> *The heedless are already dead.*
> *From craving is born grief;*
> *From craving fear is begotten*
> *There is no grief for him who is freed from craving:*
> *Whence then can there come fear?*

Let us then free from hate live happily among those who hate.
Among men filled with hatred, let us dwell free from hatred.

In a land torn and tortured by fear and hatred Gandhi had discovered in South Africa that love is an active revolt. The fruits of his discovery were his *satyagraha* movement, based upon love and respect for his enemies. Britain and India had learned much from one another through his *satyagraha* movement. But Gandhi was shot, just as Socrates was poisoned and Jesus Christ crucified, by his own people.

The message of all of them to us who had come from all over the world in search of peace seemed to be first, before all practical questions, a need for those who would be prepared to give themselves to the uttermost in the service of peace and the methods of peace. Only an army of the trained, disciplined, efficient, and of those wholly consumed by a love which is unearthly and universal, having no reservations, no racial or other barriers, but dedicating themselves through selfless action to the creative purpose in human history, could save the world.

This was the theme of a paper I was asked to give in August 1957, to a conference of the Internationale Christelijke Vredesbeweging at the Château de Boissy in which I tried to express the immense possibilities of this way.

Passive resistance is no new method of facing evil, as we know, from the early martyrs, to the Quakers with their refusal to bear arms. What is new is the common action of large numbers of ordinary people—the Indians taking their stand at Durban, the crowds at Johannesburg who walked to work, and those other Africans who deliberately break the pass laws or use seats and public buildings for "Europeans only" as a protest against discrimination, and the negro people in America who passively resist the discrimination against them. All this with prayer in their hearts and the discipline to resist the temptation to use force if they are attacked.

Satyagraha, for want of a better word, as Gandhi developed it, has been described as a universal religious ethic governing all social relations between father and son, between neighbours, groups and nations. Its values are expressed in the vows of the satyagrahis—Truth is God, the quest for truth is the quest for God, and the quest for God is the quest for truth.

In personal and social relations this quest is governed by ahimsa, *by non-violence in thoughts, words and deeds, but more positively expressed as—universal love.*

Bramacharya: *perfect chastity in thought, word and deed, including complete celibacy and control, not only of sex, but of all the organs of sense.*

Non-possession or non-attachment. Vow of poverty, reduction of possessions to the minimum necessary for the continuance of life; extinction of the desire for the things of this life. Fearlessness, freedom from fear whether as to possessions, false honour, relatives, government, bodily injuries, or death.

When applied to resistance, satyagraha *has been defined as a method of securing rights by the personal suffering of the resister rather than of the person resisted. To Gandhi, the principle underlying the whole system of law implied consent and willingness to accept the penalties imposed by society for non-compliance with its laws.*

This is no easy matter, as I pointed out:

Let us not have any illusions about it. Such a movement of non-violent resistance as is required to save our world can only come from the most sincere conviction and readiness to engage in training and self-discipline of a very high order.

What seems to be urgently needed by our world is a peace force drawn from people of every country and race and colour, and from every religion and none, who will be the pioneers of a new and undiscovered country. It will not be an army of bigots and fanatics. But it will have a divine enthusiasm for tolerance and forgiveness. It will glory in the maximum of uncertainty and doubt on many matters of doctrine, definition and name-calling. It will have no loyalty oath to any race or nation or tribe, to any earthly boundaries or arbitrary limitations, because it will be an army more like a religious order with its citizenship in heaven. . . . Such an army will not be afraid of breaking laws that are unjust, or of the methods of boycott and non-co-operation where laws and customs prevent people living in peace and friendship with one another and, where they wish to, being educated together and worshipping with one another. . . .

The watchwords of this army will be prayer and action. Never one without the other, always together, prayer and action; as from Bethlehem to Gethsemane, its members will never cease from the struggle for right and justice on earth. They will build and work with their brains and their hands for what Lewis Mumford calls "a more co-operative and serviceable civilization."

In its liberation struggle against all forms of self-enslavement, the members of this army will make their prayer something like that of the Franciscan order:

> Lord make me an instrument of thy peace.
> Where hatred is, let me show love;
> Where doubt is, faith;
> Where despair is, hope;
> Where darkness is, light;
> Where sadness is, joy.
> Divine Master, grant me to seek;
> Not to be consoled but to console;
> Not to be understood but to understand;
> Not to be loved but to love.
> For only by giving do we receive;
> Only by forgiving are we forgiven;
> Only by dying are we born to life eternal.

The new idea which is to be found in that undiscovered country is not new except in the sense that it has been so little tried. And that is the idea of overcoming evil with good. It will be out of this that a new civilization will be born, one in which we shall learn not to be always in agreement and conformity, but how to differ and how to express our differences in a most vigorous but civilized manner. That is the great task to which we must be selflessly dedicated.

That the right people exist, there can be no doubt, and that the people who want peace and good will on earth vastly outnumber the cynics, defeatists, and warmongers is to me abundantly evident. Though they lack leadership from the elderly minds which belong to the end of an age, it may be all to the good that they should feel the need of leadership and should look for the Kingdom of God within themselves. The way must be found or we may again be overwhelmed by a war which might truly end all wars. For now we are entering a new age, the age of nuclear power. The choice before us is ever more pressing and urgent between the use of this power to destroy not only "the enemy" and our-selves but others, or on the other hand to construct something that we could call a "civilization."

We are faced with the nemesis of violence in an ultimate or apocalyptic sense, as an instrument of policy, as a means of settling the issues that confront us—in particular the issues between communism and democracy no less than the spread of unbridled nationalisms.

We cannot solve these questions by the nuclear bomb even if only kept as a deterrent. For that, if used, can only destroy the world, not save it. It may be possible to resolve these issues by the intelligent use of nuclear energy and new techniques in underdeveloped countries and in freeing impoverished and oppressed peoples.

This nemesis of violence in our time also challenges mankind to speed the evolution of a federal form of international law which will be able effectually to outlaw international war.

Everywhere people in their frustration are beginning to march and dem-onstrate against the nuclear bomb, not so much it seemed at Aldermarston because they were afraid only for their own existence, but because of their revulsion from the thought of using methods of mass murder of men, women, and children as the answer to anything.

They demand of their statesmen a real answer to the economic problem of full employment through the fulfilment of the tasks of civilization—the feeding of the hungry, the clothing of the naked, and the housing of the homeless and refugees and displaced persons of our time.

To replace the arms programmes which in the past have stimulated industrial growth and prosperity, we must find the economic answer to the problem of increasing the purchasing power of the impoverished masses of cultivators and primary producers so that their human develop-ment instead of armaments programmes may become the stimulus to in-dustrial and agricultural production.

But above all, there is the challenge of our time to discover the methods and means by which tyrannies in every quarter of the globe can be over-come by an international force of non-violence, of men and women dedicated to the methods and tasks of peace. And for our statesmen there is the question too long delayed of improving the processes and proce-dures of international discussion and negotiation and, where necessary, the application of peaceful pressures of persuasion as alternatives to the force man has accepted as arbiter in the past.

The speech of the delegate of Haiti in the Fourth Committee comes back to me: "I would say that in all their naïve confidence despite the subjection into which they have been thrown, these people (the Hereros) are willing to collaborate; they do not wish to hate the leaders, but are constrained to be no more than beasts."

Such has been the nemesis of frustrated goodness in the world. These forces must find an instrument to break with non-violence the resistance of evil, an instrument commensurate in organization, method, and efficiency with the task of saving the world and our civilization from descent to a level lower than the beasts. We must rediscover the wisdom of the Bhagavad Gita and the gospel of selfless action, and not be afraid to apply it in ways which the old forms and ceremonies of institutional religion may at first find strange, till they recognize what manner of spirit it is that is moving in the world. But perhaps they do what they can and would do more if more were moved to give more—not of their "means" but of themselves.

There is a hidden quality about the life and spirit of Jesus Christ which has to be rediscovered in each age. Often it is manifest in some obscure action in particular situations which may have far-reaching consequences. The familiar words of the gospel are known, but their inwardness must be sought before their spirit is almost unconsciously applied in unexpected ways. To the historians these uprushes of the spirit at different ages have a sameness and form an inevitable pattern.

There is evidence of the beginning of a resurgence of the spirit of resistance to evil, not only in the churches but in the laboratories and seats of learning where men are engaged in extending the frontiers of human knowledge. History is in fact overtaking their discoveries and is forcing them to look into their conscience in the use of their knowledge and skill.

But for the Divine Love it is no mere matter of preaching or intellectual persuasion. The creative purpose in the "Word made flesh" had to work itself out in the form of resistance to evil and by the methods and means compatible with its own ends—the redemption of the world from its enslavement to the rule of passion, hatred, and prejudice and in fulfilment of the constructive tasks enjoined by Christ—the feeding of the hungry, the clothing of the naked, and the sheltering of the homeless. In this conflict there is joined the long cosmic struggle to give birth on earth to freedom, intelligence, and co-operation in man.

The spirit of resistance which had been born at Bethlehem with the promise of peace on earth among men of good will then went through the process of its own inner logic to Gethsemane and the fulfilment of his own prayer, "Not my will but thine be done." And that inner logic issued in its final action on the Cross which today in other forms is still the penalty for treason against the State. To others, the oppressed and the dispossessed of the earth, the Cross is the symbol of non-violent resistance to man-made laws. And to some it is its own answer to the immortal prayer: "Father, forgive them for they know not what they do."

In T. S. Eliot's *Journey of the Magi* one of them asks:

> . . . *Were we led all that way for*
> *Birth or Death? . . .*
> > . . . *This Birth was*
> *Hard and bitter agony for us, like Death, our death.*
> *We returned to our places, these Kingdoms,*
> *But no longer at ease here, in the old dispensation,*
> *With an alien people clutching their gods.*
> *I should be glad of another death.*

Appendices

APPENDIX I   *Extract from a letter from Charles Andrews to Gandhi, November 12th, 1932*

"Such a practice as this may be used by fanatics to force an issue which may be reactionary instead of progressive. Human madness or even doting affection may become tyrannical in this way. How far my anxieties and fears are mixed with human affection I can hardly myself understand. I do know that I finally saw you giving your life itself for depressed classes, in your last fast, and I was glad—I saw in it the 'greater love.' I can see you now preparing to do the same thing on Jan 1st if the Temple authorities do not give way. . . . It seems to me that I would very gladly lay down my life to remove 'untouchability' between the white race fanatics who call themselves Christians and the other races. But you have evidently come to the point of *forcing the issue*—literally *forcing* it and I have to think that out in terms of Christ. I think he *did* force the issue when he set his face steadfastly to go to Jerusalem. He saw then, I think, that only his own death could call the Jewish leaders to a halt. There is one strange saying of his 'The Kingdom of Heaven suffereth violence, and the violent take it by force.' Again I am not sure whether his act in cleansing the Temple was not of the same character, i.e. of forcing the issue. But the method of fasting, committing suicide, still instinctively repels me."

APPENDIX II   *Quotations from the* South African Sunday Express *exposing the Broederbond*

MAY 12TH, 1957
    "As Prime Minister, General Smuts ordered a secret enquiry to be made into the Broederbond. The enquiry was carried out by three well-known South

Africans who worked in the greatest secrecy, and in a conspiratorial atmosphere as exciting as that of a detective thriller. . . . This astonishing report, on which General Smuts placed a ten-year publication ban, is now among the private papers of a person connected with the secret investigation.

"The report is headed: 'The Afrikaner Broederbond. Its efforts to usurp the Government of the Union and to establish a Nazi Republic.'

"After declaring that General Hertzog's attack on the Broederbond was well-founded, the report describes the ritual and organization of the Broederbond in the following terms, which are quoted directly from the report: the organization of the Bond is Masonic down to the smallest details. [There follow the details, and an account of the gruesome initiation ceremony, where a dagger is thrust into a dummy corpse wrapped in a black winding sheet with letters of blood] . . . while the Chaplain intones 'He who betrays the Bond will be destroyed by the Bond. The Bond never forgives and never forgets. Its vengeance is swift and sure. Never yet has a traitor escaped his punishment.'

"The outward forms of Masonry are slavishly imitated; but Masonry's spirit of charity, its absolute prohibition of politics and its fundamental creed, that all men are brothers, are conspicuously absent. The Broederbond is ostentatiously Christian. There is much psalm singing and Bible thumping throughout its ritual; but there is nowhere any reference to or recognition of the Brotherhood of Man.

"To the secrecy of its character the Bond owes much of its success; but it owes more to the extraordinary care with which members are recruited. A prospective 'candidate' is watched and tested for years. . . . He must be over 25 years of age and a man of standing, active in local or party politics, and a member of as many public bodies as possible. . . .

"Scores of Government servants, occupying important positions, have to look upon the Government merely for their meal ticket. It is the Bond they serve; because promotion, their whole career, lies in its hands." [Cases quoted, though not in the paper.]

MAY 19TH, 1957

"A CLOSELY-GUARDED SECRET OF THE BROEDERBOND CAME INTO THE HANDS OF THE *SUNDAY EXPRESS* LAST WEEK.

"It is a top secret, hush-hush application form, filled in by a school teacher in Krugersdorp on February 18 of this year, in which he applied for membership of the Broederbond.

"THIS IS THE FIRST OFFICIAL SIGNED DOCUMENT OF THE BROEDERBOND EVER TO BE MADE PUBLIC. [Facsimile printed in full.]

"The Krugersdorp school teacher says, in his application that:

"He gives preference 'to his own people' in business and professional circles.

"He is a church elder, a member of a skakel committee and of the Transvaal Teachers' Association.

"He undertakes to pay an entrance fee of £12.10s.

"He swears an oath of secrecy which binds him to keep confidential 'to death' anything he may learn.

"He swears that he will divulge his own membership only in threatening circumstances; but never that of his fellow members without their permission.

"To subscribe to the principles and aspirations of the Broederbond."

In the facsimile, candidates are seen to have to sign certain "Principles of our Aspirations," parts of which read as follows:

"As unswerving Afrikaners we believe that the Afrikaans people were brought into existence in the southern part of Africa by God with an individual Christian vocation of worshipping His name. . . .

"We accept the Christian National principles of our national life (and) their preservation, extension and application in our own independent Republican state of life, in our own judicial system based on Roman-Dutch law, our own mother-tongue educational system, our own art and science, our own healthy bond of communal life and our own independent domestic management to ensure an existence worthy of a human being for each of our people.

"We accept the prerogative of our conscious organized and purposeful Afrikanerdom, which entails that we must stand faithfully together to ensure the fulfilment of our people's independence in all spheres of life.

"I the undersigned adhere etc. etc. . . ."

APPENDIX III   *Records of author's conviction for living in a native urban area, 1947*

"I am the senior superintendent of the Orlando Location in the employ of the Johannesburg City Council. . . . Nobody is taking any responsibility for this camp. There are undesirable elements in the camp. There are three factions there and each intimidates the other. Violence is always in the offing amongst themselves. I agree it would be good for some influence to break the tension. Yes, I think accused has tried to exercise his influence in this direction. . . . Accused has told me he wishes to get some authority to take over responsibility. At present all ears are deaf. I would not call the infant mortality high—28 for January and 25 in February. There is no room for the Tobruk camp school children at the Orlando schools. The Congregational Church is built of hessian sacks. . . .

"FACTS FOUND PROVED

"a. The accused was charged with contravening Section 9(8) of Act 25 of 1945, as read with section 44 of the said Act, in that he resided in the proclaimed location of Orlando without the approval of the Minister. . . .

"h. Accused, despite the warning received continued to reside in the location.

"j. He was accordingly found guilty of the charge and sentenced to a fine

of £5 or 14 days imprisonment with hard labour suspended on condition he be not again convicted of a similar offence or any contravention
of the Native Urban Areas Act for a period of 12 months."

*Four months later, in August 1947, my appeal, which was dismissed, re-
corded that:*
"The circumstances under which the alleged offence took place must be
traced back to the year 1944 when the appellant organized a deputation consisting of delegates from the Churches, the Native Representatives, the Trade
Unions and other bodies to the Minister of Native Affairs. The purpose of
the deputation was to call the Minister's attention to the beginnings of the
shantytown movement and the very serious situation that was then developing for the Native people in the Urban areas on account of overcrowding
and the prolonged failure on the part of the local authority to make provision
for its urban Native population in the matter of housing, health, transport
and the like.

"The Minister did not take seriously the appearance of a few Native shacks
which he said he had inspected by air, but assured the deputation that he
would give careful consideration to the memorandum submitted in which the
'shantytown' was foreseen as a development dangerous to health and public
order which for the sake of the Native people and the City of Johannesburg
as a whole should be taken seriously.

"During the three years which followed further representations were made
and attempts at relief measures were carried out while the numbers of squatters
grew from a few score families to a number variously estimated at between
fifty and a hundred thousand souls in the several squatters' camps that at the
end of three years had grown up.

"When the appellant was invited to stay in the squatters' camp known as
'Tobruk' in order to investigate and seek to improve the internal conditions
there, he did so in the conviction that a very serious position had developed
with the threat of small pox and other epidemic diseases, and the growth of
lawlessness and gangsterism whereby the poorest section were being terror-
ized and their ignorance and defencelessness exploited by armed gangs.

"The authorities, in the opinion of the appellant, had shown the utmost
irresponsibility in the matter and persistently refused to intervene or make
alternative provision on the grounds that all these thousands of people, the
vast majority of whom were legitimately employed in Johannesburg, were
'pari delicti' to use the phrase of the Chief Native Commissioner. . . ."

*I further deplored the continuation of these conditions in the proposed
measures for forming a new camp, Moroka.*

Extract from the local paper De Echo, *Bethal, Friday, May 30th, 1947*

"FARM FOREMAN CHARGED WITH ASSAULT WITH INTENT

"Balthasar Johannes Brenkman, farm foreman in the employ of Mr. R. A. Visser/Kalabasfontein appeared before Mr. B. H. Wooler, R.M. in the local magistrate's court on Tuesday and Wednesday in two cases in which he was charged with assault with intent to do grievous bodily harm.

"In the one case there were five counts and in the other case one, the complainants in both instances being native labourers employed on the farm.

"Mr. P. W. Holtzhausen prosecuted and Advocate R. Hill, instructed by Messrs. Roogland, Louw and Hoffman, appeared for the defence.

"Aron Ngulube the first complainant said that accused had assaulted him repeatedly with a sjambok. In reply to Mr. Hill he said that the bossboy also used to hit him. Paulus Shumba said that the accused hit with a sjambok and set a dog on him which bit him at the back of the knee. In reply to Mr. Hill this complainant said that he and another boy had deserted the farm, were overtaken by accused and a native Makalapen on the road 12 miles from the farm, that the accused hit him, striking him to the ground and while he lay there the accused had kicked him above and below the eye. Makalapen at the same time assaulted his companion. He had been assaulted before he ran away. The bossboy also used to hit them and he could not say which had caused which injury. John Phitu said that accused would come into the lands while witness was working there and hit him and set a dog on him. He also saw accused striking other boys with a sjambok while in the lands. The bossboy as well as accused used to strike the boys. The other complainants in the first case all gave similar evidence; each said that the accused and the bossboy assaulted them with a sjambok, one said that the accused struck him with his fists, none of the complainants wanted to go back to the farm and asked that their contracts be cancelled.

"Dr. L. Albertyn, senior district surgeon, gave evidence of marks of bruises he found on some of the complainants.

"In the other cases Jabangwo Ziziba said that on the evening of the first day that he worked on the farm he and certain other boys went to Mr. Visser and witness asked whether they could not be allowed to stop earlier as they had worked till after sunset. Mr. Visser demanded who he was to give orders on the farm and accused told someone to bring a sjambok. Two of the boys who were with Ziziba ran away and a boy named Joseph went after them, Ziziba and a boy named Enoch remained. Visser, the witness said, struck him and he fell to the ground and while he lay there accused and Visser struck him and kicked him. He and the other boy were taken to a storeroom where Visser ordered them to undress: the accused was not there at the time, but after Visser had thrown their clothes outside the accused arrived with the farm police boy, Visser left and the other two struck the two boys several blows with a sjambok after which they chained Ziziba and Enoch to each other, each by one leg with some donkey trekchains that were in the store. Naked and chained as they were the boys were chased to the compound where they slept still chained together.

"Dr. Albertyn in the report on his medical examination of Ziziba said he found a number of healed wounds on him. There were three lineal wounds twenty inches long across the back, a healed laceration half an inch in diameter over the right shoulder blade, and another over the left thigh, one a quarter of an inch in diameter below the left eye and one an inch in diameter below the knee joint.

"In reply to Mr. Hill the doctor said that he would have expected double marks on the legs from the wounds said by some of the witnesses to have been caused by bites from a dog but he only found single marks in each instance.

"The accused, giving evidence, said he had worked for Mr. Visser, who was his brother-in-law, for three and a half years as farm foreman. There were from 15 to 20 boys employed on the farm but the complainants were the only Nyasas on the property. He had no trouble with the other boys and his only trouble with contract boys were with those who had appeared in Court. In general they were a cheeky lot.

"He described in detail what had occurred between him and the natives. Ngulube he had never hit and had never seen him being hit. Shumba and Moyo had run away and when they were overtaken on the road Makalapen, the farm police boy, had struck them with a sjambok while witness was still in his car; they had to force the boys into the car and Shumba may have got hurt. He had flicked these boys a couple of times lightly with a sjambok to frighten them when they persisted in burying potatoes which they had been instructed to reap. John was lagging behind when reaping mealies and he had flicked him also lightly. Weki was leaving mealies behind unreaped and witness had touched him with the side of his boot; the boy ran away and would not stop when called upon and witness ran after him and caught him: as he did so they both stumbled and fell, Weki striking his lip on the ground.

"He had never struck any of these boys to hurt them but only to frighten them to do their work properly.

"Regarding Ziziba the accused said that he had gone to the storeroom to see whether Enoch, who was the only one whom he had had placed in the room, was there and as he entered Ziziba grappled with him. He struck him two blows with his fists. He did not hit him with a sjambok and he did not chain the boys together, there were no chains near by. Later he again went to the storeroom accompanied by the boy Joseph. Witness told Ziziba and Enoch to undress to see whether they had any false passes with which they might try to run away or matches with which they might set the fodder in the room on fire. Joseph struck each of the boys five blows with a sjambok but witness had not told him to do so. It was possible that Joseph might have chained the boys without knowledge of the accused.

"The magistrate reserved judgment until Tuesday."

From De Echo *June 6th, 1947:*

"Gaol without the option of a fine will be imposed in any future cases of this type, declared Mr. B. H. Wooler R.M. on Tuesday when sentencing Balthasar Johannes Brenkman, whom he had found guilty on four counts of common assault and one count of assault with intent to do grievous bodily harm.

"The complainants were native labourers on the farm of Mr. R. A. Visser of Kalabasfontein, where the accused was farm foreman.

"In reviewing the evidence the magistrate said that accused had said he carried a sjambok in the lands with him for protection, that he always had a dog in the lands with him presumably also for protection but the accused admitted that he had at times used the sjambok to chastise the labourers, which he had no right to do, the bossboy had on two occasions according to the admissions of the accused in his presence used his sjambok on the labourers, and some of the boys had complained that accused had set his dog on them, which was borne out by medical evidence.

"The conditions disclosed in this case are tantamount to slave driving the magistrate said. On a farm of 400 morgen 25 native labourers were employed and they were driven to do their work by means of the sjambok. It was akin to slavery to drive the boys on in this manner and practices of that type would not be permitted.

"In the course of an address to the Court on the subject of sentence Mr. P. W. Holtzhausen, the prosecutor, said there had been numerous cases before the Courts during the last five months in which farmers were charged with assaulting their native farm labourers. I wish it to be clearly understood that I, as prosecutor, bear no grudge against the farmers, but I also want it to be clearly understood that in all complaints of assaults of natives by farmers I shall prosecute those farmers with all my power, with all my vigour and with all the evidence available, no matter who the farmer may be, he said. The colour question in the Union had reached a serious stage and conduct such as disclosed in the present case served to aggravate it. The farmers could not obtain sufficient labour at present and a case of the present nature would only deteriorate the position. I had seriously thought of asking the Court to impose a sentence of imprisonment in this case but I will not do so now, he said. I should like the Court to issue a severe warning however that if these practices continue farmers who are found guilty will be sent to prison and if this does not help I will ask that lashes be imposed.

"I endorse the remarks of the prosecutor, the magistrate said. The number of assaults in the district had been prolific.

"The accused in his position had a duty to protect the natives not to injure them. You as a European are supposed to be of superior race because you have had an education of which the native has not had the benefit, but to act as you did is disgusting, he said. The whole affair is sordid and your part in it was despicable. It is reminiscent of slavery. It is also no credit to Mr. Visser.

"The accused deserved corporal punishment and had the complainants suffered any permanent injury the Court would have felt itself compelled to impose such punishment. You have offended against humanity, you have offended against the law and you have injured your district, the magistrate said. Through the conduct of the accused, the farmers of the district who already had difficulty in obtaining native labour, would find that difficulty increased tenfold.

"The magistrate treated the four counts in which he had found the accused guilty of common assault as one and sentenced him to a fine of 25 pounds or one month imprisonment. On the charge of assault to do grievous bodily harm he sentenced the accused to a fine of 50 pounds or three months imprisonment, and a further three months imprisonment without the option of a fine suspended for twelve months on condition that the accused be not within that period found guilty of assault."

APPENDIX V   *Referendum "To the Natives on the First of February 1946"*

"In regard to the incorporation of South West Africa into the Union of South Africa.

"The representatives of the Great Nations of the world will meet in Europe within a very short time to consider matters, and His Honour, the Administrator, would gladly like to receive your answers in connection with the above so that he may inform Field Marshal Smuts, the Prime Minister of the Union of South Africa about it; when he leaves he may then give your decision to the Nations.

"You remember that about thirty years ago the Forces of the Union fought against the Germans in South West Africa. There raged a great war in the whole world, a war which had its origin in Germany. Germany had several Nations on its side while the Allies consisted of nations such as Great Britain, France, Russia and America.

"It was a bitter war but the Allies won the war. At this time the Allies concluded that the Union Forces (Military) should conquer the Germans who ruled over South West Africa.

"Within a short time the Union Forces took possession of this territory and took over the Government of the country.

"They found chaos in every part of the country. The different tribal organizations were destroyed by the Germans, and you had no land which you could call your dwelling place. Your cattle were taken away from you and you were not allowed to own cattle. You were on the verge of starvation and your families and relatives were scattered all over the country. You lost courage and thought that you were made slaves. Gradually, the Union Government restored order.

"One of the greatest purposes and tasks of the Union Government was to find the necessary area of land, and to create Reserves for the Hereros and other Native inhabitants, so that they may feel free again, and so that they may find homes for their families and accumulate numerous cattle. The Union Government helped to get water where it was possible. You remember that it was not always possible, especially during periods of depression and drought, but the Union Government succeeded in creating for you better and happier circumstances. It results in open market for your cream, marketing for your cattle, and the education of your children, etc.

"After the First World War the territories such as South West Africa, East Africa and other regions in the Far East were taken away from the defeated Germans.

"The Great Nations could not at once decide what to do with these Territories. They soon rather came to an agreement to put these Territories under the rule of other Nations. These Nations were not allowed to annex any of the Territories taken away from the Germans including South West Africa. They may rule and send each year a report to the great Nations overseas on how the former German territories are ruled.

"It then happened that the Union Government had to rule over South West Africa and over all its inhabitants. This system is called the Mandate System. The Union Government has now governed South West Africa for thirty years. . . . After a short time Germany prepared for war, and for the return of her former colonies.

"She began to be more and more aggressive, and for the past six years she made war, and one which was more serious than that which took place thirty years ago. Countries such as Japan, Italy and Austria stood on her side. She was terribly strong and well armed. Within a very short time she nearly conquered the whole of Europe and robbed the smaller nations of their possessions and made them slaves. As you know she was again defeated. The Nations which fought against her are England, Russia, France, America, South Africa and the other Dominions. This time she suffered a serious defeat, and the troops of the Allies are still in Germany. These Nations will now take decisions over the former German and Italian Colonies.

"They have already had big meetings overseas about these questions, and they will within a short time have another meeting in London.

"They will perhaps like to know now whether you yourselves the inhabitants of the Mandated Territory, would like to be under the Union and retain your rights, and whether you would like to be governed by another nation or nations whose names I have named, and which want now to constitute the United Nations. It is about that that you must now decide. On that I want to have your answers. Do not be in a hurry, there is a lot of time today.

"I shall give you a document on which the points which you should decide about are put in your own language.

"And in order to convince Field Marshal Smuts about your decision, His Honour the Administrator would like to see that your leaders, if they want to, should sign this document, seeing there will not be any chance for them to meet His Honour in Windhoek.

"Remember that the same words which I have said to you are also being said today to all the Natives in all the Reserves within the Police Zone.

"I shall now give you an opportunity to consider the case amongst yourselves. If you arrive at a decision then you could send a messenger to me to say that you will give your answer. Then I shall come back to the meeting place. I would very much like to telegraph your answer to His Honour in Cape Town, where he and Field Marshal Smuts are awaiting your answer."

And the document given to the headmen of the various tribal units in South West Africa reads as follows:

"We, the undersigned Chiefs, Headmen or Board Members of the people of the ...... tribe, who live in the ...... Reserve in this Mandated Territory of South West Africa, acting with full authority of the people of the tribe of the ...... Reserve, wish to say that we have heard that the people of the world are talking about the Administration of countries such as ours, and that the Administration of those countries may be changed.

"We and our people wish the following matters to be made known to the peoples of the world:

"1. That our people have been happy and have prospered under the rule of the Government of the Union of South Africa and that we should like that Government to continue to rule us;

"2. That we do not wish any other Government or people to rule us; and

"3. That we should like our country to become part of the Union of South Africa."

APPENDIX VI   *Letter from Hendrik Witbooi to the magistrate at Walvis Bay, August 4th, 1892*

"I write this letter to Your Honour in the hope that you will, in reply, advise me of the full truth in regard to my questions concerning the coming of the Germans; because the works of the Germans are encroaching on my land and now even my life is threatened. They come to destroy me by War without my knowing what my guilt is. I have been told that it is their intention to shoot me. And I ask Your Honour, perhaps you can tell me why . . . the German introduces laws into the land according to his own opinion, and those laws are impossible, untenable, unbearable, unacceptable, unmerciful and unfeeling. He personally punishes our people at Windhoek, and has already beaten people to death for debt. It is not just and worthy to beat people to death for that. . . . Five Berg-Damaras and one of my red men. . . .

He flogs people in a scandalous and cruel manner. We stupid and unintelligent people, for so he regards us, have never punished a human being in such a cruel and improper way. . . . He stretches persons on their backs and flogs them on their stomach even between the legs, be they male or female. . . . So Your Honour can imagine no one can survive such a punishment. . . .

"Therefore, my dear Magistrate, I write to you as a true friend, that you may know the depth of my feelings, for I complain to you of the inmost heavy feelings of my heart and it hurts and pains me much when I consider that your people have allowed such persons into our country. I send you this letter and I request you to give it to the Cape Government—let all the great men of England know of it so that they may have another meeting and consider this position of the Germans and if possible call these people back. Because they are not following the Agreements and Resolutions on the strength of which you let them enter this land. . . ."

In August 1894 Leutwein sent an ultimatum to Witbooi.
"You have so utilized the two months of consideration given to you that you still refuse to recognize German supremacy. The times of the independent chiefs of Namaqualand are gone for ever. Those chiefs who rightly and openly recognised and attached themselves to the German Government were more clever than you are: because they have gained only advantages and have suffered no loss. I take you also for a clever man but in this matter your cleverness has left you because your personal ambition has overclouded your understanding. You fail to understand present-day circumstances. In comparison with the German Emperor you are but a small Chief. To submit yourself to him would not be a disgrace but an honour."

Hendrik Witbooi replied:
"You say that it grieves you to see that I will not accept the Protection of the German Emperor, and you say that this is a crime for which you intend to punish me by force of arms. To this I reply as follows: I have never in my whole life seen the German Emperor; therefore I have never angered him by words or by deeds. God the Lord has established various kingdoms on the earth, and therefore I know and believe that it is no sin and misdeed for me to wish to remain the independent Chief of my land and my people. If you desire to kill me on account of my land, and without guilt on my part, that is to me no disgrace and no damage, for then I die honourably for my property. But you say that 'Might is Right' and in terms of these words you deal with me because you are strong in weapons and all conveniences. I agree that you are indeed strong, and that in comparison to you I am nothing. But, my dear friend, you have come to me with armed power and declared that you intend to shoot me. So I think I will shoot back, not in my name, not in my strength, but in the name of the Lord, and under His Power. With His help will I defend myself. . . . So the responsibility for the innocent blood of my people and of your people which will be shed does not rest upon me as I have not started this war."

Leutwein answered:

"The fact that you refuse to submit yourself to the German Empire is no sin and no crime, but it is dangerous to the existence of the German Protectorate. Therefore, my dear Chief, all further letters in which you do not offer me your submission are useless."

APPENDIX VII   *Contemporary accounts of the defeat of the Hereros, 1904*

1. FROM THE PRIVATE LETTER OF A GERMAN SOLDIER:

"Settling down on my knees, and creeping for a little way, I saw tracks of innumerable children's feet, and among them those of full-grown feet. Great troops of children led by their mothers had passed over the road here to the North West. I stood up and going to a low tree by the road climbed a few yards in my heavy boots. Thence I could see a broad moonlit slope, rising not a hundred yards distant, and on it hundreds of rough huts constructed of branches from the low entrances of which the firelight shone out, and I heard children's crying and the yelping of a dog. Thousands of women and children were lying there under the roofs of leaves and round the dying fires. I gazed at this great night scene with sharp spying eyes, and I observed minutely the site and the camp at the base of the mountains. Still the thought went through my head: there lies a people with all its children and all its possessions, hard pressed on all sides by the horrible deadly lead and condemned to death, and it sent cold shudders down my back.

"Through the quiet night we heard in the distance the lowing of enormous herds of thirsty cattle and a dull, confused sound like the movement of a whole people. To the East there was a gigantic glow of fire. The enemy had fled to the East with their whole enormous mass—women, children and herds.

"The next morning we ventured to pursue the enemy. The ground was trodden down into a floor for a width of about a hundred yards, for in such a broad thickly horde had the enemy and their herds of cattle stormed along. In the path of their flight lay blankets, skins, ostrich feathers, household utensils, women's ornaments, cattle and men, dead and dying and staring blankly. . . .

"How deeply this wild proud sorrowful people had humbled themselves in the terror of death: wherever I turned my eyes lay their goods in quantities, oxen and horses, goats and dogs, blankets and skins. A number of babies lay helplessly languishing by mothers whose breasts hung down long and flabby. Others were lying alone, still living, with eyes and nose full of flies. Somebody sent out our black drivers and I think they helped them to die. All this life lay scattered there, both men and beasts, broken in the knees, helpless, still in agony, or already motionless. It looked as if it had all been thrown down out of the air.

"At noon we halted by water holes which were filled to the brim with corpses. We pulled them out by means of the ox teams from the field pieces, but there was only a little stinking bloody water in the depths. . . . At some distance crouched a crowd of old women who stared in apathy in front of them. . . . In the last frenzy of despair man and beast will plunge wildly into the bush somewhere, anywhere, to find water and in the bush they will die of thirst."

2. MANUEL TIMBU'S RECORD:

"She was quite a young woman and looked tired and hungry. Von Trotha asked her several questions, but she did not seem inclined to give information. She said her people had all gone towards the East, but as she was a weak woman she could not keep up with them. Von Trotha then ordered that she should be taken aside and bayoneted. I took the woman away, and a soldier came up with his bayonet in his hand. He offered it to me and said I had better stab the woman. I said I would never dream of doing such a thing, and asked why the poor woman could not be allowed to live. The soldier laughed and said 'If you won't do it I will show you what a German soldier can do.' He took the woman aside a few paces and drove the bayonet through her body. He then withdrew the bayonet and brought it, all dripping with blood, and poked it under my nose in a jeering way, saying, 'You see, I have done it.' Officers and soldiers were standing around looking on, but no one interfered to save the woman. . . . On our return journey we again halted at Hamakari. There near a hut we saw an old Herero woman about fifty or sixty years, digging in the ground for wild onions. Von Trotha and his staff were present. A soldier named Koonig jumped off his horse and shot the woman through the forehead at point blank range. Before he shot her he said 'I am going to kill you.' She simply looked up and said 'I thank you.' I was an eye witness of everything I have related. . . . I was for nearly two years with the German troops, and always with General von Trotha. I know of no instance in which prisoners were spared."

APPENDIX VIII   *Native commissioner's report of proceedings at United Nations—issued February 24th, 1948, to Native Advisory Board.*

"This statement simply tells you briefly what happened at U.N.O. during the last session in October and November. I want to emphasise that I am not here to ask you what you think of what happened there, nor to ask you what you think of the Union Government's decision. I am simply making the statement for your information so that you may pass it on to the people you represent.

"On question of statement to be made to natives of South West Africa, regarding proceedings at U.N.O. General Assembly, Second Session, October–November 1947.

"The question as to whether South West Africa should be incorporated in the Union or placed under the Trusteeship supervised by U.N.O. was again discussed at the second session of the General Assembly of U.N.O. in 1947 because, during the previous session, U.N.O. had asked the Union Government to consider a trusteeship.

"The Union Government's reply to U.N.O. was that it could not agree to place South West Africa under trusteeship because the Union Government in becoming a member of U.N.O. had not agreed to do so, and the majority of the people of South West Africa did not want it. The Union Government further stated no steps are being taken to incorporate South West Africa into the Union, and that South West Africa would continue to be governed in the spirit of the old League of Nations Mandate.

"After discussion at U.N.O. a resolution was passed noting that the Union Government was not proceeding with incorporation and requesting the Union Government again to consider placing South West Africa under Trusteeship. The Union Government's representative at the Conference, however, made it clear that the Union Government had no intention of submitting a trusteeship agreement."

Chair: "I thank Mr. Allen on behalf of the Board for his statement and hope that from now on we can forget these political agitations and get on with more worth while things such as the welfare of the people."

APPENDIX IX   *Resolutions of the General Assembly of the United Nations, December 1949*

"RESOLUTION I

"Whereas the General Assembly noted, in resolution 141(II) of 1 November, 1947, that the Government of the Union of South Africa had undertaken to submit reports on its administration of the Territory of South-West Africa for the information of the United Nations.

"Whereas, in resolution 227(III) of 26 November, 1948, the General Assembly recommended that the Government of the Union of South Africa continue to supply annually information on the administration of the Territory of South-West Africa.

"Whereas the Government of the Union of South Africa in a letter to the Secretary-General of 11 July, 1949, which was transmitted to the Member states, stated that no further reports would be forwarded.

"Whereas the Trusteeship Council, in resolution 111(V) of 21 July, 1949, has called to the attention of the General Assembly the decision of the Government of the Union of South Africa not to transmit further reports and has informed the General Assembly that this decision precludes the Trusteeship Council from exercising further the functions envisaged for it in resolution 227(III) of 26 November, 1948.

"THE GENERAL ASSEMBLY

"1. EXPRESSES REGRET that the Government of the Union of South Africa has withdrawn its previous undertaking, referred to in resolution 141-(II) of 1 November, 1947, to submit reports on its administration of the Territory of South West Africa for the information of the United Nations;

"2. REITERATES in their entirety General Assembly resolutions 65(I) of 14 December, 1946, 141(II) of 1 November, 1947, and 227(III) of 26 November, 1948;

"3. INVITES the Government of the Union of South Africa to resume the submission of such reports to the General Assembly and to comply with the decisions of the General Assembly contained in the resolutions enumerated in the preceding paragraph.

"RESOLUTION II
"THE GENERAL ASSEMBLY

"RECALLING its previous resolutions 65(I) of 14 December, 1946, 141(II) of 1 November, 1947 and 227(III) of 26 November, 1948 concerning the Territory of South West Africa,

"CONSIDERING that it is desirable that the General Assembly, for its further consideration of the question, should obtain an advisory opinion on its legal aspects,

"1. DECIDES to submit the following questions to the International Court of Justice with a request for an advisory opinion which shall be transmitted to the General Assembly before its fifth regular session, if possible:

"What is the international status of the Territory of South-West Africa and what are the international obligations of the Union of South Africa arising therefrom, in particular:

"(a) Does the Union of South Africa continue to have international obligations under the Mandate for South-West Africa and, if so, what are those obligations?

"(b) Are the provisions of Chapter XII of the Charter applicable and, if so, in what manner, to the Territory of South-West Africa?

"(c) Has the Union of South Africa the competence to modify the international status of the Territory of South-West Africa, or, in the event of a negative reply, where does competence rest to determine and modify the international status of the Territory?"

APPENDIX X   *Extracts from a statement made by the author at the 653rd meeting of the Fourth Committee, September 26th, 1957*

"I have asked to be allowed to make this statement firstly because I have been requested to continue making representations to you by those who asked me to speak for them, since their own nominated spokesmen are prevented from reaching you to speak for themselves. . . .

"On July 30th 1957, a leading article appeared in the *Windhoek Advertiser,* as follows:

" 'The rather misguided United Nations Committee on South West is at it again. They intend to create the impression to the General Assembly of the United Nations that South West is suppressing its non-European residents and that these people should be given more say in the affairs of the country. In the Northern Kaokoveld Ovamboland and the Okavango Native Reserves and in all the other reserves in the Territory, the Native is spoonfed to such an extent that the European taxpayers who mostly foot the bill are beginning to wonder where it will all end. South West has a sound native policy which is an example to the rest of Africa and even to the rest of the world where the less fortunate sections of the population are often not even taken into consideration. South West has at the head of its native affairs men who have devoted their lives to the welfare of people who are slowly being educated to become productive and self-supporting. This gigantic task is guided carefully by these officials who not only take into consideration the traditions of the Native, but also know that he cannot be rushed into a responsibility for which he is not mentally equipped. The Native himself is consulted continuously in every move concerning his own welfare and in his own reserves has more freedom than the European.

" 'The Native is a care free person who is being given the opportunity to develop the best land available in the country. It is time the United Nations realizes that it is also time that some of the countries who point the finger at South West with no justification look into their own affairs. Few of them have anything to be proud of.'

"It is difficult for anyone who knows South West Africa and the conditions of the African people there as compared with other parts of Africa such as Ghana, Nigeria, Uganda and some of the Trusteeship territories to understand this.

"By way of supporting and supplementing certain conclusions of the report of the Committee on South West Africa, I should like to quote from the *Windhoek Advertiser* and other sources some facts and figures which demonstrate an extension of the trends they have observed.

"There has been no wish either on the part of your Committee or your petitioners to minimize the little that is being done for the health, education and welfare of the African people.

"What is maintained is that it is all totally inadequate and disproportionate to the great expansion and increasing wealth of the mining industry, for example, which is dependent on African labour for the production of its wealth, and also the prosperous but cruel karakul sheep farming which employs its shepherds at less than twenty shillings a month. . . .

"The latest figures published in the *Windhoek Advertiser* on 10 May 1957 show that 'The mining industry has maintained its rate of development. During last year minerals yielded 34,795,175 pounds, that is 6.5 millions more than in 1955. During the year, the industry provided work for 2,032 Europeans and 11,637 Natives. 2,783,674 pounds was paid out in wages.' (As compared with 2.4 million in 1955.) 'Diamonds again provided a major contribution. Sales of gem and industrial diamonds realized 17,609,488, 2,583,607 pounds in excess of the figures for the previous years.'

"Nevertheless, the prosperity of the mining industry, and for all that it contributes so large a proportion to the revenue of the territory, is, as the industry is at present organized, entirely dependent upon the policy of the State for its continuing supply of cheap native labour.

"That the farmers are no less dependent on the supply of cheap native labour is shown in the figures given by the new South West Africa Native Labour Association of Grootfontein. In a supplement of the *Revue Française,* which has a foreword by the Administrator Mr. Viljoen, it is stated that 'the number of Natives handled annually by the Association has grown from 2,887 in 1928 to 45,500 in 1955.'

"In the same report, it is stated that during the past thirteen years (the period in which South West African Affairs have been most debated overseas), the minimum wage for all classes of labourer has increased by 200 per cent. If this be so, the fact remains that the minimum wage for labourers is 20/- per month. Wage rates for all classes of labour range from 20/- to 65/- a month, in rural areas, as a starting wage.

"In the fantastic economy of South West Africa, the wage structure is based upon the real or supposed occupancy by a man's family of a piece of land with which to maintain his wife and children in a reserve many hundreds of miles away from his place of work or in another country. The tentacles of these farming and mining recruiting agencies extend ever farther and farther afield to Bechuanaland, Basutoland and Swaziland, to Portuguese Angola and even to Nyasaland and Tanganyika. . . .

"The whole apparatus of the State is designed to keep control in the hands of the privileged white caste and to enforce the restrictions on ownership of land and restrictions on movements and opportunity of acquiring education and skills, so that cheap labour is kept available for the master caste where it needs it on the mines and on the farms.

"The ugliness and evil of apartheid is its essential hypocrisy and duplicity. There is evil in its face, in the greed and fear that peep from its eyes, which will not allow people to think in terms of what is rational and what is possible. And it is that greed and fear in the white people that can be so easily transformed by unscrupulous politicians into hatred and cruelty.

"Contrariwise, there are limits to the patience and endurance of the African people in the face of the spread of this evil doctrine. The heaped up humiliations and the insecurity of having no recourse to any representative institutions or to any legal processes of redress, to having no ultimate security of tenure for the land or incentive to improve it.

"The world and South Africa will do well to heed the warning lessons of history that you cannot stop up all the channels of orderly and constitutional methods of change without one day opening up the flood gates of human resentment and sense of outraged justice.

"This Assembly of the United Nations has witnessed the strenuous efforts of African chiefs and people to keep to the processes of orderly discussion and the processes of peaceful change which it has been the labour and the purpose of this organization to devise.

"Where the Africans have resorted to political movements of resistance to injustice it has been by the methods of non-violent resistance, of boycott and non-co-operation and strikes which, in South West Africa, are met by police action and the use of firearms. And these are, I submit, civilized methods of resistance which the most technically advanced and so-called civilized nations of the world could very well emulate in place of those methods towards which so much of their national effort and revenue are directed.

"It seems as though the time has come for the United Nations to find the ways and means of intervening in this great crisis of Africa and the world whose limits for good or evil cannot be foreseen. . . .

"There followed a report from Mr. Kozonguizi.

"The indigenous population lives in an agony of slums, poverty and wretchedness, while the European section is enjoying boom prosperity and lives in beautiful newly-built dwellings. The non-whites suffer the sharpest discrimination in housing and other health provisions, and while numerous housing schemes have been devised and built for whites, a single plan put forward for non-white housing as early as 1948 received no attention whatsoever until recently. Dr. Verwoerd, the Union Minister of Native Affairs, however, has brought pressure to bear upon the local authorities to implement residential isolation for the non-whites. That the living conditions themselves were of little, if any, interest to him is clear from his directive, despite the repeated protests of the non-whites affected, that the new Windhoek location be built five miles from the town, and from the type of hut, not fit for human habitation, that is being put up in the new Okahandja location.

"There has been a continued expansion of medical services in the Territory, especially in the establishment of new hospitals for non-whites. But even in this field, discrimination is rife. Expenditure for the maintenance of the various hospitals is so ludicrously small, that even when new hospitals are established they cannot satisfy the needs of the people. For a white population of less than 50,000, £40,000 is spent in annual subsidy on State-aided hospitals, while only £20,000 a year is spent to maintain the State-owned hospitals of nearly 400,000 non-whites. This grotesque disproportion makes the facilities of the new non-white hospitals often as useful as stage scenery, which is possibly why they were built. . . . There is not a single clinic in the Reserves.

"Social and residential segregation is strictly enforced and no non-whites, except for a handful of coloured, live in white areas. The non-white have no access to the best cultural shows, which are unfailingly staged in the white areas. Embodied in the Mandate is the obligation to raise the social and cultural standards of the people, though surely the behaviour of the Administration would not suggest it.

"Immorality in the South African sense, or private relations between white and non-white, is strictly prohibited by law, whilst the Mixed Marriages Proclamation of 1953 has made all marriages between whites and non-whites illegal. By law the non-whites may not be in possession of liquor—either so-called European or home-brewed—though this is the salary many chiefs receive in private from administrative officials for silence in the face of discriminatory legislation. Coloureds may have special documentary exemption. In spite of all these paper restrictions, however, drunkenness and immorality in the proper sense are lavish in the slums, and only a raising of the living standards of a desperate and miserable people can really eradicate the evil.

"Most horribly of all, the Pass Laws are strictly enforced. In terms of the Native Urban Areas Proclamation of 1951, all the towns in South West Africa have been declared 'proclaimed' areas, areas in which the various curfew and pass regulations apply. All non-whites, African or coloured, have to carry passes once they leave the 'Reserves.' Women, also, cannot move from one place to the other without a pass similar to that required of the man. The 'Permit' system for non-white women is scrupulously enforced in the Territory. No non-white woman may remain in an urban area without a permit, even in the slums of her people. It seems that the whole Pass system, with all its terrors and cruelties, will be extended to women next year, when the deceitfully termed 'Abolition of Documents Act' will be made applicable to S.W.A.

"The description of economic conditions which follows will reveal the absurdity of the contention that the social facilities for non-whites are commensurate with their contributions to the State.

"ECONOMIC CONDITIONS

"At the bottom of the non-white sacrifice and suffering in South West is land allocation. . . . Now the Administration has embarked upon a new invasion of the non-white areas. The Damaras have been moved from Aukeigas Reserve to a dry, infertile area. A portion of the Reserve has been turned into a Game Reserve, and the rest of the land has been given to European settlers. The Hereros have been ordered to evacuate those areas in the Aminuis Reserve which are well-watered and best suited for farming and to move instead into the dry corridor lands between the Reserve and the Bechuanaland boundary, lands incidentally which the Administration claimed were too dry to be opened up for settlement when the Hereros requested their annexation before. (In parenthesis I may mention that on this point I have a record of a solemn promise given by the Administrator to the Herero chiefs in 1933. This is taken from a record in the archives of the League of Nations.) The Nama people were told last year to move from Hoachanas, where trade in vegetables and fruit has been flourishing, to the already overcrowded Berseba Reserve, and the Administration has threatened to use force if they do not move promptly. All the land, of course, is to be given to white settlers. . . .

"The standard of living in the Reserves is particularly low. Africans have been forced to occupy the dryest parts of the Territory, where the subsistence capacity reaches its lowest ebb. The Administration does not deny the deplorable conditions, but seeks justification by claiming that the inhabitants themselves are lazy and indifferent to progress. The truth is, of course, that the inhabitants can have little enthusiasm for improving their land if the moment they have done so, they are required to give it up to white occupation. Even were they to feel sufficiently secure, they are never provided with the training necessary if they are to be equipped to carry out developments themselves. In point of fact, the Reserves are used as vast reservoirs of labour, and little attention is paid to them as long as the labour supply is steady.

"Non-Africans are liable to income tax (low by any overseas or even South African standard), diamond tax, land tax, transfer duties, etc., whilst Africans are affected by direct taxation only through the dog tax, wheel tax and stock fees. But indirect taxation affects both Africans and non-Africans similarly; both groups pay the same for cigarettes and tobacco and various imported items. And the incredibly low wage paid to the African means that he pays a much higher proportion of his income in taxes, mainly indirect, than the non-African.

"WAGES

"*In Towns:*

Average for Men	£2	0 0 a week
Recruited Labour[1]	£1	5 0 a month
Average for Women	£2	0 0 a month

"*On Farms:*

General Farm Labourers	£1	0 0 a month
Shepherds		18 0 a month

"(In parenthesis, I should mention that food rations as provided in addition to these wages, inadequate as they undoubtedly are.)

"EDUCATION

"Apart from economic advancement, education is the key to the development of a people. But in S.W.A. the Administration, apparently, has a different view; proper education is for whites only. Small wonder then that the Territory had its first African matriculant in 1948 and its first African graduate this year. At the moment only six non-whites from S.W.A. are studying at South African universities and abroad, and not a single one of them has a grant from the Government. The whole policy of the Administration could

---

[1] African Workers from the Northern Reserves, recruited through the South West Africa Native Labour Association.

not have been more clearly exposed than in the remarks made by a Government official in S.W.A. to a non-white student who had applied for financial assistance. The Government, he said, would have no place for a post-matriculation qualified teacher in the African schools, as it was contemplated introducing 'Bantu Education' in South West, and that did not need highly qualified teachers.

"The invariable discrimination infects the provision of educational facilities. Of the £803,853 public expenditure on education in the 1952–53 financial year, £659,781 was spent on white education. During the 1952–53 financial year, the average Government expenditure per pupil was as follows:

White	£42 13 0	African (Police Zone)	£10 15 0
Coloured	£21 5 0	African (Elsewhere)	14 9

More vividly than anything else, these statistics indicate how enormously the education of the majority of the people of the Territory has been neglected. Many of the teachers are of very poor quality, and there are no prospects of any improvement at the present rate. Not a single African teacher in S.W.A. holds a Matriculation Certificate. . . .

"POLITICS

"The Africans and Coloureds have no political rights at all, and the present Administration has made it quite clear that it has no intention of changing the situation. The Tribal Councils and Basterraad in the Reserves are of no political significance: for a long time now they have been used to rubber-stamp the Government's repressive and discriminatory measures.

"Political movements such as the African National Congress are non-existent, and the basis of non-white politics is on the whole tribal. This is, to a very great extent, encouraged by the Government's strict enforcement of ethnic grouping in all non-white residential areas. But a Consultative Committee at a chieftain level has been established to communicate with the United Nations Organization.

"Politically the most vocal element are the Hereros. The other groups are just as aware of the injustice meted out to them, of course, but fear victimization. . . ."

After re-stating the legal international position my statement concluded:
"On behalf therefore of those Africans of South West Africa whom I represent, I would appeal to each Member State and particularly the countries of the Commonwealth for conscience' sake to bring South Africa's conduct to the judgement of the International Court. . . .

"It may be asked what is the ultimate sanction behind international law more than the moral sanction. This is an urgent question for the world of to-day where the resort to military force as an arbiter of disputes may threaten the very existence of life on this planet. But what, in the event of a judgement by the Court, could happen if South Africa disregarded this judgement.

"There are other and more civilized forms of pressure than brute force, even if the pressure of world opinion should not prevail. In reality, South West Africa would be extremely susceptible to such pressures. Just as the mining industry and agriculture are dependent on cheap native labour, as I have pointed out, so the mining industry and agriculture, and particularly the white master caste, are dependent on the export trade in diamonds, copper and furs and upon the import also of petroleum and machinery. Its economy of privilege and discrimination could be brought to a complete standstill in a very short time if the conscience of the world had the will to exert this pressure. In support of international law and justice, voluntary organizations could also exert their own forms of pressure in such spheres as athletics, art and culture, with the initiative and leadership of UNESCO.

"I could give some examples of how effective even these seemingly mild forms of pressure have been in influencing opinion in South Africa, notably that of the Churches, in their opposition to the claims of the State, in the sphere of Church order and worship.

"It must not be forgotten that there are many peoples of all races in South West Africa, Afrikaners, British, Germans, Africans, Asians and coloured people, who are sick at heart and afraid of where they are being led by this irrational myth of apartheid. But they are waiting for a positive lead and this could be given them by the U.N., by UNESCO and by the specialized agencies of the U.N.

"By all such and many similar means may the divine urge towards justice and freedom which exists in people of every race and religion and is the monopoly of none be brought nearer to their realization, even in this complex of political procedural and human problems that now confronts you.

"But I must thank you and members of the Committee for their patience and not presume any further on the forbearance you have shown me."

APPENDIX XIA *Sections of a petition to Her Majesty Queen Elizabeth II against federation, made by chiefs and citizens of Nyasaland*

"We, the undersigned, Chiefs and citizens of Nyasaland, offer Your Majesty our respectful greetings, and express to you our undying loyalty. . . .

"2. We are a delegation sent to Your Majesty by the Chiefs and people of Nyasaland to ask you to permit us to present to you the objections of the majority of the African people of Nyasaland to the proposed federation of Nyasaland with Northern Rhodesia and Southern Rhodesia. We are Chief Maganga, one of the Chiefs of the Central Province of Nyasaland, Chief Somba, one of the Chiefs of the Southern Province of Nyasaland, acting Paramount Chief Gomani (Regent during the protracted illness of his father) of the Central Province of Nyasaland, Paramount Chief Mbelwa, of the Northern Province of Nyasaland, Chief Kuntaja, of the Southern Province of Nyasaland, I. C. K. Muwamba, delegate from the Northern Province, B. W.

Matthews Phiri, delegate from the Chiefs' conference, and Dr. Hastings Banda, representative in the United Kingdom of the African National Congress of Nyasaland and a native of Nyasaland.

"3. At a conference of the Chiefs of Nyasaland attended by more than a hundred Chiefs of Nyasaland, held at Lilongwe, Nyasaland, on the 15th and 16th days of November, 1952, it was decided to send a delegation comprising the above to England to ask Your Majesty to receive us and hear the objections of the majority of the African people of Nyasaland to the proposed Central African federation.

"4. We are aware that Your Majesty is, according to constitutional practice, advised by Your Ministers in forming policy, but while we have every confidence that justice will prevail in the councils of Your Majesty's Government, we have lost confidence in the wisdom and justice of the Ministers who at present advise Your Majesty on Colonial policy; hence, we ask Your Majesty to receive us and hear us. . . .

"8. In March 1951 a conference of officials from the three territories and from the Commonwealth Relations Office and from the Colonial Office was held in London which prepared a Report (Cmd.8233). That Report recommends federation of the three territories with a constitution which would give the European minority in the three territories the political dominance which it desires. In a Legislature of thirty-five members there would be twenty-six elected for European interests, seven elected for African interests, and two appointed for African interests. Of that number Southern Rhodesia would have seventeen representatives. It is not stated why over six million Africans should be represented by one quarter of the Legislature and less than a quarter of a million Europeans by the other three quarters. The European members would always have an overwhelming majority over the Africans. Moreover, it is provided that once the Parliament of the United Kingdom has voted the federal constitution, power to amend the federal constitution would be vested in the federal legislature and in the federal legislature alone. The Parliament of the United Kingdom would be able only to reject such amendment. It could not amend an amendment bill. Moreover, constitutional amendments must be passed by a two thirds majority. Under the constitution Africans would never have a two thirds majority. . . .

"11. The overwhelming majority of the African people of Nyasaland are opposed to Central African federation, and we humbly pray Your Majesty to protect us from it. . . ."

APPENDIX XIB   *(after petition). Extract from debate in Parliament on Rhodesia and Nyasaland Electoral Bill, February 18th, 1958.*

Mr. Creech Jones: ". . . Let us examine the Bill. Let us remember that there are roughly seven million Africans, two thirds of whom are protected persons, living in their own countries—countries which have not been subject to conquest by this country. As compared with the seven million Africans, there are 275,000 Europeans—roughly one twenty-fifth of the number of the Africans. The Europeans inhabiting the three territories are there primarily for the purpose of making a livelihood. Many of them have no roots in the country, although they have been conceded political power. In the case of two of the three territories, many of them entered knowing full well that the territories enjoyed protected status. The Government of those States must therefore be a question for determination by this Parliament.

"The Secretary of State takes the view that it is a good conception of partnership to give the Europeans, whose numbers are only one twenty-fifth of the African population, 42 out of the 57 seats in the House of Representatives and, in addition, to give them full control without a seat in the Cabinet of the Federation. This European minority is put in permanent possession of Government. On the general roll for election to the House of Assembly there will be 81,000 Europeans and possibly 2,500 Africans. That is what we are told to accept as partnership.

"How is the right to be placed on the general roll secured? First, we must bear in mind that the average income of the European is £1,100 per year and that of the African in employment £70 per year. A person is eligible for registration upon the general roll if he receives £720 per year and is literate; £480 a year and has completed a primary course of education, or £300 a year and has had four years of secondary education. With those qualifications a person can become one of the 81,000 who have the right to vote.

"It is obvious that in the present state of African development the imposition of such qualifications and conditions makes it virtually impossible for Africans to qualify for the general roll and thus have the right to vote in the election of 42 of the Members in this small Chamber. They are too poor, and they are not sufficiently educated. They cannot hope to achieve the qualifications now required for admittance to the general roll.

"The Federal Government admit this lack of balance and inequality and shelter behind the argument that with the passage of time the practical effect must be for Africans to influence the elections and possibly secure the election of African Members, although it is admitted that the vast majority of the people on the general roll are at present Europeans. The Federal Government say, 'The Africans must wait for the economic development of the country.' If they are to do that they will have to wait for an indefinite period.

"How can we ever hope for fast progress by the Africans towards the attainment of the high standard of qualification needed for the general roll when they are repressed by segregation principles, colour bars, the denial of trade union rights, and a whole series of other discriminatory clauses, and have poor facilities for education? Sir Roy Welensky, and Lord Malvern before him, made it perfectly plain to the Africans—and certainly to the Europeans —that it was very unlikely that the Africans would assume any definite place in the political life of the country for 100 years.

"In the meantime, the European community has possession of the machinery of government. Political ascendancy in the political life of Central Africa is established. The Africans have no influence whatsoever in the election of the ordinary Members.

APPENDIX XII   *Chain letter received by the author from South Africa and referred to in evidence for the prosecution in the South African "Treason Trial" (1957/58)*

"The Black Man is being persecuted, prosecuted, jailed, fined, assaulted, murdered and denied education.

"God will help us if we try to help ourselves.

"We have no leaders to speak for us—they are in jail, banned and ostracized from us.

"Every non-European must burn the white man's property.

"You are ordered to set a light to the veld and also to European schools and post offices, Dutch churches in town.

"Use paraffin and dry wood. Break the air-bricks under the floor and start a fire between 1 o'clock and 4 o'clock in the night. Travel in motor cars to distant towns to burn European schools.

"You have been appointed as captain in the Chesa-Chesa-Army to carry on with legalized destruction against Malan's Nationalists.

"When travelling, pull down telephone and telegraph wires and road signs.

"Burn farmers' tractors, cars, barns, veld, haystacks and stores especially Nat. Afrikaner enemies.

"Post this to all friends—black and white or be cursed, unlucky and damned to hell for ever and ever—amen!

"COMMAND!!!

"Copy out this 6 times and post them to 6 different addresses, African or European.

"If you fail to do this you will break the chain and you will be cursed for your whole life.

"You will be a traitor and God will punish you everlastingly. . . ."

APPENDIX XIII   *Press statement, August 8th, 1957, by the delegation from the elected African members in the Kenya legislature, Mr. Tom Mboya, M.L.C. and Mr. Ronald Ngala, M.L.C.*

"The visit of our delegation comes to an end to-day. To-morrow we fly back to Kenya arriving in Nairobi Saturday morning.

"In the course of the visit we have met Members of Parliament of all Parties and addressed several meetings. We have also had three meetings with the Secretary of State for the Colonies, one of which was attended by the Governor of Kenya. We are satisfied that we have fully explained the African case for increased representation and fully interpreted the African attitude in the present constitutional crisis. We are also satisfied and convinced that this visit was both necessary and justified and that on the whole it was worthwhile. In general everyone we have met is in agreement with us that a case exists for increased African representation and many M.P.s and other people agree with us that a declaration of the ultimate objective of British policy in Kenya should be made immediately.

"Our talks with the Secretary of State for the Colonies were friendly and encouraging and we are glad that he has decided to pay a visit to Kenya and to be able to participate, and help, in the discussions on the constitution. This is a step in the right direction and we shall look forward to his visit hoping that in the light of our discussions no effort shall be spared to seek a solution. We have fully emphasized the urgency of the situation and we are convinced that this point is acknowledged.

"With regard to the present crisis the following statements made in the last few days are worth noting.

"Mr. Shirley Cooke, European Member of the Kenya Legislative Council for the Coast, has not only resigned from the European Elected Members' organization and condemned the European Members' statement, issued on July 5th, 1957, but has been reported to have called the organization 'the mischievous and reactionary European Elected Members' organization.' He said that 'a reactionary caucus controlled the organization which was full of intrigue and political manoeuvring but objected to other races behaving in the same way.'

"Mr. Cooke, at a meeting in Mombasa, called for an immediate increase of seven African Members. Mr. Humphrey Slade, another European Elected Member, speaking at Gilgil a few days ago, referring to the African demand for increased representation and refusal to participate in the Council of Ministers under the Lyttelton constitution, said: 'We see no reason to be stampeded by any so-called demand. Liberalism is too often misunderstood for defeatism and not being defeatist we (Europeans) prefer to be liberal in OUR OWN TIME.'

"Referring further to the possibility of constitutional discussions, Mr. Slade said, 'So far as I am concerned we shall not finally agree to any constitutional changes (other than those already agreed) without first telling you (the European electorate) and being assured of your majority.'

"These statements reveal beyond doubt that the stumbling block in the Kenya situation is the European community. So far it is evident that they are neither united nor of the same opinion. It is also evident that whatever liberal talk European leaders may engage in in London is negative and ineffective so long as they intend to act in the manner suggested in Mr. Slade's statement. There can be no question, therefore, of anyone blaming the African Elected Members for the present situation. The African Members' readiness to discuss has been repeated and emphasized. The European Members want to lay down conditions even before the discussions have started. This is very definitely unacceptable to the other Parties.

"The Lyttelton constitution included an escape clause which in the present circumstances, and if the Europeans persist in their current attitude and confusion, the Secretary of State should be called upon to invoke. The African case is supported by the Arab and the Asian Groups.

"The White Highlands

"A few weeks ago Mr. Blundell stated in the Legislature that in a decade there may be Africans fit to farm 20, 30 or 40 acre plots in the White Highlands. This has been interpreted as a sign of a changing mood and a growing liberal opinion among the Europeans. Let there be no illusion that the White Highlands remains the bone of contention in Kenya politics. This anachronism must be removed without compromise and immediately.

"Mr. Blundell's statement is curious and illogical since he, as Minister for Agriculture, has been known publicly to praise African farmers in other parts of Kenya for their efficient and effective farming on larger plots than he suggests for them in a decade hence. To the best of our knowledge there is no requirement for any European settlers coming to Kenya to produce either a certificate of qualification or of past experience in farming. It is disappointing that the Kenya Government is still engaging in recruiting white settlers.

"State of Emergency

"The conditions which justified the declaration of the State of Emergency, namely to combat Mau Mau terrorism, do not any longer exist. There is the danger that the conditions of the State of Emergency may lead to the exploitation of Emergency regulations in an otherwise normal situation. A declaration ending the State of Emergency should be made forthwith. There is an urgent need to review the situation as regards Pass regulations for the Kikuyu, Embu and Meru tribesmen. It is urgent that a review of the position of all people in detention camps and under restriction orders should be made immediately.

"Military Base in Kenya

"We emphasize once more the fact that the Africans do not support the establishment of a military base in Kenya.

"Public Meetings

"The present Government restrictions in Kenya limit the freedom of association and the freedom of assembly by denying Africans the right to organize on a Colony wide basis and also to address open-air meetings. The African Elected Members demand that these restrictions be lifted. The requirement to take a tape recording of African leaders' speeches is also abhorred, especially when no copy of such tape recordings is left with the speaker and no explanation is given as to what use would be made of such tape recordings. It should be noted that these restrictions are discriminatory since they apply only to African leaders' meetings and organizations.

"The African Elected Members are conscious of the need for the economic and social development of Kenya and of the fact that there are limitations as to the capital resources available to the country. The African Members are aware that the speedy development of Kenya is dependent on outside capital and on imported knowledge and skill. It does not, however, support the continuation of indiscriminate European settler immigration. The African Members are convinced that increased African representation in the Legislative Council is part and parcel of their desire to see greater economic and social development among the African people, since it is only with an effective say in the affairs of the country that the Africans can participate fully and effectively in the formulation of policies and programmes and the implementation of same."

"TOM MBOYA, M.L.C.   RONALD NGALA, M.L.C."

APPENDIX XIV   *Memorandum to Dr. Nkrumah, 1957: South Africa Versus the Conscience of the World*

"1. The fact must now be faced by the international community that South Africa has for ten years defied all the resolutions of the General Assembly relating to the question of Apartheid, the Treatment of People of Asian Origin in South Africa and the supervisory authority of the United Nations over the Mandated Territory of South West Africa. The latter have been upheld by three advisory opinions of the International Court of Justice, the Africans' right of oral petition has now been recognized, but the African petitioners themselves are prevented from attending the United Nations.

"2. So far from making any concessions to world opinion, South Africa has steadily continued her defiance by enacting increasingly repressive apartheid legislation and measures for the absorption of South West Africa into the Union. Proposed legislation now before the Union Parliament seeks power to make it illegal for persons of different race to worship together in the same building and to study together in the same Universities.[1] The Anglican, Roman Catholic and various Protestant denominations have declared themselves unable to accept this interference by the State in matters of religious belief and worship.

"3. Thus the challenge of South Africa to the 'outside world' has extended from the sphere of international law and politics to the sphere of religion,

---

[1] This was subsequently amended to give the Minister of Native Affairs power to prohibit this under certain conditions.

education and medicine. This must be reckoned with by all organizations which have the integrity of the Commonwealth and the United Nations at heart.

"4. The question of what can be done must be thought out and a plan of strategy devised which will achieve what moral persuasion and ten years of debates and attempted conciliation in the United Nations have failed to achieve.

"5. At the United Nations a more vigorous leadership is needed and in this the initiative should come from other African States. It should be made quite clear to South Africa that henceforth other African countries will not content themselves with passing resolutions and making speeches in the United Nations deploring the injustices which are being increasingly inflicted on the African people in the Union. Action will be taken both individually and jointly which will adversely affect South African trading and other relations with their territories in Africa. This could include commercial exchange as well as communications including air travel, servicing of aircraft proceeding to and from South Africa, etc.

"Strong representations should be made by States having vital interests in the African continent and in the Commonwealth regarding the continued financing of South African gold and diamond mining enterprises whose migrant labour system is disrupting the social organization of the African people as far away as Nyasaland, Tanganyika, Bechuanaland, Basutoland and Swaziland despite the cash wages offered which, however high in relation to those prevailing in adjoining less developed agricultural countries, nevertheless depreciate the standards of wages and labour conditions in the Union itself.

"6. The karakul sheep farming of South West Africa is producing fabulous wealth for some of the landlords who employ African shepherds at a wage of considerably less than a pound a month for tending five or six hundred sheep whose lambs, slain at one day old, fetch for their skins between two and three pounds apiece. This is a cruel luxury trade which women with consciences could well take the lead in boycotting. The African labour employed in it could be more usefully employed elsewhere and with more profit to the labourers, most of whom are on contract service, recruited from many hundreds of miles away. West Africa could set an example by boycotting South African foodstuffs, eggs, tinned fruit, wine and other products from the Union.

"7. In the social sphere, in music, entertainment, the arts, athletics, sport and education much could be done to exert a healthy pressure of world opinion on the South African public. In the past voluntary organizations have been timid in the expression of opinion as well as in action, believing that the South African people, by which is usually meant that section of the white people which supports the Government's policies, will be hardened by 'interference.' There is however growing disillusionment with the philosophy and policy of the 'Nationalist' Government and this argument fails to take account of the nine-tenths of the population which is showing itself increasingly opposed to this policy in the form of boycotts, strikes and other measures forced upon them by their lack of any constitutional means of redress, representation in

Parliament and the repression of their leaders and their political and trade union organizations.

"8. The dangers not only to South Africa but to many surrounding territories of this total stoppage of all channels of peaceful change and remedy for injustice are too great to be evaded any longer by pious resolutions and oratory.

"9. The time has come for other African countries to take carefully planned and co-ordinated action both outside the United Nations and within the United Nations to induce other like-minded countries to join them in more effectual measures. Such will help to convince the South African government of the error of its ways and assist the people opposing it. It will demonstrate the unwillingness of the world to wait complacently for some inevitable disaster or explosion which would cause unlimited human suffering and leave Africa with a heritage of racial hatred which would take centuries to overcome.

"10. The question of South West Africa offers all those countries who sincerely want it, an international procedure for maintaining a hold on the obligations assumed by South Africa as a member of the Commonwealth. The Mandate of South West Africa was entrusted to the Union by international treaty as a 'sacred trust of civilization' to be administered 'for and on behalf of His Britannic Majesty' and his rightful heirs and successors.

"11. Article Seven of the Mandate agreement with South Africa could now be invoked by members of the League of Nations which includes those countries which belonged to the League through their being subject to the jurisdiction of His Britannic Majesty at that time. Article Seven of the Mandate provides that in the event of any dispute between South Africa as the Mandatory and one or more of the members of the League which entrusted the Mandate to her the compulsory jurisdiction of the International Court of Justice could be sought by one or more members and South Africa would be compelled to accept the judgement of the Court even if she absented herself and took no part in the Court's proceedings. Continued defiance by South Africa of the Court could be referred to the Security Council and could result in the invoking of any of the active steps open to the United Nations including the 'collective measures' usually referred to as sanctions. Meanwhile consideration could perhaps be given to the question of whether travel documents could be issued by the United Nations or a friendly State to recognized petitioners from South West Africa whom the Fourth Committee has expressed its readiness to hear. The delegation of Liberia once raised this question in connection with the possibility of petitioners from Trust Territories being prevented from attending the United Nations. Since then the International Court of Justice has upheld the right of the United Nations to hear oral petitioners from the Mandated Territory of South West Africa and I was heard in their enforced absence.

"12. The calling of a Conference of African sovereign states has already been suggested by the Prime Minister of Ghana, Dr. Kwame Nkrumah. Such a conference could discuss, in addition to many other matters of mutual interest, possible policies and lines of concerted action to deal with the problem of South Africa, also the part which non-governmental organizations could play in the various fields of education, sport, culture, trade etc. in the form of both negative and positive action. South Africa could be invited to be present as Dr. Nkrumah has suggested, and discuss her present and future relations with other States of the African continent. She could thus be made aware of the likely consequences of the continued pursuit of her present policies of repression. On the positive side such a conference would do a great service by exploring all the possible ways in which Africa could be helped by the Specialized Agencies of the United Nations and the constructive ways by which technical and financial assistance can be, and are being, extended to undeveloped areas of the world.

"The purpose of the courses of action outlined above is to reinforce the principles of the United Nations Charter in face of South Africa's defiance and not to counterpose one form of racialism against another. Procedures must be devised which will make the Charter principles and the rule of international law effectual or confidence in peaceful methods may be undermined in that part of the continent and peace and security threatened."

"Accra 22.3.1957   "MICHAEL SCOTT"

The first conference of eight sovereign African states was held in Accra in April 1958. South Africa was invited but did not attend. Discussions took place which will have far-reaching implication for economic and technical assistance in Africa and will be followed up in future conferences.

APPENDIX XV   *A conference sponsored by the Africa Bureau on political, social, and economic development in Africa for 1959 has set itself the following aims:*

A. *The Aims of the Conference*
The Conference will consider the usefulness, relevance and adequacy of present and projected plans for development in Africa: it will examine (with special reference to the problem of trained personnel) the relevance of the assistance made available, or likely to be made available by the Metropolitan countries, the United Nations, the Council of Europe, the Commonwealth, the United States, the Soviet Bloc, the Commission for Technical Assistance South of the Sahara and the Foundation for Mutual Assistance in Africa South of the Sahara.

It will consider to what extent this provision reflects the actual needs of the African people; what are the plans of the individual African territories; and how African development is likely to be affected by the Common Market.

It will discuss the factors essential to establish African confidence and co-operation; the geographical, physical, ecological and social obstacles to development, and how African initiative can be encouraged.

It will examine and compare the political and economic objectives of the Metropolitan countries and the independent African territories in relation to development. It will consider the challenge of communist conceptions and the problem of development in multi-racial communities.

B. *Preliminary Research*

Information papers on the principal subjects to be discussed will be prepared and circulated before the opening of the Conference. These will include:

1. *Background facts on underdeveloped territories in Africa,* comprising brief notes on: area and population; economic position; social services; the percentage of Africans in public service; development programmes (in progress or projected) and aid received; constitutional position; Government policy.

2. *Descriptive notes on agencies engaged in financial and technical assistance projects in Africa:* their organisation, policies, activities, and the funds at their disposal.

3. *A short descriptive bibliography*

C. *Membership of the Conference*

Invitations to attend the Conference will be extended to scientists, technicians, administrators and other people with relevant experience, representatives of African Governments and of international agencies concerned with African development. It is hoped that those who attend will later spread information about the findings of the Conference.

D. *Conference Arrangements*

The Conference will meet in regular plenary sessions in the afternoons or evenings, and in three or more separate study groups in the mornings.

STUDY GROUPS AND SUGGESTED TERMS OF REFERENCE:

Group 1.—Finance: Can the supply of capital be increased: is the present machinery adequate, can it be improved, or should additional machinery be set up? What are the advantages and disadvantages of price stabilisation schemes? Should African territories and investors formulate a mutual policy on foreign investment, defining the rights and obligations of investors and borrowers?

Group 2.—Technical Aid Programmes: What is the magnitude of the problem being tackled by the African territories and the various agencies? What purposes have they in common? What should be the relationship between (a) the various agencies, (b) the agencies and the governments of the recipient countries? What are the local obstacles to development schemes and what are the best means of overcoming them?

A Sub-Committee of Groups 1 and 2 will meet to discuss the problem of how technical assistance programmes can be co-ordinated with investment.

Group 3.—Political objectives and Development Programmes: What bearing have the political objectives of the Metropolitan countries and the independent African territories on development planning: for example, on the use and allocation of land; local cooperation; ownership and management of enterprise and development; the improvement of communications; wages and labour legislation; migration; immigration; education; training for and recruitment to the administrative and technical services? What are the special problems facing the smaller territories that are not economically viable, and how are they to be overcome? What are the likely political and social effects of the competition in economic aid programmes between the Western and communist blocs?

Each Study Group, including the Sub-Committee representing Groups 1 and 2 will present a Report for discussion in plenary session.

Index